Production Racers of the 1960s
Where *Super Bike* Was Born

Peter Crawford

Dedication

To Ray Knight, without whom none of this would have been possible. Literally.

Production Racers of the 1960s
Where *Super Bike* Was Born

WIDELINE

Published & designed by **WIDELINE**

www.wideline.co.uk

A catalogue record for this book is available from the British Library

ISBN 978-1-8381336-3-4

Printed in the Czech Republic via Akcent Media Limited

CONTENTS

Foreword

When I first started my embryonic motorcycling career, back in the early 1950s, Norton and Matchless singles embodied the peak of British racing machine development. They were lusted after by anyone who aspired to join the band of trade supported racers – those assisted by the larger high street dealers - to compete against the foreign challengers of the day.

At the time direct factory support in the UK was mainly focused on off-road competition, as both scrambles and grass tracking were popular enough to even attract television coverage. However, while road racing was largely neglected the emergence of long distance races for production machines took place at around the same time, with the Southampton & District Club giving birth to the *'500-miler.'* This generated a lot of publicity and became the highlight of the year for production racers, until the emergence of the Production TT. I was fortunate in playing my part in those early events, both as a credible racer - a personal career highlight was a TT win - and as a commentator, since I was also a regular columnist covering production racing, initially for the magazine *Motor Cyclist Illustrated*.

Production racing rapidly grew from the Clubman's TT of the 1950s, through to specialised championships and one-make series and while these attracted riders who would go on to become household names I managed, somehow, to remain near the centre of things. This resulted in discussion with the then ACU Secretary Derek Jackson on legality and eligibility issues, through to persuading Brands Hatch to be the first major circuit to stage production races. Manufacturers and dealers would also contact me to offer test rides and ask my opinion of their latest machines, in which I would like to think my comments and feedback had some influence. The icing on the cake was the offer of *'works'* rides, particularly 24hr rides at Le Mans and Montjuïc Park, which no doubt did no harm to my reputation as *Mr Production Racing,* a title I somehow acquired along the way.

The story is therefore something of a personal narrative for me, as this book traces the development of production racing - as well as the machines and personalities involved - from humble beginnings at the start of the 1960s through to the point by the end of the decade where production racing started to take over as the entry point and bedrock of national racing, as we see it all around us today.

Ray Knight
Jurby, Isle of Man - August 2022

Acknowledgements

Motorcycles for the Road Racing Superbike and Supersport World Championships must be motorcycles with a valid road homologation in one of the following areas: USA, EU or Japan. These motorcycles must be available for sale to the public in the shops and the dealerships representing the manufacturer in at least one of the above areas

- FIM Regulations [1]

It's all production racing today. We take it for granted now, that racing motorcycles are road bike derivatives. This wasn't always the case and in the 1970s in particular production machines stood out from the two-stroke racing machinery around them. I was attracted for this very reason - that they mirrored the big four-strokes most popular on the street - and I was obviously not alone. Over the years the production-based bikes multiplied, the pure racers dwindled and the rest is history.

Back then production bikes still didn't get the publicity they deserved though - for some they were still racing's black sheep - so I like many others avidly read the columns of a guy called Ray Knight, initially in *Motor Cyclist Illustrated* and then *Motorcycle Sport* magazine. A new breed of journalism, spearheaded by the likes of Mark Williams at *BIKE* then crashed the party and it took production racing to its heart. Ray Knight was still the go-to guy however and it was only when writing for *Classic Racer* magazine subsequently that I came to understand quite how big a role Ray had played. Not just in recording the history of the class, but in helping to create it in the first place, both on and off the track. He was the obvious person to ask to write a foreword for this book and happy to oblige, but suddenly I had a problem. As Ray offered: '*A few pieces of paper. Do with them as you want.*' They were actually 190 pages of an unpublished book, developed with the help of respected editor Alan Wilson, of Redline Books. Both parties had it seemed run out of steam - it happens in publishing - and I could use what I wanted. This was a gift beyond value, not least as it included the donation of Ray's entire seventy year archive of material and hundreds of photographs, but of course a huge headache too. Since I now had two books, both three quarters written. The solution was obvious. Ray's formal contributions to the book are limited to the foreword and direct quotes you will see within. You will see his hand throughout however, where I have quoted verbatim and lifted chunks complete from his and Alan's original text. This has been possible as our intentions were, unsurprisingly, quite similar, though this book deviates in one critical regard. While Ray's intention was to chronicle the development of production racing from his own unique perspective – much as he had done previously in his excellent autobiography *'Ever More Speed'* - this volume incorporates the contributions of more than fifty additional tuners, sponsors, club officials and racers, who shared the paddock and track with *Mr Production Racing* during the 1960s.

In this regard I'd particularly like to thank Graham Bailey, David Boarer, Mike Bowers, Peter Brown, Rex Butcher, Martin Carney, Bruce Cox, Dave Croxford, Norman Curley, Clive Davies, Pete *PK* Davies, Brian Davis, Dave Degens, Declan Doyle, Hugh Evans, Graham Falcke, John Gleed, Rod Gould, Norman Hanks, Reg Hardy, Bob Harrington, Lester and Steve Harris, Geoff Harris, Bob Heath, Ray Hole, Chris Hopes, George Hopwood, Graham Horne, Mike Jackson, Frank Kateley, John Lancaster, Chris Lodge, Joan Milligan, Gerry Millward, Alan Peck, Ralph and Phil Ridley, Rod Scivyer, Ron Smith, Tony Smith, Malcolm Stanley, Richard Stevens, Bob Trigg, Chris Vincent, Ken Vogl, Clive Wall, Norman White, and John Woodward. Additionally I'd also like to thank Alan Cathcart for allowing me to quote from his 1984 interview with Syd Lawton. Rollo Turner of Panther Publishing and Andrea Sintich for permission to reference Claudio Sintich's *'Thruxton Triumph Bonneville 1959-1969'* and to quote Percy Tait, Ken Buckmaster, Stan Shenton and John Hedger. Fred Pidcock and Bill Snelling for source material from *'The History of the Clubman's TT races 1947-1956'* and quotes from Alan Brodrick. Barry Smith for permission to quote from his autobiography *'Whispering Smith',* Mick Duckworth for quotes from his notes on Geoff Dodkin and the Cotton Owners and Enthusiasts Club, for permission to quote Bill Southcombe from the August 2020 edition of their club magazine *Cotton Pickins*.

Many photographs within this book come from Ray Knight's large, personal, archive. They also draw on the personal and family collections of many of the contributors listed above. The ever helpful Bill Snelling of the TT Fotofinders Bikesport Archive also provided a prodigious number of TT photos, as did the Sid Lucas archive, care of son Malcolm - Sid Lucas being the photographer for the *TT Special* newspaper. Other photos have come from the extensive VMCC photo library, the highly regarded Jan Burgers - chronicler of the last days of the Continental Circus, the BSAOC, the Darley Moor Collection/Bob Brown care of Chris Sammons, the Boyer Archive care of Deborah Brand, Mortons, the John Stoddart Archive and the Gus Kuhn Archive care of Valerie Davey. Individual photos have also come from Deryk Wylde, Geoff Harris, Mike Cook, Dave Mason, Roy Topping, Lionel Goulder, Richard Bailey, Bill Riley, Len Thorpe, Howie Millburn, Jim Kanka, Doug Mogano and Ted Reading. I would also like to thank a number of marque specialists and the current owners of some of the historic racing machines mentioned, including Michael Oliver and Roger Charles James. As a note, some of the images used within are not of *coffee table* standard, but neither were the cameras of the time. As such the photos are included for reason of their content rather than their quality. Lastly, I'd also like to offer special thanks to Nick Jeffery, Pat Crawford and Kevin Moore for proof-reading and much appreciated editorial advice.

It's all *Production Racing* Now

The Clubman's was often a more interesting race than the TT proper. It had been prophesied that the TT course *'would run red with the blood of all these novice riders,'* but this did not happen, even though the lap speeds were not a lot less than they were in the TT races

- Alan Brodrick

The 1990s were a low water mark for Grand Prix motorcycle racing. The 350cc capacity had been dropped in 1983 and the 50cc class went a year later. It was superseded by a short-lived 80cc class, but this was gone itself before the end of the decade. Sidecars were downgraded to *World Cup* status from 1997 and only the 250s seemed to flourish. The 500s soldiered on, into the dying days of the new century, but their days were numbered too. They went in 2002, they had to.

World Superbike, WSBK, was booming. Six figure crowds flocked to Brands Hatch, while as many as 60,000 *British* fans alone crossed the English Channel to watch the Dutch round of the championship, at Assen. The TT was also, miraculously, flourishing even though it had been dropped from the World Championships over twenty five years previously for being out of step with the times. In comparison spectator numbers at the British Grand Prix, part of that very same World Championship, were down in to the tens of thousands – rumored to be as low as 15,000 in 1998 – which showed quite how far the pendulum had swung in favour of road-based race machinery. Who cared about peaky 500cc two-strokes, who rode those on the road? On the domestic scene things were similar. The British 500cc Championship collapsed through lack of affordable machinery in the early 1980s, to be replaced by a revolving door of championships. These had only one thing in common, production bike engines at their heart through to 1993, after which the production formula spread to the whole machine, when *Superbike* rules were adopted. These required both engine and chassis to be road bike derivatives and its all been production racing from then on. From the Isle of Man TT to *British Superbikes*, Moto 2 through to *World Superbike*. The link is either direct or very thinly disguised, with Moto GP's CRT rules in 2012 actively encouraging race bikes which flaunted their road bike DNA. Many would cite the rise of *World Superbike* as the start of the turnaround. But WSBK was the beneficiary, not the cause. Others would go back further, to the TT Formula classes of the late 1970s, or the rise of F750 racing earlier in the decade, when a class initially based on road bikes competed for the biggest money in the sport. The roots are more prosaic however, dating to another period when, similarly, the gulf grew too big between race bikes and those ridden on the road.

A Golden Age?

The 1960s are held up as a golden age, when the impossibly sophisticated multi-cylinder machines of MV Agusta and Honda slugged it out on the global stage. Their presence undoubtedly caught the imagination, but they also created predictable and non-competitive racing in an increasingly anomalous class. 500cc was no longer the preferred capacity of the road bikes on which fans arrived at the track. You needed a

Eddie Crooks' name is synonymous with racing Suzukis. In 1953 he was still learning his trade however, on a production Norton International in the Clubman race. He took 2nd place among a gaggle of BSA Gold Stars

650cc, or better still a 750cc, and back then virtually all the fans *did* arrive on motorcycles. When Suzuki and Yamaha entered the fray, adding water-cooling to machines already beyond the means of the average racer - let alone the general public - measures were introduced to limit the technical disparities. From 1969 the FIM - the sport's international governing body - limited machines to four cylinders and six gears, but the horse had already bolted. The 1976 German Grand Prix was the last time a four-stroke motorcycle would win a Grand Prix run under the classic capacity classes and the 350cc MV Agusta responsible was already a racing anachronism. Two-strokes had taken over in every class from 50cc to 500cc and there was no small irony in this, since the move coincided with a global oil crisis, growing environmental awareness and the Japanese manufacturers' wholesale move to four-stroke technology for their flagship road bikes, all of which were bigger than the 500cc ceiling maintained in GPs. How had it come to this?

In the immediate post-war period 500cc *was* the premier class, both on the track and in the high street. British manufacturers contested the World Championships with machines such as the Manx Norton and AJS 7R but never claimed a title after 1952. This was because Gilera were followed by MV Agusta, Honda and ultimately Benelli with four-cylinder machines. British riders continued to compete at the highest level, winning world titles every year without fail until 1972, but it was never on a British machine again. At the time the manufacturers were criticised for not countering with multi-cylinder machines of their own, but the British business model was totally different to that of the opposition. The Italian firms were largely family owned and in many cases they made road machines to fund their racing activities, not the other way around. While the Japanese used racing to build their reputation and credibility, creating awareness for previously unknown brands.

The British manufacturers were not blind to racing as a shop widow, but they were controlled by shareholders and money spent on racing reduced their owners dividends. These were derived from the profits of the manufacturers' *cash cows* – the models which delivered the highest unit profit for the least investment – and these were all big motorcycles, particularly in the all important export markets. Here the United States called the shots and their races, governed by the AMA - the American Motorcyclist Association - were primarily for 750cc side-valve and smaller push-rod machines run under their '*Class C*,' production-based formula. This had been introduced in 1933 to make racing more accessible and by 1954 - when the Grand National Championship series was introduced - it was the only class in which anybody was interested. It incorporated all the disciplines - mile, half-mile, TT, short track and road racing - under one championship umbrella. This outlawed even the obsolete British Manx Norton and AJS 7R and when Dick Mann tried racing a Matchless G50 road bike – AMC *did* make a few G50 CSR homologation specials, to circumvent the rules - it was banned. As far as the Americans were concerned racing already *was* production racing and the G50 was clearly an OHC GP bike in disguise. Initially UK domestic racing was unaffected by either of these developments. The Italians and Japanese rarely brought their machines across the channel – remember, there was no British Grand Prix until 1977 - while British fans were indifferent to developments in America. Who knew about flat track racing in 1965?

Mr Gold Star, Eddie Dow, taking the Clubman TT win in 1955, on the shorter Clypse course

However, with the passage of time racing machines in the UK became as long in the tooth as they were short in supply. You couldn't buy a new Manx or 7R after 1962 meaning that the British Championships were increasingly contested by museum pieces. Expensive ones at that, as they were as rare as hen's teeth. It was also frustrating for the 1960s café racers, who lined every British circuit. Their Thunderbirds and Constellations, Road Rockets and Dominators were the hottest machines on the road, and filled car parks at race tracks up and down the country. Yet they were without exception excluded from the sport. These machines were all over 600cc and the ACU – the national sport's governing body – still sanctioned races only in the same solo classes as the FIM, from 50cc to 500cc.

A Chink of Light

Briefly, in the immediate post-war period, production machines ran at the TT. Such a race had been discussed between the ACU and representatives of the Manufacturers Union in July 1939. Hitler put the kybosh on that but, post-hostilities, a set of rules were agreed in 1947 in time for the first post-war TT. The aim of the races was to encourage the participation of racers and manufacturers who did not normally race at Grand Prix level and in this the initial race was entirely successful. Ten different manufacturers contested the Senior class - which was for machines up to 1000cc, rather than the more traditional 500cc – eight different manufacturers competed in the 350cc Junior class and four in the 250cc Lightweight class. However, the organisers were too far ahead of the times for their own good.

In 1947 the 650cc vertical twin, which would soon dominate the roads, hadn't really appeared yet and the 500cc versions struggled against full 1000cc opposition. As a result a further 500cc sub-division was added and it proved as popular as the 350cc class. This popularity created two further problems though. The 1000cc class became a Vincent V-twin benefit, while worse still, the 250cc class became dominated by pre-war machines, particularly Excelsiors and Rudges. Post-war British manufacturers focused exclusively on utility machines in the sub-250cc market, meaning the Clubman's TT was in danger of promoting the world's first *'classic'* class, racing ten year old machines. 1951 therefore saw both the 250cc and 1000cc classes axed, with the Clubman TT settling down to just a Senior (500cc) and Junior (350cc) format.

These classes saw very healthy entries but as early as 1951 the wide diversity of manufacturers seen in 1947 had gone. The 350 class was a BSA monopoly and by 1954 that had spread to the Senior. In 1956 things came to a head, when all but two of the fifty finishers in the Junior race were on BSA CB/DB32 Gold Stars, with twenty of the twenty eight Senior finishers being on the 500cc version, many the latest DBD34 model. The race was cancelled the following year with the organisers citing *'deviation from the original intention'* as the justification. The reasons were actually more complicated, but the dwindling number of manufacturers competing was the major factor.

With some forward thinking the races could have survived, specifically by reinstating the 1000cc Senior class capacity to encourage the now abundant 650cc twins. Instead the Clubman's TT was dropped though the concept, in part, survived. The ACU's Cheshire Centre was one of the most vocal groups to support the continuation of the races and they instituted Clubman races at Oulton Park, every Whit Monday, until the late 1970s. However, these races missed a trick by focusing on the riders, the *clubman* rather than the machines. This could have left the riders of big road bikes kicking their heels again, but there were simply too many to go away. Indeed, outside of the official British Championships, on disused WWII airfields, events were already being held for just such machines. Around oil drums and straw bales production races were already being run, creating the blueprint for racing as we know it today. The Clubman TT had let the genie was out of the bottle, production bikes weren't going away.

Frank Perris would go on to become a works Suzuki GP rider and manager of the John Player Norton team. In 1952 he was still learning the ropes at the TT though on a production Triumph Tiger T100

DBD34 Gold Star

Production	1956 - 1963
Predecessor	DB34 500
Bore	85mm
Stroke	88mm
Capacity	499cc
Compression	8.75:1
Front wheel	3.00 x 19
Rear wheel	3.25 x 19
Front brake	190mm SLS
Rear brake	7"
Power	42hp @ 7,000rpm
Weight	380lb
Top speeds	110mph

The *Goldie,* as the Gold Star was universally known, was born out of Wal Handley's 1938 Brooklands speed record and was launched initially as the M24 Gold Star in 1939.

Over the following twenty years it underwent continuous evolution in both 350cc and 500cc capacities, excelling on the road and in every single discipline of the sport. Developments went through ZB, BB, CB and then DB designations before the Gold Star reached its definitive, final, DBD form, by which point the race track was the only place where its performance could be safely enjoyed

The Tabloid's Ton-up Terror

By the turn of the Sixties the Gold Star was only available in the UK in the classic café racer style, complete with close-ratio RRT2 gearbox, clip-ons and rear-set footrests. It was the RC30 of its day, a racer on the road, thirty years before Honda claimed the accolade. The Goldie exemplified what could be done with a basic product when developed, incrementally, to the *nth* degree and it was no surprise that it dominated production racing during the 1950s

It rapidly fell from favour a decade later though. BSA stopped development of the Goldie toward the end of the 1950s as its hand-built nature made it an unprofitable anomaly among the cheaper unit construction models BSA was currently promoting. The company was also uncomfortable with the rebel *'rocker'* culture the

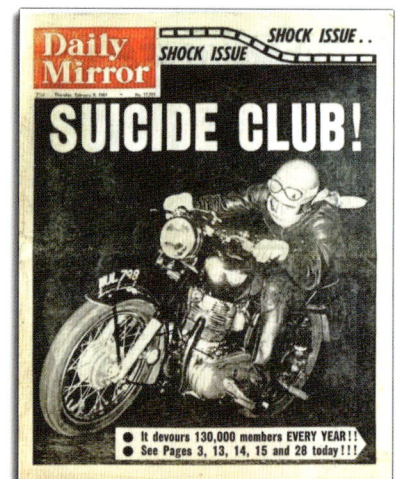

machine was associated with on the road, where it remained the epitome of café racer style and performance years after it had actually ceased production. It had speed and handling ideally suited to the Queen's highway and looks to die for, parked up at the Salt Box, Busy Bee, or Ace Café. On the track things were different however. Production racing grew partly as a result of the capacity classes being out of step with the most popular machines of the day. No club offered a 350cc class in production racing after 1960 and 500cc was no longer the premier class.

650 twins were now in vogue, but the BSA singles still provided sterling service as entry level machines, through virtue of the same characteristics which made them peerless during the glory years of the Clubman's TT. Tractable yet high revving, fine handling and easy to work on, yet infinitely tune-able, not least through the products of Banbury dealer Eddie Dow.

The Gold Star as more often seen on the UK roads. Covered in Taylor-Dow goodies

Indeed Dow continued to provide the same go-faster goodies which stars such as Rod Gould and Phil Read had used while learning their trade on Goldies ten years earlier. Riding the bikes to the circuits, racing them, then riding them home again, in a manner familiar to many of their peers who first went racing on this the most iconic of all BSAs, identifiable by its signature twittering exhaust note and lashings of alloy and chrome

Bernard Codd on his way to his unique 1956 double. Winning both the 500cc and 350cc Clubman's TT races on the same day

In the Beginning

Run *What You Brung*

In those days, I was what was usually referred to by serious, boring, clubmen, as a *'cowboy'*. Johnson's Café on the A20 was my haunt at the time, the equivalent of the Ace Café on the North Circular. Not half as many people as north London, but the same sort of customer. Anyway, about this time, 1958, our hard-riding group of six local lads attended the 500-mile race at Thruxton. Because it was an event for production machines, those that we were familiar with, unlike *'proper'* racing machines in which we had little interest
- Ray Knight

The race which Ray Knight witnessed had first taken place three years previously. The future of the Clubman's TT was in doubt but interest in the road machines participating was not, quite the contrary. To fill the void Thruxton aerodrome was suggested as the venue for a marathon race modelled along French, Le Mans 24hr lines, but the meeting's organisation was not a seamless or bloodless affair. Indeed the proposal was highly controversial at the time as witnessed first-hand by a future Norton Managing Director.

Mike Jackson: It almost split the club in two at one point. The Southampton & District Club was a strong club here in Hampshire, where we had the Portsmouth-based Waterlooville Club and the Bournemouth-based XHG Tiger MCC clubs. Each of these three clubs had very strong membership. Our membership was four hundred and fifty fully paid-up members and when we had our annual dinner, we had not one but two tables for trade folk. There would have been two hundred and fifty people there for one of those events and can you imagine forty blokes from Lucas, Dunlop, Girling, Amal and the like would be there for the annual dinner. As cleverly we always had it on a Wednesday, not a Friday like most clubs would have done, because the trade and industry people would never have pitched up so far away from home on a Friday. The idea of inviting all these trade barons was of course to ensure support for our events, such as this idea for a marathon road race.

However our club was also very strong on scrambles, grass track and trials. Personally I'm a trials and scrambles rider and we felt we were being ignored at the time, at the expense of promoting road racing. So, there was a break away and a dozen or so members left Southampton and joined the Ringwood Club, which was a rival club and ran the Ibsley event, the Hants Grand National and the Perce Simon Trial, actually it was the only club in the country to run three National events. It was a dramatic event, a dozen of the Southampton Club's best trials riders walking out and while I was only a peripheral part of it, as I had only just joined and got a licence to take up trials, my older brother was one of the rebels who left. People slowly trickled back, but that was how important it all was for the Southampton Club at the time as politically it caused quite a rumble.

Not everyone agreed with the road racing idea but Neville Goss, our whizz bang secretary, he foresaw that Grand Prix racing would ultimately become too expensive and that the manufacturers would want to focus on production racing. That was his thinking and the Southampton & District Club, with its huge membership and that, it was big-time back then. Neville Goss was a very dynamic Secretary who became a Vice-President of the FIM and ended up as production manager of the Métisse, at Rickman's. His arrangement with Derek Rickman was that he'd work an eleven month year, as in the month off he did FIM business, as he was so important to the FIM and ACU by then. He was a very clear thinking sort of bloke and one of our other club members, a Vice-President at the time, Wilf Paskins also happened to be a bit of a boffin. A very high powered scientist and it was he who was able to cope with and devise a means of dealing with the lap scoring issues. Can you imagine the logistics? I scored once at one of the Brands Hatch 500 mile events so have a great appreciation of what was involved and what they'd done.

What the Southampton Club had done, due to the problems of providing lighting, was evolve the 24hr idea into into a shorter daytime, nine-hour, race. As the inaugural event was sponsored by *The Motor Cycle* magazine, it was billed as *'The Motor Cycle Nine Hour Race'* and Gold Star singles won it three years running, 1955 to 1957. The 1958 race was seminal however, as Super Bikes, 1950s-style, were front and centre.

Bigger 600cc-plus machines made all the running, with Royal Enfield, BMW, Triumph and Norton twins trading paint and places in the top six. There wasn't a Goldie in sight. The riders changed too. Few would have recognised the leader board in previous years, but in '58 the lap scorers chalked up *'Hailwood'*, *'McIntyre'* and *'Shorey'* as though at a continental Grand Prix, with Hailwood's Triumph pipping McIntyre's Royal Enfield for the win. The event looked more professional too. Previously the Thruxrton circuit had hugged the old WWII perimeter road and main runways so that riders had to dodge the potholes that the airfield's previous residents, USAAF Thunderbolts and RAF Whitley bombers, had bequeathed. Weeds grew out of the cracks and marshals would move straw bales around during racing, covering new potholes but altering the racing line simultaneously. In 1958 that all changed.

The circuit length was reduced, bringing in the swerving Campbell, Cobb and Segrave section, while the event was shortened too. The thermos flasks and corned beef sandwiches would never last nine hours - less was more when it came to spectator appeal - so the Southampton & District Club's shorter *'500-miler'* was launched and it instantly took on the mantle of being the country's premier production race. In truth the choices were limited so Ray Knight took the next opportunity - the MCC Silverstone Time Trial – to enter, pumped with post-Thruxton enthusiasm.

Ray Knight in his first race. By 1958 a touring fairing and greatcoat were unconventional, but not uncommon

Norman Surtees (Royal Enfield Crusader 250) leads Ray Knight (Royal Enfield 700), Peter Inchley (250 Ariel Arrow) and John Holder (650 Triumph Bonneville) through the Thruxton hay bales at the *500-miler* in 1961

Ray Knight: McIntyre's furious pursuit of Hailwood's Triumph in 1958 to retrieve lost time in the final stages had been the talk of the day. He only just failed, despite reeling in the Triumph by some three seconds a lap at one stage, passing all the other bikes like a dose of salts up the long Hangar Straight. As a consequence I bought my own to make my competition debut. My Super Meteor it should be said really was a standard machine and presenting it to the scrutineer for his approval, it was rejected. Even at that embryonic stage of my racing career I'd discovered, while playing *cowboys* on the open roads, that lying flat on the tank would confer several extra miles per hour. The worthy individual intoned that my drop-bars were illegal on a touring machine, but my riposte that the aforesaid bars were exactly the same ones that were fitted when the Enfield factory completed the birth of this mechanical marvel, and that I had merely turned them upside down, left him metaphorically scratching his head, and so he let me through. The first lesson I learned when competing out on the track was that several of the machines I encountered were somewhat faster than similar bikes I had come across while enjoying a joust on the roads. Another was that standard exhaust systems bounced on the tarmac when the bike was leant right over, leaving a trail of sparks for track marshals to admire, which later earned comments from the Clerk of the Course to the effect that if I was: *'trying to break my neck, would I do it elsewhere'* and not at his meeting!

Red Rag to a Bull

Knight was ex-Royal Navy and not averse to a bit of verbal argy-bargy. His *'dialogue'* with the ACU continued – it would for another 50 years – and by chance it came to a head at the very first production race of the 1960s. Promoters still perceived production races as a way to entice manufacturers back into the sport but, as the Clubman's TT had already discovered, competitive obsolete stock was a major spanner in the works. Though discontinued from BSA's catalogue 350cc Goldies continued to dominate the smaller classes, with a problem among the big bikes too.

Ray Knight and the big Royal Enfield. The Constellation was possibly the fastest machine around at the turn of the decade and it could have dominated on the track

Massive Vincent V-twins, ridden by the likes of George Breach and Mick Bennett, could harry Britain's newest parallel twins and this wasn't what the manufacturers wanted to see at all. The last Vincent was made in 1955 and to avoid embarrassment Oulton Park's Clubmans Championship, on 21st May 1960, advertised its production race as being for machines between *'400cc and 650cc',* excluding the 350cc Gold Stars and 1000cc Vincents with one stroke of the pen. At 692cc Ray Knight's Royal Enfield became collateral damage, which he challenged and promptly won. The revised programme now stated 400cc to *700cc*, with a 4th place and £10 cash as Knight's reward. He followed this up with a Silverstone lap record and second place at Trophy Day run by Bemsee - as the British Motor Cycle Racing Club was universally known. This was behind George Breach's Vincent which, Knight's hand written records noted, he swapped places with over thirty times during the race, due to its rapid straight-line speed, but equally wayward handling. There were other Vincents on the entry list too, which was both varied and wide, which was also reflected in the line-up for the same year's *500-miler*. Here the outright victory went to an AJS Model 31 CSR, a Norton Model 88 took the 500cc class and a Royal Enfield 250 won the lightweights. These were critical results for the manufacturers concerned as the *500-miler* was rapidly becoming the industry's shop window and Royal Enfield were pleased for more than just their 250's showing.

As well as riding Ray Knight wrote race reports in the Royal Enfield Club magazine, whose readership evidently went wider than just the membership. The company management read it at the Redditch factory too, the consequences of which Knight could not have possibly foreseen. It was hardly how it was done in Hamamatsu or Varese, but by the following year Royal Enfield not only had dealers Lawton & Wilson preparing a Constellation for Bob McIntyre again, but one for Ray Knight too.

Ray Knight: Well, the Owners Club Secretary conceived the idea of them entering a bike in the *500-miler*, and in the first instance it was supposed to be a Club member's bike. However, it wasn't too long before the factory was giving a hand, and then a complete bike was to be loaned, while the Club took out a competition licence to make the entry officially theirs. Now, there were not many actual racers in the Club, and even fewer who held an International Licence for road racing. One character was Harry Voice, by then retired from active competition and just having the odd gallop in vintage races on an Excelsior, who was persuaded to come back for the occasion. The offer of the other half of the racing seat came as a surprise, after which I was on my way to the doc for a medical certificate of fitness, a trip to ACU Headquarters, and I was ready for my first International race. I rode down to Southampton from London for a fitting on the bike and to meet Harry. Fortunately we were the same size and with minor mods made by Syd's race mechanic we were ready to race. On the ride home I thought to myself, they were actually changing a works bike to suit little old me - couldn't be true! Dawned the day when for the first time all I had to do was turn up at a meeting and ride. I hauled my ancient, ninth-hand riding kit out of the Thunderbird chair that had just about made it to Thruxton, but at least I did have a '*jet*-style' helmet instead of the more prevalent pudding basin variety. Thus I did not feel quite as out of date as I obviously looked with leathers decorated with patches and scuff marks from many previous owners' misuse.

It wasn't just the British taking an interest in production racing. Rod Coleman (AJS 27) and John Hempleman (Norton 33) at Pukekohe, New Zealand, in 1963

Ray Knight's more 'normal' Royal Enfield at Oulton Park in 1960. The factory/Syd Lawton bike was only for the Thruxton 500-milers

Ray Knight and Harry Voice subsequently pushed into the pits, twice, their petrol tank as dry as a bone, calculating that the *Connie* could only manage an eye-watering 15mpg at race pace. This wasn't something that Royal Enfield would be publicising and it spoke as much about race-preparation, or the lack of it, as did Knight's sidecar transport to the meeting and his threadbare riding kit. There was more to production racing than building a fast engine and turning up, as seasoned entrants knew only too well.

Syd Lawton: Enfield were initially keen and competition manager Jack Booker prepared an engine which was fitted with W&S valve springs, Gold Star alloy valve caps and collets and Nimonic BSA exhaust valves cut down to fit. That way we could go as high as 7,000rpm without any problem. Strictly speaking these modifications were not legal on the Meteor but when the Constellation came out the following year it incorporated them. The parts by then were manufactured by Enfield, but then a dispute arose over carburetion. Tony Wilson-Jones the Enfield Chief Engineer, wanted to fit a 1¾" TT9, but I knew that this was prone to giving trouble with fuel surging. He wouldn't be told though, so I decided to present myself at MIRA – the Motor Industry Research Association - test track when they were trying the bike. In my pocket I had a 1¾" Monobloc which I knew suffered a lot less from high-frequency vibration than the TT9 with its bolted-on float chamber. The Meteor was doing 113-114mph through the lights, but it was misfiring at high revs. They fiddled with it for a long time without improving things, so at last I whipped out my carb and asked Jack Booker if I could fit it. I'd already worked out what main jet and needle to fit, so it was all ready to bolt on. I borrowed a helmet off their tester and tucked my trousers in my socks. The first run through the traps with the Monobloc produced 118.7mph which wasn't hanging about in those days. We had a good eight to ten mph advantage over the rest. A good

Triumph would do 110mph and the 600 Norton about 107mph while the 500 Gold Star was pretty quick, but didn't accelerate as well as our twins. The fit of the fuel tank over the frame tube was a bit stiff though and one day Pat Wilson had given it a thump on the sorbo rubber pad on the top of the tank to get it back on again. What nobody noticed was that in spite of it being a steel tank he'd put a dent in it under the rubber and inevitably the tank split in the race. The following year I fitted Norton fork tubes to the Meteor because I knew McIntyre would be riding it that much harder. We also put in a lot of Constellation parts, but in general the Constellation wasn't as fast as the Super Meteor on acceleration because of the siamesed exhaust. At the start Bob just cleared off but incredibly enough we had another leaking fuel tank, only this time we were prepared and had a spare that we fitted in under 3½ minutes. Then the bike started misfiring, which we eventually traced to swarf in the carburettor jet-well, it probably got there when the tank was changed. Before that we'd changed the plugs and magneto rotor arm in an effort to cure the problem and so we ended up spending too much time in the pits. That was when I learnt the first rule of endurance racing – *Stay out of the pits!*

We never had the slightest problem with the Enfield engine. It was a wonderful unit, strong and dependable until Wilson-Jones took it into his head to fit new big-end bolts which were supposedly stronger. They also fitted new conrods, but I wasn't at all happy about all this and at one stage seriously considered entering Bob and Alistair King on a Triumph Bonneville. We used the Enfield in the end, after persuasion from Jack Booker, but this time it didn't even last long enough for Alistair to get a ride. Bob was miles in the lead as usual, but coming up the hill flat-out at over 115mph a big-end bolt sheared, the engine locked up and off he came again. He was very downcast afterwards though: '*I don't bring you good luck Syd*' he told me; '*I'm too hard on the bikes for this kind of racing.*'

There was no definitive production racer in the 1950s. Big Vincents would run strongly into the 1960s too

I told him it was nonsense, which it was. None of the reasons for retirement on the Enfields had been his fault. It was just that because he rode them harder than anyone else, he exposed the deficiencies sooner. The potential for the Enfield to be the best British vertical twin was there, but though I gave them a list of thirty different points that needed attention, very few of them were acted upon: It was as if some people thought I was treading on their toes.

ROYAL ENFIELD

Constellation

Production	**1958-1963**
Predecessor	**Super Meteor**
Bore	**70mm**
Stroke	**90mm**
Capacity	**692cc**
Compression	**8.5:1**
Front wheel	**3.25x19**
Rear wheel	**3.50 x19**
Front brake	**6" twin sided sls**
Rear brake	**7"**
Weight	**427lb**
Power	**51hp @ 6,250rpm**
Top speed	**112mph**

Launched in 1949, Royal Enfield's take on the classic British parallel twin started with the 500cc Meteor and then evolved through the 692cc Super Meteor and Constellation to the 736cc Interceptor. Followed by the mighty MkII Interceptor of 1969 with a completely new, reworked, wet-sump engine.

By this point Royal Enfield had been bought up by Manganese Bronze Holdings however and with Norton, AJS and Matchless names already under their belt they found themselves with too many irons in too many fires. As such the promising, final, 800cc twin prototype never saw the light of day

One Step Beyond

Royal Enfield played a canny game during the 1960s ensuring that their big twins were always ahead of the opposition in the capacity arms race. When others enlarged from 600cc to 650cc they were already making a 700cc and they matched Norton with a 750cc too. Their twins somehow always played second fiddle however, partly as they lacked the dealer network and overseas distribution of Britain's *Big Four*, BSA, Norton, Triumph and AMC - the latter the owners of the Matchless and AJS brands.

Royal Enfield nevertheless successfully sold their rugged large capacity machines off the back of their *'Built like a gun'* reputation and impressive early racing results. In 1958 a Super Meteor was prepared for Bob McIntyre to ride at the Thruxton 500. He was sensibly paired with experienced Clubman's TT winner Derek Powell, who had brought a similar machine into 3rd place the year previously. Both machines were prepared by Syd Lawton and while the 1958 entry was visibly the fastest machine in the race, time lost in the pits was sufficient to lose the lead to the Triumph pairing of Mike Hailwood and Dan Shorey.

Second place was still a fantastic result, though attempts by McIntyre to better it in the two following years ended with a spill and a broken connecting rod respectively. Ray Knight continued to wave the Enfield flag for another couple of years, but with declining road bike sales there was less factory investment in the big twins as the company's learner-friendly 250 singles were also a high priority. Subsequently the big twins, now in enlarged 736cc Interceptor MkI form, became a rarity on the track, partly due to rumours of bottom end frailty.

The twins outlived their single cylinder counterparts however and when Enfield's main Redditch plant closed in 1967 production continued at the smaller Bradford on Avon site. From here the final evolution of the twin, the fabulous, much re-worked, 750cc MkII Interceptor showed great promise in the hands of development tester/racer Richard Stevens. Sadly, with the company's owners championing Norton there was no desire for an in-house Commando competitor and Interceptor production ceased in 1970. As a final fling a small number of the final 200 engines were sold on to Floyd Clymer in the United States, to be put into Italian, Tartarini designed frames and sold as Indians. The majority of the engines went to Rickmans however. These were housed in their legendary Métisse road racing chassis, though they were destined for the road, not the track.

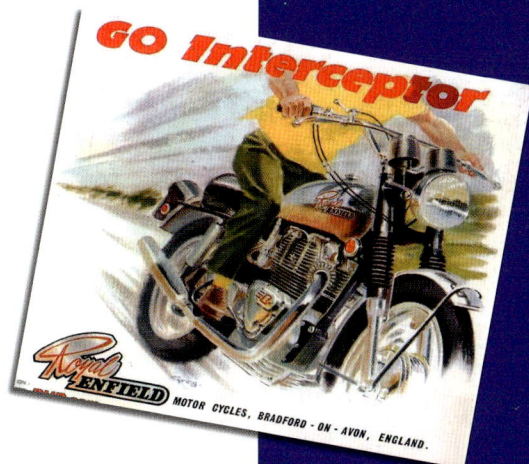

GO Interceptor

Royal ENFIELD MOTOR CYCLES, BRADFORD - ON - AVON, ENGLAND.

Royal Enfield's final fling. The Interceptor MkII

Too little too late. A glimpse of what could have been in the form of the glorious Rickman Métisse Interceptor MkII

The '60s Get Off to a False Start

The big Enfield twins would never achieve their racing potential. But production racing generally was still finding its feet and manufacturers, riders, tuners and race promoters were all learning on the hoof. With the *500-miler* established however, the promoters concluded that imitation was the sincerest form of flattery and Bemsee announced that a 1,000 kilometre race, the *'Silverstone 1000',* would be run in 1961. Competitor and trade support was forthcoming, but spectators were not and Bemsee needed the punters' gate receipts. The 1962 running was little better, with bad weather and a thin, disappointing crowd. The organisers of Thruxton's earlier 9-hour race could have warned them – at 1000km the race was just too long - but Bemsee persevered, shifting from the backwaters of Northamptonshire to Oulton Park, in the more densely populated North West. It was a good idea, but bombed and Club Secretary Guy Tremlett shared his thoughts later in the Bemsee club magazine:

> After the 1963 version of the 1,000kms had finished one could well ask this one question: 'Is it worth it?' As someone who did his part in getting such a meeting run by the Club, my answer now is emphatically: 'No.' It is now clear that the manufacturers are not interested. They are presented with a golden opportunity to show just how good their wares are, and to improve them as well. Instead it is left to a few keen dealer types.[2]

It was a major blow so early on in the development of production racing, but the whole concept was ill-conceived. In 1963 British factories didn't actively race. Not even at the TT. It was all dealers and private entries and the production racers were firmly at the private end of that spectrum. Riders like Knight, in scuffed helmets and borrowed leathers,

Graham Horne: *We all rode up together to our first ever production race with the Midland club at Perton, where it was always pretty packed. We were all very young but the guy with the Rocket he was getting on a bit, he must have been nearly 24!*

had to count every penny and distance events were invariably machine wreckers, so not what they wanted at all. Without exception, self-funded proddie racers simply wanted a circuit near enough to ride to, race at, then ride their bike back home from again. As next morning they might be dusting off the very same machine for the daily commute. Dealer bikes might arrive in vans for the *500-miler*, but they were the exception, not the rule. The backbone of the class was the ride-to-work racer and, at first, their opportunities were few and far between.

Getting ready at Perton. The latest *'Jet'* helmets and old two-piece leathers made an odd combination

Ray Knight: To begin with most promoters wouldn't put on a production race. In those days it was difficult to get race entries as there were too few meetings for the many wanting to ride. The sport was beginning to boom but I still had to get a register of names, as they'd say: *'Well, we'd never fill a grid. Where's these guys who would like to ride?'*

Where's These Guys?

Knight provided the names and despite the demise of their marathon event Bemsee were the first club to regularly run production races. These were at Silverstone and Snetterton initially and the meetings had names which would go on to become synonymous with the sport - Trophy Day, the Baragwanath Trophy and the Guinness Cup among them. Meetings started to be held elsewhere too, at Snetterton and Cadwell Park by the new Bantam Racing Club. While the Midland Motor Cycle Racing Club, like the Southampton & District, extended their activities beyond trials and scrambles, to test the road racing waters at Prees Heath and Perton. These were basic, decommissioned WW II airfields, but races here and at other similarly long forgotten circuits slowly multiplied as word got around. You didn't have to wait for the *500-miler* if you had a proddie bike, you could now race one any time, with one of these new rider-run clubs.

Ray Hole: Kenny Matthews got me into racing. He was a local lad who'd been going to a motorcycle repair class at night school which was run by Phil Hillstead who was a big cog in the Midland Racing Club. One of the founders, along with Len Vale-Onslow and Jim Stephens. Kenny bought this Gold Star off Phil, 'asked if I'd have a look at it, and said: *'I'm racing at Perton at the weekend. Do you want to come along?'* I went, 'found the problem - it was the float on the old GP carb – and old Kenny led the race for four laps. His first race! I thought: *'Bloody hell, if he can do it so can I.'* So, I entered the

The start line at Perton. Qualification wasn't an issue when everyone was automatically on the front row

next meeting on my A10 and, more or less, did the same. 'Led it for several laps before Oscar Dixon passed me on the last corner. He pipped me a couple times like that, on the last lap or last corner, that first season. But after that we did a lot of racing together, my friend Pete and me. As I used to prepare most of his bikes in those early days and over the winter it was always a case of: *'How can we get a few more horses?'*

Pete Davies: Kenny Mathews he found out that Bill Boddice, the sidecar racer, lived in Selly Oak so he decides to go knocking on his door and ask a few things about racing. Bill was a really big help, he brought him into the house, showed him round the garage, encouraged him to have a go and told him who he had to get in contact with. How to get an ACU licence and what have you, and we did the same. The A10 just happened to be what I was riding at the time, on the road, as you used the bike that you'd got. It was the only way for us to go racing, as everyone was short of money in those days and we started with the Midland Motor Cycle Racing Club. One of the founder members was called Phil Hillstead. I'd love to meet him if he's still around, as that guy changed my life.

He encouraged us to get into racing, so we - me, Ray and my buddies - we thought we'd have a go. The first season, we didn't do too much racing really, just four meetings at Perton and at Ragley Hall, as they used to do a hill-climb up the drive at the Hall and that was intended to be my first competitive event. I thought that would be a good way of getting used to the competitive atmosphere, but without having bikes all around on track. But as it turned out Perton came up first and the thing that struck me about Perton, I'll never ever forget it, was the start. As the first race I'm looking up and down the start line and bugger me if they didn't just line everyone up across the track. It was an airfield, so they had as much room as they wanted, so *everyone* was on the front row. Which was, if you're in your first race and you've got thirty, forty-odd guys all hurtling down the straight together toward the first corner, well, let's just say it was memorable! It was a push start and while I can't remember much about the rest of it I do remember that we had two races me and Ray. He finished the first race second and I fell off and in the second race, I came second and he came off.

Pete Davies would memorably dominate production racing in the 1970s on a thundering bright orange Slater Brothers Laverda Jota triple, but in the early 1960s his A10 was a popular choice, particularly if you actually worked at BSA, as Graham Horne did.

Graham Horne: I never went to a race meeting before I rode in one, I just knew I wanted to go racing and it stopped me becoming a yob and hooligan, as I was a budding one! Ray Hole I remember from before I was even old enough to ride a motorbike, as he used to be one of the local Bromsgrove coffee bar racers, ton-up boys, racing on the road. So, though originally my wages were only about £4 a week, I just about managed to do something with them. Like many others, I rode my bike to and from the circuit and I think Prees Heath was my very first race, arriving with sandwiches and tools on the back. There were a lot of A10s about then and I distinctly remember beating Pete Davies when he was still on one and Ray Hole a couple of times too. But the BSA went eventually as one meeting I had a great big tank slapper and the bike ended up cart-wheeling so badly I had to hacksaw the engine bolts out of the frame. And anyway, Oscar Dixon - ask Ray Hole about how good he was back then - he zapped everybody, as boy, that guy, was he brave on his 650SS. He reigned for two or three years, so that's why I got a Norton too, though I did get a bollocking off Brian Martin, the BSA Competition Shop manager when I wheeled that in. He said: *'What's wrong with our Rocket Gold Star!'* Well the Rocket Gold Stars weren't quite cutting it like the SS was at the time, though I wish I'd gone down the A65 route now.

Graham Horne (in glasses) at the *500-miler*. Norton mounted this time, rather than BSA, much to his boss's dismay

I could have saved myself a lot of money with access to parts that way and I'm not convinced by that featherbed handling thing at all. Phil Read thought the Norton he rode at Thruxton didn't handle and mine shook its head something rotten too.

Sacrilege? It would certainly seem so, as by the time the 1960s started swinging so too were Norton's production race results. The 650SS was clearly the thing to have, not least since Syd Lawton was now campaigning them in preference to Royal Enfields. In the hands of Brian Setchell, Lawton-tuned Nortons won both the Silverstone 1000-kilo and Thruxton 500 in 1962, came second at the Oulton 1000-kilo and won the *500-miler* in 1963, then won the *500-miler* yet again, in 1964. In 1962 and 1963 Setchell was paired with Phil Read and in 1964 it was Derek Woodman, since Read was away in '64, winning the 250cc World Championship for Yamaha. Those wins ensured that the 650SS took the prestigious MCN *'Machine of the Year'* award in 1962, the paper stating:

> *'The sleek 120mph Norton won as convincingly as it did in the production races at Silverstone and Thruxton, the races that prove a bike's speed and endurance. So popular was the Norton Super Sports that it polled 23.66% of the total vote, which was the biggest in the competition's history.'* [3]

Such announcements must have really annoyed Bemsee as that message had been exactly what they were trying to prove with their 1000-kilometre races. *Race on Sunday sell on Monday* was the adage and Norton sold. On the road the featherbed twins had never been so popular, helped when Norton launched their even bigger 750cc Atlas. Many racers were equally impressed, transferring their allegiance after those fabulous *500-miler* results.

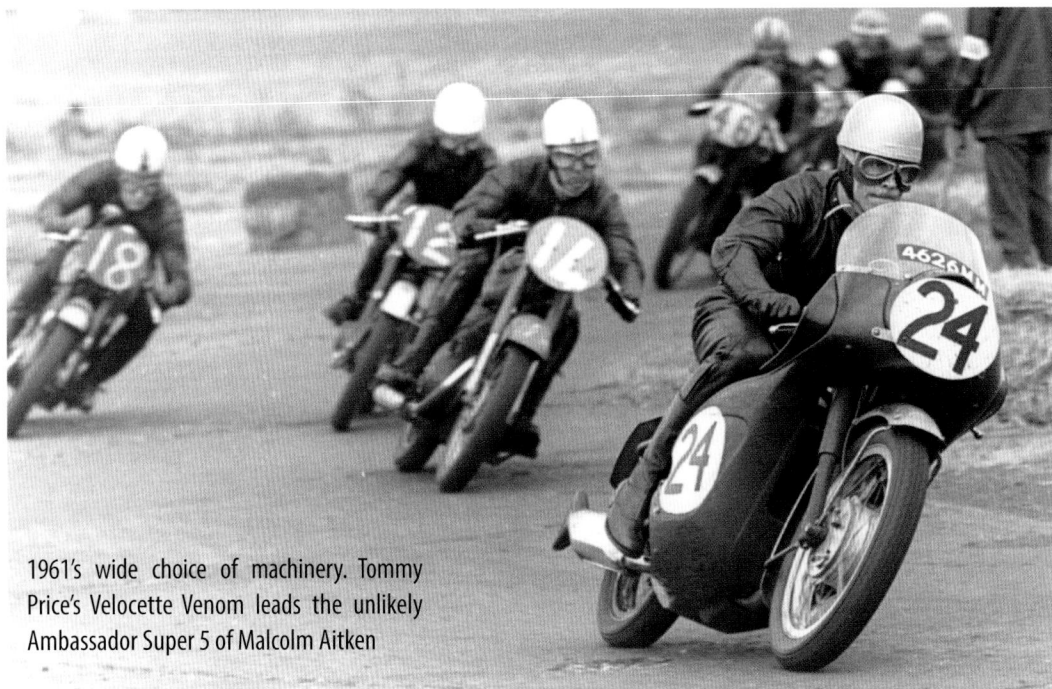

1961's wide choice of machinery. Tommy Price's Velocette Venom leads the unlikely Ambassador Super 5 of Malcolm Aitken

Declan Doyle in 1967. It was early days for coloured leathers, let alone a matching fairing

Declan Doyle: For me it all started with a 1961 CSR, an ex-TT marshal's model, as there were six models sent to the TT and this was one of those back. I got it through Slocombes, in Neasden, an AJS CSR, 'went to Brands Hatch on the Saturday afternoon for practice and went production racing after that. That's just how it happened back then. As what you raced wasn't so much a question of choice, it was more a case of racing what you had, because of the money of course. Some of the other guys were sponsored. They had a motorcycle shop behind them or another source of income. Like Peter Butler and George Hopwood later, they were *'in'* with the lot up in Coventry. But I was just working in a factory and you'd do all the hours you could get, everything under the sun, six, seven days a week, so you'd have some money with which to work on your bike, in your shed and I didn't even have one originally, I had to hire mine.

You couldn't throw money away, as you didn't have any and that CSR, virtually new from Slocombes, I had problems. I worked on Staples Corner and I always had to really rev it to take off from the lights. Well, one evening there was a cop besides me, on his own bike and he says: *'I'm watching you!'* 'Cos I was revving it so hard, I had to! As if you went off normally you just couldn't hardly pull away. So I decided it wasn't right, AMC came to pick it up and when I got it back it was a different bike all together. Well, it seems the timing was set at 39°, instead of 35° and as I had a bench in the attic, the guy who ran the service shop at AMC, in Woolwich, I forget his name now, but he came over and set up the camshafts for it too. As the marks on the cams and timing gears, as standard, were all in the wrong places. He changed them all around using a disc on the crankshaft, to measure the lift properly, and after that it was a much faster machine. With the CSR what you also did was you took the dynamo off the front and took the middle out of it, so it was there in looks only, and you weren't losing any energy from the engine driving it. Then, as you had the magneto for ignition, you didn't need the battery either. Little things like that you'd do. As those production bikes, from A to B, traffic light to traffic light sort of thing on the road, those little things didn't matter. But for competition you had to polish the valves, reduce the valve seats and the pistons you had to relieve perhaps a bit more around the valves too. You'd balance the crankshaft and polish the ports and I did that on the Norton as well.

I can't remember quite why I went to the Norton really, but the frame, the handling was superior and it had a better reputation I suppose. Somehow I'd acquired a 750 engine too. So I built a 500 out of parts as well and as before you just polished the head, increased the compression ratio and put a cam in. I got Dudley-Ward to put in needle rollers on the camshaft and was able to get away with bigger carbs too. The Norton Amal carb was 1¹⁄₁₆″ but as it happens the body of the 376 was the same as the body on the 1⅛″. So I got my friend to ream it out and put the 1⅛″ gubbins in, as it went better like that, but you still had the 376 part number stamped on the side. It was the same frame I used for both though. I just changed the engines around, as the 500 was actually a better bet than the 750, as the Nortons weren't as fast as the 650 Triumphs by then.

That wasn't something Oscar Dixon would have agreed with as he was pick of the bunch on the Bracebridge Street twins winning at club level, while Lawton-tuned machines similarly dominated the *500-miler*. As a result publicity was on a high though, bizarrely, Norton was in trouble. 1961 was the last time a Manx would win at the TT races while the production bikes had largely remained competitive due to the work of engineer Doug Hele and the bad news was that while Norton was shortly to move south to join Matchless and AJS in London, Hele would not be going with them.

Velocette were another company in trouble. They were, endlessly fighting a rear-guard action with their bankers but always looking for ways to publicise their road bikes' prowess too. In 1961 they broke the world 24hr speed record - 100.05mph - at France's banked Montlhéry circuit

Rob Herring and Syd Lawton's son Barry still worked on the Lawton & Wilson twins however and Barry Lawton took a landmark win on 13th October 1963, at Brands Hatch. This was no club event, but a full National meeting, being sponsored by Redex Oils. Other winners that day included Phil Read, Derek Minter and Tommy Robb, and Lawton took the production bike win ahead of an impressive forty five bike field. This wasn't actually the first time a production race had been run at a National however. A similar race had been held at Brands Hatch on 25th August, at the instigation of Ray Knight, with John Bowman's Pat Keeble Motors Bonneville going down as the first ever winner of a production race at a British National championship round. This gave production racing real credibility and it did Triumph's reputation no harm either. As Declan Doyle pointed out, while Norton had the handling Triumphs were faster, and their handling would soon catch up.

The reason was that Doug Hele had moved to Coventry rather than London so, both spreading his risk and hedging his bets, Syd Lawton entered both a Triumph and a Norton in 1962's *500-miler*. Lawton was a shrewd observer of what was going on behind the scenes and realised that Triumph had started to move to the fore. Ray Watmore was a regular performer on the club scene along with John Bowman, with both reeling off the wins. Bowman's Bonneville was rumoured to feature many factory parts, but

A feature of the 1960s was circuit practice days and speed trials where budding racers could mix with the real thing. Declan Doyle (top) mixes it with the part-timers at Brands Hatch, while Malcolm Hancox (centre) and Mike Cook (bottom) test the water at Silverstone and Brands Hatch respectively

this was actually quite early for Triumph to have a direct hand in the bigger twins. The reason was that they were in the process of moving from pre-unit to unit construction and just seven of the new versions were prepared for racing in 1963. Keeble got one, but otherwise for most racers it was still older, pre-unit models. It would take a bit more time to make the new model competitive but on Triumph's smaller twin Meriden had already had that time. Triumph's pre-unit 500 had been no match for BSA's singles at the Clubman's TT, while on the short circuits it was Norton's Dominator Model 88 which, well, dominated. Norton's smaller 88 twin won the *500-miler* in 1960, 1961 and 1963, but it started to struggle against Triumph's new unit construction 500s, as annual updates moved the T100s sporting potential along.

The Triumph T100 was the coming thing in the 500 class for the average clubman as Norton's 88 Dominator's star waned. The Velocette Venom was also far from done

Not Just the Big Stuff

Unit construction, where the engine and gearbox were all in one casing, made for a much more compact and robust unit. The Triumph 500 twin also had an improved single down-tube frame which, while not in the featherbed Norton league, marked real handling progress. There were also small benefits to the twin which we'd take for granted today. A Gold Star or Velocette Venom might be a match for a T100 on the track, but the Triumph could equally be used as a ride to work machine. It could nip to and from the corner shop for a packet of Senior Service in the same time that it took to run through a single's complicated starting rituals. This was not to be laughed at, as production races were all dead engine starts. A slow getaway with a recalcitrant single might not matter at the *500-miler,* but one-kick starting, at a five-lap Cadwell Park club meeting, could make all the difference between first place and last. It made a difference on the road too and as a result the Triumph not only out sold the performance singles but all the competitor 500cc twins too. It meant that Royal Enfield's Meteor Minor was pulled from their range as early as 1958, the AJS/Matchless equivalent by 1961, and the Norton 88 was dropped in October 1966. BSA's A50 only soldiered on through virtue of its almost total parts interchangeability with the bigger A65. Pretty soon if you wanted a 500cc twin, there really was no point in looking beyond a Triumph and that domination of the market started on the track in 1963 when a T100 took Triumph's first ever 500cc class *500-miler* win.

Brian Davis: I was very fortunate in meeting a chap called Bill Scott, who Ray Knight actually knew quite well. My father always had motorbikes, that sparked my interest and after a trip to Brands Hatch with a group of guys one Easter I thought: *'I've gotta do this!'* and bought a Gold Star. My first race, at Brands Hatch I fell off and my second, a National race, I was last. My transport was an old Morris J-Type van, which was so rusty that you had to keep the doors from flapping around by tying them up with bailing twine. But it was around then that I met Bill through the Witley & District Motor Cycle Club based in Guildford, which I became a member of to make it easier for me to get race entries. Well, Bill took a shine to me, not least due to my ability with the spanners and it was brilliant after that as I got these bikes supplied for nothing. Francis Beart did the G50 and 7R engines, but the production bikes were mostly done by Hughes of Tooting and Wallington, who at that time were mainly Triumph dealers.

The 1962 *500-mile* race was actually my first ride on a production bike for Bill. A blue, silver and black Triumph T100 and I only got the ride as stand-in for Bill, as he had crashed and broken his shoulder in another race. I rode with a guy called John Tanswell. He quickly found beer and women, so fell by the wayside as a racer, but he was a real tearaway

Up to the early 1960s production racers still looked like road bikes, though even then fairings were appearing on the grid

and would wear his boots away till his feet bled. But he fell off it somewhere in '62 and the bike was too badly bent to continue, the steering was all over the place after that. But those Hughes production Triumphs were very well put together. We had an electrical fault at the 1000 km race at Oulton Park 1963, which Doug Hele fixed actually, he just came along as Stan Brand, the Hughes owner, had a word with him and he just put it all back together again. We rarely had mechanical breakdowns however and '63 was our very best year.

1963 was the first year when the 500 Triumph had points on the side and we raced that bike exactly as it left the factory, other than the footrests and handlebars, which you were allowed to change. Oh, and one thing I'll come on to. The Bikini skirt and an exhaust pipe with a little kick, where it goes into the centre entry silencer, was one year only that, as the silencer was bottom entry after. But Hughes stripped that bike and totally rebuilt it, checked every nut, bolts and bearing, it was a thorough rebuild, even though it was brand new. They were very thorough. I can't remember the name of the young lad now but there was Ronny May and this one young lad who were the main team to get their race bikes ready and that bike was perfect. I remember at the start I ran across the track and Dave Pierce, one of our team had the handlebars ready to go. You know, standing one side. He'd already tickled the carburettor, because that was a thing about them, if you didn't tickle the carburettor, even if they were hot, they wouldn't start. So first kick it started, 'clicked it into gear and away and as you'll see from that Oulton Park photo I was always one of the first away.

The Oulton Park 1000km race 1963. Brian Davis (no.12) gets away as the quickest 500, in pursuit of Phil Read's 650 Norton (no.2)

The bike didn't miss a beat all race but a funny one, well not funny at the time, was that when we were trying to refuel at the first pit stop, nothing was coming out. Well Dave Pierce he grabbed the hose from the next pit and filled us up. It was a change of riders too, so he sent William on his way, then went on to the gantry, looked into the big fuel hopper and there was a rag wedged in it. Was it sabotage? Who knows, but what was interesting about that bike was the alteration I mentioned earlier. It had this brake which looked like a single leading shoe brake, but was actually a twin leader. It was done by Hughes, but I didn't know about it beforehand. It had an extra cam where the pivot bolt was, with the link inside. It made a difference until it was hot, when it faded fast and when William came in after the second session he said: *'It's got no brakes!'* and I said: *'I know, it didn't in the first!'* But with the *500-miler* it wasn't so much the speed which was important as the reliability. You see we had a lot of opposition from the Geoff Dodkin Velocette over the years, with Tom Phillips riding it, Dave Croxford one year too I remember. But their bike was unreliable. They might have won in '63 had it been in the pits less. As there was only about forty five seconds in it at the end, with it being a case of just keeping it going for us, and because we did, we won.

Brian Davis (top and middle) and William Scott (bottom) hassling the big bikes at Thruxton in 1962

It was Triumph's first ever 500cc class win at the *500-miler* but it certainly wouldn't be their last. Not least since the electrics-fixing Doug Hele was well into his stride at Triumph's Meriden factory by 1964 and more dealers, along similar lines to Hughes, were coming on board, supporting production racing, realising the publicity benefits of racing the bikes that they sold. The twin leading shoe brake also told another story, of which many similar would unfold. As while some manufacturers and dealers were scrupulous in their *'production'* machine preparation, there was a whole tale to be told about modification, cheating and interpretation of the rules.

Matchless
ASSOCIATED MOTOR CYCLES LTD. PLUMSTEAD. LONDON. ENG.

G12 CSR

Production	**1958-1966**
Predecessor	**Matchless G11**
Bore	**72mm**
Stroke	**79.3mm**
Capacity	**646cc**
Compression	**8.5:1**
Front wheel	**3.25 x 19**
Rear wheel	**3.50 x 19**
Front brake	**7" sls**
Rear brake	**7" sls**
Weight	**381lb**
Power	**35hp @ 6,500rpm**
Top speed	**108mph**

AMC announced their 500cc parallel twins in late 1948. The Matchless/AJS engine – it was always identical, just differently badged - was an odd-ball among British twins in having a separate central crankshaft main-bearing. It was there to quell vibration, but didn't, as this only increased in proportion to the size of the engine, which reached 650cc by 1958, the same year that the CSR models - universally dubbed the *'Coffee Shop Racer'* - were unveiled. These were the AJS 31 CSR and Matchless G12 CSR respectively and they were the final Woolwich designs as subsequently parts from their new bed fellows, Norton, slowly started to creep in

The *Coffee Shop Racer*

With an AJS CSR winning the 1960 *500-miler* and an identical Matchless achieving the same result at the Oulton Park 1,000 Kilometre race in 1963 AMC were quids in. The CSR was one of the industry's first, genuine, 100mph road machines and it had real racing pedigree behind it. Did they have a contender on their hands? Well, yes and no.

AMC had developed the G45 Grand Prix racer off the back of the standard 500cc twin and the CSR's similarities went more than skin deep. Production of the G45 ceased in 1957 however after just eighty machines had been built, since it never became the winner that the company hoped it might. It was replaced by the G50, an enlarged version of their older, but very successful 350cc 7R racing single and Jack Williams, the brains behind that machine, was brought in to gee-up the G12/ Model 31 project. *500-miler* results of 3rd in 1961, 2nd in 1962 and 4th place in 1963 flattered to deceive however.

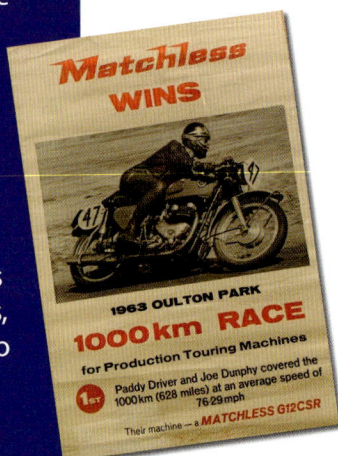

Matchless
WINS

1963 OULTON PARK
1000km RACE
for Production Touring Machines

Paddy Driver and Joe Dunphy covered the 1000km (628 miles) at an average speed of 76.29mph

Their machine — a MATCHLESS G12CSR

As AMC were strapped for cash a move to unit construction was never on the cards for the road bikes on which the development then stagnated and stalled. 100mph was a fantastic top speed in the 1950s, but a decade later twenty more were needed. Peter Butler harried much faster machines, week in week out in club racing on his AJS, but this was down to the skill of the rider, not the CSR's latent ability. A 750cc *'Matchless'* CSR, entered by Tom Kirby, did later, take 4th place at the Castle Combe *500-miler,* in 1965, but this wasn't all that it seemed.

Sponsor Tom Kirby with Joe Dunphy and Paddy Driver after winning the Oulton Park 1000 kilo in 1963. It was the CSR's last big win

This final model had two exceptional riders pulling the throttle cables - Ron Chandler and Bill Ivy – and it was powered by a Norton Atlas engine, as AJS and Matchless were finished as independent brands. Manganese Bronze had snaffled up Norton along with AMC and Norton would be their focus from now on. With lashings of chrome and huge *'juke box'* tank badges these final Norton-engined CSRs did briefly appeal to café racers, but on the track their time had already gone.

AMC Road testers Bill Corne, Frank Pollard and Tony Botting admire the final version of the CSR. By 1967 the 750cc *'G15'* had a Norton front-end and engine. A Matchless? Buyers thought not

Rules   *Lies, Damned Lies & Statistics*

The 250cc line up for the TT was a nightmare for the scrutineers. The rules stated that no refuelling was permitted for the three lap production machine event, tanks had to be standard, and that manufacturers had to prove that the machines had been homologated with two hundred of each model produced. How Cotton got over this I do not know. It must have represented their entire production in 1968. Most teams fell foul of the regulations. I was warned by Bob Havers, Chief Scruntineer, that if I won on the Cotton that he'd disqualify me, otherwise I could take part. Some others were not so lucky, and there were seventeen protests at the end of the race
— **Bill Southcombe**

'Every motorcycle entered for these Races shall be a two-wheeled vehicle propelled by an engine and shall be a fully equipped model according to the manufacturer's catalogue which shall have been published before 28th February 1947, such catalogue to be submitted to the Union by the entrant not later than 3rd May 1947. At least 25 of each model entered shall have been produced by the makers and such motorcycles shall include in their equipment, kick-starters and full lighting equipment.' [4]

The original Clubman's TT regulations set the basic parameters for what was, and was not, a production motorcycle. But even these were an amendment. An earlier communiqué had omitted any reference to lights and kick-starters. As a result rumour had it that Manx Nortons and Velocette KTT models were being prepared for entry as, in fairness, both were listed in their respective manufacturers' catalogues as motorcycles which were part of their general production. Why not? They could be bought through any dealer and the small number of machines of the type required made their eligibility a possibility. Twenty five *was* a very small number, but in the immediate post-war period to have set the bar any higher would have excluded many of the smaller concerns. The following year the requirement did rise, to seventy five machines, but it was back down to fifty by 1949 through manufacturer pressure.

By the time the *500-miler* was established on the mainland, the post-war economy had improved markedly and the ACU were stipulating that 100 machines had to be produced to make any model eligible. By 1965 it had risen to 200. But it dropped back again to 100 in 1966 and subsequently no one at the ACU seemed overzealous in keeping tabs on what had and hadn't been manufactured. The rules were pretty clear though:

(a) *Machines must be fully equipped motorcycles built from new components according to the manufacturer's catalogue, details of which, including all optional extras, must have been notified to the ACU and made available to the technical press before 1st March each year.*

(b) *The general specification of the motorcycle as supplied by the makers must be strictly adhered to. It may comprise only the type of original optional equipment with which, according to the manufacturer's published specification, similar models of the same year could have been fitted before leaving the factory. The total value expressed as the retail selling price of optional extras fitted to any machine must not exceed 25% of the basic retail price of the machine when new, excluding any government sales taxes.*

(c) *No less than 100 machines equipped with the maker's original or optional equipment must have been manufactured and sold. An accountant's certificate will be required as proof.*[5]

When production bikes *were* production bikes. The Clubman's TT 1956. John Righton on the sole Velocette next to John Eckhart's BSA Gold Star. Behind is Arthur Taylor, partner with Eddie Dow in the Taylor-Dow Gold Star performance company

The one hundred bike rule was still genuinely challenging for smaller manufacturers. Greeves, Cotton, DMW and even Velocette could struggle and this resulted in some *creativity* in the calculation and presentation of the production figures. The clause covering *'optional extras'* was similarly open to interpretation which, in many cases, bordered on flagrant abuse.

The rear-set footrests on the 1965 Lightning Clubman. Try getting those over the counter from a BSA dealer?

Clive Davies: My first race was at a BFRC Cadwell meet in early 1967. I finished three races mid-field or lower and it was quite an eye opener. I thought I was really motoring along but I was over-taken either side by two 250 Aermacchis. I'd bought the *Spit* on the strength of David Dixon's MkII road test in *Motor Cycle*. The fastest road bike tested at that time. But my MkIII was a huge disappointment. 'Vibrated very badly and top speed was probably about 110mph. At the time Tom Kirby was fielding a Spitfire production racer so I wrote to him asking if rear-sets, performance exhausts and things like that were available. He wrote a very courteous reply saying: *'No, BSA didn't make such things'* and that he'd actually tried to get them for his own customers without success! Owen Greenwood lived nearby and ran his own tuning business, so it was engine out and over to Owen's. He stripped the engine down, balanced the crankshaft, fitted 10:1 pistons, as per the MkII, did some porting work, lightened the rocker gear and fitted a close-ratio gear cluster. He recommended keeping the Amal Concentrics, saying the MkII's GP's only gave an advantage at very fast circuits like the TT. His bill was about £40 and when I got the bike back the performance was amazing. Very little vibration and a top speed around 120mph, give or take. The next BFRC meeting at Snetterton was much more fun. Very fast and open, I could really motor.

That was a typical story of *optional parts* non-availability and recourse to a degree of tuning with which few would have objected - blueprinting, as practiced by any assiduous engine builder. Declared *'Supplementary parts'* also provided another loophole which not only allowed manufacturers to *not* provide parts listed, but to submit lists to the ACU, for their *'works'* machines, which the public wouldn't have even been aware of – Cotton and Triumph being culpable. A provision which, conversely, could favour privateers over the factories, was the ACU rule that stated; *'The bore may be increased without changing the pattern of the cylinder and providing that the increase does not result in exceeding the limits of the original capacity class for which the machine is recorded by the ACU.'* [6] This meant that smaller machines such as Honda's 305cc CB77 could be quite legally over-bored to help it get nearer the 500cc of the capacity class in which it competed, while Triumph and BSA 650cc machines could be bored out to get nearer the 750cc of the Norton Atlas and bigger Enfield twins. This wasn't really feasible on a Triumph - 688cc was the most you could achieve until the homologation of Sonny Routt's 744cc barrels on the US market-only T120RT - though savvy BSA owners could get an instant boost, through a judiciously selected barrel.

> **Reg Hardy:** I'll come clean mine was a 750 in the end, as we used to go to Syd Tappers scrap yard in West Bromwich, or was it Wednesbury, anyway where BSA used to throw all their old castings away and I got a barrel casting there which had the tappets machined, but hadn't been machined at all otherwise. As the top fin had sagged on cooling, I got it for a song and we bored it off-line so we could get as much of the meat as we could around the pistons and put 79.5mm pistons in, BSA Victor pistons in, which were .020 oversized. That made it about 736cc and that's when it became what I called the yellow one, on which I won the Darley championship, as then I had a little more go.

There was nothing wrong with Hardy's approach, as he had used a standard barrel. But one additional regulation could have rendered his machine ineligible, if he didn't keep a careful eye on his log book. Age limitations were originally put in place for a specific and well intentioned purpose. In 1951 a regulation was added to the Clubman's TT rules that all machines had to have been manufactured after 1st September 1945 to exclude pre-war machines in the 250cc class in particular. By the 1962 *500-miler* the ACU rules stated: '*The machines used in this competition must be standard catalogue models which must have been manufactured after 1st September 1958*'[7] and this morphed into a generally accepted '*5 year rolling rule*' thereafter. It was rarely adhered to however since who was worried about mid-field Gold Stars or tail-end Ariel Arrows in the late 1960s? The Japanese perhaps, as they dug out the regulations in the early 1970s, when the Triumph Trident *Slippery Sam* won the production TT five years running, was called out for being too old, and promptly banned!

Reg Hardy on his home-tuned Darley Moor championship winning machine. At 736cc it was a good 12% larger than the standard 654cc but 100% legal by ACU if not club rules

Going electric

The starting rule of 1947 was also one with unforeseen consequences. Races throughout the 1960s were for *'dead'* engines, which meant the rider - as envisaged by the Clubman's TT rules onward - had to use the mandatory kick starter. Or did they? The original rules said they had to be *'fitted'*, but nothing about their use. The advent of electric start Japanese machines obviously threw a curve ball in here, as a press on the button could now give some riders

The electric starter button on the Honda CB72's right handle-bar was rocket science when it appeared on the UK shores

a half lap lead over poorer starters. This was rectified by some clubs, by them requiring that all bikes be kick-started, though a judiciously placed finger might still *'accidentally'* hit the starter all the same. This could be a potential race-winner over a five-lap club race at Cadwell Park, though it was less important during a *500-miler*, particularly if the Japanese machine in question had been banned from the race to begin with.

La Fédération Internationale de Motocyclisme (FIM)

ACU rules prevailed in the UK but on the continent the FIM held sway. This meant that British production machines competed against thinly disguised racing machines in the 24hr races and from 1960 the *500-miler* came under those rules, once incorporated as a round of the *Coupe d'Endurance*. The International Hutchinson 100 did too, but there were odd contradictions in the FIM rules which the Southampton & District Club - which organised the *500-miler* along ACU production lines - noted in their regulations:

> *'The machines must also conform to the production machine specification of the FIM. This is in most respects far less strict than our own standard machine specification and allows many alterations. On the other hand it specifically excludes certain features of design, such as double overhead camshafts, rotary valves and fuel injection. Because of this restrictive rule it has not been possible to accept in today's race, certain machines of advanced design, which are production machines according to our standards. Machines which comply only with the FIM specification, but do not meet the Southampton & District MCC's standard machine specification are marked thus * in the programme. They compete for all the awards and score points in the FIM Endurance Championship series but will not qualify for a standard machine certificate of performance.'* [8]

The result? Honda was crestfallen, as Mike Hailwood's entry for the 1966 *Hutch* on a DOHC Black Bomber was rejected, while other riders' hopes of racing CB450s in the *500-miler* were also dashed. Gallingly most continental machines, which were heavily modified, had to be accepted by the Southampton & District Club, albeit under duress.

Damn foreigners! As a rule the British clubs and the ACU allowed the Honda however, and ACU rules applied to the TT once production machines were added to the programme from 1967, as those races were initially run as National races (ACU rules) within an International (FIM rules) meeting. Clear? No, not really.

Interpretations, Flexibility, Foreign Rules and Open Cheaters

Even when rules were clear some elements were interpreted differently and some rules of course were openly flouted. The highest profile cases of this, as will be seen later, were probably at the 1967 and 1968 TTs, as while they were hugely successful races overall behind the scenes it was chaos. In practice for the 250cc race in 1967 the Suzuki twins had looked as fast as anyone, with Barry Smith less than 1mph slower than fastest qualifier Bill Smith. It was three Suzukis and three Bultacos in a close mix in the top six, but come race day everything changed. The Bultacos of Bill Smith and Tommy Robb had been fitted with road legal silencers in practice but as they were wheeled on to the Glencrutchery Road for the race they now sported expansion chambers and competition cylinder heads. After the initial fog of two-stroke smoke had cleared no one saw them again they were so fast and while the post-race objections were dismissed the *TT Special* newspaper spelt it out when it pointed out that: 'The Bultacos were thinly disguised racers and it was

Home snaps of the 1968 Trevor Burgess Ossa. In practice (top) it had a silencer fitted, while in the race (bottom) it had an expansion chamber

a tremendous credit to the Suzuki T20s that they were able to keep within a couple of minutes of them.'[9] The same objections were raised in 1968, when it was Ossa's turn to field a *'ringer'* in the hands of Trevor Burgess, but by this point the rules had been amended, not to protect those running genuine production bikes but to cover the organisers behinds:

> 'Maker's modifications introduced to machines of the maker's home market in subsequent years may be incorporated in machines which are listed as the same type or model but of earlier manufacture, provided that they may be incorporated by the simple process of exchanging one part for another.'[10]

In the 1968 regulation the *'maker's home market'* caveat was critical as in truth no one knew what they sold in Spain, nor how many. The same would have been true for the Japanese, were it not for the fact that they tended to document these things. The importers said that expansion chambers were legitimate and that's the way the decision went. Though as events would prove it wasn't just the Spanish playing fast and loose with the *'maker's home market'* clause.

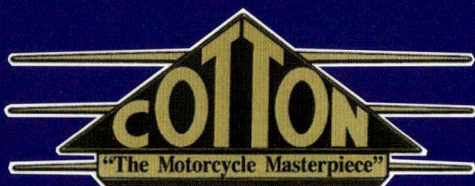

Cotton
"The Motorcycle Masterpiece"

Conquest

Production	**1965-66**
Predecessor	**Telstar Racer**
Bore	**68mm**
Stroke	**68mm**
Capacity	**247cc**
Compression	**12:1**
Front wheel	**2.75 x 19**
Rear wheel	**3.25 x 19**
Front brake	**7" tls**
Rear brake	**6" sls**
Weight	**230lb**
Power	**30hp @ 7,500rpm**
Top speed	**105mph**

Cotton like many small British manufacturers relied on Villiers for its engines, but was unusual in preferring their highest performance options.

Cotton were Villiers' biggest customer for the Starmaker, their high performance 250 engine, and while the Cotton Conquest was only made in penny packet numbers – somewhere between 30 and 60 being built – the race results brought publicity and notoriety in equal measure. The sun shone brightly but briefly for Cotton however, as with the demise of their engine supplier so too Cotton's fortunes waned

The Gloucester Rogue

Cotton was a tiny, virtually dormant firm, when bought by Pat Onions and Monty Denley in 1954. The pair had ambition however and by 1960 Cotton had grown to over twenty staff when Fluff Brown joined as Competitions Manager. The Villiers two-stroke engine was the Hobson's choice of small manufacturers, but Cotton got lucky in 1962 when supplied with three prototype Starmaker engines.

As a result a close relationship was formed with Villiers development engineer Peter Inchley and the Telstar racer was the happy and successful result. It was rapidly followed by the Conquest roadster for which they claimed 185 sales. It was pure fantasy of course, it wasn't even close. But the Conquest became eligible for proddie racing through a *'typographic error'* when the accountants produced build certificates covering Cotton's entire annual output and it was expedient not to query the results!

The *'works'* (far left) racing Conquest had very little in common with the production road version (left) and there were precious few of these

The works machines, of which there were probably just two, differed markedly from standard, but the press version was reported as more user friendly than could reasonably have been expected, even if there were some downsides to a racer with lights on the road. It was bloody noisy, had no stand, terrible ergonomics, Christmas tree wiring and dubious build quality. These could have been addressed on a mass produced, cheaper, 5-speed successor, since the race engine was soon delivering 32bhp at 7,700rpm. That it never happened was, ironically, in part a result of the Conquest's own success.

Bill Southcombe on his way to 13th at the TT in 1968. The ex-Derek Minter Conquest was timed at 112mph but stopped at Ramsey, explaining the lowly finishing position

In 1966 Manganese Bronze took over Villiers, along with AMC, to form Norton-Villiers. At the same time they ceased supply of engines to other manufacturers adding salt to the wounds by pinching development engineer Fluff Brown to continue Starmaker development. Why? Well, the Conquest and Telstar had so impressed them that they earmarked the engine for their own new AJS branded machine, the Stormer. It was cold comfort to Cotton but in retrospect perhaps the Conquest's death was a mercy killing. As in politics, a year is a long time in two-stroke tuning and the Cotton was in truth a bit of a one hit wonder. The Japanese soon moved expectations along making the Conquest rapidly look very dated.

Bruce Cox: Our 1963 *500-miler* performance on the Yamaha YDS2, that got us 150 quid start money for the following year's Barcelona 24hr race. That was two months' wages at that time, when I was on £17 a week. I teamed up with Rod Gould as Alan Kimber was going to provide us a Suzuki, but the only model that could be provided in time was a T10 tourer, rather than the T20 six-speeder sports model. But we couldn't bring ourselves to miss out on the £150 still on offer. I'd just ridden the TT, on a Greeves and got round respectably and remembered the *500-miler*. We'd been racing the Montesas, Bultacos and that, which were just race bikes with headlamps on, so we decided to play them at their own game, as essentially the Greeves was no different in concept to the Bultacos and Montesas that had masqueraded as *'road bikes'* at Thruxton. We figured that the Spanish organisers could hardly object if we did the same and they didn't. So on went lighting equipment and a kick-starter and we were Barcelona bound!

The kick-starter was really there just to satisfy the *'road bike'* rules for the race but there was no way that the Greeves, with its massive Amal GP carburettor, would respond to any attempt to kick it into life. The penalty for a push start was four laps, so we were already four laps down as I sprinted across the track and pushed away from the Le Mans-style start. But I think I was up to 27th from somewhere in the mid-40s on my first stint, as when it was going it was really very good. Faster, in fact, than the AJS 250CSR being ridden by another pair of young Englishmen on their first trip racing abroad. Peter Williams and Tony Wood had won the 250 class with it at

A 250 Fleetwing trying its best. Greeves never produced a genuine performance road bike of their own however, which was probably a missed opportunity given the dominance of their off-road competition machines

The Greeves Silverstone as raced by Cox and Gould at Barcelona in 1964. A production bike? Not even close

Thruxton that year. Despite this, the hefty four-stroke single cylinder road bike was no match for the lightweight Greeves racer so I was able to pass Peter on the long climb up to the Montjuïc summit, which of course, was very definitely the one and only time *that* would ever happen as normally we shouldn't have belonged on the same piece of track. But the next corner was a downhill hairpin and it was in its braking zone that Peter came back by me with the Ajay locked up and crossed up and went straight off into the trackside shrubbery! He was still tearing away the rhododendron branches to extricate the bike when I came around on the next lap and years later said *'Back then I hated being passed by anybody and certainly not by you, on that bloody Greeves! In those days, if I was passed I always made it a point to at least try and get back by at the very next corner. But that was one time it didn't work.'* Not that Peter had to worry about *'that bloody Greeves'* for much longer, as an hour or so later it ended up wrapped around one of the cast-iron lamp-posts that lined the picturesque parkland track.

Our mutual friend, Ron Herring, who was also in the race stopped by our pit for a chat, telling us about a big crash that had happened right in front of him. *'One of those Spanish riders on a racing bike came flying by me into that first left-hander and got it so crossed up that both wheels came off the ground and he smashed straight into one of those lamp-posts. The straw bales exploded but I don't know if he got away* with it.'

I replied *'You can ask him yourself. He speaks English'* and with that I pointed to Rod Gould who had just returned from the medical centre and was sitting groggily in a chair at the back of the pit! That was the end of us playing the Spaniards at their own game, although we did have the dubious pleasure of seeing our totally written-off bike pictured on the front page of the Barcelona daily newspaper. *'Any publicity is good publicity'* is a well-known saying but, after paying the bills incurred in our Barcelona excursion, it is certainly not one that I'd agree with!

They'd never have got away with passing off a full blown Greeves Silverstone as one of the company's more mundane Sports Single roadsters in the UK. But, incredibly, it wasn't far from what others did. By 1966 Cotton claimed to have built 185 Conquests – they hadn't – a thinly disguised Telstar racer with lights. The Conquest *'no two the same'* according to *MCN*, was accepted by the ACU however and the governing body's dealings with other *'manufacturers'* were even more difficult to fathom.

Ray Knight: Dunstall, there's a mystery there, I never did find out the inside story with that one. I did, later with Dave Degens and his registration of Dresda as a manufacturer. But with Dunstall I was there when they tried to compete with double discs for the first time at the TT. I know as at first the ACU wanted to throw them out. But somehow he also managed to register as a manufacturer and that's how he got away with it. With Degens first attempt, with a Triton at Snetterton he blew everyone away, but then there was a riot, I know as actually I led it! And the win was taken away.

Cotton's and Degens' situations are covered later on, but Dunstall's is worth exploring here, not least for the fact that his machines very rapidly became so dominant. For the ACU the critical issue for any machine was that it had to come

Dunstall didn't only do Nortons. He customised Triumphs too, though his name was always synonymous with Norton when it came to production racing

from a *manufacturer* and that manufacturer had to list any optional parts. What constituted a manufacturer was not stipulated however and, as Paul Dunstall registered himself as such with Companies House, a manufacturer was what he became. Even if he was clearly a tuner, or customiser in reality, as he received complete machines from Norton like any other dealer.

Rex Butcher: I was the shop manager back then and we only sold Norton at the time. They used to come in as standard twin-carb 650 Dominators or a 750 Atlas but they then went into the workshop at the back, where the Curley boys, Norman and Ken were the mechanics for years. As the other Curley, Reg, he had a fibreglass business and used to make all the fairings and tanks. As they were used on the Curley Nortons too, which quite a few good racers rode.

So anyway, the Nortons came in as standard bikes, but they then stripped off the exhausts, tank, seat, the battery cover and all that sort of stuff, then fitted the Dunstall equipment. The special exhaust system, racing seat all that as that's what we used to sell as Dunstall Nortons. He *did* used to do engine stuff as well, pistons and cams, but the gearboxes and disc brakes they only came later, along with parts for other machines.

There was no denying Dunstall turned out attractive and competitive machines which included the 650 Dunstall Dominator (top) 650 Dunstall Lightning (middle) and the 750 Dunstall Atlas (bottom). All of which could be provided in different states of tune. Were they production bikes? Not really

Norman Curley: Yeah I was one of the mechanics, as it was me and my brother Ken, we stripped them all down then built them back up with all the special gear. As my other brother Reg, he did the tuning with the engines. So it wasn't just the cosmetics. We did the cam followers, the pistons, opened all the ports up, and fitted bigger valves. That's what my brother did to them originally, as Paul Dunstall used to race a Norton at Crystal Palace and my brother, Reg, started tuning his bike for him. That's how it all started. Paul had three shops on the go at one time. The main one at 156 Well Hall Road, on the corner, then we had another up on the High Street in Eltham, selling

A later Curley Commando. Ironically the parts were legal on a production bike as they were marketed by Dunstall

scooters and every type of moped, along with another motorcycle shop over at Bostall, at Belvedere. Though that one only lasted a little while I suppose we were doing possibly one or two full Dunstall Nortons a week by 1967. We'd maybe strip five down at a time in the workshop, strip the frames right the way down to get them diamond chromed or whatever, all different specs, as some wanted them chromed, some standard black. And all the standard bits then got sold off in the shop. As Paul was just another dealer as far as Norton were concerned, regardless that he'd bought all the Domiracer bits off them previously. Though Norton benefited from it of course, because as far as Nortons went at the time, Paul was *it* really.

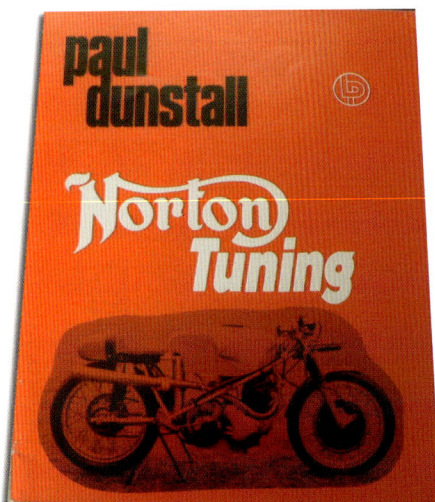

Those Dunstall Nortons, I used to run them in on the road, all round the south east, doing it on trade plates with no lights or anything and often they'd be raced the next day believe it or not. The discs back then were Lyster ones, discs floating on pins and Griff Jenkins was one of the first riders to use them in 1967. That *was* very early for discs, but the thing was every bike was different. They were all built to order, as people wanted them specially made to different specifications, so there wasn't a standard Dunstall as such, just a catalogue of optional parts from which they could choose. So there were lots of variations of the machines that were sold as Dunstalls.

Perhaps the most contentious of these parts, as mentioned by Ray Knight and Norman Curely, were the brakes. The 1967 Dunstall catalogue did *not* include disc brakes and while they appeared on a model tested by *Cycle World* magazine in the United States, in September 1967, they were big news at the TT, as they were on the Norton works bikes as well. The *TT Special* noted: '*Non-starters include the two massive 745cc works Norton Atlas's of Ron Chandler and Peter Inchley – the official reason being because of brake troubles.*'[11] Well, they certainly did have brake trouble, because everyone was protesting about them! So was Norton's a tactical withdrawal? Possibly, as brakes would remain a contentious issue, being the single

Rex Butcher outside the main Well Hall Road branch of Dunstall. Although he was the manager he oddly didn't ride for Dunstall that often on production bikes

area where road bikes most notably differed from pure racers. Triumph would list Italian four-leading-shoe drum brakes as optional extras on their triples– the like of which no private entrant could buy from a dealer - while Norton would similarly list disc brakes for their 750cc racing Commando a long time before they were seriously considered as options on the road machines.

There again, riders had been fiddling brakes for a long time as highlighted by Brian Davis on his 1963 *500-miler* 500-class wining Triumph T100. This concealed a twin leading shoe brake inside a single leading shoe exterior which others also tried, including Slater brothers' mechanic Ray Hole on his and friend Pete PK Davies machines.

Ray Hole: I remember when Dave Nixon and Peter Butler came out with these twin leading shoe front brakes, as they were probably 20-30% better than the standard ones we were using. I went to Triumphs, but you could not get one for love nor money. They were just for the export bikes and the very favoured few - Tait, Butler and that lot. So, I thought; '*How could you improve these brakes?*' and converted a single-sided, 8" sls BSA brake to tls myself. But I put all the mechanism inside, so apart from a tiny adjuster you couldn't see any difference. It had a Ferodo AM2 lining on one shoe and an AM4 on the other and it was brilliant. So, I converted Pete Davies' too and he promptly broke the lap record at Snetterton! The way I did it, it worked like a servo. It was so good I even looked into patents but found out something similar had been done on some 1920s aircraft brakes or similar, so didn't take it further. But for the year or so that we were using those twin leading shoe front brakes, we could out-brake the best of them. Though I do

Ray Hole leads the Nortons of Dave Draper and Graham Bailey

remember one time at Snetterton the scrutineers picked up on this little adjuster, on the brake plate. They were like; *'What is this here for then?'* But I just said it was to stop the brake plate rattling or something, brushing it off and they let it go. The other thing I did, on the front-end, was that I always used *'helper'* springs on the forks. On the outside, under the rubber dust covers, as to begin with the forks we had, had internal springs.

These extra springs weren't full length, so only came into play when you were hard on the brakes or when you were leant right over. I did those on Pete Davies bike as I remember at Snetterton he just couldn't get this thing round Corams, but with these fitted it knocked nearly two seconds a lap off for him. You were always looking for little things like that, to give you an advantage, as some of the *'production'* bikes you were up against, like the Boyer Triumphs, were factory bikes really, full of special bits.

Tweaks were even easier to conceal within engines, though in the case of Dunstall these would have been difficult to call out, since the specification of a Dunstall was never fixed. But what of the bigger manufacturers, who had some parts listed and some parts not?

Clive Wall: Oh, Tony Smith he had a 5-speed gearbox in his works A65. Well I sussed that they'd got one in because at Snetterton one day I'd got a flier and it took Tony quite a while to get by me, as his bike wasn't actually any quicker than mine really. Maybe one or two miles per hour quicker, but it *accelerated* faster I suddenly realised, when we were coming out of the hairpin. He was changing gear quicker than me and I thought; *'You can't get through the gears and into top that quick?'* So I spoke to him about it after and said what I thought he had in that engine; *'What are you going to do about that then?'* And he said; *'Well, if I give you all the bits, the same, you've got to keep your mouth shut, haven't you?'* and they did. BSA gave me all the bits apart from one cog. But that particular gear, which I think was the sleeve gear, I never did actually locate one, so I never got to use it!

This was a dodge Triumph were at too, as while five-speed clusters *were* later listed as extras they were also being used in advance of approval. Triumph fitted them to the Bonnevilles for the 1969 TT but removed them when they had trouble in practice. It was the same for BSA, so as neither actually used them it avoided the inevitable protests.

Clive Wall's BSA Spitfire. He won plenty of trophies on it, but none of them with a five-speed cluster

Steve Brown: Actually when we were in the Isle of Man Brian (Martin) asked me to test the five-speed first, instead of Tony. In case it went wrong, as he didn't want to hurt his top rider! The trouble with the one I was using was that it would change gear, but then stick. You could go up the box, but you couldn't come down again which I found out the hard way. I had to come back round the course in top gear and of course everything ended up knackered. The clutch and that, as I was slipping it everywhere, just to get around.

Crash test dummy. Steve Brown, this time on a TT Marshal's bike. These were much coveted, as built to racing spec

Hugh Evans' *'big'* A50. It went directly from 500cc to 750cc, without the normal 650cc intervening phase

Tony Smith: I had the odd Quaife gearbox to work with. We tried them to be fair. But the thing was they crammed five-speeds into a four-speed space, and they were really just too fragile. You certainly wouldn't want to be racing round the Isle of Man on one. I actually pulled off after half a lap of TT practice as I thought: *'Stop it. It's gonna get you.'*

As mentioned previously engine sizes could also legitimately be increased but only using standard barrels. As such Reg Hardy's approach was legitimate, though oddly the factory did not follow suit. Tony Smith's works machine and others prepared for the Blue Riband events always ran just the maximum standard over bore - 670cc – since taking the barrel beyond this size was felt to make it borderline reliable. Bored too big the barrels could break-off at the base flange. It didn't stop riders getting full 750cc engines though, through an entirely different route.

Hugh Evans: I had an A50 and when I converted it I didn't bother with a 650 I went straight to a 750. So I got a long-stroke crank, an A10 crank, but then thought: *'Great, now the piston comes out the top of the barrel!'* So what to do? Get another barrel, cut the top fin off that, machine it, joint it, pin it and attach it to the top of the original barrel. Then hone it and you got 750. No liner down it, just honed. It never caused a problem with the rings and no one ever did count the fins on that barrel, to see if it was over-sized, though Ray Knight did come close one day when he said: *'How come your 650's so bloody quick*?'

Another area where the factories had no advantage was over foot rests, as rules were universally applied, largely for safety reasons, that: *'Control and footrest positions may be modified to suit the preference of the driver'* though these could – and were – challenged on occasion as the mounting type should not have been changed. i.e. the popular clip-on type handle bars should not really have met the rules. It was the same situation with exhausts and silencers, a regularly controversial issue. As while some kept religiously to the standard items some alterations were allowed and others not. Most clubs worked around the variations of the ACU regulations which allowed:

> *Exhaust pipe/s and silencer/s, with the exception that the actual line of the pipe/s and silencer/s may be varied to avoid alternative footrest position fitted by the manufacturers, providing that the pipe/s and silencer/s are eventually directed rearwards parallel in plan to the direction of the motion of the vehicle and not more than 10˚ inclination to the horizontal.*[12]

Most clubs actually allowed more, so that exhaust pipes could be altered to give increased ground clearance, with the first Oulton Park Clubmans National actually *requiring* silencers to be removed. Clubs normally required silencers however, though even in this case they could be *improved*.

> **Malcolm Stanley:** My first meeting I rode there and took a mate on the back. A Racing 50 Club meeting at Cadwell Park. The footrests dug in at the hairpin, as it was all standard and fetched me off, so it was a case of just straightening the levers out and banging the footrests back before riding it back home again. Then I got a lift to my first Darley meeting. I was still very green, not knowing much about it, but had started as an apprentice mechanic at the time, so was soaking it all up, all the information which was going around, and everything was cross referenced to the bike. The bike had high level pipes and short A10 silencers with their ends cut off. As what you used to do was weld a circular plate back in the end, with holes in it, no baffles, then put it all back together again. There used to be a thing called Metaloid filler and you'd smear that over the weld, then spray it black, so when they put a broom handle up the silencer, to see it had baffles or not for production racing – which is what they did at Darley Moor - it would just hit this metal plate and they'd think it did!

Malcolm Stanley's non-standard A10 silencers were nothing unusual.

Tony Smith's works BSA concealed megaphones inside standard looking silencer bodies, while the Triumph Thruxton silencers achieved the same with a catalogued part

In terms of the factories BSA did their bit by listing their least restrictive 1965 specification silencer (part number 68-2733) on the *'optional parts list'* for the remainder of the 1960s. While Triumph did the same with their Thruxton silencer (part E6238/9 for 1965 and part E6971/2 from 1966), listing it for both the T120 Bonneville and T100 500cc twin, since it was in essence little more than a tuned megaphone, with a long tail piece added on. In truth however there was a fair bit of flexibility with exhaust systems, without actually cheating. This was exhibited by the pipes on Mike Hailwood's 1965 Hutchinson 100 winning production machine, but as these were not available from the factory a pair of enterprising brothers filled the breach.

> **Lester Harris:** We had this idea that we'd start making things, like exhaust pipes, frames, whatever, that would allow us, if we weren't good enough to earn a living out of racing, to at least pay for our racing. But of course it actually finished it. All the experienced chassis people and tuners said the current bikes coming out were too big. We erred towards the bigger bikes, and we were young enough and foolish enough to think that we might know better, and over a time we obviously did, as that's how we've arrived with our chassis business as it is today. But those pipes on the A65, which came out and are tucked right under the bike, then came back out again, we made two or three sets of those initially and they were actually the first thing we ever sold.

Lester was half of the partnership which created Harris Performance, a company now owned and run by Royal Enfield to spearhead new model development. But his views and those of his partner, brother Steve, were illuminating on other aspects of the top production bikes too.

> **Lester Harris:** Production racing was popular. Really popular and on the face of it, the production racers, they looked like a standard motorcycle. But the really competitive bikes, the factory bikes, I mean everything was different, absolutely everything. There was a lot of prestige involved and they did whatever was necessary. Because the factories, they really wanted to win.

Steve (left) and Lester (right) Harris came through the fertile breeding ground of Dick Rainbow Motorcycles before developing their own chassis business. They knew a thing or two about race preparation and with production bikes they recognised a *'ringer'* when they saw one

Steve Harris: Yeah, the factory bikes were quite different. To give you an example, I went to work for another local motorcycle dealer, Les Rugg, who had Longstaff 's. He said one day, out of the blue: *'There's a bike here for sale in MCN. Buy it.'* It was Malcolm Uphill's Bonneville. You know the Isle of Man one, from the TT100 tyres adverts. But over time it got modified back to standard, as gradually we couldn't find the bits. Everything was different on it. Every damn bit of it. It was a genuine one-off. Well, maybe not a one off, but really just one of a handful.

These observations were telling as while there were dodges which most privateers could manage, depending on their wallet, technical nous and brass neck, the factories had an advantage. Tony Smith's works A65 had a one-off, Ken Sprayson-welded, lightweight frame while, as the Uphill Bonneville story reveals, the Triumph factory took rule bending to a whole new level.

The Triumph T120/T100 build books for 1967 and 1968. 18" x 18" and an inch thick they listed hundreds of parts unique to the *'production'* bikes prepared exclusively for the factory. Little of the information ever got outside of Meriden

TRIUMPH

T120 Bonneville

Production	**1962-1975**
Predecessor	**Pre-unit T120/T110**
Bore	**71mm**
Stroke	**82mm**
Capacity	**649cc**
Compression	**9:1**
Front wheel	**3.25 x 19**
Rear wheel	**3.50 x 18**
Front brake	**8" s/tls**
Rear brake	**7" sls**
Weight	**399lbs**
Power	**46hp @ 7,000rpm**
Top speed	**112mph**

The Bonneville was the quintessential British motorcycle. Internally it was very similar to Edward Turner's original 650cc design, the 1953 pre-unit T110, but it took a big step up in 1962 when it went over to unit construction.

This brought in a very neat engine/gearbox unit and a new single down-tube frame which instantly transformed the beautiful, but previously wayward Bonneville into a serious scratcher. Triumph's top of the range model went as good as it looked and it was no surprise that it outlived its T150/160 Trident replacement, in the form of the 750cc Bonneville T140

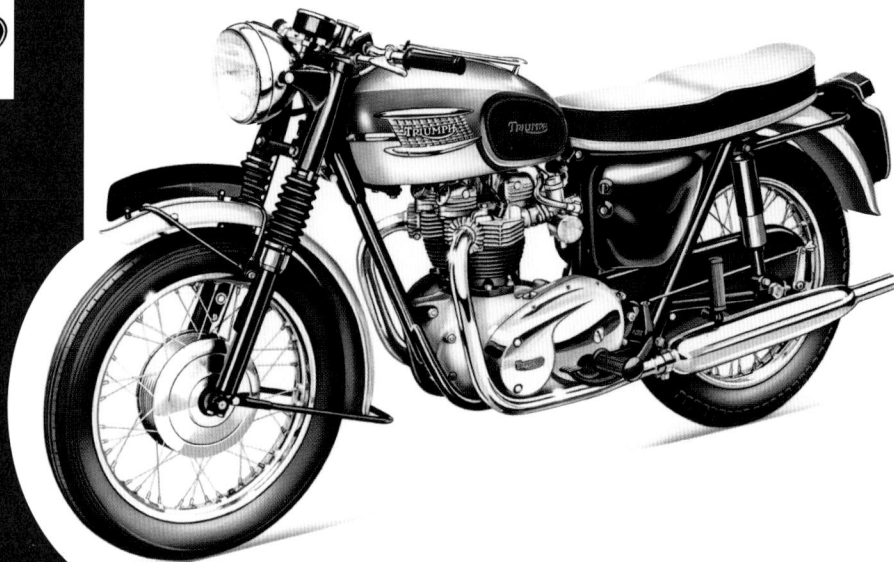

The *Bonnie*

An American name for a British motorcycle explained all you needed to know about Triumph in the 1960s. Export was everything, which makes it even harder to explain quite how *right* the Bonnie was for the UK market. Famously styled by Jack Wickes - Edward Turner's *'pencil'* - it was Doug Hele who got under the metaphorical bonnet to work his wonders mechanically and hone the fabulous machine. The much vaunted Thruxton version was what all the racers wanted, but in truth the standard Bonnie was already difficult to beat. In the early 1960s there were arguably machines which could match it in every area - handling, braking, speed and reliability – but as a package it was peerless. Style-wise it was a killer too.

Meriden's tills rang to the sound of pounds and dollars pouring in and sufficient of those slipped through the shareholders' fingers to improve every aspect of Triumph's top of the range machine.

Sales Manager Bert Thorn outside Comerfords of Thames Ditton. Like many other dealers they could never get enough *Bonnies*. They raced them too

None of this was lost on those thumbing *The Motor Cycle* over coffee at the Salt Box, or a cold beer and *Cycle World* in Santa Fe. If the Gold Star defined 1950s black and white cool, the Bonnie did it in 1960s *Technicolor*. The T120 was the go-to bike for Hollywood celebrities and pop stars, putting Coventry on the American map. Demand on both sides of the Atlantic was huge with Meriden's production capacity, soviet-like, ultimately being the only limiting factor. Triumph could sell every one that they made, helped by the fact that they started to dominate domestic production racing and could match Harley-Davidson and BSA on America's flat-tracks. Then, the wheels fell off the bus.

The Trident, the model earmarked to replace the *Bonnie* failed to hit sales targets, while a raft of proposed new models from BSA-Triumph either bombed or failed to appear at all. Americans still wanted Bonnevilles however, so a workers co-operative kept them coming before a case of *Back to the Future*, in 2001. Care of the resurrected Triumph Company, some heavy 1960s styling cues and the vision of new owner, John Bloor, the *Bonnie* was reborn.

Another successful competitor on the earlier, 1950s pre-unit Bonneville

1964

Birth *of a Legend*

In the '50s and '60s you had a Bonneville if you wanted to go quick, didn't you? The roads were better and I rode a Triumph until I lost my licence. 'Cos you could lose it easy in those days. 60 in a 30 limit, straight away. But the Ace Café had a few racers come out of it and I thought; *'I'll have a go at solo racing too. Let's get Tuning for Speed. Phil Irving.'* Right, so you had the book, you'd sit down in the Ace Café and the others, it'd be like; *'Oh look, there's Dave over there, he's a real racer.'* But you could not get an entry back then. You could not get an entry anywhere.

So, I had to go to Chatter Hall, Scotland, to do my first race. When I got there, with all my mates and bike in an old Commer van, they were like; *'Well Dave, what do you think then?'* I said; *'Well I've learnt the circuit, it's OK, but what I'll do, is I'll follow them round and on the last lap I'll out brake them all'* and added that I thought I could probably win it, as I really thought I could. 'Course, life doesn't work like that, does it. So, come the race, where am I? Yeah, last!

– Dave Croxford

Getting on the grid could still be difficult for the production racers. But once they did the playing field could be a real leveller in comparison to the other classes. One day International licenses required little more than a postal order and stroke of a pen, meaning first timers could do a few club meetings then, within weeks, be rubbing shoulders at Thruxton with returnees from a European Grand Prix.

Chris Lodge: As a 16 year old I had an old Douglas and 'was pottering round the back roads somewhere all dead quiet one Sunday when suddenly, activity! I looked in this field and there were motorcycles tearing around in circles. So, I thought I better have a look. I paid my 3s 6d or whatever it was, went in and there was stone and mud flying all over the place and all this noise and I thought: *'I've got to get into this!'*

I started in '62 actually, on a little 250. It didn't go too well, as I didn't have much knowledge or money, but I was determined to ride and got a 1960 Tiger 110, picked up an *MCN* one day, looked at it and saw they had things like that racing. I guess I was the right age at the right time. As you'd just come out of the austerity of the 1950s but suddenly you had road bikes which could get up to the power of a real race bike, in what was called production racing. There was a new era building up wasn't there, as I couldn't have had done it before. So, in '63, I decided to stick it on the track. I was reading *MCN* all the time and saw the Bantam Club were doing one, a meeting, wrote off for the regs and stayed with the Bantam Club after that, as once you'd entered one race you got your regs sent automatically after that. Back then it was the British Formula Club, the Bantam Club and Brands Hatch running the odd production race, on and off and within a couple of meetings you were in with the crowd. Everybody talked to everyone else, saying: '*See you next week!*' or next month, or whatever, a great scene and I raced from '63 to '68, the same bike, as I couldn't afford anything else. And while I should have been outclassed, as it was a pre-unit T110 against unit Bonnevilles, I won on it a fair number of times and had plenty of places. You know, first three, sort of thing. Though like most everyone else, I did just meeting to meeting, as I didn't know there was anything else.

In my first full season if I'd known what I was doing I could have won the Bantam Club Championship. But I didn't know they even *had* one until halfway through, when someone comes up and says: '*Oh, you've got an awful lot of points!*' I asked what for and they said: '*Well, the club production championship.*' I was in with a sporting chance up to the last meeting of the season and I got three rides. The first ride I think the carburettor came off. The second ride the mag pickup fell off. So, I said to my girlfriend; '*The only thing that hasn't fallen off yet is me*' and of course I ended up in hospital. I finished third in the end behind Ray Knight and Colin Dixon, but I wasn't really bothered.

I just liked the riding and racing, though 1964 it was a bit more serious as I did my first *500-miler* and we were going very well. We had one of the ex-works Thruxtons, an ex-works 1962 Bonneville, pre-unit. They prepared two bikes for the '62 race. Syd Lawton prepared them, he always prepared them, as Triumph never entered them in their own name. Then a friend of mine, Eddie Webb, at the end of

Chris Lodge (top) and Chris Hopes (bottom) negotiating the same Cadwell Park corner, as they approach the famous Mountain. Bathtub enclosures, tank racks, trackside *'furniture'* and bikes parked within feet of the racing line weren't seen as issues in 1964

Paddy Driver (no.40) threading its way through the Thruxton hay bales. In 1964 it was a case of 'close but no cigar'

the year he bought that bike and that race was a pity really. The bike was going well, going quick and handling, which was unusual for one of those frames, when a pin came out of the gearbox selector fork. It was one of those things which wouldn't happen in 20,000 miles on the road. It was annoying as I'd been out an hour or so when someone came by and I nipped in behind. Well, what I wasn't aware of until later, when I read the report of the race, was that he was actually in the lead, as it was South African Paddy Driver. I hung on to him for quite a while, perhaps fifteen minutes, but then I fell off at the chicane, got chucked off.

It didn't matter too much as I was in the paddock within ten minutes, but then unfortunately my mate Eddie pulled in about half an hour later with that gearbox selector pivot I mentioned having come out. Which was a shame, as after an hour or so we were still on the same lap as the leaders and the bike was going quick. Though bad luck could hit anyone. Near the end I remember Paddy Driver comes in again, close to us, pushing. The Renold's guy comes rushing up to put a new chain on but I walk round the front and says: 'Forget it mate, you've got a rod sticking out' which was bad luck, as I think they were still leading. But it was bad luck for us too, as I was surprised how well our bike handled actually. Only the works ones seemed to handle well with the duplex frame, as I rode a standard one a couple of years later, and it nearly threw me off.

The mention of *'works'* Triumphs and *'Thruxtons'* was highly significant in 1964, as while Meriden twins typically packed the grids, contrary to popular belief they didn't always dominate. With the launch of the pre-unit Bonneville in 1959 Triumph arguably had the fastest machine on the road, but this did not translate on to the track. The handling was poor to evil, depending on who you talked to, while the unit construction version introduced in 1963 was initially only marginally better. In comparison however the smaller, 500cc Triumph, was already several years into development and Ray Knight was one of the beneficiaries of the T100's rapidly improving performance. He was in the right place at the right time, as a result of events in that very same *500-miler* where Chris Lodge had just broken down.

Ray Knight: I'd thought that having blagged the factory Constellation once more for the 500-mile race it might provide a good chance of competitive racing mileage at National level, with not too much pre-race maintenance. But a broken connecting rod early on in the event soon terminated that effort. I was later asked whether my maintenance had included fitting new rods but I confessed that even if I'd had the time, which I surely hadn't, I'd never really considered it, thinking that a factory bike would go all the way. I don't think my interlocutor from the factory was impressed.

It was the need to upgrade finances and the desire for yet more pocket money to spend on entering more races that prompted a move to a senior draughtsman's position in a company whose offices overlooked a row of shops, one of which

The shape of things to come. The Thruxton Bonneville in full flight. It was the Ducati 916 of its day. A racer on the road

The trademark *'Thruxton'* giveaway. The long, tapered silencer which worked as well on Triumph's 500 twins as it did on their 650s.

happened to be Hughes, a Triumph motorcycle dealer. The lines of sparkling new bikes were parked in rows on the pavement presenting a tempting sight whenever I glanced away from my drawing board and those bikes began to look ever more attractive. That I sold the Royal Enfield and bought a 500cc Triumph from that local dealer was to have consequences I could hardly have anticipated. I'd calculated that with a 500cc bike there would be a greater choice of races available and that the T100 was probably more competitive in its class than trying to win races outright - as production race grids usually accommodated all classes of bike with *'tinware'* for each. I guess I was what was called a *'pothunter'* in those days. Chancing into the shop one day when it was devoid of customers, giving Stan Brand time to chat about racing, Stan enquired if I'd be riding in the Manx Grand Prix again. I said that I'd got nothing to ride and as a result of a general conversation about racing it brought me to asking about their racers. Stan then offered them both to me. *'Might as well'* said Stan somewhat laconically. And in the event, the bikes came with their mechanic, Ron May, from the Tooting branch, who would choose to *'holiday'* with us. Some holidays they were.

The Thruxton Bonneville

For Ray Knight the culmination of those holidays came in 1968, but in the meantime a far more significant Triumph than the T100 was in the offing, the first victory of which would be scored, by chance, by Knight. Various motorcycles are highlighted throughout this book as staples of the production racing scene. But the one which would supersede Chris Lodge's 1962 model stood head and shoulders above the rest. Triumph's unit construction T120 Bonneville, specifically the *Thruxton* model, introduced to the general public at the Earls Court Show in November 1964. A detailed analysis of these machines is outlined in Claudio Sintich's excellent *'Triumph Thruxton Bonneville 1959-69'* but, as the dates in the title of this book imply and Lodge's comments on his 1962 bike confirm, works-prepared machines appeared a long time before the *'Thruxton'* designation became official. While the meagerness of the resources available to Triumph's Experimental Department – they had no competition department as such – would look comical by today's standards the Meriden factory prepared race machines in industrial quantities in comparison to other

British manufacturers. These might assist with one or two carefully prepared, but largely standard machines, entered through a favoured dealer for the *500-miler*. Alternatively they might offer tuning advice or parts, but Triumph's involvement was in a different league. In 1959 when the pre-unit Bonneville was launched they supplied thirteen machines, in 1960 it was eleven, 1961 saw eighteen bikes prepared and in 1962 in was ten. These were always supplied to preferred dealers and always on the understanding that they were for competition purposes, not for use on the road. When the unit construction version was announced things went up another gear. As Chris Lodge alluded to, the earlier Triumphs, while powerful, were poor handlers and the reason so many Tritons - a Triumph engine in a Norton frame - were built at the time. As such while the new unit construction twin was interesting for its engine of greater significance was the work carried out on the new single down-tube frame. This was a real improvement on what had gone before and of the seven machines built for competition in 1963, the most notable was that despatched to Bennett's of Southampton, as it came second in that years' *500-miler*. However, it was in 1964 that things really changed.

In October 1962 Doug Hele exited Norton for Triumph and it was the nineteen racing T120s which left the factory under his auspices in 1964 which were the first to benefit from his hand. Well, eighteen which left the factory and one, registered AUE 37B, which was retained, to be entered as a *'dealer entry'* through past masters Lawton & Wilson. This machine took what was fast becoming Triumph's traditional second place at the *500-miler,* though under conditions which were a little bizarre.

Lawton entered both a Norton and Triumph in 1964 and at the end of the race it was his two machines which led, Percy Tait's Triumph taking the flag as Brian Setchell's Norton pulled into the pits. The organisers decided they'd both run a lap too long however, the flag coming out too late. The win therefore went to the Norton which Triumph could hardly protest since it would have required the entrant, Lawton, to challenge himself for a win he'd already achieved. He was sufficiently impressed by the Triumph to switch allegiance subsequently however which proved a very wise move on Lawton's part.

The ubiquitous Ray Knight coming in after the first win recorded by an officially designated 1964 *'Thruxton'*, at Snetterton, 3rd July, 1965

Doug Hele's Little Shop of Delights

By the time the Thruxton Bonneville was launched the ACU was getting wise to bikes deviating markedly from standard, built purely to win. This was undermining the principles of production racing and as such only *'extras'* listed by the manufacturers and freely available to the general public were legal to fit. Triumph's response was a list of *Alternative Extras* on the official Triumph *High Performance Specification* list, from engine number DU101 (the first unit construction engine) which ran to over 80 parts. By 1965 this had risen to 120 parts, *including the entire front frame,* and with Doug Hele at the helm that number would rise annually. It made for a better bike and created a virtuous circle, of more riders moving to Bonnevilles, more wins being scored by Triumphs and thus yet more racers being convinced that this was the way to go. On both the road and track pre-unit models were traded in with almost evangelic zeal.

> **Chris Hopes:** The first time I ever raced was Snetterton in 1963 and I finished 3rd to Peter Butler and Ray Knight. That was on a Trophy, a pre-unit Triumph. I borrowed an engine off a friend who had a Bonneville, put his engine in my bike and Snetterton was just easy for me. We had Thornaby airfield near us, which had been a race circuit, and we had full use of it. This airfield was a Mecca for motorcycling, a hell of a circuit, the equal of Snetterton really. So when I went to Snetterton even though I'd never seen it before it was easy. But then I went to Cadwell Park and my bike right, it was bloody annihilated wasn't it. I realised the pre-unit was no good, so traded in my Trophy for a unit Bonneville. I part exchanged it at Cowie's who sponsored Mac Hobson in the sidecars. He was canny, a good bloke Cowie, that's how I got my '64 Bonnie and that was it then. I used to go to Cadwell Park or Snetterton nearly every weekend and Perton I did too, as I won the Midland Club championship that year, so had to race there as well. Though I haven't got anything to show for it mind, as if you didn't go to the awards you didn't get the trophy!

Chris Hopes and '64 *Bonnie*. As with Lodge's machine it still retained the tank rack and all the roadster parts

Chris Hopes, his Triumph now fully faired, moves up on Declan Doyle's similarly streamlined Norton.

The fitting of fairings was always a bit contentious as while Triumph and BSA listed them for their twins most of the other British manufacturers did not

It was a close family among the production racers though, as a lot of us started at the same time. It got more popular and it got more and more competitive every year. Though in the 1960s there was only Ken Redfern that we got involved with around Newcastle, as there was no one and nothing else, not production race-wise up here. The Croft circuit wasn't open yet and you had to go where the production racing was. That was the up and coming class and the unit Bonnie was the one to have, as you got so much feedback from it. It was a tremendous bike, though standard it was slow! I remember we went to Snetterton one time and someone had got a timer on the Norwich Straight. It said 120mph on the speedo, but the timer said 99mph. That's what we were doing on the straight back then, just 100mph. We still delivered the lap times, racing against the likes of John Hedger, Peter Butler and Dave Nixon, though on that big long straight they'd all just come steaming past. Butler and Nixon were phenomenal, as they were on Stan Shenton's bikes, Boyer of Bromley, with George Hopwood doing the tuning and I remember Peter turned up at Aintree one year and really pissed me off. It was me through the corners and what have you, that's why they used to call me *'horizontal Hopes'*, but Butler would come past on the straight bits and in the end you just had to give up, it was a waste of time, as he was through you down the straight.

I got really friendly with Peter though, even though Hopwood and him would go on about us having an axe to do the mechanic-ing with, as we were northerners. And I remember John Hedger taking the piss out of us, for asking to use his pump. As they'd pronounce it *'pamp'* of course, all being southerners. Nixon and Butler were the ones I really got friendly with, while Hedger was the real opposition later on, no one else. As Hedger was a pioneer of hanging off. Mick Andrew was alright, a normal sort of type and Clive Wall I was friendly with too, he was more my sort of person. I remember we went to a Bemsee meeting driving with Clive through London, central London this is, in his Thames van. He was driving along with the sliding doors open, switching the ignition on and off, the exhaust going *"Bang, bang, bang!"* Can you imagine doing that today?

Golden Arrow

Production	**1961-1965**
Predecessor	**Leader/Arrow**
Bore	**54mm**
Stroke	**54mm**
Capacity	**247cc**
Compression	**10:1**
Front wheel	**3.25 x 16**
Rear wheel	**3.25 x 16**
Front brake	**6" sls**
Rear brake	**6" sls**
Weight	**305lbs**
Power	**20hp @ 6,650rpm**
Top speed	**81mph**

In 1959 Ariel took a huge gamble when ditching their entire four-stroke range, for a two-stroke 250. And it very nearly paid off. The initial, fully enclosed Leader was hugely innovative, while the stripped-down Arrow was hugely popular. Ariel won *MCN's* prestigious *'Machine of the Year'* award three years running – from 1959 to 1961 – but then Selly Oak production faltered.

Moved to parent company BSA, investment for further development was not forth-coming and ultimately the Arrow became no one's baby. 36,000 machines were made in total but more sophisticated Japanese offerings had already sounded its death knell

Defeat from the Jaws of Victory

In the early 1960s Golden Arrows, complete with white wall tyres and red handlebar grips were parked outside cafés and coffee bars up and down the country. Val Page's revolutionary design was an instant hit, as while the Arrow and Leader were an engineering tour de force, they were also both stylish and quick.

Handling was exemplary too, through virtue of a ground-breaking beam frame, to the extent that a Herman Meier-tuned version was soon lapping the Isle of Man at over 80mph. Other Arrows rapidly hit the track and Ariel came close to success first time out. At the 1960 *500-miler* Cecil Sandford led, but when co-rider Sammy Miller took a tumble, second place was the result. The production Arrow's engine was not quite the double of Meier's either, so in 1961 it was

get together **with an**
ARIEL

second place again, for Inchley and Good, which they repeated in 1962. Incredibly they then replicated the same results at the Silverstone 1000km races, Inchley and Good coming second in both 1961 and 1962. Talk about ever the bridesmaid! The Arrow really was second best however, as unfortunately, it was the same story on the street. With changes in Britain's learner laws the 250cc market was moving on apace.

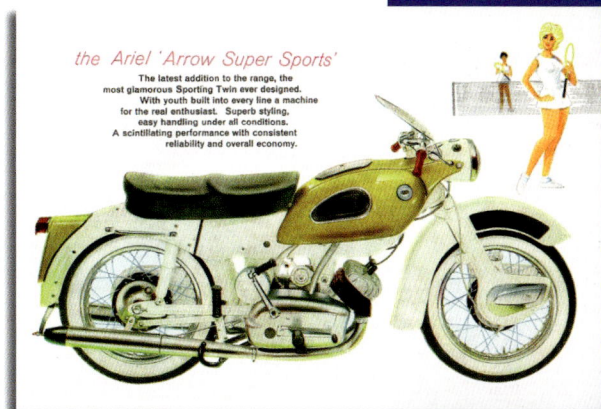

the Ariel 'Arrow Super Sports'
The latest addition to the range, the most glamorous Sporting Twin ever designed. With youth built into every line a machine for the real enthusiast. Superb styling, easy handling under all conditions. A scintillating performance with consistent reliability and overall economy.

The Arrow's pressed-steel box-chassis and dummy petrol tank could have made it look weird but it was actually very stylish and quick for its time too

The sloping, two-stroke, twin had the same bore and stroke dimensions as the incoming Suzuki Super Six so, theoretically, all it needed to stay competitive were twin carburettors and more gears. But both were problematic. The carburettors required a wholesale redesign of the chassis and while Ariel tried a tubular Arrow frame - and even a four-stroke 350cc twin - those were never going to fly. With the gears even keeping four was problematic. The Arrow used a Burman gearbox and with Burman cosying-up to the car industry they'd soon be losing them. The Ariel business was small beer in comparison to Austin-Morris and while Ariel experimented with a BSA C15 gearbox, that was still two gears too few. The Arrow had scored a bull's eye on launch, in a year of record registrations, but as the market headed downward so the Arrow headed south too.

The Leader and Arrow pioneered many new ideas which would be picked up on by the industry in subsequent years. The two-stroke twin cylinder engine was never sufficiently developed however and lacked such refinements as *Autolube* which were becoming standard on comparable foreign machines.

The box-chassis concept was further developed by designer Bob Trigg however, who went onto use it in his later work on the DeltaBox frame for Yamaha

Plenty of wrist and ankle on display on this early bathtub, unit 500. In future years the Triumph T100 would go faster, handle better, stop, and become virtually bullet-proof reliable too, as one of the few British middle-weight machines which actually improved year on year

The mix of stiff competition but equally strong camaraderie was a hallmark of the production racing scene, while Chris Hopes' comments on the competitiveness of the Meriden twins were confirmed by the aforementioned Dave Nixon, Peter Butler and John Hedger all soon appearing on Triumphs. Initially Butler persevered with his 650 AJS however, taking the 1964 season opener at Snetterton from Ray Knight and Chris Hopes, followed by wins in April at Brands Hatch and Snetterton again. The pickings became slimmer thereafter, so while Butler won again at Snetterton it was his and AJS's last. He took the season closer, at Brands Hatch, on a Triumph and it was much the same for Ray Knight. He included three wins at Cadwell Park among his first on a Triumph and there were Triumph wins for Bill Penny, Tony Smith, Chris Lodge and Ray Watmore before the end of the season. It wasn't all Coventry bikes however.

Syd Lawton wasn't quite finished with his Nortons in 1964 and son Barry tried out his father's 650SS at Snetterton on 26th April, in preparation for the *500-miler*, scoring an impressive last to first performance over just six laps. Tony Carlton also scored a double at Oulton Park on a similar machine, but when it came to Nortons, Oscar Dixon was still very much the star. He racked up wins at Perton, Oulton, Silverstone, Snetterton, Cadwell and Aintree over the course of 1964, with the last mentioned event, on 11th July, being the first production race ever held at a circuit better known for horses than motorbikes. It was another indication if one was needed of the increased profile production racing was achieving, as while the *500-miler* had always dominated four or five pages of the weekly papers - *Motor Cycling* and *Motor Cycle News* – now club results featured too. Critically, there was also a new kid on the block when it came to race reporting.

Read all About it!

Launched in 1958 *Motor Cyclist Illustrated* soon became pre-eminent as *the* sports enthusiasts' monthly. There were plenty of papers and magazines to choose from in those days, but many were worthy rather than engaging and they presented news and stories in a public information message sort of form. To be a columnist you required a pipe and letters after your name, while at *MCI* as it was known, things were a little different. *MCI* featured colour photography for a start, while the columns were written by participants in the sport, not observers, including off-road World Champion Jeff Smith, top road racer Joe Dunphy and, in a highly progressive move for the times, production racer Ray Knight.

> **Ray Knight:** It started, when I met Barry Ryerson, the first editor I came across. He was racing with his son down at Thruxton and we met in the paddock, got talking about this and that and I mentioned I wrote bits for the Royal Enfield Club magazine, as I was still racing an Enfield Super Meteor at the time. So, he said: *'Send me something'* and I never looked back after that. It was MCI, *Motor Cyclist Illustrated* initially, then *Motorcycle Sport* in the late 1970s. I'd write up race reports, offer advice and I then started to actually test race machines. I'd take 'em out and try to break them, as that was my forte but, as I rarely crashed anything, after a while people started to come to me with stuff. Offer it and I'd say: *'Yeah, OK, I'd really like to test that.'* So, I was *'it'* for a long time, until Alan Cathcart came along to do a similar thing.

That was a long way in the future when Knight joined *Motor Cyclist Illustrated* in May 1961 but his *PR Notes* column and track tests soon became mandatory reading. *MCI* tapped a rich, un-mined vein, with there being such demand for Knight's agony aunt services that a number of books soon followed, on the subject of how to start racing in this new branch of the sport. The interest never really abated, so his writing moved to *Motorcycle Sport*, *Bike* and *Motorcycle Racing* subsequently as different magazines vied for top spot as production racing's standard bearer. Knight maintained his mantle of *'Mr Production Racing'* however and if there was anything lacking in his columns it was always simply space. Which resulted in one omission which was detrimental to himself. 500cc and 250cc machines ran concurrently with the big bikes and the results of these classes were, out of necessity, often missed. Which was a shame, as Knight and riders such as Dave Nixon actually favoured the 500s, while the 250s had been given a whole new lease of life.

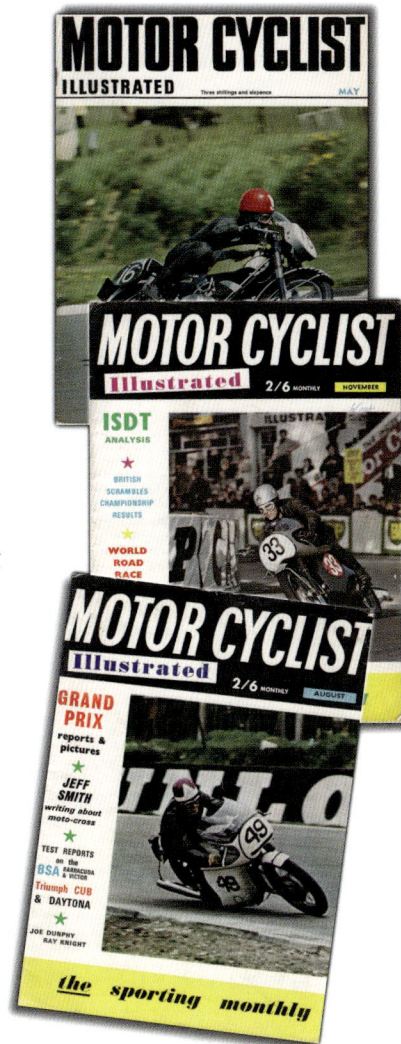

'L' Plate Rockets

The 250cc class was only added to the *500-miler* in 1959, running alongside the 350s which had traditionally been the smallest capacity raced. Bemsee had similarly run the 350 class at its 1000-kilo events and its club meetings until 1962. In 1960 the 350s were dropped from the *500-miler* however and while many believed this was because of the Gold Star monopoly, nothing could be further from the truth.

In 1963 the 1000-kilo had a brace of Triumph Tiger 90s in the lead - the T90 being Triumph's largely forgotten 350cc performance twin - with a Norton 350cc in third place. In 1961 a 350 Norton appeared again, Mick O'Rourke being one of the riders guiding it to second place, while in 1962 the same bike actually won, entered by Norton racing legend Harold Daniell. This was not an OHC International of the type which had harried the Gold Stars a decade earlier however, but a Navigator, the 350cc version of Norton's rather lack lustre 250cc Jubilee twin. It was a factory prepared special, timed at well over the ton, as were the two Tiger 90s entered by Dugdales and Hughes respectively. They'd remain just a foot note in the production racing story though, as the ACU was in constant communication and discussion with the Ministry of Transport and the government had landed a bombshell on 1st July 1961.

Cecil Sandford (top) on the Ariel Arrow, Derek Woodman (middle) an a BSA C15 and Bill Scott (bottom) on a Honda CB72, demonstrating the diversity of the 250cc class. The British machines would soon be gone however leaving the class to the Japanese and Italians

Previously learners could ride any bike, but from that date onward budding café racers would be restricted to 'L' plates and 250cc machines. These had previously been the preserve of ride-to-work commuters. Now, suddenly, every seventeen year old wanted the hottest, fastest, version available and Ariel was sitting pretty with a real ground-breaking, if unorthodox, machine. They launched their innovative if rather sensible Leader tourer in 1958, but they soon had it

The Triumph 'Cub' was a popular machine on the road but lacked the cubes once the learner law was introduced

totally stripped down. The result, the Arrow, was made available a year later and to coincide with the new learner law an even hotter version, the Super Sport – universally known as the Golden Arrow – was released in 1961. Royal Enfield landed on their feet too. Their foray into the 250 market started earlier, with the Crusader of 1956, but their clean and sleek unit construction model lent itself to tuning with plenty of scope for a restyle too. The standard model took the 1960 250-class win at Thruxton and constant updates and re-engineering came to fruition in the form of the Continental GT of 1965. This was arguably the first bespoke café racer built by a major manufacturer, but Royal Enfield had already caught the others napping with their 1962 Super 5. This not only produced a class leading 20hp but came with a 5-speed gearbox. It was a rare mould breaker, as otherwise British manufacturers largely failed to rise to the challenge. There were few, genuine, sporting 250cc machines.

Norton's twin-cylinder Jubilee was an anaemic non-starter and while Triumph's Tiger Cub was raced - particularly in Ireland and Scotland where they had a 200cc class - it was really too small at 199cc. BSAs 250, the C15, lined every high street as the UK's best selling four-stroke 250cc learner machine, but it was also the living embodiment of 1960s *'grey porridge'*. A utility product, of lacklustre performance, on which the accountants counted every bean. Hot C15s *did* exist, in scrambling and other off-road sport, so the loosely related SS80 was BSA's lukewarm offering to learners in July 1961. It had a bit more chrome and a lot less reliability than the standard C15 and did little to stir the pulse. Privateers did campaign them, but road racing singles learned to live in the shadow of Jeff Smith's motocross ambitions at BSA.

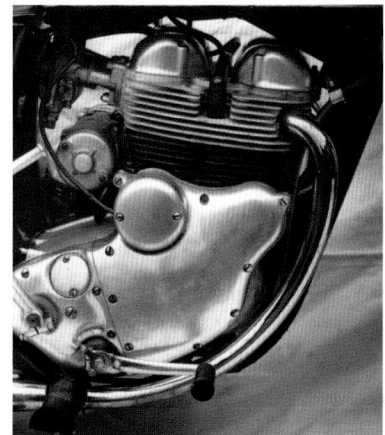

Norton's smaller unit construction twin looked great, but wasn't. The Electra even had an electric start, but won ever less fans than it won races

Chris Vincent: Originally they asked me if I wanted to run one of the hot A10s at Thruxton. They were standard but the engines were doing 120mph at MIRA. A mean of 117mph. We prepared two and Derek Minter had the other one through Comerfords. I could get the bike round OK, but you weren't talking Featherbed Norton and in my first race I was paired with someone who was twelve seconds a lap slower! Second time out, in 1959, I was 7th, but by then they'd changed the brakes. I lost my Gold Star 8" brake and had these full-width Ariel things

Even in top of the range, Sports Star, SS80 specification the C15 was a poor thing, though enlarged it would go on to greater things

on instead. Again the engine was good enough to match an Enfield Meteor or a Norton, but dealers were fiddling quite a bit and BSA wouldn't change a thing. Air filters and gear ratios, they all had to stay standard and after that they put me on a C15, twice, and believe me it was twice too many. By then the Montesas and Bultacos had expansion chambers and were virtually racing spec, but I managed to *'squeeze'* close ratio gears into mine and the engine was done by the bloke who did Jeff Smith's, John Thickens. That bike was fast, really fast, but again too fast for the chassis. The forks were only glorified Bantam jobs really and I told them how bad they were. They sent Brian Martin to the second meeting, from the Comp Shop, so he could see the thing jumping about. But after that race I said: *'I'm not riding that no more'* as they weren't interested in getting some one in like Phil Read or Bill Ivy. If they'd said to me: *'Pick a rider and we'll see what we can do'* we could have done much better.

In truth that was doubtful with the C15 and BSA probably knew it. Vincent's comments on getting hold of top line riders were valid however and given the lower profile of the 250s it was surprising who the manufacturers managed to get. In the early years Grand Prix regulars John Hartle, Derek Minter, Derek Woodman and Bill Smith all appeared on the tiddlers and that level of ability could really deliver the results. In 1964 it was Peter Williams partnered by Tony Wood who took victory at the *500-miler,* but it was on a machine which was arguably one of the worst designs to ever grace a track. The bike, an AJS Model 14 CSR, was entered by Tom Arter, but was prepared at AMC's Woolwich factory by Peter's father Jack, the designer of the 7R. With a 100mph top speed it bore little relation to the abject standard machine and in the wake of race victory many an unfortunate seventeen year old was relieved of £209 17s 9d believing they'd bought a road rocket when they'd actually been sold a pup. The truth was that by 1964 British 250s were already struggling against the foreign opposition, so if any of those AJS owners got their money back a Honda was the way to go. Bill Smith first took a CB72 to victory at the *500-miler* in 1961 with John Hartle then, in 1962, he did it again with *The Mint*. Derek Minter. They were of course exemplary racers, so what impressed learners more was when a genuine dealer version came close again in '65, without an ounce of factory support.

Brian Davis: All we had to do was put petrol in it and ride it. It was from Minear & Bruce in Guildford, dealers who were there for donkey's years. Now Max Minear he was the workshop side of things and Gordon Bruce, big moustache, ex-RAF, a very flamboyant man, he was in the showroom. He said: '*I want to get a Honda on the race track and I think the 500-mile race would be the ideal spot.*' So he provided the bike free of charge and my friend Dave Pierce, he used to run all our production bikes in, he did 1000 miles on it, on the road.

Davis on a less successful machine. A 350cc BSA B40 at Silverstone in 1962. It would be a few years before '*big*' C15s would feature

It was serviced by the American Marty Lunde, as he knew Hondas inside out, those little CB72s and CB77s and he said that with just the standard gearing you could do what he called 'X' the gears. I still don't know what this is exactly, but I think you could swap the standard gears around, putting them on the opposite shafts and it meant we had a close-ratio gearbox for that race, using just the standard parts. We also had the ace-type bars and race seat and rear-set footrests, as they were all part of the Honda race kit. I was racing with Bill Scott and someone complained about these bits, an ACU bloke, called Coleshill. So Bill just opens up the brochure, points at the pictures and says: '*There we are.*'

Brian Davis' partner Bill Scott, this time on the giant killing Minear & Bruce Honda CB72. It was fast but perhaps its biggest asset - as would be the case with many subsequent Japanese machines - was its total reliability. Distance races were won on the track, not in the pits, so the less time spent on running repairs the better

A factory race-kitted CB77, the CB72's bigger brother.

At 305cc the CB77 fell in to a no-mans-land capacity-wise, but it could legitimately be increased in capacity to around 350cc with big-bore kits from Leytonstone dealers Reads. In this guise they proved highly competitive in the 500 class and ultimately would prove a more successful racer than the bigger CB450 which followed

We won the *500-miler* in 1963 on the Triumph but that little Honda in 1965, compared to the opposition we were up against, outgunned by the 650s and that, to finish 7th overall wasn't bad either. It rained like blazes at the start, but we were allowed to use the electric start so you used to leave it in gear, run across the track, pull in the clutch, press and be away. But it rained so hard that an hour in I was thinking: '*I've got another ¾ hour to go before we change over, I hope the weather clears up?*' But just then whipped my goggles up and it was already sunny. It was just that there was so much filth on them I could hardly see. But that little Honda it didn't miss a beat the whole race. No problems. Others were in with clutches and chains, but we were behind Peter Inchley and Derek Minter on that Cotton Conquest, which was a race bike with lights just bolted on of course, and there was also a works Montesa, with the Spanish riders Busquets and Rocamura, which again was just a race bike, with lights on really. So technically we were the first genuine production 250 over the line and 7th overall. Which was bloody good, as I remember the works 500 Velocette of Joe Dunphy and whoever it was, Dave Dixon I think? Every ten laps or so we'd lap them! They won the 500 class but we were *seventeen* laps ahead of them by the finish. We were lucky though, as once we finished the bike went back to the shop and when Gordon Bruce sent one of his mechanics out on it, the timing chain only went and broke!

The Honda CB72 of veteran George Leigh and Fred Stevens also won the 1962 Silverstone 1,000km race and the 1963 version too, at Oulton Park. Where, like Brian Davis, they beat the class-winning 500cc Norton Dominator in the process. The reliability of Honda's machines - the facet the company were most keen to promote - was amply demonstrated and featured heavily in Honda's advertising. An aspect where one manufacturer and competitor missed out mightily, by a curiously noncommittal approach.

Yamaha Miss a Trick

Bruce Cox: I had track tested one of the first Honda CB72 twins in 1961 when I was a feature writer for the weekly magazine *Motor Cycling*. It had actually been prepared for racing by Honda UK and naturally, I raved about it and its potential for success on road or track. In 1962 I moved over to *Motorcycle Mechanics* as Assistant Editor to find that a motorcycle due to be pictured on the front cover of the issue awaiting publication was one that I had no idea was even in the UK. It was actually the very first Yamaha to come into the UK and it certainly earned its keep.

It was provided to us by Mitsui and as I recall, their London operation back then was just one Japanese guy in a prestige office on Exhibition Road, in Knightsbridge, with a secretary/PA. One of the swankiest addresses in the city. He chose *Motorcycle Mechanics* as in those days it was the world's biggest motorcycle magazine with a 150,000 circulation. Hard to believe, isn't it? But I guess he found out what he needed to know as once we'd given it our seal of approval he couldn't be bothered to hawk it around the other magazines, or to ship it back to Japan. So they just told us to keep it and that Yamaha was a bit of a game changer. Staff mechanic Dave Weightman fitted it with a fairing, a racing seat and large capacity fuel tank, plus some expansion chamber exhausts (of questionable efficiency!) and rode it in the 1963 250cc Lightweight TT on the Isle of Man. There were only two other Yamahas in the race, Fumio Ito who came 2nd and Hiroshi Hasegawa who was 4th and Dave was going well himself until it ate a piston mid-race. Other races that the YDS2 contested included the 1963 British 250cc Championship, which at that time was a single international race at Oulton Park. In '63 it attracted a full factory Honda team, on the CR72 twins used for non-Grand Prix international races. Listed in the programme were Jim Redman, Tommy Robb, Luigi Taveri, Bill Smith and Kunimitsu Takahashi. I can't remember where I finished but it was on the same lap as the winner, Tommy Robb, on what was still a standard road-going model under the fairing.

Then we took it to the Thruxton 500-miler where Dave Weightman took the first stint and was going really well. He was involved in a four-way battle for the lead of the 250 class but was knocked off by another rider who centre punched him in the chicane and took him out, breaking his collar bone and dislocating his shoulder. The rules allowed a single rider to do a series of two hour stints provided he rested in the pits for half an hour intervals in between. So I got all the track time I wanted and the bike ran fast and faultlessly all the way through to the chequered flag. It also provided me with a couple of items for the memory bank. First of all,

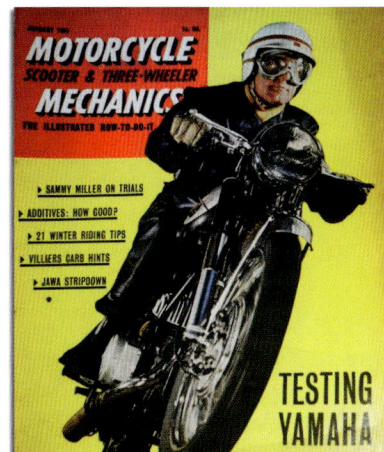

The YDS2 on test in Motorcycle Mechanics. All in all it got a lot of use but Yamaha were slower on to the market than Suzuki

The Yamaha YD series went on through various Marks from the YDS2 to the YDS6.

The YDS7 was actually a ground-up redesign - the first variant of the hugely successful RD series - and it was only with this model that the Yamaha 250 really took off in the UK

the organisers of the Barcelona 24 Hours race paid a visit to our pit box with a contract in hand and an offer of 150 pounds in appearance money. That was at a time when my take home pay was £17 a week! So, in as long as it took for me to make a hastily scribbled signature on the bottom line, I went from being a club racer to an international professional. The other memory I have is that the race gave me a chance to ride wheel to wheel with a personal hero of mine, Grand Prix legend and former MV Agusta team rider, John Hartle. A dice which seemed to go on for an hour, but was probably twenty minutes, with Hartle on a Super Five, riding it for *Scuderia Duke*. Our Yamaha was good for around 90mph and, somewhat surprisingly, the Enfield was able to match that. Obviously it had a very special camshaft and we were side by side down the straights. But him, being John Hartle and me being me, he'd pull away going into the corner, but coming out, him trying to get back on the cam, I had a super amount of low down power in comparison. I had more bottom end so could pull away and, as it was the only time I ever shared the same bit of track with Hartle, it was frustrating having to pull off for a rest. But it proved that the YDS2 could outpace the hitherto all-conquering Honda CB72. George Leigh and Fred Stevens had won the 1000-kilo on one of those, beating all the 350s and 500s, well, we never saw them, as we were in front of them the whole time, on a par with the factory Bultaco and Montesas. But Mitsui was an advance guard trading company, which might well have bought in sewing machines and what have you as well. So while it all went into a report back to Hamamatsu or wherever, it was two or three years later before the Yamaha road bikes started to really come along.

By the end of the sixties Billy Ivy had taken two world titles for Yamaha and Phil Read an impressive three. Yamaha's dominance was so complete that within a couple of years there was little point competing in the sub-500cc categories unless you had a TD or TR2, their all-conquering *'customer'* Grand Prix racers. It was different on British high streets however. That two or three years delay meant that Yamaha were slower than their Japanese competitors in setting up a dealer network, so while Yamaha won the 250cc World Championships learners bought 250cc Honda CB72s or Suzuki T20s instead.

In 1964 while Nortons were being bettered by Triumphs in the club championships they were still proving dominant in the higher profile events. Charlie Vance was typical, seen here at Castle Combe on an early Dunstall Model 88

If it was frustrating for Yamaha it was frustrating for Triumph too. The 1964 Bonneville was an outstanding machine, the best out there, but it was mainly older Triumph models on the track. They won, but not habitually and the *500-miler* was a case in point. The top five here were Norton, Triumph, Velocette, BMW and Velocette again. The class wins went to Norton (1000cc), Velocette (500cc) and AJS (250cc) and those results had real impact on the street. In 1963, the year the unit Bonnie was launched, Norton won the *Motor Cycle News* machine of the year award with the two year old Dominator 650SS. The *500-miler* win by the Syd Lawton entered machine was a huge influence and race results told again in the 1964 awards. For the first and only time the *MCN* title, voted for by their readers, went to a pure racing model, the Greeves Silverstone. It became a runaway success and just shy of two hundred were sold. It demonstrated quite how important race results were becoming for manufacturers and for 1965 Triumph thought they finally had things nailed. Further improvements were made to the standard T120 Bonneville and for the first and only time the bikes were given the official *'Thruxton'* designation by the factory itself. The machines were built between December 1964 and May 1965, to meet the ACU stipulation of two hundred machines to qualify for the *'production'* criteria. There were actually only ever fifty two, but presumably the ACU never asked how many were made and Triumph never offered? The parts for these machines included an entirely different frame, with an altered head-stock angle, but the most obvious modification was a unique exhaust system which effectively enclosed a racing megaphone within a long, cigar shaped, silencer. Their performance was felt by Doug Hele to be easily sufficient to see off the dominant Nortons, but as history would prove, Nortons weren't the only problem.

In October 1964 a small *'advanced warning'* leaflet went out to BSA dealers in the UK announcing that the previously export-only, twin-carb, Lightning 650cc and Cyclone 500cc models would be available in the UK in 1965. Additionally there would be a limited run of 200 *Clubman* versions – and 200 *were* genuinely made - at £4 extra, fitted with cosmetic, café racer, parts. What difference could £4 make?

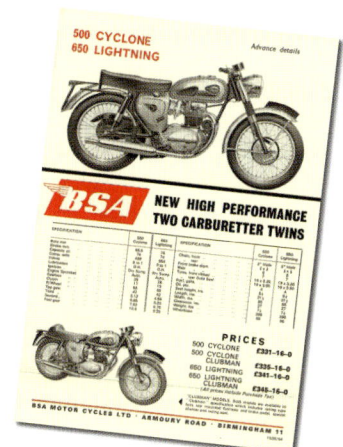

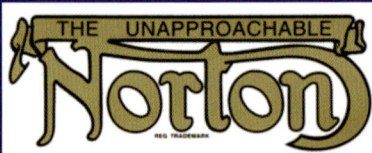

THE UNAPPROACHABLE Norton

Dominator 650SS

Production	1961-1968
Predecessor	600cc Dominator 99
Bore	68mm
Stroke	89mm
Capacity	646cc
Compression	8.9:1
Front wheel	3.00 x 19
Rear wheel	3.50 x 19
Front brake	8" sls
Rear brake	7" sls
Weight	398lbs
Power	49hp @ 6,800rpm
Top speed	115mph

The reputation of the *Best Handling Motorcycle in the World* came courtesy of a Featherbed frame in 1952, when the Bert Hopwood designed Model 7 become the 88. It was joined by a 600cc version too, the model 99 in 1956 and the 650cc Dominator Sport Special, or 650SS, in 1962.

The same basic long-stroke design then spawned the 750 Atlas and Commando, which you could still buy in 850cc form in 1976. The 650SS was the archetypal 1960s featherbed however and it was available in any colour you wanted, as long as it was Norton's classic racing colours of black, silver and chrome

The World's Best Road Holder

Norton's Dominator was dominant in name only during the 1950s. Norton won Grands Prix with the Manx single, but their biggest twin was a bit of a slow burner. Until the 650SS. This had the new *slim-line* version of the famous featherbed frame, being narrower and more comfortable, and Norton quickly landed a broadside with a unique treble at the 1962 Silverstone 1000km race, where they won all three production classes. This was followed up by a win at the Thruxton 500-miler later in the year, which also became a treble. Since they won the *500-miler* three years running. It wasn't surprising the 650SS won *MCNs 'Machine of the Year.'*

Norton was on a roll. Except that they weren't. 1962 also saw the last Norton leave their historic Bracebridge Street factory, as behind the scenes all was far from well.

N 650/SS

As part of the bigger AMC conglomerate production was moved to Woolwich and there was little time for the frivolity of competition. Indeed, the *500-miler* results were always down to tuner Syd Lawton, rather than Norton. So when Lawton switched to Triumph the wins switched to Triumph too. Though there was some life in the old dog yet.

During the 1960s there was a resurgence in the café racer scene and ambitious south London dealer Paul Dunstall was at its heart. He bought from Norton their entire cache of parts for the Domiracer - a planned twin-cylinder replacement for the Manx, based on the Dominator – and got himself registered as a manufacturer at the same time. Through this he was soon entering blisteringly fast Nortons as Dunstalls, in souped-up, customised form.

On the track Ray Pickrell in particular proved unbeatable on them and while Dunstall's very heavily modified Nortons weren't always universally popular in the

production racing world, through extension they prolonged the 650SS's reputation as a genuine high performance road machine. Realistically the standard *Bonnie* was still the thing to have on the road but, customised, a Norton from Dunstall had similar if not better performance and a lot more racing credibility and bling.

The Dominator came in many guises over the years but the 650SS was always the one to have

Lightning *Strikes*

I'd got mates with motorcycles and we often went up to Bridgnorth. Not just riding but racing on the road and ending up in coffee bars. Then we went to see some road racing at Oulton, Mallory and Darley Moor and realised that we could actually race a road bike in the production class. Four of us joined different motorcycle clubs and I joined Darley Moor. I'd seen a BSA Lightning Clubman at the Blackpool show and I finally found one at the Coventry Motor Mart. Norman Vanhouse, the local BSA Rep. was there when I collected it and years later, at a TT function, he told me he'd thought: *'That lad won't last long'*

– Bob Heath

Nineteen sixty five was all set to be Triumph's year. Everything was in place to end their run of second places at the Thruxton 500-miler and the gloves were off in terms of factory involvement. Everyone knew the bikes in which the Meriden factory had a hand. Triumph also had their eyes on a new, Blue Riband, production event, but it didn't all go quite to plan.

Tony Smith: I started off at sixteen with a second-hand BSA 250 C11G and as no one had ever had a motorcycle in the family I went very slowly initially. As there was no one to show me and I didn't really know what I was doing. But after six months I understood, 'was quick and by seventeen I had a brand new Triumph Thunderbird and was flying. I could get it sideways on the road and my first race came soon after, at Snetterton. John Bowman and Barry Lawton were there, the guys to beat, but by now I'd sold a Mk 1 Zephyr for a brand new Bonneville and got red flagged I got so excited, as I ended up doing two extra laps! But I finished fourth out of thirty five or forty riders and second time out I was third. My second event I went to Cadwell Park. I'd never practiced there as I couldn't afford it, so I just walked round the circuit beforehand, but won both races. This was the Bantam Racing Club and I won my first championship in '62. But it took off for me really in '64, as Peter Butler had a new Thruxton Bonneville and with that we came fourth in class at our first attempt. At the

Thruxton *500-miler* would you believe, and we were just a couple of kids. I was working for Dick Rainbow Motorcycles by then, after Clarkes Engineering and though they were very small, Rainbow's were a full BSA dealer. So, the logical thing was that we would run a BSA in races, to promote the business and that's how it all began.

I was so keen to do well that we bought one for racing and one for the road. It was the only way to do the job properly. I literally lived on it. Dick bought the race bike and I bought the road bike. We went to the factory on the Wednesday to collect the race bike, as I had an entry at Brands for the opening race of the season, March 1965. They said they'd have one ready, but it wasn't, so Fred Green, the Sales Manager, promised they'd deliver it Friday and Dick said: *'You better have your bosses there, my boy's gonna win'.* I hadn't even sat on the bike! Not only that but I hadn't raced for six months and come race day it was raining. Can you imagine, a brand-new bike, unknown, in the wet, Brands Hatch on the long circuit? Anyway, they dropped the flag and I disappeared. I never looked back and apparently at the end of the race there was no one else in sight. I thought; *'This bike's pretty damn good!'* and that season I had a hard time not to win.

That first victory for Tony Smith and the Lightning Clubman was on 21st March, at the Brands Hatch Redex Trophy National meeting, where Smith rubbed shoulders with the other winners, Minter, Simmonds, Vincent and Degens. This was headline stuff, as were the announcements of Oscar Dixon getting beaten at the second meeting of the season. It was not the result which made the headline - Dixon and his Norton weren't invincible - but the venue. As Darley Moor was a new circuit and from their very first meeting there was a production race on the programme. It was the UK's first one circuit Production Championship. New ground was being broken.

The Darley Moor circuit ran production races from its very first meeting in 1965

Another win for a T120 Thruxton Bonneville at Snetterton. A few years earlier *'real'* racers wouldn't have given a Triumph twin a second glance in the paddock, but suddenly they were everywhere and posting very impressive lap times

Brian Nadin's Triumph took the honours that day, Good Friday, after which wins were divided pretty evenly between Triumph, Norton and BSA riders throughout the early season. Dixon and Doyle were joined on the top step by the Nortons of Bill Bate and Dave Vallis. While Brian Nadin's victory was added to by the Triumphs of Knight, Butler, Watmore and Nixon. Dave Nixon's wins at Snetterton and Cadwell being noteworthy as taken on Triumph's smaller, 500cc twin, over full 750cc opposition, while to Knight went the privilege of taking the first win on a Bonneville officially designated as a Thruxton. It wasn't just the newest models at the head of the field though. Reay Mackay's Vincent 1000cc won Trophy Day, at Silverstone's wide, open, expanses, Barry Boase showed a BSA Gold Star could still cut the mustard at Darley Moor and both Ray Hole and Kenny Matthews had wins on the Birmingham firm's older A10s twins. Publicity-wise these were yesterday's news however as all eyes were on BSA's latest, the Lightning Clubman twin.

On Saturday 24th April Tony Smith claimed the fastest lap at Snetterton, which *Motor Cycling* reported as *'a shattering 86.95mph'*[13] and while he was subsequently out with a suspected broken neck – it wasn't – his sponsor, Dick Rainbow, bought two more Lightning Clubman models. Fortune had it that Mick Andrew's dad owned the chemist shop over the road from Rainbow's dealership and on 29th May he had a try out at Cadwell Park, coming 5th and 3rd, each time ahead of a presumably peeved Ray Knight. With Smith recovered the Dick Rainbow runners then returned to Snetterton on July 18th as a warm-up to the following week's Thruxton 500-miler. It couldn't have gone much better. Andrew and Smith won three of the four big bike races with another Lightning rider, Bob Lovell, taking the final victory. Indeed, the final production race was a BSA A65 clean sweep, of Andrew, Lovell and Smith, so things looked good for Thruxton, or Castle Combe, as it turned out to be.

When the Thruxton 500-Miler….. Wasn't

Triumph had a lot riding on the *500-miler*. Not having won the race since 1961, wheeling out a machine officially named the *'Thruxton'* came with no small reputational risk. Triumph were also blindsided somewhat by the Southampton & District Club moving the event. The Thruxton circuit badly needed resurfacing so the race suddenly became the *Castle Combe 500*, which didn't have the same ring to it at all. It also ruined Triumph's publicity when the Lawton-entered Thruxton Bonneville duly took the victory, in the hands of his son Barry and Dave Degens. Publicity-wise the story was also further spoilt by Triumph loading the deck. Those in the know were aware that at least seven of the Triumphs entered were factory-tuned Thruxtons from the latest 1964 production run, with other Triumphs making up two-thirds of the 750cc class entry. It was long odds on anyone else getting a look in especially as there were some untested machines in the field, including the Eddie Dow A65.

Tony Smith on the Dick Rainbow Motor Cycles Lightning Clubman. They were the surprise package of 1965

Barry Lawton (in glasses), Syd Lawton and Dave Degens receive the *500-miler* trophy. Triumph's success rate at the Blue Riband events - the *500-miler, Hutch* and Production TT - was good, but actually less than popularly believed

John Gleed: I remember making a solid head gasket for that bike out of a piece of copper, with a hacksaw and file, buggering about because we knew the head gaskets were suspect as they were. They were composite and of course after a short while BSA started making them solid too. But there were none available for the bikes being prepared for that race and what happened to the bike was that there was a problem with the oiling. The return feed-pipe hole wasn't big enough and it allowed oil to back-up in the crankcase, which then got very hot. It rattled the bottom-end out which is why Rod Gould never got a ride. I remember it as Tony Smith came up to me - I didn't know him from Adam at the time - and started talking about the oil feed. I mentioned we had the same problem and he said: *'We had to drill out the hole in the top of the return pipe, to allow more oil to come back into the oil tank, to keep the temperature down.'* And of course his bike went very well, so we did that afterwards too.

Smith's bike did go very well, as did the other Dick Rainbow-entered Lightning, both acquitting themselves admirably. They were second and fourth overall and had they not split their two best riders, Smith and Andrew, who knows, they might have taken the win. This was a fact which was not lost on BSA, several of whose staff were watching. They were impressed and, as a result, wheels were set in motion back at Small Heath which would result in a dramatic one-off ride.

That was three weeks away however and there were still other significant stories to tell at the *500-miler*. In the 500cc class no one would have bet against winners Joe Dunphy and Dave Dixon on their Velocette Venom, as they were rapidly gaining a reputation. The 250s were less predictable however. With the *500-miler* being part of the *Coupe d'Endurance* series continental riders on Montesas, Ossas and Bultacos were to the fore, with the Busquets/Rocamura Montesa Impala ultimately claiming second place. It was two laps adrift of a left-field entry from one of Britain's smallest manufacturers however, which raised lap speeds and eyebrows in equal measure. The Cotton Conquest might rightly have been named the Cotton Conflict and arrived at Castle Combe shrouded in a spare *'Norman Motorcycles'* cover to avoid too much unwanted scrutiny. Factory records showed that the engine had no generator - a dummy wire was tucked into the appropriate casting – and when presented for scrutineering there was much head scratching and comments along the lines of: *'We can't pass that. It's nothing like standard'.* They were hard to counter. Since even the supposed standard Conquest of Roger Corbett and Dave Browning looked nothing like the road bike, while the factory entry had completely different steering geometry to both. The waters were smoothed by Neville Goss, who stepped in to take personal responsibility and to sign-off the required documents himself. Why was he so lenient? Well, Pat Onions of Cotton had previously checked with the ACU on what special parts were allowed and Goss had confirmed that

John Chubb in striped jumper, John Gleed with hand to mouth and rider Ron Langston in leathers, discuss the finer points of the Eddie Dow Clubman with an unidentified well-wisher. The bike went out with an oiling problem before co-rider Rod Gould could even get on it

Cotton had carte blanche to list whatever they wanted to, as long as people could genuinely buy the parts over the counter. Which, in the case of the Conquest they could, as the engine was essentially the same as in their full racing machine, the Telstar. Pat Onions wasn't going to let this opportunity slip so passed on the Telstar list, wholesale, to be typed up by the company secretary, Doreen Denley. Onions was then faced by her husband, his business partner Monty Denley, wanting to know: *'What the hell was this all about'* with Denley stating emphatically and firmly that he'd have nothing to do with something which looked illegal.

As such, after everyone else had gone home, Onions sat over the typewriter, tapping out, one-fingered, *'The approved parts list'* for the Cotton Conquest and posted it himself to the ACU office in Holborn. Hell, it was one better than Edward Turner at Triumph. He probably couldn't type at all and Cotton's list was far less creative than the Thruxton's. You *could* genuinely buy the Cotton parts.

Derek Minter gets the plaudits for his Cotton performance while a wreathed 750cc class winner, Dave Degens, looks on

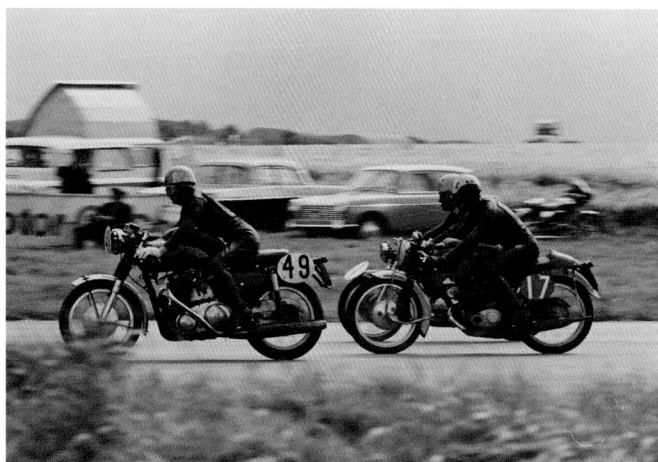

Minter's co-rider Peter Inchley closes up on Billy Ivy's Norton powered Matchless G15

Everyone knew that the Derek Minter/Peter Inchley machine was a wrong 'un, but in this regard it was no different from the Spanish machines around it. The ACU were going to sign off these bikes as eligible so Neville Goss probably thought; *'Why not the Cotton too?'* in a case of *'What's sauce for the goose is sauce for the gander.'* Even if it made a bit of a mockery of what production racing was meant to be all about.

No seventeen year-old was ever going to buy any of the machines involved in the debacle. The Cotton was too expensive and impractical – for God's sake, you had to lean it against a wall, it didn't even have a stand - while some of the Spanish machines weren't even imported. It meant that the third and fourth placed machines at the *500-miler*, Honda's CB72 or Royal Enfield's Continental, would Hoover up the sales. This was because production race results were now routinely used to promote the road machines, a fact which was nowhere better demonstrated than in the adverts following the result of the UK's *'premier one day meeting.'*

A grid dominated by Triumph twins. Many were still pre-units however and these older models would continue to be campaigned into the early 1970s, many very successfully

BSA

A65 Lightning

Production	**1965-1972**
Predecessor	**A65R Rocket**
Bore	**75mm**
Stroke	**74mm**
Capacity	**654cc**
Compression	**9:1**
Front wheel	**3.25 x 19**
Rear wheel	**3.50 x 18**
Front brake	**8" sls/tls**
Rear brake	**7" sls**
Weight	**395lbs**
Power	**51hp @ 6,750rpm**
Top speed	**110mph**

Replacing the popular A10 was always going to be a tall order for the A65 and the original model didn't help itself. Staid, conservative and mildly tuned, it arrived in pastel shades with similarly tepid performance. The Star struggled to reach 100mph, but it spawned the Lightning which America appreciated particularly, for its in-your-face style and thundering performance.

Other models followed but the Lightning was always the biggest seller among the 100,000 A65s BSA produced. And while it arguably emerged from a 1971 restyle better looking than it had gone in, financially BSA had already cooked their goose.

The Birmingham Bonnie Beater

The A65's groundbreaking, smooth, engine design always divided opinion. It initially struggled to emulate the popularity of the A10, particularly when the anaemic Star was lined up alongside the final, stunning, A10 Rocket Gold Star. It was no competition. However, the A65s over-square motor and modern, flat, combustion chamber design knocked its adversary's gas flow into a cocked hat and once a twin-carb head was launched so too was an engineering epiphany. There was not just a Lightning, but a *Clubman* too, on which Mike Hailwood won the Hutchinson 100 in 1965. John Cooper matched him in 1966, but this was on the Spitfire, a Lightning with attitude.

At 128mph the Spitfire MkII was the fastest road bike ever tested and those tests were ecstatic. With a caveat. Fantastic performance came at the price of wayward ignition timing, finicky carburettors and rumours of bottom-end frailty. It meant that subsequent versions of the *Bonnie-beater* were de-tuned, marginally, though they always looked glorious and re-established BSA's credentials for making serious road burners. In racing terms BSA missed a trick however.

With its class-leading 68-473 Spitfire camshafts - so good Triumph copied it – the Clubman and subsequent Spitfire had all the makings of winners, but then BSA stood back, non-committal, expecting dealers and privateers to do all the work. Chris Vincent, Norman Hanks, Peter Brown and Mick Boddice – all TT winners or British Champions – worked at BSA and raced A65-engined sidecars. Their knowledge was never really exploited however and it was a similar story with the development of the road bikes.

Dealer feedback was largely ignored, though the final oil-in-frame 1971 Lightning was a fabulous, flat track-inspired, eyeful. Its launch coincided with Dick Mann winning the American Grand National title and coveted AMA No.1 plate, but BSA invested too little and it was also far too late.

By the time Mann picked up his trophies, the last A65 was rolling out of Small Heath. BSA arguably had the right product at last, but they had unfortunately missed the boat.

Ray Jones with the Lightning he bought new in 1965. A happy customer? In 2022 he still owned it

The ultimate seal of approval. Mike Hailwood on a road-going
BSA Lightning Clubman at the UK's premier one day event

The *'Hutch'*

The Hutchinson 100 is now long forgotten. But it was billed as Britain's premier one day meeting up to 1976, when Barry Sheene won the last running of the event on his World Championship-winning Suzuki RG500. The meeting had started at Brooklands in 1925, but moved to Silverstone post-war and took a big step up in 1963 when the *Daily Express* moved in as title sponsor. 1964 saw huge crowds witness the MV Agustas, Hondas and MZs which they could otherwise only read about in the absence of a British Grand Prix and 1965's event was even more significant. With the cash and clout of the Beaverbrook publishing empire behind it, the *Hutch* – as the Hutchinson 100 was universally known - saw every reigning World Champion lured to compete. But that was not enough. The *Daily Express* wanted close racing, popular appeal and ideally a British bike winning and there was only one formula which could deliver that. A production race.

At the time Mike Hailwood was winning all before him. He had just claimed his third 500cc World Title for MV Agusta and had won every race so far in 1965. While Hailwood is revered today as a virtual deity, he was still not the finished article in 1965. Skepticism abounded, particularly that his success was down to the money of his father, *'Stan the wallet'* and that, fundamentally, he might not actually be as good as his results made out.

Tom Kirby: This upset Mike no end. He was frustrated with the lack of equal competition which would put the others in with a chance to beat him, if they could. His tarnished public image badly needed restoring. It worried Mike to the extent that he approached me on the subject, asking my advice: *'What do you think I should do 'Uncle'?'* I said that there was only one thing he could do: *'Get a bike for the production race at Silverstone and blow them all off! Nobody can say it was the bike if you win on a standard road machine, identical to everyone else's.'* Mike was amused at first, but the more he thought about it the more he liked the idea: *'I'll do it'* he said. And how.

Peter Brown: I had instructions from Clive Bennett that Mike Hailwood was going to ride an A65. *'Would you build the engine?'* So, I did, and we went down, with Clive in tow of course, to Silverstone. 'Would have been the Thursday as then we had another day messing about, when Clive says: *'Oh, we've made another frame for you as well. It's got a so and so head angle. We can change that tonight and you can try it tomorrow.'* Hailwood just says: *'Well if you want to. But this is OK, it doesn't worry me.'* He just got on the bike, rode it as it was and blew them all off. And with a virtually standard engine. Nobody believed us but there was hardly anything in those early engines that wasn't standard. We always used production camshafts and pistons. We didn't have anything else. It's just that the design of the engine lent itself to development.

Mike Bowers: The bike that Hailwood won the Hutchinson 100 on was actually my *'going-home'* bike. They did do a special bike for Hailwood, but Hailwood didn't like the bicycle. He liked the engine, but he just didn't like the bicycle. So, he rode several, differently set-up. My old knackered going-home bike was well fettled, fork-wise, suspension-wise and everything else-wise, as I was into that sort of stuff, and the chassis did everything he wanted it to do. Being a motocross-er mine was slightly different in that it had got different length dampers and stuff on it, which jacked it up slightly at the back, and that's probably where stories about a different head-angle came from. Mike liked the chassis, so they pinched basically most of it and Hailwood won of course, beating Percy Tait, which the Triumph people weren't best pleased about.

Hailwood and fellow Continental Circus rider Paddy Driver share a joke during practice for the *Hutch*. The participation and endorsement of riders of this calibre was a huge coup for the production racing world with multiple World Champion Phil Read being another A-list rider who would continue to support the class

While the three foreign world champions, Jim Redman (350cc), Luigi Taveri (125cc) and Hugh Anderson (50cc) watched from over the railings, Britain's two youngest and brightest World Champions, Phil Read and Mike Hailwood, were among the grid which formed up for the new International Production Race. Frank Perris, John Cooper, Peter Williams and Paddy Driver added a bit more Grand Prix dash. *Motor Cycle News* also came in as the race's title sponsor, to stamp their name on a piece of production racing history, as Hailwood won for BSA, Birmingham and for Britain. That sounds slightly more poetic than it was for those in attendance, and there were thousands, as the 1965 Hutchinson 100 was largely memorable for the horrendous weather in which it took place. The rain was torrential, but it didn't seem to worry Hailwood, who pulled away to win, with two other Lightnings having also briefly led. Tony Smith's Dick Rainbow entered machine and an Eddie Dow version, ridden by another British World Champion in the making.

Rod Gould: The first bike I raced was a 350 Gold Star which I bought from Eddie Dow. It was about the fastest 350 Gold Star out there and I could give Manx Nortons a good run for their money. Eddie was very good to me after that, when I was a sort of semi-professional, as I worked for him when I wasn't racing and in the evenings I could use the workshop to work on my race bikes. Though the people who built the A65 were John Chubb and John Gleed. The first race we were entered in was the Thruxton 500 and I did the road testing on it, ran it in and everything else and while I practiced Ron Langston came off in the first hour so I didn't actually get to ride. But I raced it again

Rod Gould on the BSA Lightning Clubman. Like many other dealers Eddie Dow used the bike as a mobile showcase for his Taylor-Dow tuning parts and cosmetics, as an adjunct to his better known Gold Star components

later in the production race at Silverstone. A friend of mine, the journalist Bruce Cox, was on the inside of the corner at Woodcote and next to him was Mike Hailwood, who was also with a friend. I was coming round on this A65, wide open, and it was weaving all over the place, and Bruce said Mike's mouth fell open and he said: '*Faaarkin'ell...! Just look at this!*' It *was* incredible, as I didn't really know much about setting a bike up back then. So, it was a case of wide open and hang on hard. That was in practice. It was alright in the race as I was used to it by then, 'got a great start, led the field away until half way round, when I ran wide on a corner and Percy Tait and Mike Hailwood passed me. I sort of got back in mid-field, got through them again and if I hadn't been so young and the blood gone to my head I think I could have been a bit closer to them by the end.

He was still fourth behind the two works Bonnevilles ridden by Percy Tait and reigning 250cc World Champion Phil Read. So whichever way you looked at it, it was a big day for BSA. '*Hailwood's Hutch*'[14] ran one headline '*Mike kills that MV myth*'[15] was another. BSA themselves perhaps lost the initiative by not pushing Hailwood's win better in the press, but what wasn't lost on them was the opportunity seen by Sales Manager John Hickson. He was equally impressed by the recent performances of youngster Tony Smith. His second place at the Thruxton 500 was noteworthy, but what really caught Hickson's eye was Smith's little publicised achievement at the Hutchinson 100, since Gould's wasn't the only A65 to have pushed Hailwood.

Tony Smith was one of the nearly men of British racing. Employed by BSA from 1966 to both race machines and prepare them for others he worked in the shadow of the company's off-road focus

BSA's *'Comp Shop'* circa 1964. All of it - Graham Horne, Arthur Crawford and Jeff Smith. It would grow and though Horne was a road racer the focus would always be on off-road competition

Tony Smith: When it came around to the Hutchinson 100 this was like *the* big race of the year. Hailwood was the cat's whiskers and they were going to give him the best bike they could. So we figured that we had to do something different, to try to close the gap. And what we did was exactly what the factory had done to his one. Which was increase the inlet valve size, to the size of those going in the '66 road bikes. But we'd never seen in his bike of course and the problem was we didn't have the right valve springs for it. So, it was actually 1,000rpm down on what it would rev to before. But I was blessed, as in the race it rained, which virtually eliminated the deficit of the speed it lost. So I managed to stay ahead of Hailwood for a while, though the writing was on the wall. He wasn't bad was he? Probably the best the world has ever seen.

Once the B40 developed into the B44 it would actually become a formidable endurance racer. But for now the Victor remained just for the mud

So, it was inevitable and at Chapel Curve I aquaplaned off the circuit and on to the grass, stood it up and had to jump off. But what I'd done impressed the factory sufficiently for them to give me a call. A month later I was working there. I walked in that first morning and asked what to do. The foreman just said: *'Build us a race bike.'* I was like a kid in a sweet shop. It was the best job in the world! I asked John Hickson why he wanted me and he said: *'Because your bloody bike was beating the factory one!'* and I inherited that bike after. It was good, but in the space of twelve months it was transformed. If Hailwood had the same bike a year later, he'd have been even further away.

Smith at the *500-miler*. He was still on a very standard machine

The Factories Get Involved….*a bit*

He wouldn't, tester Norman Hanks actually wrote the bike off while testing it on the road, but the big take away from the whole *500-miler/Hutch* story was that the country's biggest manufacturer was taking production racing seriously. Well, reasonably seriously. BSA's subsidiary, Triumph, had been investing more time and money than they'd like to admit for several years. This was new ground for BSA however and new enough for the A65 to be shunned by the *Comp Shop*. For the time being race preparation would continue to take place in Engine Development, where Peter Brown worked, as BSA had a long history in off-road competition and this wasn't going to change. Jeff Smith had just won BSA's first 500cc Motocross World Championship title and he was *MCN*s *'Man of the Year'* too. He was well on his way to winning the 1965 World Championship and scrambling was televised every winter in the UK. Whether people bought stodgy C15s off the back of seeing Smith's roaring 440cc Victor, who knows? But motocross would continue to hold the purse strings at BSA even if there was now tacit acknowledgment that production racing was free advertising and being promoted through an increasing number of clubs. The Bantam Racing Club being one of the first.

David Boarer: The club started originally as odd people were already racing BSA Bantams in the 125cc class and someone said: '*Why not set up a club and just race each other?*' As there were loads and loads on Bantams back then. We set it up at Jeremy Shaw's house actually, on the edge of Kensington and Hyde Park Corner, a really posh place and I was a founder member. Along with Roy Bacon, *'Mole'* and Sam Benn, Fred Launchbury, Bob Smart and a few others. This was 1961 and one of the first things we started to do was buy old GPO Bantams from the Post Office, £100 for 20, then sell them on to the members for a fiver each would you believe, so they could start racing too. It was Cadwell Park and Snetterton, they were the main circuits, with Brands

A typical mid-60s Bantam Club Snetterton grid - Triumph, BSA and Norton, but Suzuki and Velocette too

occasionally after and my job was travelling marshal. Which I did for years, probably going on into the late 1960s and I remember I got paid a grand total of £1 a meeting, to cover my petrol costs. They were all one day meetings back then, and as a marshal you were responsible for the safety on the race track. So before the racing started you did a lap of the circuit to check everything was OK and all the marshals were in place. Then after the end of every race you'd make sure there were no bodies lying around! If there was an accident during the race you'd go round in the middle, while they were still racing to sort out the incidents, which was great fun of course, though the St John's Ambulance was always on board.

I did it mainly on an Arrow, as I bought a new Arrow in 1960, then I got a Velo Venom Clubman, though thinking about it I did it a bit on a Leader for a while too. As of course the Ariels were quick and the Bantam Club were one of the first to have production bikes in the programme, as people were racing things like the Arrows. We added a 250 race and the production races as essentially if you were hiring Snetterton for instance it was £50 or whatever for the day, so you needed more than just 50 or 60 Bantams to ride, to make it all pay. So we opened it up to these other classes as they were the ones becoming really popular at the time. I can't remember what the total membership of the club was, but with all the production racers it ran into several hundred for sure, as outside of the racing the social side of things was big too. Here in the south east we met at a place on the road that ran alongside the railway line between Richmond and Chiswick, near Mortlake, a church hall it was or something like that. I was in the South East section with the writer Roy Bacon and *Mole* as everyone knew him. Maurice Benn, an authority on weapons of the civil war period, muzzle loaders, who was always being called in by the British Museum to look at things. Which was typical really, as if you looked at the people racing back then some were really interesting, as they came from every walk of life. The club was all very hand to mouth though and entirely volunteer run, with the newsletter and programmes all done by the members on an old Roneo reproduction machine. Someone would type up the entries, letters, programmes or whatever it was on a special piece of paper, then it went in the Roneo which printed out the pages while you cranked it by hand, time after time. They'd all end up as chip paper after the meeting of course, so you'd be back on it again, though I don't know where we found the time.

Bemsee were unusual in having paid staff, but for all the other clubs, like the Bantam's, it was a labour of love, with that labour growing exponentially as production racing grew. The launch of the Thruxton Bonneville, Hailwood and that first *Hutch* were all huge boosts to the scene and they would all influence events in 1966. But for the rest of the 1965 season Triumphs proliferated on the track and while Matchless and Enfield twins seemed to disappear, pensioned off under the dust sheets, wins were notched up by everything from Vincents and A10s, to Gold Stars and Norton 99s. The season was seen out with wins for Tony Carlton's Norton at Darley Moor on the 10th October and Peter Butler's Triumph at Snetterton on 17th October. But it was two other Snetterton results during October which told all you needed to know about production racing at the time.

The weekly newspapers reported that the result of the Bantam Racing Club event on Saturday 16th October was a win apiece for Peter Butler's Triumph and Tony Smith's BSA. But this wasn't actually the case. Smith's prodigiously fast Lightning had broken down in the first race and seeing his misfortune Butler stood down in the second, lent him his bike and watched Smith take the second win. It summed up the camaraderie among the racers, but events on 3rd October showed another side. This saw Snetterton hosting the final round of the Bemsee championship and the results were finally declared as *1. Butler (Triumph) 2. Vallis (Norton) 3. Davidson (Norton)* and *4. Smith (BSA)*. But not before a serious ruckus and protests to the ACU.

Peter Butler, his normal blur of speed. On 3rd October 1966 he didn't win but there were extenuating circumstances

What is a Production Bike?

Over June 10th and 11th the annual Spanish 24hr races had been run at Montjuïc Park in Barcelona. Dave Degens had ridden in 1964 and off the back of that, and the start money offered for 1965, he had decided to enter a Triton. This was a Triumph engine in a featherbed Norton frame, a *'special'* he had helped to popularize and constructed commercially for customers, through Dresda Autos, which he owned. By the continent's more liberal interpretation of production rules his machine was eligible, as road legal and registered for the road, even if it was initially wheel-less and sported other borrowed parts.

Dave Degens: I borrowed the wheels from Rex Butcher, who pulled them off his Manx. I wanted Rex with me because he was a good friend and I'd never seen him fall off. The silencer we added was the most efficient you could buy. It was designed to perform like a racing megaphone. Even when Triumph produced the Thruxton race version of the Bonnie they used a silencer based on the Goldie's. But then on ours the tube at the end broke off. Ducati protested I was running with a racing megaphone and the scrutineers called me into the pits. I was in the clear because it was a two-into-one and the volume was smaller than the maximum allowed, but they still made us swap it for straight-through pipes. That protest cost me five or six laps and the chain was so worn out that it was almost dragging on the road. We fitted a new one at half-distance, but that was knackered by the end as well. For the last hour or so I could feel the brake grinding as there were no shoes left, but we were so far in front that I didn't have to ride that quickly.

Rex Butcher at Barcelona on the winning Dresda Triton, fitted with straight-through pipes

Butler leads Smith and Hedger. For much of the 1960s these three were the class of the field

The reason Ducati had protested was that the factory had put up a cash prize for anyone who broke the record they had set the previous year, but it didn't really matter. At the end of the 24hrs the Dresda team of Dave Degens and Rex Butcher had covered 631 laps, three more than the best works Montesa and six more than the third placed Velocette. Importantly the Dresda Triton had passed the test in Europe's most prestigious production race, so Degens thought: *'Why not race it in the UK as well?'* At the final round of the Bemsee championship, on 3rd October, there were objections as soon as the bike arrived and rightly so, as the opposition didn't see which way Degens had gone. He won the race easily and more protests soon came flying in. These were both at the track-side and in the letters pages of the weekly newspapers, with Jim Swift, the editor of the Bemsee journal, summarising the situation in the next edition:

> *'It is very interesting to read the opinions of our contributors to the production machine problem, whose letters have been recorded in this issue. What immediately springs to mind is the fact that each has his own personal idea of what should be done but few can really suggest a remedy. This is not surprising. It is going to take a long time to reach a really satisfactory conclusion and I fear that, even now, the manufacturer still holds the aces. Peter Butler's protest was upheld by the stewards on the grounds that the stewards considered that a production machine was one on which purchase tax has been paid. This, to my mind, was a very commendable decision, but does it really answer the problem? Personally, I don't believe that it does.'* [16]

It didn't and the issue of eligibility would run and run.

ROYAL ENFIELD

Super 5

Production	**1962 - 63**
Predecessor	**Crusader**
Bore	**70mm**
Stroke	**64.5mm**
Capacity	**248cc**
Compression	**9.75:1**
Front wheel	**3.25 x 17**
Rear wheel	**3.25 x 17**
Front brake	**7" sls**
Rear brake	**6" sls**
Weight	**308lbs**
Power	**20hp @ 7,500rpm**
Top speed	**86mph**

Royal Enfield's 250cc single of 1956 was their only model to move to unit construction and it was unusual for a British design in having the valve gear driven off the engine drive-side. Its big-bore cylinder dimensions made it ripe for tuning though and this saw the 13hp of the neat but understated Crusader rise to 21.5hp with the launch of 1965's rip-roaring Continental GT.

Better still the styling of 'Britain's fastest 250' - weren't they all? - kept pace with the opposition, though ultimately it wasn't really enough. Royal Enfield was on the skids by 1967 and when their main plant ceased production the 250 went with it too

Close But No Cigar

With Britain's 1961 250cc learner law Royal Enfield had it on a plate. At 78 mph the Crusader Sport was already the fastest 250 *Motor Cycling* had ever tested and a class win at the 1960 Thruxton *500-miler* put it at the top of every 17 year-olds' shopping list, vying with Ariel's Arrow. That top speed became 85mph when the Super 5 was launched in 1962 and John Hartle helped one to second place and a moral victory at Thruxton in 1963, since he was on the same lap as the winning Bultaco, which everyone knew was a race bike in disguise. The Super 5 was *'super'* through its five-speed gearbox, a unique feature among British manufacturers. The Japanese would soon have more though, along with fewer neutrals. It was soon common knowledge that the Enfield five-speed gearbox was a stinker and owners were soon retro-fitting four gears feeling that they'd been rather conned.

Enfield dealt with warranty issues while they should have been fitting an electric start and indicators. At 85mph they'd also pretty much explored the performance envelope of the basic pushrod single, but in 1962 Royal Enfield were taken over by E&HP Smith and the new managing Director, Leo Davenport, made one last roll of the dice. He asked dealers what they wanted, then left the rest to a team of young apprentices. The glorious Continental GT was the result which, for publicity purposes, was thrashed from Lands End to John O'Groats in under 24hrs, then around Silverstone, at record speed, by John Cooper.

Unfortunately as a production racer the GT never really caught on and following John Hartle's 2nd place at the *500-miler* in 1963 Royal Enfield's 250 never appeared on the podium again. The Continental GT was actually a fine motorcycle, but it was simply too late in coming.

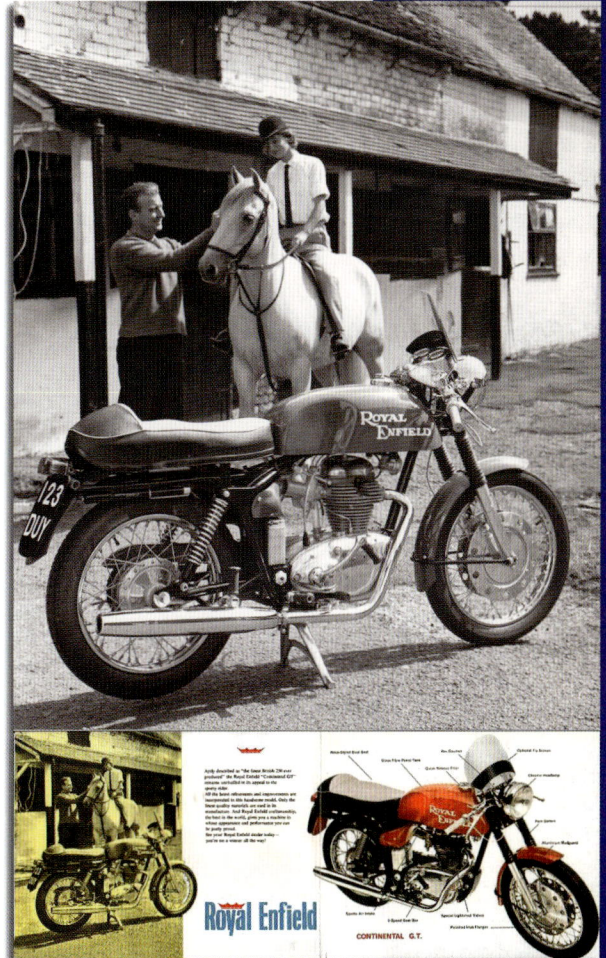

The Suzuki Super Six had another gear and the Ducati Mach I another 10mph. The Ducati also had even more style and that told on the street. Worse still a group of property developers had designs on Enfield's main Redditch factory, so when it went the singles went with it too. It had been great while it lasted but by 1966 *'Britain's fastest 250'* was gone

The Royal Enfield Continental GT was probably the most stylish British 250 ever made. It went well too but was several years too late to really make a mark

Barcelona!

I was just a normal teenager, but a friend of mine started racing and when I went to watch him at Crystal Palace I thought; *'I wouldn't mind having a go at that?'* So I got them to order a 175 Ducati Silverstone road bike for me, as it was so easy to start back then. I just sent off for my ACU licence, went up to London on the Saturday to get some leathers and boots from Lewis Leathers and was at open Brands practice the same afternoon. My first time on track was the next day, a National at Brands, where I came seventh, won a pound and was away

— **Rex Butcher**

Rex Butcher hit prominence in 1965, sharing Dave Degens' Triton in their historic Barcelona win, but British riders had been dipping their toe into the continental waters for a few years by then. In fact since the FIM Autumn Congress of 1959, where it was announced that an *'Endurance Cup'* for production motorcycles would be started in 1960, with points scored on the Grand Prix system across a number of international events. The Thruxton *500-miler* was an immediate addition, though initially the championship gained little traction among British riders. Most continental rounds concentrated on the smaller, sub-250cc class, but larger machines started to creep in and as the decade progressed participation, at Barcelona in particular, became a rite of passage.

Ken Buckmaster was one of the pioneers, competing without break from 1963 to 1971, taking a couple of second places with Irishman Austin Kinsella along the way. What was most notable to outsiders however was the unbelievable, almost clockwork reliability of his machine, as across nine races, 216 hours of flat out relentless racing, his Triumph never ever let him down.

> **Ken Buckmaster:** It was one of the best-kept secrets. I was a Triumph sponsored rider. I was a pal of Frank Baker, who was head of the Experimental Department at Triumph. I started on the Tiger 100. When Percy (Tait) tried the first unit Bonnie he did not like the way it steered. To alter the steering angle they took off the petrol tank, heated the frame tubes and so modified the trail. I then bought this bike and raced it in 1965 and 1966. I bought my Thruxton Bonneville, HDD 49D from H&L, Triumph dealers in

Stroud, for £300. I still have the original log book. It was delivered to me in early 1966 directly from Meriden and at the end of each season the bike would be returned to Meriden, where it would be updated and even painted in next year's colours. The bike was then bench tested by Doug Cashmore on the production engine test bed. He even came with me to the races and worked as mechanic.

It didn't entirely explain the reliability but that support was not untypical of what Triumph would put in to *their* riders, if they thought they had a chance of success. For others it was a far more hand to mouth affair, including Degens original Barcelona entry, which relied on BMW Owners Club volunteer support.

Ken Vogl: I'd been in the Isle of Man spectating when I got a call from Charlie Lock the BMW dealer from London, who ran MLG, who said: '*Would you like to come down to Barcelona with us for the 24hr race?*' That year there was Norman Price, Peter Darvill, Ginger Payne and Dave Degens. Anyway I went all the way down to Barcelona on my bike with a bloke from Bracknell. He said he'd show me the way as I didn't even have a map, but we had a week to get down there, then we were on duty like at the track. Charlie said: '*You'll do the time keeping and lap scoring*' so I had all the sets of watches and that. We'd rigged a BMW sign up but we'd needed to pinch a load of bulbs from other places, due to the different voltage, and we told the different bikes what the signalling was, 'cos my job was to lap score and do all the timing for the full 24hr. The fuelling sign was about ¼ mile before the pits, so you could tell the riders when to

Ken Vogl (far right), was better known as a sidecar racer, but as a member of the Leicester Query Club he was at Silverstone helping out Dave Pickett (41) and Mick Wordsall (49) in 1964. Wordsall was probably the most successful rider at the time on the rare YDS Yamaha

come in from the two hour stints and it worked really well. But Dave Degens, before the racing had started or anything, he'd never been on a BMW before, so he says: *'Can I have a go on yours, round the track?'* so I said; *'OK, but don't thrash it, remember I've got to get back home to England on that!'* So, he rode my bike for just a few laps, then went out for the full 24hr race.

Dave Degens: I was 24 and fit, so I ended up riding for about 18 hours! There were plenty of Montesa, Ossa, Bultaco and Ducati bikes there – the track was ideal for nimble lightweights – but there were a few English teams as well. Velocettes were having the usual

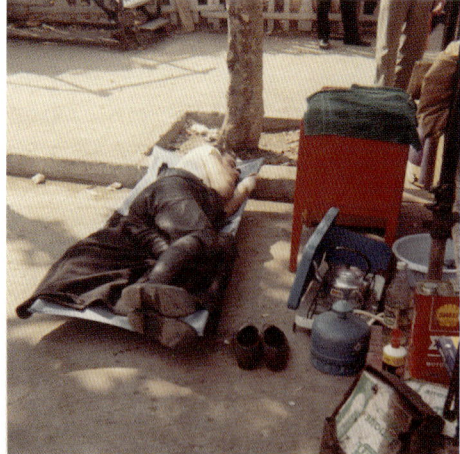

Rex Butcher benefitting from Barcelona's 5-star track-side facilities in 1965. You slept where you could

problems with clutches and primary chains, and of course there were Triumphs and Nortons. But the BMW was disastrous! It was too easy to ground the heads on the long downhill left-hander, so I had to keep the bike upright and hang out to stop it dragging on the road. It was a bit of a plodder and a bit lollopy – it certainly wasn't a short-circuit bike - the generator packed up, and towards the end I lost third gear. The rule was that you had to push it to the pits within three minutes and it took me five.

Ken Vogl: When the race was finished the bikes were impounded 'cos our bike won it in '61, Peter Darvill and Norman Price, and the bikes had to go to the other side of the track from the pits. So myself and Charlie Lock went to fetch them after, because as soon as the bike race finished a car meeting was on. They released the bikes for us but remember by then we'd been on our feet for about 28 hours, what with the set-up before the meeting and so on. So we were all about half dead and as I'm shoving the winning bike out I'm suddenly surrounded by this mad mob. I couldn't speak the language so Charlie says; *'Start it up'* and, as it was the noisiest bike on the circuit, it scattered the crowd. I thought; *'thank goodness for that I can breathe now!'* went off to the end of the track and next thing I know there's a copper in front of me getting his pistol out, pointing it at me and I thought: *'I understand the language now!'* What we didn't know was that the Lord Mayor was coming round in a car, so once he was past the copper waved me on and I had a lovely ride back to the prize giving on the winning BMW, as they kept the roads clear and I didn't have to worry by then if I blew it up!

Break-downs, attrition, unexpected incidents and plain bad luck were what it was all about. And that could just be the trip to the circuit. It didn't deter the British production riders however, nor the sponsors, with Chris Hope's experiences in 1967 and 1968 being typical. As were Rod Scivyer's and Chris Lodge's, in 1966, when they shared the track with Rex Butcher and Dave Degens, though on vastly different machines.

Rod Scivyer: It was a cheater bike, of course it was the Cotton, but I tell you what, that engine was so reliable for a full-on race bike's. The actual power plant, I'm not talking gearbox or clutch, the actual power plant, all the times I rode it, it never let me down. It was Frank Higley who got me on to Cottons first, as Bill Ivy was riding one but got scooped up by the Yamaha factory. I can't remember exactly who recommended me, but someone put my name forward as while I wasn't 125cc British champion yet, I was doing well. With Cotton the deal was that I just got a free ride and if I'd won anything I would have kept it, but on the short circuits, on the Telstar, the full racer version, there was nothing over exciting. I had a few thirds and top tens, that was the best you could say for that. But then there was the first long one on the Conquest, with Dave Browning, at Barcelona. Pat Onions sorted everything out and we took the bike down in Dave's van. All was well then, all of a sudden, as we were coming up over the mountains through Andorra there was this eff-ing great rattle and the cab filled with smoke. We all looked at each other as we coasted to a stand-still, and thought that's it then, we're not even going to get to Barcelona. But we stripped the rocker cover off the engine and saw it was bone dry inside. Not only that but you could take hold of the rockers and pull them up and down, as the holes in the middle had worn oval, what with them having no oil. There was an oil feed to the top on the engine, with a little rubber seal on it, which had perished. But we had some tubing of the same dimensions, stuck that on, smothered it all with oil then started the engine up with the rocker cover still off. Because we couldn't set the tappets as per usual, so did them as the engine was running. Winding them down till they went quiet! And it went all the way to Barcelona and back to the UK like that, never making a sound.

When we got there, Jesus was it hot! But practice went relatively uneventfully and we were in the top ten overall which we thought was pretty good. Nothing broke and the morning of the race, we were staying on a camp site just south of the circuit, right on the coast and Pat Onions says: *'You two, go off to the beach and take the van.'* We laid out on the beach for about half an hour and I said to Dave; *'Its eff-ing hot here, I think we better get out of the sun before it's too late.'* But when we were getting dressed not only was it painful

Hugh Evans was another endurance regular who went on to factory supported rides with BMW and Honda. He learnt his trade in the mid-1960s however, on Dick Rainbow entered machines

but my legs had swollen up! I had heat stroke the next day too, but once I got my leathers on it wasn't so bad. Once you got on the bike, on the tank, the draught went down your neck and through your leathers sort of thing and the start of the race was relatively uneventful. It was all quite straightforward, but when I was out on the bike I discovered if I turned left it vibrated but not when I went right. It was gradually getting worse and I thought it must be something to do with the chain, as that was the only thing which was asymmetrical. But why would it be like that? So I went into the pits where we found that every single engine and gearbox mounting bolt had fallen out, or was about to!

We hadn't got enough bolts of the right diameter and I believe, I don't know as I went for a lie down, that they managed to scrounge enough off Mead & Tomkinson, who helped get it going again. So, we gradually climbed back again into the top ten but it was getting dark by now and then all the lights went out! In the end we changed the entire electrics and while the lights came back on they were tantamount to an excitable glow worm. As I remember rightly about a third of the Barcelona circuit wasn't lit, so the only way we could go fast round that bit was to wait for something bigger to come round and hook on to it until the street lights came on again! But it was around then that the beginning of the end set in. A clutch cable broke, which was odd, as they'd never had that before not even on the road bikes. The clutch is held on to the shaft with a circlip, so if the circlip comes off, which it did, the clutch moves outwards. Well I don't know if you know where the clutch cable runs on those engines, but it runs between the clutch and the outer cover, so it just cut it in half. An hour later it broke again, so in the end we were put out as we ran out of clutch cables. It was as simple as that and when it happened it was daylight, so about 18 hours through the race and we were still circulating well up at that point. Everybody saw the Conquest as a bit of a joke, but it was surprisingly good. The brakes could have been better, but there was plenty of bigger stuff behind us and the engine never let us down once.

Chris Lodge emerges out of the Barcelona gloom, with an improvised chest-rest on his standard Triumph tank-rack

Chris Lodge: We were all production racing at the time, so knew each other and the ride came about as I happened to phone Dick Rainbow's one day for….. I don't know what? Some spare parts or something. Anyway, Mick Andrew answered the phone and said: '*We need a rider for Barcelona?*' So, I said: '*Yeah, I'm coming!*' and that was that. I rode with Hugh Evans, as when Tony Smith moved out to the factory that sort of gave a place for me and space for Hugh too. One of the problems with the BSAs was that when you put a lot of load on the gearbox the main-shaft bent a bit and caused the selectors to rub up against the gears. Well Barcelona that first time, we went out did a couple of laps of practice and the gear was jumping out, out of third. We pulled out all the bits the next day and the selectors were all burnt out. They were blue. Well Dick bought a fair amount of stuff, so he could rebuild the gear-box, but because of that we got hardly any practice. I really didn't know the circuit well at speed, so went straight out into the race and on the fastest part of the circuit all the lights had gone out! So, we had a 35watt headlight bulb doing 110mph round a series of fast curves, at the top of the circuit. It was ludicrous.

Dick Rainbow on the bike and Chris Lodge holding the torch, search for missing sparks late in the sweltering Barcelona evening

Then either Degens or Butcher came past, in company with another Bonneville and I found I had no trouble whatsoever staying with them. They'd just won the *500-miler* but I hung on to them quite easily, as the handling of that bike it was lovely. A standard A65 wouldn't have been able to do that. It wouldn't have been as stable, and this bike was quick too. The ones we had were a bit special. I mean an ordinary A65 wasn't worth racing. '68 I rode an almost brand-new Spitfire, with all mod cons. You know, twin GPs and that and I couldn't ride it properly it was so slow. But Rainbow had a lot of help from the factory you see and was almost like the unofficial works team.

But even so those distance events really did punish bikes. It was always down to attrition and with Hugh that year we had a bit of a stop-start sort of race. Niggling problems. The bike stopped one time up at the top of the circuit and I was exhausted. I leant forward onto the tank and as I did so I saw the top of my boot had rubbed through the battery lead. So, 'borrowed a penknife off one of the spectators and screwed it all back together again. Same day the bike stopped again and looking around the fuel tap had come undone. So, I'm soaking with petrol from the waist downwards and suddenly there are all these Spanish guys round me with fags on! It must have looked ludicrous, me pushing and flapping my arms but I had to keep all these guys away or I would have gone up in flames. While another time the whole of the left-hand exhaust system departed. I pottered round on one cylinder, went past Dick at the paddock - who must have thought: '*Oh that's the end of that then!*' - but went 'round again, found it and hooked it over my shoulder so the bloody thing was dangling down my back. A whole exhaust system! That pleased old Dick as he said: '*I didn't believe you'd do that.*' But then, I think it was early morning the second day, there was a sharp left-hand bend after the start line and as I come 'round there's a fella walking across the zebra crossing with a dog on a lead! I thought: '*If I go left I'll hit the railings over there and if I go the other way I'll hit him.*' As I reckon he was ten-foot from the kerb. Well, I passed between him and the kerb and if he'd run we'd both have been dead. Tony Smith was behind me and saw it all.

Chris Hopes: In '67 there were three of us in the van and we were followed by Gary Green with a Vauxhall Viva and a trailer. There were four of them in the car then, near Limogese, they broke the back axle. So we put his bike in the van, so there was us three and those four in this three speed – well two speed really, as first gear wasn't syncromesh - Thames van, all the way down to Barcelona. So it was quite a journey, monumental really. Pioneering! And of course we'd never been abroad before. So the first day we laid out in the sun and I woke up with sun stroke. They were really pissed off weren't they? I was burning but shivering too and drinking loads of tea. But anyway next day it was alright. I got over it but then I had a run-in with Dave Degens and Rex Butcher in practice. I was still getting used to the bike and there was this left-hand corner where I overtook Rex. I

Chris Hopes under the Barcelona floodlights

lost control a bit but didn't fall off so got 'round and cleared off. But after practice Dave Degens and Rex Butcher came marching over going: *'We've come here to win this race!'* Really bollocking me, but I just laughed it off and said: *'Rex, you shouldn't have been going so slow then'* and I got on really well with him after. Though, the race itself, was quite peculiar. I was talking to Gary Green as it started, so was a bit slow running across and getting going. But that ended up being a good thing in the end as Pirelli had given tyres to everyone and no one had scrubbed them in. As no one knew about that sort of thing back then and they were falling off left right and centre. Armageddon it was. But as I didn't get such a good start I survived it and don't remember really any problems with the bike at all.

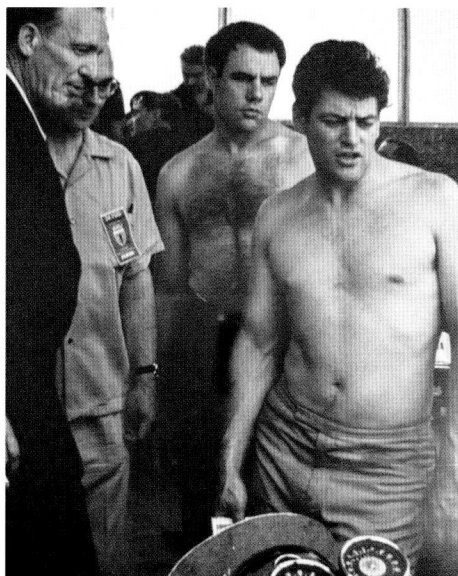

Butcher and Degens stripped for action. The heat was always a major factor at Montjuïc Park

And it handled too, as we finished well up against all those two-strokes, which were full race bikes really, perhaps as I really liked the circuit, like Cadwell, just twice as big. The 24hr races were a bit of a holiday for us though and one of the things I'll always remember was getting a fridge full of Fantas and Coca-Colas. You got them at the beginning of the race and it was like being given a pot of gold. The other thing I particularly remember was coming up the top of the hill, after the start finish line, as where you came into a lefthander everyone was just sitting there at a café, drinking. So, you peeled off just before you hit 'em. It was surreal. But I've never ever heard anyone mention that before, having people sat drinking on the racing line. It was bizarre, like after the race, when we all went to the Town Hall to get the prizes and there were these guys in flashy old military helmets and what have you. All pomp and ceremony.

Waiting for the off. It was always a running, *Le Mans*, start

Then in 1968 we drove to Southampton didn't we and got the ferry across, but we broke down again. A friend had a van with a flashy Sunbeam Alpine engine in it but the water pump broke and went through the radiator, so it was just us again in our trusty old Commer van. When we came back we actually cracked our wind-screen, so we punched a hole in it and got back to Le Harve like that. When we crossed, as we drove off, the guy in customs opened the back and there was Ken Redfern sitting on a deckchair in the back, with the bike and someone else sitting in the middle, on the floor, eating lunch. The customs guy just stands there with his hands on his hips, shakes his head and says; *'By heck lads you know how to live well don't you. Now bugger off and go home!'* It was so amateurish, but you got paid for going and we got a free holiday didn't we, both years. Though in '68 we had to get a carnet and we were completely naive. I went to the bank manager and Ken Redfern had to put a deposit on the bike, £350. Anyway, we finished 4th or 5th, so we had loads of Spanish money which we hid round the van, as there were all sorts of money restrictions then, with Harold Wilson's government. But at the Spanish border they just waved us through, didn't stamp the carnet or anything, so when we got home they wouldn't release the money of course. I ended up having to take the bike to Stockton police station, for them to read the chassis number and that, to get a letter confirming it was back in the country, so Ken could get his money back. It was a hell of a job, but we were only 22 years old at the time and we really didn't have a clue.

That might have sounded like a comedy of errors but it was the same for the winners too. Dave Croxford and Tom Phillips won the 500 class on a Velocette Venom in 1966 and it had been Degens and Butcher in the largest class in 1965. These were the big names in the newspaper headlines, but the realities of endurance racing were vastly different from what they'd become a decade later on.

A pensive Butcher awaiting his ride. This time at the *500-miler*

Rex Butcher: Dave Degens had a MkII Jaguar. There was Dave and Donna his wife, Butch his mechanic me and Angela, five of us towing a trailer with the bike on it and it was a typical 24hr race. Bloody hard work, incredibly hard work actually, your wrists and arms were aching, as there was lots of tight down-hill braking. Montjuïc was a dangerous circuit too, a bloody dangerous circuit. It was all potty really and it was mayhem towards the end, because the Spanish Bultaco works team were trying to get us disqualified, for any reason they could, because we were looking good towards the end. They were looking all round the pits for things and yet they had been cheating like mad. They'd crash a bike then just wheel another one out of a van. All sorts of things like that. That was the first year we did it and won. Then when we went back in 1966, we were 4th riding a Triumph for Syd Lawton. He came down as the spanner

It was all back of an envelope stuff, but in Butcher and Degens' case at least the envelope contained 4,000 Pesetas. Not a fortune, but a tidy sum and there were add-ons from trade suppliers

man, but from memory we had I think four punctures in the race and I crashed it as well. I remember I had to extract myself from the hay bales and fight the guys off who tried to put me on a stretcher. They wanted to wheel me away but I pointed out that I wasn't hurt and pulled the bike back. But I think I'd punctured the tank and ripped a clip-on off so, after all the repairs, we went out and finished 4th. Syd was backed by the factory, so we were sort of an off-shoot of a factory ride, but I was very naive. I'd dearly love to go back, as you didn't know what was going on really. You were just pleased to get the ride. It didn't cost you anything and if there was any prize money you got that, as I don't remember anyone taking any of the money. But in those days we didn't know anything about start money. Dave might have got some money to take the bike down, as we'd won it the year before, but I wasn't really aware, though by the end I got start money at pretty much every circuit.

But back then we didn't have a clue. We didn't sign contracts for the year or anything like that. It was all done by word of mouth, gentlemen's agreements. So after the first ride in '66 Syd would have just said: *'Are you going to ride for us again then?'* and it would be a case of: *'OK, go on then, yeah.'* It was the same with the Boyer's bikes later. I don't think I ever got paid by Stan Shenton for riding his bikes? It was just a case of: *'Would you ride for me in the TT?'* As you were just pleased to have a good bike and good mechanics working on it. Because remember back then it wasn't like it is now. Some of us were riding 250, 350, 500 and unlimited bikes as well, so it was a really big help having a well sorted proddie bike sitting there waiting for you to ride.

Rex Butcher and crew in the Barcelona pits

It wasn't all twins in the endurance events. Expatriate Dutchman Jan Strijbis on a Velocette, a legitimately streamlined machine since a fairing was listed early on for the Clubman, it being the Avon fairing later listed for the Thruxton

Butcher was of course a big name, while the majority of production racers were confined to just one machine. The products of Stan Shenton were not entirely beyond their wallets however and Shenton's Boyer of Bromley concern was not the only dealer fielding production racers or marketing performance parts. The factories, Triumph in particular, might have a focus on the *500-miler* and *Hutch*, but dealers had an interest throughout the season. Their priority was promoting their name, their services and their special parts and the first meetings of the 1966 British season highlighted the growing opportunities. With no production race at the chilly Mallory Park National, on Saturday 5th March, Peter Butler turned up none the less, taking third place in the 1000cc event

Rex Butcher in practice at Brands Hatch. This time on one of his employer's Dunstall Nortons

on his road-legal production Bonneville. While on Sunday 13th Rex Butcher took Paul Dunstall's 650 to victory over the thoroughbred singles of Ivy, Cooper and Minter. This latter machine wasn't a true production bike, but neither was Bob Heath's road-registered A65 according to the Darley Moor stewards. Since while Heath won the first actual production race of the season, on March 27th, he was then unceremoniously disqualified for running illegal, open, pipes. It handed the win to Bill Bate's 600cc Dominator 99, which was fortuitous, as during the first half of the 1966 season, Norton victories were few and far between. Future notables Terry Haslam and Roger Bowler harried the leaders at Cadwell Park on theirs, but neither could take a win and it was slim pickings for BSA riders too. Mick Brogdale and Pete Davies's A10s were now realistically too long in the tooth to seriously challenge and with the A65s of Tony Smith and Mick Andrew off the pace, Triumphs had a field day. The previous quartet of leading riders – Butler, Knight, Nixon and Hopes – being joined by a newcomer, John Hedger, on an Ivor Kilbourn tuned machine.

> **John Hedger:** Kilbourn Motorcycles was a total one man band. It was his own business which he ran himself, no mechanics, and that included selling bikes, repairing bikes and of course preparing and tuning bikes himself. Ivor was an extraordinary engineer and whenever I took a bike to the starting line I had 100% confidence in his ability to provide me with the best bike, allowing me to concentrate on racing and get the results he craved. He received a new Bonneville in 1964 and again in 1965, neither of these bikes were registered for the road, so whenever they required to be tested I would take them out on Trade plates, which were issued to motor trade concerns. I don't know why, but I preferred the way the 1964 bike went and the 1965 was eventually sold.

The Hedger-Kilbourn combination was new for 1966 but they were immediately up to speed as they took wins at Silverstone, Cadwell Park, Perton and Snetterton in the run-up to the *500-miler*. Here Hedger teamed up with production stalwart Declan Doyle, but as events would prove it was not to be their day.

John Hedger's favoured Kilbourn Motorcycles Thruxton Bonneville at rest. The 1964 version. This had the standard exhausts, since it was only the 1965 model which came with the long, cigar shaped silencers. The fairing was also of the earlier type. In 1966 Triumph replaced this with a smoother, Mitchenhall version, which could be run with the lower portion detached

Velocette

Thruxton Venom

Production	**1966-1971**
Predecessor	**Venom**
Bore	**86mm**
Stroke	**86mm**
Capacity	**499cc**
Compression	**9:1**
Front wheel	**3.25 x 19**
Rear wheel	**3.25 x 19**
Front brake	**7½" tls**
Rear brake	**7" sls**
Weight	**390lb**
Power	**41hp @ 6,200rpm**
Top speed	**114mph**

The Thruxton was the last incarnation of the Venom. But an odd model to wheel out as *new* in 1966, as it could trace its lineage to the pre-war MSS. The commuter LE twin had burnt Velocette's fingers however and there was sense in retreat back to the big singles that the company knew best. There was also method in Hall Green's madness. The demise of the BSA Gold Star had left a hole where big singles used to sit and the new Thruxton brilliantly, if briefly, filled it, antiquated styling belying blistering performance. As a result over one thousand rolled off the production lines before the accountant called time on the fastest dinosaur on the track

The Hall Green Coelacanth

Velocette held the moral high ground, even if Triumph beat them to the Thruxton name in 1964. Venoms took the top three places in the 500 class that year, while Triumph had won only twice in the preceding nine. Stuff copyright, Velocette was using the name. No one was going to sue them anyway, they were on their uppers, but were lucky in having enthusiastic rider and dealer support. Back at Hall Green they also knew what they were doing with their antediluvian engine.

In the Thruxton 500 mile event Tom Thorp and Roy Mayhew had taken second place in 1961, on a very standard Venom similar to the L. Stevens Ltd. machine, which took the class win in 1964. Journalist Dave Dixon then won on his own bike in 1965, partnered by Joe Dunphy, while Ellis Boyce and Tom Phillips brought a similar model home

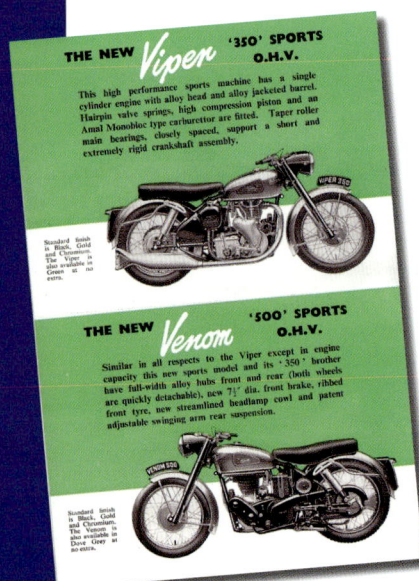

second at the Barcelona 24hr race. In 1966, a year by which time the Venom should really have been pensioned off, things then went up a gear. The launch of the Thruxton was heralded by a never to be repeated treble, when Dave Croxford and Tom Phillips took a Geoff Dodkin-tuned version to the 500 class win at both Barcelona and the *500-miler*, with Phillips going on to win the 500 class at the Hutchinson 100 too! Top that? Well Neil Kelly did the following year, by taking his Reg Orpin-tuned Thruxton to the inaugural 500cc Production TT win. Keith Heckles came second, on the reliable Geoff Dodkin version, which John Blanchard then rode to the same position at the 1968 TT, being timed at 121.6mph through the *Motor Cycle* speed trap. Some dinosaur. Then, unfortunately, the curtain came down.

The Venom was always greater than the sum of its parts, and peerless on the long, endurance courses, but it was no short circuit scratcher and that's what production racers required. Road riders also grew tired of the machine's idiosyncrasies now that the age of disc brakes and electric starters had arrived. The roof at the Velocette factory leaked worse than the balance book and by 1971 the 1950 World Champions' classic, funereal black and gold was gone.

An L Stevens machine being prepared on the road, for the track

The Velocette Venom Clubman. The direct forerunner to 1966's Thruxton

The *500-miler* Goes Walk-About

BSA had come second at the *500-miler* in 1965 but weren't even close in '66. It wasn't for the want of trying. They had two factory bikes entered, under the name of dealer Tom Kirby, with an interesting choice of riders too. Billy Ivy and John Cooper were one pairing, while Tony Smith and Peter Butler were on the other machine, paired as the cream of the production specialists. It came to nought however as Butler and Smith went out with engine trouble and Ivy threw his Spitfire into the scenery within a lap of Cooper passing it on. Ability on a Grand Prix two-stroke didn't always translate to a production machine.

Lapping at over 80mph, hour on hour, it was Triumph's day but not for 'Mr Triumph', as Percy Tait once again had victory snatched away. A lot of people knew he'd probably won the race in 1965, but in 1966 he was genuinely beaten, after 6hrs 20mins and 58seconds, by just 10 seconds, after a rev counter drive had come away. That detached cable resulted in a stop for his co-rider, Phil Read, which ultimately handed victory to the machine being *'run in'* for Barcelona by Butcher and Degens. It also made it win number five, on the trot, for Syd Lawton. Griff Jenkins and Dave Dixon brought Paul Dunstall's 750cc Norton Atlas into third place – many comments being made about its disc brakes - but of the other full 750s there was nothing to be seen. Both Tom Kirby and the Arter Brothers entered 750cc G15 Matchless twins, but it was a last hurrah for the brand, as neither really featured and as they were powered by Norton engines, there was little enthusiasm among the die-hard Matchless fans. If you wanted a Norton, well, buy a Norton.

They're off ! Left to right, 48 Ron Langston (650 Bonneville), 47 Dave Dixon (750 Dunstall Atlas), 58 Rex Avery (650 Bonneville), 21 James Howes (Honda CB72 250), Peter Butler obscured (650 Bonneville) and 49 Rex Butcher (650 Bonneville)

A pair of works machines, but hardly evenly matched. Peter Inchley's Cotton Conquest leads Paul Smart's Royal Enfield Super 5 in a one-sided contest. The Cotton must have been 20mph faster

In the 250 class the Cotton Conquest again ruled supreme, though they missed out on a possible one-two finish when the condenser wire on Rod Scivyer's bike broke, leaving it to Tommy Robb and Chris Vincent - on a *genuine* road bike – to bring their Suzuki in to second place. Apart from a lonely Royal Enfield, ridden by Dave Simmonds and Charlie Mates there was not really another British machine in the mix and this mirrored the situation on the club scene. Here Clive Thompsett was making a name for himself on a Ducati 250 and as Rex Butcher had discovered in his early days on a 175 version, this was the way to go. Unless you fancied a Honda that is, like Roger *'Ernie'* Bryant's, whose electric start gave him a huge advantage on the short circuits over those thrashing away at kick-starts! Results indicated that the odd Yamaha and Suzuki 250 were also starting to crop up, but in the 500cc class time briefly stood still.

At Brands Hatch Dave Croxford and Tom Phillips cruised around to score a perfectly paced win on their Geoff Dodkin-tuned Velocette, while the wisest head in the paddock was probably that of *'veteran'* Ray Knight. He'd gone for the 500cc Triumph option over the 650cc, and partnered by Martin Love he took a steady ride on the Hughes machine to take the 500cc class second place.

It was a good result for Hughes Motorcycles who, like their competitors, used the *500-miler* programme to highlight quite how successful they were. Hughes listed simply the circuits at which they'd already won in 1966 – Thruxton, Oulton, Snetterton, Cadwell and Brands Hatch, the majority of the wins being taken by Knight. Boyer of Bromley listed all eleven of their results so far that season, which included six wins and three second places for their rider Dave Nixon. Lawton & Wilson preferred to simply point out that they had won all four *500-milers* since 1962, while Dick Rainbow excused his bikes' recent poor run of form by highlighting the BSA Lightning's successes over the previous season. An impressive 53 wins out of 67 production race starts, the lion's share divided between Tony Smith and Mick Andrew. On top of this John Hedger's fifteen-plus wins for Ivor Kilbourn in 1966 could have been added, along with Peter Butler's. Since he'd taken twenty one wins combined over 1965 and '66 so far, on his privately entered, George Hopwood-tuned machine.

Apart from Lawton's these machines were all prepared for short circuit scratching, so it was only the more adventurous who subsequently headed for Barcelona where, as already noted, Lawton's Bonneville took Butcher and Degens to 4th place. One place behind them and outright winner in the 500 class were Tom Phillips and Dave *'crasher'* Croxford in a case, over more than 2000 incident-less racing miles, of a name never having been so inaccurately applied! Croxford was 100% rock solid and reliable, though the Butcher and Degens result was perhaps more important. It gave them the overall *Coupe d'Endurance* championship title for 1966, without them even having competed in the first round at Imola. It was a ringing endorsement of the basic Triumph product and races on the mainland remained a largely Meriden affair in the run up to the *Hutch*. However, as with so many of the big races previously, it didn't pay for Triumph to count their chickens before they'd hatched, which held true for Honda too.

The peerless Dave Croxford at speed on the Dodkin Velocette. He could ride virtually anything and did, usually with indecent haste. He picked up the reputation as a crasher which wasn't entirely fair

Much Ado About Nothing

Chester dealer Bill Smith had his finger well and truly in the Honda pie by 1966. He'd come close to becoming the official Honda importer a few years previously and scored brownie points by taking a win on a *Black Bomber*, at Darley Moor, on 1st May. It was quite possibly the first ever win for the machine in the UK and two weeks later Willie Dey won again on a CB450 at Crimond, where John Cooper graced a circuit hosting its first race in nearly eight years. Bill Smith then took a second place in June, again at Darley Moor, on the same, standard, production machine. Honda's great white hope looked promising.

The Bill Smith/John Hartle 1962 500-miler winning Honda CB72. Ultimately Smith, like other Honda riders, had more luck with the smaller CB72/77s than he did with the 450cc *Black Bomber*

500cc World Champion Mike Hailwood's win a year previously at the *Hutch* had been a high watermark for production racing and had generated huge publicity for BSA's A65 Lightning. MV Agusta evidently had no problem with Hailwood riding the Lightning Clubman, perhaps as it was no rival for the lightweights they made for the road? He was contracted only for the Grands Prix anyway and could look elsewhere for other rides. But now Hailwood was with Honda, who were a different kettle of fish. There had been rumours of a big Honda for some time before it arrived in September 1965 and initial reports of the CB450 were sufficiently terrifying for Triumph and BSA to hastily carry out feasibility studies for DOHC versions of their own T120 and A65 twins. Honda were dominating Grand Prix racing and for the British manufacturers a high performance, road going, DOHC 500 production racer was their worst nightmare come true. It got worse when it was announced that Mike Hailwood would be riding one at the forthcoming Hutchinson 100 though, as it transpired, it was an idle threat.

Both the European FIM and American AMA governing bodies banned the Black Bomber because, with its dizzyingly sophisticated double overhead cams, it could not possibly be considered a production machine. These were clearly crazy rulings but, in the United States in particular, it was the manufacturers – read Harley-Davidson – who pretty much wrote the rule book. If they didn't like it, it didn't race which, to show impartiality, went for British twins over 500cc too. It was harder to fathom what lay behind the FIM rules, but as the *Hutch* was an International meeting, it used theirs. On May 25th *Motor Cycle News* announced that Bemsee secretary Jim Swift was looking to get the race classified

The CB450 engine was quite sophisticated but in truth to no great effect. It vibrated like a British bike too

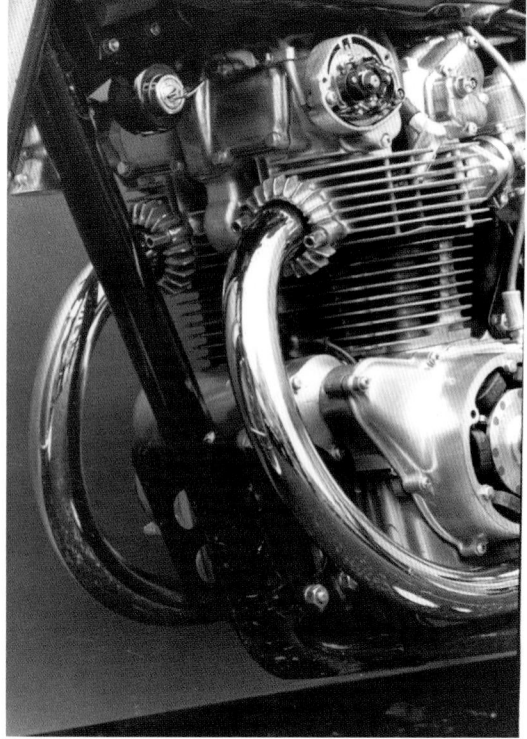

as a National, so the ACU's more liberal, and sensible, rules could be applied, but it never came to pass. As a fig leaf to Honda Hailwood was allowed to run a Black Bomber around in the interval and perhaps it was a blessing in disguise. The Honda was a sound and capable machine, but it was over priced and as a racer over-hyped. Honda's less heralded 250cc CB72 and 305cc CB77 twins would ultimately prove more successful on the track, as while Honda CB450s filled both the newspapers and dealer windows, that was where they largely remained. The new twin was not the game changer Honda hoped it would be

The MkI CB450 – dubbed the *'Black Bomber'* – perhaps wisely mimicked a British look, with its chrome tank and conservative styling, but it benefitted from an electric starter and the sort of refined ergonomics which the British opposition could only dream about. It would prove itself reliable, like all Hondas, but two factors worked against it. Firstly, at a list price of £360 it was as expensive as a British 650, the weight of which it also unfortunately matched. It was also no racer. When *Motorcycle Mechanics* tested one in June 1966 they managed a wheezing, asthmatic, 102mph which the American *Cycle World* matched when they tested the supposedly improved, 5-speed version. Hailwood and Honda were saved their blushes, but who now was going to provide the *Hutch* sparks?

The Honda-less *Hutch*

In one stroke Hailwood had established BSA's new, unit construction, A65 twin as the machine to be seen on in 1965. The Small Heath factory built on this in 1966, by launching the raucous Spitfire. Tested at around the 125mph mark on both sides of the Atlantic it looked the business too. But early in the racing season A65s hadn't featured as they had in 1965 and there was that nagging doubt as to whether it was Hailwood or BSA who'd won previously. The rider or the bike? Well, everyone knew it was Hailwood, so massed ranks of Triumph lined up at the *Hutch*, in a case of not which manufacturer, but simply which Triumph, would take the win at Brands Hatch, to where the *Hutch* had relocated.

Well it wasn't the luckless Percy Tait to whom went the unenviable accolade of scoring a double, coming second in the *Hutch* two years on the trot. Indeed, it wasn't a Triumph at all taking the victory, as Hailwood's stand-in, John Cooper, caught the nay sayers napping. Worse still his BSA clearly wasn't handling well, the slides, weaves and lurid corner exits simply emphasizing how much faster the Birmingham bike was than those from Coventry. Cooper's win couldn't even be nailed on the door of greater circuit knowledge, since the entire race was run backwards, the wrong way around the circuit, to mitigate the advantage of the *Brands Scratchers*, such as Minter, Degens and their ilk. Behind Percy Tait it was Mick Andrew on the year older, 1965, Hughes Bonneville in third, followed by Rod Gould in fourth. It was the same result for Gould as the previous year on the Eddie Dow Lightning Clubman, but a pretty good result for Small Heath all round, as they had only six machines entered while rivals Meriden had twenty two, nearly a dozen of which had a degree of factory support. It was quality over quantity in the smaller classes too as a Cotton Conquest, Dave Browning's, won the 250cc class while Tom Phillips won the 500cc category on the all-conquering Dodkin Velocette Venom again. The model appropriately named the *Thruxton* from 1966.

Cooper Man did the business for BSA in 1966. John Cooper taking an evil handling Spitfire to the win at the first Brands Hatch *Hutch*, run backwards round the circuit to hinder the *Brands Scratchers* who rarely raced anywhere else

Bob Heath as a blur of speed. By 1966 he was already making a name for himself, taking his first win at Darley Moor in August. Within a season he'd *'own'* the circuit, his production bike proving unbeatable in both Production and Open classes

Kings, Queens, Squires and Conquerors

Two weeks after the *Hutch* Triumph got a further wake-up call when a new meeting was held at Cadwell Park. The *'King of Brands'* crown had caught the imagination of both promoters and spectators alike and similar titles grew over the years. The Lord of Lydden, Laird of Croft, Master of Mallory and Squire of Snetterton were among them. In 1966 Charlie Wilkinson, the convivial owner of Cadwell Park, was first on the band wagon however with the Conqueror of Cadwell event. Grand Prix regular Billie Nelson took the title, but only after Rod Gould dropped out, fuel-less, while leading. Gould was clearly fired up so then went out and won the big Coronation Trophy race on his Manx Norton and capped the day with a magnificent win on the Eddie Dow Lightning Clubman in the big production race. It was from the Bonnevilles of Triumph test rider Steve Spencer and John Hedger, while Tony Smith on a second A65 was fourth. BSA's A65 was still very much in the hunt then and in August it was announced that Alan Shepherd, the former works MZ and Honda rider, would be joining BSA to spearhead their expanded road racing plans. The latest Spitfire was clearly worth considering as a Bonneville alternative and the rider taking one to fifth place, first time out, on 18th September, clearly thought so, though benefiting through a bit of good luck.

> **Clive Wall:** I started racing when it was all in black and white. 1964. But I spent the whole of '63 going down to Brands, doing practice days as often as I could. I probably did one or two a month and it was 17s 6d for a half day, 27s 6d for a full. They were proper race practices though, not like track days today. You'd run into Derek Minter and who ever, getting in their way, but it taught me the short circuit and a bit about racing. With the National scene there were only two bikes really, a G50 or a Manx, or if

you like a 7R or a Manx and a Manx was an expensive bike. There wasn't even much choice, as so few were around. So, realistically, production racing was the way to go. The first meeting I did was a Good Friday International, and although the production race it was only classed as a National, it was a full grid, on the long circuit, and I'd never been out the back before.

The Triumphs of Chris Lodge and Melvin Rice, lead the BSAs of Hugh Evans and Kevin Moyes in a typical Snetterton scrap

But I finished midfield and I completed two more Brands Nationals that year, and at one of those I was third and won my first cup. There weren't many meetings at Silverstone in the mid-60s, but the MCC ran a thing called the Speed Trial. It was actually just a race meeting, run under an auspicious name to keep the old timers happy I think. But I went there as I'd never been, on my Gold Star, and I came up against this guy called Kevin Moyes. He raced this A65 for RH Smith Motorcycles, which was stock, but a Spitfire MkII, so fast. Well I harassed him for quite a while then went and had a look at it, 'cos it was so quick down the straights compared with mine. I thought: *I gotta get off of this Gold Star. It's just too slow.*

Anyway, I started chatting to him and he said he couldn't actually justify the money and that he was going to pack up: *'If you want to come and meet Dick Smith with me, he might help you out?'* I did, he did, and I ended up buying half the bike. Dick used to pay all my entry fees and sell me all the parts at trade price as he was a BSA dealer, and while that doesn't sound a lot now, it certainly was back then. As when you weren't paying your entry fees you could do three times as many meetings, as you paid by the race in those days. So, I could do two proddie races and two or three 1,000cc events in a day.

Clive Wall and newly acquired Spitfire MkII. Spitfires became slightly more refined over the years but the first 1966 model was the fastest

A typical mid-1960s production grid. Four pre-unit Triumphs, a BMW, a diminutive 199cc Tiger Cub and not a unit construction British twin in sight. It wasn't all Thruxton Bonnies and Dunstall Nortons on the Club scene

Those extra races would help Wall to get up to speed rapidly on his A65 but Tony Smith sprung back into life on the works version at the same time, winning the last four races of the 1966 season. The first two on 15th October, at the Bantam Racing Club meeting and the second pair next day, as Bemsee's season signed off at Snetterton. This final meeting was interesting as while the pack behind Smith was predictably made up of the usual, dominant, Triumph runners - Butler, Nixon, Buckmaster, Hopes and Knight - Graham Penny appeared among them taking a 5th then 4th place. It was on a Honda CB450 and while it demonstrated there was still some mileage in the new Honda twin, history would prove that in racing terms they never really cut the mustard.

Nick Warwick: I had a CB72 originally, my first bike, but everything went wrong on that and this lad, Maurice Eccles, he had this CB450 and was a bit of a fiddler. He took everything apart, polished everything and took the ports out accurately checking that the volumes were identical. As the Honda ports were actually pretty rough as standard and put back together this thing would rev. It would really go, but it was too fast for him and he swapped it with a mate, Sparky, for a Thruxton Velo. Well, eventually

I said I wanted it and paid £200, which I borrowed off my boss, who was a big help. It was quick, it was smooth and while it would rev to 9,000rpm at anything over 6,000rpm it just took off like a scalded cat. But the problem was it had been rebuilt with old piston circlips, as you just couldn't get things like that off the dealers, parts were always a problem. Well, of course one came out and scored the bore. I rebuilt it again with oversized pistons and a new camchain from Reads, as they were the big Honda specialists back then, but unfortunately it never really went the same after that. It was a brilliant starter off the line though - well you could hit the button! - and at Silloth, later on, I remember I was up against Frank Whiteway on the Crooks Suzuki Cobra and Tony Jefferies on his Thruxton Bonneville and I managed seventh in a big field with plenty of good bikes behind me. Actually I only got pipped for sixth as a Rocket Three overtook me on Hangar Bend under a yellow flag. I asked Tony Jefferies how his bike went so well and he said it was because he went through every part at the factory, weighing pistons and conrods, as they were all slightly different, to make sure everything matched. While I rode my bike to the circuit and we were still running on Japanese tyres! The fairing was from a Thruxton Velo, as Sparky bought one the same for the Honda and it was good he did as it saved me a few times. I was down several times on it, as the the tyres were useless. But, otherwise, it was a perfect little bike, it left 500 Triumphs.

By chance my brother had a Tiger 90, converted to 500cc with Thruxton pipes and cams and it would leave that for dead. But the Honda silencers rotted and the asbestos pieces which were between the pipes and the silencers they would always fall to bits. It wouldn't run properly like that, so you had to keep repairing them with asbestos tape and silencer repair paste and even Honda dealers didn't want to work on the CB450s. I don't know why, it was a simple bike really, but eventually I swapped it for a Triumph T100, a Daytona. I shouldn't have, it gave me nothing but trouble, but the Hondas of course though they later fitted a disc and fifth gear, they just got heavier and slower and that was what really killed the Black Bomber off as a racer.

Nick Warwick and Black Bomber. It was fast, when well-fettled, but the Honda CB450's Achilles heel was poor parts availability and excess weight

Jim Kanka would go on to become one of the top genuine privateers on the scene, taking many top places on southern circuits, on a standard Bonneville brought up to Thruxton specification

It was a neat summing-up of the Honda's abbreviated racing career which was at odds with the burgeoning, broader, production racing scene. New bikes and new riders were appearing all the time, with the names Robinson, Ridley and Kanka all appearing in the top six over the first weekend in September, when the British Formula Racing Club and Midland Racing Clubs both held meetings at Cadwell Park. Terry Haslam's 750 Norton appeared that week-end too, taking a fourth place, with the Bantam and the British Formula Clubs being the two he and his brothers Phil and Ron raced at most, as recounted by one of the organisers.

Joan MIlligan: Most of the racers actually seemed to race with both the clubs. We did a lot of production racing and if you looked at the people racing they came from every trade under the sun. I remember there was a vicar, from Eaton Socon, who raced and one lad, a student from Wales, I remember he rode a Tiger Cub all the way across to Cadwell Park one year, took all the road equipment off that he didn't need, did all the races then re-fitted all the road equipment and rode it back home again. It was like that and anyone would lend anyone anything so people could keep running. They just wanted to race and if your bike blew up on the Saturday you lived on baked beans to save up enough money to buy spares, so you could go racing again the following weekend. And remember a lot of people were very good, they just didn't know the right people or have the right connections to progress further in their racing. We had a lot of very good riders racing with us. Dave Potter, Roger Winterburn and Greg Page later, and Pete Davies as well. *PK* was a good friend as was Hugh Evans, one of our stars, as was his wife Eunice, who was a good racer herself of course. Dave Railton was another one and Ron Haslam rode his first ever race with us, riding his brother's bike, though it goes without saying he was probably under age.

He was still very young then and it had just become compulsory for everyone to have their leathers and helmet checked before they went out to race. This was up at Cadwell Park again, at the little old office that we had for signing on, as when I looked up this very small, slight, creature came staggering through the door, weighed down by leather boots and helmets, and it was Ron. I said: *'Are there any more at home like you?'* As of course his older brothers Terry and Phil had always been milling about. But his first race it was on the big bike, perhaps it was Terry's Norton? As we were short-handed I was doing the starting, down at Mansfield, the start finish line for the Club circuit. Well, the bike took off with Ron hanging on to the bars, everything else flailing behind him, and as we were one of the first clubs to use a radio for connections, between the start and the office, well the call comes through from the clerk of the course; *'I think we better get another person down there, to the start, as if he does that again he'll take half the field out!'* But he was always so polite, even when he was famous and if he saw me Ron would always enquire: *'How is Mr Milligan?'* As me and my husband ran the club, took it on in the mid-60s, right up until the end of 1985.

Len Read queuing up for scrutineering at Snetterton along with the other production runners. Huge effort went in to running the clubs

The younger Haslams and the best years of the British Formula Racing Club were yet to come in 1966, but the scene was growing irrespective, with a number of new clubs and circuits being added to the list. The Bon Accord, Lincoln & District, Cardiff Eagles and Louth & District clubs had all come on board running production races at their meetings. While Crimond and Llandow were added as new circuits on the production racing scene, for anyone willing to travel. Through the international *Coupe d'Endurance* Imola could also be added to that list, as while the influence of British racing on Italy might be stretching the imagination, the announcement of racing on another *'new'* circuit for 1967 was entirely down to the growth of the domestic scene.

Come May, the production racers would be heading to Liverpool, the Steam Packet ferry and off to the Isle of Man.

HONDA

CB450

Production	1965-1974
Predecessor	N/A
Bore	70mm
Stroke	57.8mm
Capacity	444cc
Compression	8.5:1
Front wheel	3.25 x 18
Rear wheel	3.50 x 18
Front brake	8" tls
Rear brake	7" sls
Weight	412lb
Power	43hp @ 8,500rpm
Top speed	105mph

Laverda made no bones of the fact that their SF750 – a successful production racer of the 1970s – took its inspiration from the CB72/CB77 in designing their 450 successor, Honda thought otherwise, starting from a blank sheet of paper. The four gears which emerged looked miserly by 1966 however and while torsion bar valve operation was innovative, as the CB450 Black Bomber only revved to 8,500rpm it begged the question, why the fuss? A disc brake, five gears and indicators all followed and, while the CB450 soldiered on as the CB500T until 1976, Honda's first *big bike* in truth was one to forget

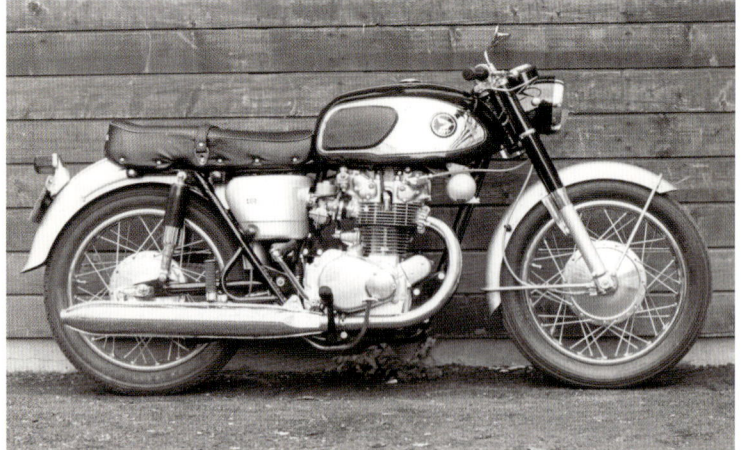

Black Bomber/Red Herring

In 1969 a Honda CB450 *Black Bomber* ridden by Graham Penny won the 500cc production TT. It marked Japan's first ever Production TT victory and staked the Honda's claim as a 1960s racing success. Unfortunately for the CB450, that win was three years too late. The Black Bomber had failed on the high street, in the UK at least, and Honda had shifted focus in early 1967 to the development of the machine which *would* take it into big bike territory, the époque defining CB750/4. How had the great white hope grown into a great white elephant?

Meet the big black bomber...

Sit astride this black beauty. Feel the size. Feel the power. Don't worry any more about capacity or revs—the Honda 450's got both. 444 c.c. 9,500 r.p.m. in waiting. What makes it go? Turn over and see . . .

The smaller, sloping, CB72 twin won both the *500-miler* and 1000km 250cc class races in 1961 and 1962. Up to 1965 Hondas were only once off the podium. CB77s over-bored to 350cc also did well in the 500 class, so it was reasonable to presume that the Black Bomber would clear up in the class. The problem was that the CB450s greater power came at the expense of extra weight, while archaic

FIM and AMA race rules virtually banned it from the sport. Had Mike Hailwood been allowed to run one at the Hutchinson 100, as planned, in 1966 then the story could have mirrored the A65's. But he wasn't, and it didn't, while the CB450 suffered the Honda curse. Namely, that each road model was both slower and heavier than the one which went before. Club racers *did* race them, but they were no more numerous than they were on the high street and herein lay the rub. The general design, combined with the electric starter, meant the CB450 weighed as much as a British 650, cost the same, but delivered less. It also suffered from under-damped, period, Japanese suspension with some customers experiencing remarkably high levels of mid-range vibration for a machine with a 180 degree crank.

Nevertheless, the CB450 *did* win a TT, had moderate success as an open class racer and set the blue print for the vertical CB250/350 twins which would replace the CB77/72. These, while no more successful than the CB450 in production racing, currently dominate the modern classic racing scene. A case of '*the older I get, the better I was*?' certainly, but their success

also demonstrates what *could* have been achieved by Honda, if they had moved away from Grand Prix racing sooner, to focus on the production racing side of the sport.

You met the nicest people on a Honda. Just not going that quickly if it was a CB450

My enthusiasm took me as far as a session with the Charles Mortimer Racing School at Brands Hatch and I remember it poured with rain. We plodded around on Greeves Silverstones and for my £25 - not a small sum in those days - I received a detailed report stating that *'this man shows promise.'* God I bet we all did at that price!

- Ted Reading

Riding at the
TT Races

Deja Vu. 1967 started much as the previous year had finished. Tony Smith's factory Spitfire added four wins at Snetterton over the opening weekend. All the top Triumph riders were there, but the speed of the BSAs was highlighted in the final, fifth race. As while Smith was out of this one, A65s came home first and second anyway, in the hands of Melvin Rice and new boy Clive Wall. As March moved into April there were more good results for BSA riders too. Bob Heath won at Darley Moor, the first of four, one for every round of the Darley Moor championship he contested. Those results would bring him the club Production Championship in 1967 which he'd repeat in 1968, by winning six out of six this time. There were also four wins for A65s on 22nd April. One for Clive Wall on the RH Smith bike at Snetterton, then three at Cadwell Park for Dave Vickers. Vickers hadn't bothered the leaders in 1966 but he was now on the ex-Rod Gould, ex-Eddie Dow machine and the difference really showed. It was the same with Melvin Rice's machine, as his win on 19th March had been achieved on an A65 sharing similar provenance, coming through Tony Smith and the BSA factory.

In general this was to be a feature of production racing as it moved on. Not of BSAs winning, Triumphs would dominate again, but of the leading machines having factory or dealer provenance, or at least a history of benefiting from the same. Bikes started to be known by who had *previously* owned them, as the top riders started to acquire the latest models and their previous machines, sometimes just twelve months old, moved their way down the food chain. This allowed new names to shine, with three being particularly prominent during the first two months of the 1967 season. Howie Robinson was all over the club results on an ex-TT marshal's Triumph and was helped by the fact that these machines were always meticulously prepared in Triumph's Experimental Department, to the latest Thruxton specification. The second who raised his profile was Graham Bailey, who won twice at Snetterton on 22nd April. He did it by borrowing Peter Butler's current Boyer Bonnie, while the third rider had bought his old one.

Pete Davies: In 1966 I bought Pete Butler's Triumph Bonneville. Thruxton Bonneville, the unit one. Peter was of course a super rider and great fella and he'd get one from the factory, keep it for a year or so, then sell it on. So, '67 was the first-year racing on a Triumph for me. Ray Hole was a very good friend of mine back in the day. He started racing the same time, the same day actually, so when we saw Peter Butler's bike for sale I thought: *'Wow if I could only get hold of that?'* Well Ray was a good mechanic and I mean I was hopeless, I didn't know what the hell I was doing, so I asked Ray if he'd come down to London to have a look at the bike and he said: *'Yeah I'll come.'* Well, long story short, he liked it, so I bought it and Ray just slipped into the role of mechanic for me, though I can't ever remember sort of asking him: *'Would you be my mechanic?'* But there he was every meeting and several nights in the week he'd be helping me in the garage, showing me what to do. He taught me quite a lot actually and after that we did really well.

Davies did, though Hole's racing wasn't over quite yet. He'd appear again, but in April all minds were on the *500-miler* with its usual glut of disguised factory entries and star riders.

Brands *Grand Prix d'Endurance*

The *500-miler* continued with the posh new name it had acquired in 1966 - the Brands Grand Prix d'Endurance - and as ever, a whole book could be written on the *what-ifs*, *could-have-beens* and *oh-so-closes*, but it was only the results which mattered and the big news was that Percy Tait had finally got his hands on one of the big trophies. Thirteen years since his first proddie ride in the 1954 Clubman's TT! The official entrant was *'PH Tait'* but Doug Hele would have been hugely pleased as Tait's was a works machine and it was actually a Triumph top four.

Come 1967 fairings were a growing fashion on the mainland production grids, perhaps with the TT in mind?

The other machines were entered by Comerfords, Hughes and Boyer respectively, the first pair being two of the newest, coveted, 'MAC' registered 1967 Thruxtons, while the Boyer's bike, though a year older, was unquestionably the most highly developed non-factory machine on the track. The first non-factory supported Bonneville home was a typical, privately owned machine however, which had been appearing in the top six on the club racing scene since the first weekend of the season. It would take its first outright win against the established dealer machines early in 1968, but it was run on a shoestring by a rider whose experiences probably encapsulated those of many journeymen racers.

Ralph Ridley: The whole racing thing back then was a lot of fun to be part of. I was the same as everyone else in that I had my up-and-downs, but wouldn't have missed it for the world. Even though, like all the rest, I was skint. I was an apprentice and didn't have money or time for anything else as it was all spent on the bikes. Luckily for me I worked at an engineering company, Coventry Gauge & Tools, so I could get all sorts of what were called *'foreigners'* made for nothing. As if you wanted parts made or modified pals would do this or that for you. Lord knows how much it cost the company, but that's just the way it was back in the day.

Early days for Ralph Ridley (No.23) and Ron Ireland (No.25) at a Lawford Heath test day. In the 1960s many production racers tested the water with sprints and time trials before committing to road racing

I started on an old T100, 1954 or '55 model I think it was. I had that bike for a number of years, riding to and from the races and there was a lot of faith there, as it was my ride to work bike as well. But I guess the bug really bit, as I went on and bought a Thruxton Bonneville from Streamline Motorcycles in London. That would have been 1967 and I paid £325 quid for it. A '65 model, as in actual fact there were only two years up till then, '65 and '66, when they really made Thruxtons. The first year there were 51 or 52 made and then in the second year there were only about half a dozen of the orange and cream ones I think. A friend of mine John Lancaster had one of those and I had the silver and blue one, the '65. I never knew the history of that bike – GGF 60C - or where it came from, as I didn't take much heed of things like that back then.

Snetterton March 1967. Ralph Ridley's first ride on his 1965 Thruxton. He took 4th place

So when I went to Canada a couple of years later I ended up selling it back to Streamline and I think I got £225. Of course I wish I'd never sold it now, as there were never many of them and it was a lovely bike to ride. I can remember going along the back straight there at Snetterton, 7,500rpm on the clock and there was no vibration at all. Incredible. I was a member of the British Formula Club, and I did a few with the Bantam Club as well, though I don't ever remember being a Bantam member as such. As you'd ride at other clubs too, stuff like the Vincent Owners, the MCC at Silverstone, I did a couple of Nationals, a couple of Brands and Mallory Club events and thinking about it I was a member of Bemsee too. So, come the following year, all told I know in 1968 I rode in a dozen other meetings, plus all the British Formula ones too. So 15 to 18 meetings in all in a season, sometimes on consecutive days. Lots did. I'd do Brands of a Saturday then my grandma lived in Norwich, which wasn't far from Snetterton. So we'd ride up there on the Saturday night, kip over and race at Snetterton the next day. But, and I know this sounds strange, I can't say I really paid much attention to the results. All I knew was that if I'd done reasonably well I'd get a trophy come through from the club, maybe two or three weeks after the event type thing and I guess I got a dozen or so of whatever type over the years though, as you say, it's true, I was there at the *500-miler* in 1967, with a guy called Eric Fitzhugh. I had that Thruxton Bonneville that year, the first year I had it, but I fell off it in practice. I think it was Hawthorns? It's quite a fast right-hander, on the big circuit, and I fell off in practice and did myself no good at all. It was in April and was bloody cold – there were hardly any spectators that year as I remember - so consequently, in the race, I was five or six seconds behind my co-rider. Because I was so bloody sore. I'd got gravel rash all down my hip sort of thing, but nevertheless, sore or not, you still tried to get on the bike, that was the thing. But that was the reason I was so slow in the race, as otherwise we could have done even better.

Fifth among the big names was not to be sniffed at. As Pat Mahoney, Dave Degens, Dave Croxford, Paul Smart and Rex Butcher were among those brought in by BSA and Paul Dunstall. None of the fancied runners went the distance however and it was similar among the 500s. For once the dealer-sponsored Velocettes and Triumphs fell by the wayside, leaving the over-bored Honda CB77 prepared by Read's of Leyton - up from 305cc to nearer 350cc – to take Honda's first 500 class win, ridden by Graham Penny and Tony Dunnell. The Honda was in turn beaten by the fastest 250 however, the Super Six of Chris Vincent and Kevin Cass, with the diminutive Suzuki quick and reliable enough to clinch an incredible third place overall. In a similar vein Clive Thompsett's Ducati 250, which he campaigned week-in week-out up and down the country, came home sixth overall, five laps ahead of the fastest Norton Dominator. It was also three places ahead of the second placed 500, which was the top Triumph 500 in the race, ridden by a young, unknown international pairing, of Bob Harrington and Dutchman Jan Strijbis. It all went to show that despite the big names and fancied runners the result of the *500-miler* could still be unpredictable, especially given the performance of the latest 250s.

Read Brothers may not have been hot on the cosmetic aspects of their racing Hondas, but they went well in the hands of their favoured riders Tony Dunnell and Graham Penny.

At the TT Dunnell (left) was on the *500-miler* 500 class winning CB77 while Penny was on the newer CB450

An enraged Bob Harrington makes his feelings felt at Mallory Park. By 1967 production races commanded big crowds

Small is Beautiful

A couple of years previously Ariel Arrows and BSA C15s had contested the 250 class, but by 1967 that felt like a life-time ago. The 250 class had always been competitive, if under reported, but now the latter wasn't so critical, as 250s were regularly creeping into the top six. Neither Suzuki's Super Six nor Ducati's 250 were genuine 100mph machines on the road, but they were very, very, close. Discarding a bit of bodywork and adding some mild tuning could get you there and those tuning kits were available, off the shelf, from some very enthusiastic dealers. The Ducatis of Alistair Rogers and Pete Kilner regularly joined Clive Thompsett's in hassling the 650s, while Dave Spruce's Suzuki T20 was the most regular Super Six crashing the podium party around the short circuits. This was important for Suzuki, as they advertised heavily and reaped the benefits. Everyone knew that the Vincent/Robb Super Six was the first *real* road bike home in the 1966 *500-miler* and Vincent proved it by winning in 1967, with Aussie Kevin Cass. The result? The Super Six won the coveted MCN *'Bike of the Year'* award, two years running. Suzuki had even bigger ambitions for June however.

Welcome to the Club. The First Production TT

The significance of the Production TT cannot be overstated. Today the TT is an *entirely* production based event. They race nothing else. But back in 1967 it was an entirely different situation, with the TT holding a unique sporting, indeed cultural, status. Like the Aintree Grand National or Oxford and Cambridge boat race the TT sparked national interest out of all proportion to any other motoring event. People who had no interest in motorcycles knew all about the TT and in the national psyche a TT win trumped any World Championship. Small boys could reel off the names of winners, as they might Premiership football stars nowadays.

The TT was part of the World Championship however, indeed the oldest race in the world. So when rumour circulated that a Production TT was being considered it sent retired brigadiers into apoplexy and purists to the letters pages. The weekly broadsheets and monthly magazines were full of protests claiming that a production race would dilute and devalue the event, but things had rapidly changed. Hailwood, Read, Cooper, Minter, Gould, the list went on, they all rode production bikes now and while the ACU weren't yet of a mind to talk about a National Production Championship another, one-

Not necessarily the sort of machine the organisers were hoping to attract.

Griff Jenkins on the double-disc-ed *'production'* Dunstall Norton, which still courted a lot of controversy

off, high profile race was a different issue. The manufacturers were also increasingly keen to see their machines raced on the international stage and it was not lost on the ACU that a Production TT - like the production race at the Hutchinson 100 - was almost inevitably going to result in a British rider winning, on a British machine. The last time the fans had waved their Union Jacks at such a combination, and it was a combination, was when Chris Vincent's BSA outfit had won the sidecar TT in 1962. Ray Knight might have had difficulty convincing circuits to host a production race three or four years previously, but now grids were bursting and factory involvement was continuing to grow. By 1967 a production TT was becoming a no-brainer.

As the title implied the previous Clubman's TT had been as much about the rider, the clubman or amateur, as it was about the machine. The Production TT would be different. The organisers were keen that the race would get British *manufacturers* back on the Island, along with top riders of the calibre who now graced the grids of the *500-miler* and Hutchinson 100. They hedged their bets however by giving the race only National status. This was possibly to save their blushes if it didn't attract the riders or produce the spectacle they hoped for, but also to avoid eligibility hurdles for the regular national runners who they hoped would also enter en masse. The downside of this decision was that the winners would be awarded just medals, instead of Mercury replicas and that the race would be held early, on the first Saturday of the TT, before some of the fans had actually arrived. To some extent this also helped assuage the naysayers for whom a production race was verging on sacrilege anyway. Particularly as the organisers took one final gamble which further broke with convention, but paid off in full. A split, mass, Le Mans-type start, which would ensure that the riders would start at a run and then circulate in gaggles, if not one pack, in each of the three competing classes. The 750cc riders running across the track to their machines and departing first, then the 500cc bikes, followed by the 250cc machines, at timed intervals.

Bookies Favourite

There would be many short circuit newcomers, but it was clear that Mountain knowledge would tell and that with eight podium finishes, including a TT win, John Hartle stood head and shoulders above the rest. He was entered by Scuderia Duke, but his was one of three Thruxton Bonnevilles which were prepared by the factory. The only rider close in terms of experience was Griff Jenkins, who had a Manx Grand Prix win under his belt.

Come race day it was no surprise that these two headed the field. That was until a few miles from the finish, when Jenkins' clutch let go allowing his Dunstall team mate Ray Pickrell through into second place and BSA's Tony Smith, on his first ever race round the Island, into third. It was a hugely popular win for Hartle and just what the first Production TT needed. There were those less pleased with the machine in second place however, Pickrell's bike, which like Jenkins' sported double disc brakes and who knew what else in the engine. What a *'Dunstall'* was exactly had still to be clearly defined. It was Triumph's day though, as American Lance Weil was fourth and Peter Butler fifth. In publicity terms, Meriden also had another ace up their sleeve.

Fifth place, first time out ,was pretty good going for Peter Butler the king of the short circuit scene

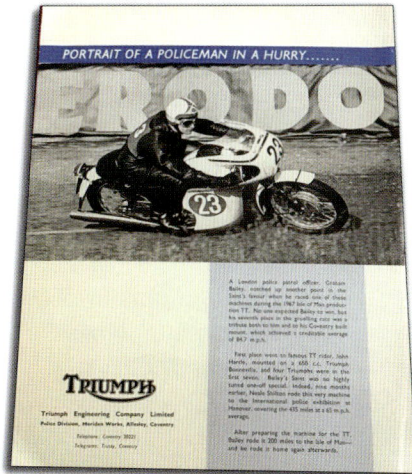

Graham Bailey's exploits provided rich copy and Triumph went to town with it to promote the TR6P Saint to police forces globally

PC Bailey's *'normal'* Metropolitan Police TR6P Saint was a little bit different to the one he raced

Graham Bailey: One day I'm nosing up a mews, a little double-up near Denmark Hill and there were a couple of blokes in this garage. One was a fair-haired chap with a Matchless CSR and the other a tall gent, with glasses, with a Constellation. The fair-haired bloke was Peter Butler and the other George Hopwood. Peter was a commercial artist and George was an engineer with the GPO. I was just crazy about racing motorbikes, talked to them and said: '*Look, why don't you come with me, down to Brands Hatch on a Wednesday, pay a couple of quid and you can have the afternoon bumming around?*' As you know you'd go out have fifteen minutes, then the cars would go out, then they'd come in you'd go out again, sort of thing. They weren't in to racing at all, just motorbikes, but they came down to Brands as I was racing a Tiger Cub at the time. Well they both went out and George decided his line was not going to be riding round and round, but more twiddling and fiddling with all the bits and pieces. But Peter clicked. So I was thrilled and privileged that I got these two guys in to racing and we became part of a gang. There was Ray Knight, Hugh Evans a smashing bloke, Peter Butler and George and we all used to meet up. I raced with Bemsee, the Bantam Racing Club and the British Formula, run by John and Joan Milligan, but it was George Hopwood who got on to me about the Diamond Jubilee TT, the first year of the production race. I'd already had a go on Peter's Thruxton, as Peter was riding for Boyer on their 500 at Barcelona. His was the most competitive non-works bike out there and if Peter went out, he pretty much won, that was it.

So I had this bike, arrived at Snetteron and everyone, John Hedger and the rest of it were going: '*What's he doing on Peter Butler's bike?*' as they didn't really know me from Adam. Well I got a 3rd, a 2nd and a 1st and it went on from there. George said, as Peter Butler was already entered in the TT: '*Ring up Sid Shilton for a bike*'. I said: '*Sid? Do you mean Neil, the Triumph Police bike Rep?*' and he says: '*No, everyone calls him Sid, but ring him up and ask for a bike*,' as George was well in with Triumph's by then. So I picked up the phone and this chap answers. I say my name is Graham Bailey, a policeman from London and that I was wondering if he could lend me a Saint to ride in the production TT? '*Hmm.. well...let's think, I've got two bikes in the Welsh, one in the Liège whatever it is...*' and you could almost hear his brain going '*publicity, publicity, publicity*'. So he says: '*Hold on, my Saint which I rode to Hanover, to the police exhibition, that's in for a service. What do you want?*' So I said, well could I have a close box and a 19" back wheel? Because the Avon GP rear was a racing profile, though a road tyre, but they only did it in 19". So he says: '*Leave it with me*' and the phone goes down. Next thing I know is that I get a phone call from Leslie Nichol, of the *Daily Express*, a smashing bloke, who says: '*I understand you're doing the TT?*' So I knew it was on and sometime later Neil gets back and says: '*The bike's ready, come and collect it. Stan Brand at Hughes Motorcycles will fix you up with an exhaust system and racing seat and I've had a word with Doug Mitchenhall and there will be a fairing for you too.*'

So George with his car and my trailer drive up to Meriden and there's this Saint standing there, sans exhaust and stuff and the bloke Freddy Swift says; '*We've put handle bars on it like Percy's, as that's how it likes it*' as they weren't clips-on. So there's this semi-prepared thing, with twin-carbs on, so I'm thinking: '*Oh, that's odd?*' But apparently they did specify twin-carbs in some countries, on police bikes, so catalogue-wise it was OK as a production model. So we brought it home, Stan Brand provided the Thruxton pipes and Mitchenhall the fairing and as I was working as the night duty reserve at the time, at Lewisham Garage, the skipper, Toby Jug we called him, after I'd done all the paperwork, he'd let me wheel the bike in and finish preparing it in the police garage. For the Island Peter Butler, George Hopwood, Dave Nixon

Barry Smith testing the waters at the TT in 1966. 12th place in a 250cc Grand Prix, on a road bike, was unheard-of

Terry Grotefeld's Yamaha leads Barry Smith's Suzuki on the opening lap of the 250 race, while Chris Vincent - in the background by the BP sign - retrieves his looped Suzuki Super Six. Graham Bailey's police bike would provide plenty of publicity in 1967 but the 250 class would produce even more

and myself, we all rode up on our respective race machines can you believe, practiced and the Triumph works people were all so friendly and helpful. Arthur Jakeman and that. But the Friday night before the race we'd all done our final practice and were in the field behind when Doug Hele came up. Arthur Jakeman says: *'Doug this is the policeman from London, who's going to ride the Saint'* and that's when he told me to forget it; *'You're wasting your time. It's too slow, not competitive.'* The Saint went through the speed trap at the pub, the Highlander, at 116mph. But his works Thruxtons were going through at 132mph, so he said I shouldn't bother. Well as you might know Doug Hele had a club foot and after the race I wheeled the bike back in and there used to be wooden posts, stakes, that you'd lean your bikes on. Well as I lent my bike against this one Doug Hele *ran* across the field towards me, going: *'Well done, well done'* and I felt like a World Champion. I only came 7th but I really felt like a World Champion after that. An ordinary copper getting the chief of contracts, for the army and that, to give him a bike and everything, then the race boss congratulating me!

The newspapers did loads of stories after that. *'Policeman, preacher, TT racer'* was one. They came to a church in Eastbourne where I was speaking and before that we went to Brands and Victor Blackman the *Daily Express* photographer, a great chap, climbed into the boot of a Ford Corsair, boot open, me following him round, to take photos of me riding. But I was at the Lewisham police garage afterwards and this bloke rings up and says I am so and so, whoever his name was who wrote the Saint books, Leslie Charteris,

Kel Carruthers' Thompson Suzuki was only fifth in 1967, but he was 250 World Champion by 1969 for Benelli

that's it: *'What's all this about you using the Saint name?'* Well I said it was a police designation and meant Stops Anything In No Time, and that I wasn't using the image - the Saint silhouette on the TV series I guess he meant - that's Neil, who has it on his helmet. So he says: *'Oh, OK, I see, alright.'* As I guess he was worried about copyright, though we never heard anything back from him again. It was probably a case of *'there's no such thing as bad publicity'*, with Leslie Chateris and his publishers being as pleased as Triumph?

Either way they were happier than Suzuki, who had every reason to expect as much success as Triumph. Suzuki had won the 250 class at the *500-miler* and Harrogate dealer Harry Thompson had tested the waters a year previously, in the 250cc Light weight TT, with a rider fresh from victory at the previous Austrian Grand Prix.

Barry Smith: In 1966 I had entered the 50 and 125 races, while Harry Thompson had entered me in the 250 race on a new T20 Suzuki. This was only a standard road bike, and when we took it through scrutineering it still had its tax disc and number plate attached. They made us take these off, but it was a good ploy by Harry, because it created a great deal of publicity. You need to remember the Isle of Man TT was a round of the World Championships in those days and it was not heard of to ride a standard road bike in a 250 Grand Prix. The only modifications Harry made to the standard bike was to fit a fairing, clip-on handlebars, larger fuel tank, racing seat and rear-set footrests. Otherwise it was a bog-standard road bike. I was very impressed with the bike but had a couple of scares during practice with marshals wandering across the track. They were so used to listening for approaching bikes which all had loud exhaust pipes, but as mine had its original silencers, it couldn't be heard easily.... After the race I was named *Whispering Smith* by all the press and it was well reported, including stories in the UK's major daily newspapers. Harry and Suzuki were over the moon.

As a result Suzuki poured a lot in to pre-TT publicity for 1967, as while Yamaha were knocking on the door of a 250cc world championship with their impossibly exotic, water cooled, V4 RD05 racer their road going YDS3 was a bit weak in comparison. The Super Six was the thing every teenager wanted and Suzuki had some choice riders to demonstrate it, including Eddie Crooks, Chris Vincent, Barry Smith and Kel Carruthers, the last two being World Champions in waiting. It was not to be however, with Chris Vincent the first to hit trouble on the machine entered directly by Suzuki GB.

Chris Vincent: The bloody stupid mechanics, they took the brake linings to Ferodo and had them lined out in AM4 without telling me, but they were too sharp a brake. They did a Le Mans start there, so I was going down Bray Hill and then I put the brake on for Quarter Bridge, I was leading, and I somersaulted. It was one of the worst accidents I ever had. I picked it up and had to satisfy the marshals it was OK and luckily I always rode solos quite relaxed. But I had to rip off the screen as it cartwheeled at over 100mph and it ended up on the traffic island among the straw bales. I was a bit battered but OK really and the screen was the worst part of it, trying to get it off. I had a real job, but they decided I could carry on and as I'd lost a lot of time I really got my head down. This brake was so difficult I had to warm it up gently before I got to a corner. And as it was an evening race that was the biggest problem. Night air you see, 6.30 in the evening, damp air coming down. I could use AM4s on the sidecar but I didn't need it on the solo. But I worked my way up quite a bit until I ran it wide at the

Chris Vincent hustles his screen-less and battered Super Six in pursuit of the rest of the 250cc field. He made it to 8th

Lap two and Bill Smith (63) and Tommy Robb (64) are already well ahead on their expansion chamber equipped Bultacos

33rd Milestone at some silly pace which wasn't really possible and I ran it off the road. I wiped off my right footrest on the posts I was that close to running it clean off the Mountain and I ran the same corner on the sidecar the year I won the TT and wiped my foot-peg off then too! Some of these near misses they never get published in the reports and for the rest of the race I had to get it up into top gear as soon as possible and then use the gear shifter as a foot peg. As otherwise I was on the exhaust, though fortunately it had a bit of a cover so it wasn't too serious a heat.

That catalogue of errors meant eighth was the best Vincent could make, one place ahead of Eddie Crooks, as while Crooks Suzukis would come to prominence in future years they were not yet really refined. The Spa Motorcycles Super Sixes entered by Harry Thompson now looked the threat, but while Thompson had been working to ensure everyone knew just how standard his production bikes were others had been working the other way, to see how far the rules could be bent.

Barry Smith: Once the race got underway the two Bultacos of Bill Smith and Tommy Robb headed the field. It transpired they fitted race kits to their Metralla 250s for the race, even though they had both practiced with a standard bike during the week. How they got through scrutineering I will never know? There was no way our standard T20 Suzukis could keep up with these supposed production bikes fitted with race kits, which even included expansion chamber exhausts, ported cylinders and high compression heads. How were they allowed in a production race that was meant for bikes that were ridden on the road? So the battle was now on for who could finish in third. Kel had got a better start than me and it was at Ballacraine, eight miles from the start before I caught him. We accelerated out of the right-hander together and as he shut off for Ballaspur, the next left-hander, I rode right round the outside of him. I then put my head down and gave it everything I had through the Glen Helen section and by the time we got onto the Cronk-Y-Voddy straight I had a quick look behind and I couldn't see him. I then settled down to my normal pace and at the end of the race I ended up in 3rd place with Kel in 5th. Harry was happy that we had both finished, but he was in a dilemma regarding the race-kitted Bultacos. We were both good friends of Bill Smith and Tommy Robb and could not comprehend how devious they had both been, so it was with heavy heart that Harry decided not to protest. But we both knew we had been robbed of our first TT win and so did the majority of the riders and journalists who reported on the incident. After the race we went back to the hotel to drown our sorrows and to contemplate what could have been.

It was the sort of adverse publicity the TT could have done without. The Metralla MkII was a formidable bike, as effectively it was a road bike fitted with a detuned version of their 1964 TSS racers' engine. There was also a catalogued race kit available for it. The problem was that this was a kit intended to turn a road bike into a racer, not a tune up kit for a road machine. It wouldn't have been legal in the UK, but was it legal in Spain? Or Ireland, as the machines were all entered by Harry Lindsay, the Irish importer. Not Rickman Bros. the official UK importers, nor Frank Sheene, Barry's father, who was also receiving racing machines direct from Spain and was the UK's number one Bultaco tuner. The obvious question which had to be asked though was, if the kit *was* legal why was it only fitted after practice, by which time it was too late for doubters to protest?

Ultimately, as with the Triumph *'Saint'* issue, for the injured party there was actually no such thing as negative publicity. It was all positives for Suzuki. No one bought a Bultaco, but learners queued up for Suzuki Super Sixes. Thompson's Spa Motorcycles also did well, as their main interest was publicising his line in customising parts, and the news coverage did him no harm at all. Overnight Royal Enfield Continental GTs and Ariel Arrows looked very dated – they were, they were no longer making them – so a customised Super Six was the way to go.

Clive Thompsett's Ducati. A far more representative and genuine 250 production machine

Half Litre

In the 500 class Honda were presumably looking for the same sort of spin-off as Suzuki. Their range topping CB450 was banned by FIM regulations from the mainland's premier events so, with the Production TT being run as an ACU organised *National*, this was their chance to shine. But herein lay a problem. As virtually no one other than Bill Smith – who was on a Bultaco Metralla in the 250s - had raced a Black Bomber on the mainland, the TT was not the place to begin. As a result, of the four Honda's entered, three were actually over-bored 305cc CB77s, with Tony Dunnell best of the bunch, taking the *500-miler* winning *'Read Titan'* to a respectable 7th place. The sole CB450 was entered by Graham Penny, who put in a great performance to come fourth, albeit a good thirty seconds shy of the podium, which was an entirely British affair. Prior to the race Triumph test rider Percy Tait was the talk of the paddock. He'd just won the *500-miler* on a Bonneville but leaving the 750 class to others, it was clear that Triumph were lining him up for the 500 win. It would be Tait's eleventh time around the Island and it was obvious that his 500 *'benefitted'* from the knowledge which had gone into the exceptionally fast 1966 and 1967 Daytona winning machines. Perhaps too much however, as his highly strung example struggled, never really running properly, leaving the door open for more standard, genuine production machines to go for the win.

Neil Kelly and his staggeringly fast Velocette

Percy Tait: That bike was virtually like my racer, very fast, I don't think the Velocettes would have caught up with me if I hadn't had trouble. One plug never fired up and I went round the first lap on one cylinder and came into the pits. Arthur (Jakeman) changed the plugs and off I went. They shouldn't let you out after a thing like that, but they did and I was really het up. I hit Bray Hill at the bottom so fast that one of the spokes came unhitched and eventually punctured the front tyre and I came off, I think at Ballacraine?

As a result Dave Nixon's Boyer T100 was the best Triumph in third, as a pair of spectacularly fast Velocette singles left everyone else for dead. Velocette were in big trouble financially by 1967 but *their* Thruxton - as opposed to Triumph's - was at the pinnacle of its development and was well suited to distance events. Neil Kelly's L. Stevens

Graham Penny did well to get the Read Bros. CB450 into 4th place. It was a full five minutes down on Neil Kelly's Velocette by the finish, but the Venom had about 50 years more development put into it

version won the race and his speed would have placed him third in the 750cc class. It showed what could be done with a big single, even if it was a pre-war design. This was emphasised by Keith Heckles, on the Geoff Dodkin-entered version, coming second, three and a half minutes ahead of Dave Nixon.

> **Geoff Dodkin:** You could say an endurance race starts with the rule book. You have to interpret the rules as favourably as possible and sometimes exceed them when you see that other people are. I can remember Doug Hele with sheet after sheet of paperwork he produced to circumvent certain rules. We were naive for the first two years running a standard Venom just put together correctly, but we got good finishes. Neil's was literally a works bike with lots of engine tweaks. We were over-geared – a big mistake – and a slight gearbox fault meant that it sometimes dropped out of gear. But I take responsibility for the failure. It wasn't Heckles' fault. I thought he was a slightly better TT course rider than Kelly.

They *were* both very good, and experienced. But following Kelly, Heckles, Nixon and Penny the battle for 5th place was contested by a gaggle of battling twins, from Triumph, BSA, Norton and Honda piloted by less experienced TT riders. The nod finally went to a BSA test rider, who was used to rather different racing lines and was only warming up for the sidecar race, which would take place in two days time.

Norman Hanks looking very neat and tidy. Fifth place was incredibly good for a sidecar racer riding his own machine

Norman Hanks: Chris Vincent had showed them he could do it, by winning first on a Honda. So we all thought we could have a go after that and being a Development Tester I thought I was the bees knees. I actually first rode a works BSA in the *500-miler* at Brands with one of Tony Smith's mates, Melvin Rice. I did the first stint and because I had been riding these things day in day out I think after the hour I was in 5th place and had lapped Chris Vincent on his Suzuki Super Six, which was good, as I knew he'd know it was me when I went past! Then they gave it to Melvin and we dropped down the field again, so I asked Brian Martin to let me have another go.

They brought Melvin in early and, of course, within a lap and a half I'd thrown it into the trees at Stirlings! I was meant to ride the same works bike at the TT, the inaugural production race, but later Brian says: '*I've been thinking about the TT*' – and I'm limping about at the time, with all these stitches in my foot – '*I think it would be better if you rode your own bike. And don't ride in the 750 class. We've got enough in that. You've got some 500 barrels haven't you? Build your own engine with those and ride in the 500 class.*' Being told to ride my own bike I knew I was in Martin's black books, but he gave me all the trick bits. The cut-off flat silencers and the other bits I probably shouldn't say, as it was all down to the interpretation of the rules! And it was just as well it was a 500 as it was a mass start, where you ran across the road to the bike.

I don't know if they thought that would split us up or not, but I went down Bray Hill side by side with Hugh Evans and it was pure madness. I frit myself to death. Mick Andrew was meant to be on one of the works Triumphs but fell off in practice and they gave it to Alan Peck, so I thought: '*I'll just keep this bloke in sight and make sure he doesn't get away from me, then try to pass him at the line.*' I thought I could slipstream him, but I only beat him as I think he missed a gear, as we were even for speed. He did an article about it afterwards, and was most put out, being beaten by this sidecar racer!

There were of course countless other TT stories but the big take away was that the production race had been a roaring success. Far from being the embarrassment purists had prophesised, it had provided some of the closest, most exciting racing, featuring machines the fans could identify with. They had undoubtedly enjoyed Hailwood's epic

Senior victory on the mighty Honda 500, where he traded blows with Agostini's MV before *Ago* was finally forced out. But it was helped by the fact that they had *eight minutes* in which to eat their sandwiches and think about it before the second place machine – Peter Williams' Arter Matchless - came through. The following day, the Junior was closer, between Hailwood and Agostini again, but once more it was eight minutes to the next finisher – Derek Woodman's MZ - leaving plenty of time to admire the view. In comparison the three waves of mass starting production machines provided a spectacle which had never been seen before on the Island, with bike-on-bike battles throughout the field. From the Highlander to the Mitre, bar room racers extolled the virtues of the Bonnevilles and Venoms, or defended the BSAs, as it was *their* bikes out there racing, not unobtainable four cylinder fantasies.

There was only one decision needed from the race organisers and the ACU. Where within the main week's programme would they move the race in 1968? The proddie bikes weren't the stars of the show, but they needed moving up the TT bill.

1967's happy campers. Left to right, production class winners Neil Kelly (Velocette 500cc) John Hartle (Triumph 750cc) and Bill Smith (Bultaco 250cc)

T20 Super Six

Production	1966-1968
Predecessor	T10
Bore	54mm
Stroke	54mm
Capacity	247cc
Compression	7.3:1
Front wheel	2.75 x 18
Rear wheel	3.00 x 18
Front brake	8" tls
Rear brake	8" sls
Weight	297lb
Power	29hp @ 7500rpm
Top speed	94mph

Suzuki's workmanlike T10 gave no clue as to what would follow. The electric start, four-speed commuter was civilised but unexciting, while the odd, pressed-steel looks did nothing for UK sales, of which there were virtually none. The T20 rectified all that through a different bore and stroke, tubular frame and Posi-Force oil supply to the race-bred six-speed motor. At 21 horse power it claimed no more than some British 250s, but the British horses must have been donkeys. The Super Six was in a different league, transforming both the learner class and Suzukis indifferent sales

Raising the Bar

Suzuki had huge racing ambitions in the 1960s. They were heavily involved in the defection of Ernst Degner from East Germany and benefitted from the technology he brought from MZ. Even if they wouldn't admit it. 50cc and 125cc World Titles resulted but the Super Six – the name came care of its 6-speed gearbox - was the first manifestation of Suzuki's technical advances on the road. Testers gushed over the performance while its civility triggered eulogies. It looked good too and even ditching the electric start was seen as a plus point since who needed the unnecessary weight on such a sporty machine?

Suzuki claimed a 100mph top-whack and while 90mph was nearer the mark it could cruise at 80mph, faster than most British twins. T20s shot out of show rooms. The writing was on the wall and dealers clambered to get a Suzuki franchise. Suzuki had arrived, with the Super Six becoming the first

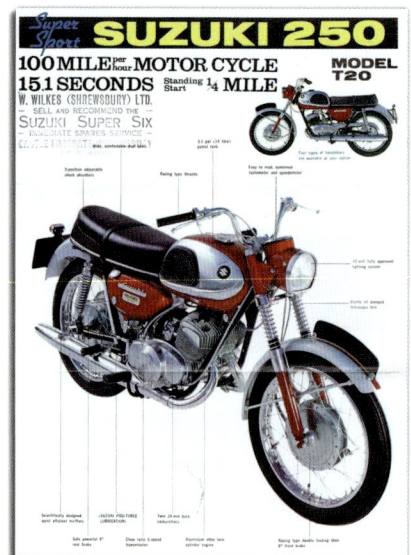

Japanese motorcycle to win the *MCN 'Machine of the Year'* poll, in 1966. It did it again in 1967 through features such as the Posi-Force oil feed to the engine. This ended the chore of measuring out oil every time petrol went in and was heady stuff in 1967. Gone were garage forecourts like ice rinks. Suzuki's prestige benefited from the race results too. They won the *500-miler* and while they were denied a TT win, everyone knew they should have had not one but two, were it not for cheating.

The T20 put Suzuki on the map as a company in the UK and a replacement, the T250-1, took care not to change the winning formula. This was also replicated on the T500 Cobra, a grown up Super Six, which would have its own racing career. The GT250 of 1971 *was* a genuine redesign, but it kept the bore and stroke of the original, to ensure a host of British youngsters could get the full performance experience during the 1970s, emulating their idol, Suzuki World Champion, Barry Sheene.

Suzuki's *Posi-Force* lubrication system was rocket science in 1966 and sounded a death knell for British two-strokes

There was a big brother too in 1968, the T350.

It never really caught on in the UK but it won the Australian Castrol 6 hour Production race at Amaroo Park and though later disqualified the exact same machine was still good enough to win the 500cc production class as late as 1973

Back on the Ferry

Production bikes were big news, it was official and nowhere better demonstrated than by a record twenty British teams making the annual trek to Barcelona. Where, as in previous years, it was actually the smaller machines making all the noise. Dodgy 250s at the TT were an affront, but accepted away from home. A 230cc Ossa *road bike* took the win and barely raised an eyebrow, but a second place and outright 500cc class win for the Hughes Triumph 500 really brought a smile. Not least since arch-rivals Boyers had a whole saga with their own. The 500 class in general was interesting, since the machine which led initially was almost totally new to the scene.

Alan Peck on the giant-killing Mead & Tomkinson BSA B44. It's results would become the stuff of legend

The Mead & Tomkinson BSA B44 single had completed just thirty laps at the *500-miler*, as its introduction to the sport. Yet at Barcelona it led the opposition for the first hour before broken valve springs put it out. Out of the lead that was, not out of the race. The need for an entire new cylinder-head, oiling issues, a new clutch and various other problems which would have beaten lesser men saw Peter Darvill and Alan Peck in and out of the pits before a loss of sparks called an end to play 20 hours in. Some might have doubted the effort put in, since the B44 had lost an hour and a half in the pits, but Mike Tomkinson never thought he could win. These were test outings for an entirely new machine and as the history books would record, the physically tiny BSA singles would go on to deliver legendary, giant-killing, performances. That was a few years hence as British crews toiled in the heat of a Barcelona evening though and none more so than the teams from Boyer of Bromley, or Suzuki GB. The latter running Irishman Chris Goosen and an injured Barry Smith on a Super Six, while their mechanics stalked the paddock stealing parts to keep them going.

Barry Smith: At the end of the first hour and a half I pitted for refuelling and to change over to Chris for his stint. I hopped off the bike and Chris jumped on while John used the quick filler to fill the tank. He didn't stop the fuel flow quick enough and a huge load of petrol spilled over the tank and onto the hot engine rapidly cooling it down. Then there was a loud bang as the front engine bolt snapped. It was about 30cm long and fired out of the bike across the track like a bullet and ended up embedding itself into the trunk of a tree. After the race we inspected it and could not pull it out. If it had hit anyone it would have certainly killed them. We sent Chris on his way as we searched the spares for a new engine bolt and it soon became apparent we did not have one. With only the rear engine mounting securing it to the frame we didn't know how long it would last before the whole thing vibrated apart. Undaunted one of the mechanics went in search of a replacement and before long he returned with engine bolts in his hand. It turned out he'd scoured the car park and found a T20 Suzuki parked among the hundreds of bikes. It belonged to a French guy who had come down to watch the race. He was nowhere to be seen, so the bolt was robbed off his bike and a note left with our pit number on it.

We left Chris out for his one and a half hours and when he came in to refuel the new bolt was fitted and away I went on my second stint just as it was going dark. Everything seemed to be going fine until one hour into my session when the exhaust noise seemed to be getting louder as each lap went by. Then suddenly on the far side of the circuit the right-hand muffler decided to part company with the bike. It was obvious to the pit crew as I went past for another lap that I had lost a muffler and by the time I came in for my scheduled stop they had a new muffler ready to bolt on. Once again the Frenchman's bike had been robbed of a vital part! By now I was starting to feel the effects of my knee injury and I struggled to get off the bike. Chris took off into the night and we hoped our mechanical troubles were over. Then at about 3 o'clock in the morning Chris had a very close call with one of the factory Montesa bikes. They somehow sideswiped each other coming down through the tight corners leading onto the start and finish straight. Luckily they both stayed on their bikes and were fortunate not to crash. At the next fuel stop I climbed on board. Chris was shouting out that the bike felt like a lump of jelly and a quick check soon revealed the reason. Apparently during the coming together with the other bike his footrest had broken several spokes on the front wheel and the rest of the spokes were now disintegrating. There was no option but to rob even more parts from the unfortunate bike in the car park!

Dave Nixon on the Boyer T100. With third place at the TT great things were expected in Barcelona, but it ended in major road-side surgery. The bike once repaired would go on to become highly successful in the hands of another rider however

The owner, on discovering the remnants of his Super Six, was actually over the moon that he'd helped as the setbacks were par for the course. In keeping going they secured sixth overall and fourth place in the 250cc class, which was much better than the result of the Boyer machine. Peter Butler and Dave Nixon had been in and out of the pits all race, but had got themselves up to fourth place before catastrophic piston problems promptly brought them back in again. The head, barrel and offending piston were all removed but, being too damaged to salvage, drastic measures were required to get them out on track again. To make the 500 rideable George Hopwood got out his hack saw and cut through the con rod, so the stump could swing harmlessly once the engine was reassembled. The revised 250 single then continued and completed the course, to ensure they picked up their prize and, critically, the finishers' money they'd need to get home again!

Doug Hele Waves His Magic Wand ....Again

The performance of the Hughes Daytona, ridden by Colin Dixon and Mick Andrew, in beating the 750s at Barcelona was hard to ignore, particularly as back home 500 Triumphs were increasingly taking outright wins. Ray Knight might have moved to a Triumph Tiger 100 through 'pot hunting' but there was a little more to it than that.

Triumph won the Daytona 100, America's premier road race in 1966 then did again in 1967. They did so with a development of the Tiger 100, as while Daytona was not strictly a production race American 'Class C' rules dictated a production bike as the base. Development of these bikes had been a huge learning exercise for Triumph and resulted in a marked step up in performance. Indeed the very success of the racer developed for Daytona meant that Percy Tait did a lot less production racing than is generally imagined. He was, by and large, campaigning the Triumph 'development' bike in the 500cc class with the machine's ultimate achievement scored in 1969, when it came second to Giacamo Agostini's 500cc MV Agusta at the Belgian Grand Prix. This engine produced about 52hp @ 8,500 revs, but could reach 11,000rpm if need be. Though externally very similar, there was virtually nothing in this engine that was standard T100, but there were huge spin offs for the production machines. The most obvious of these was that the new for 1967 'Daytona' road bike sported twin carburettors and a much

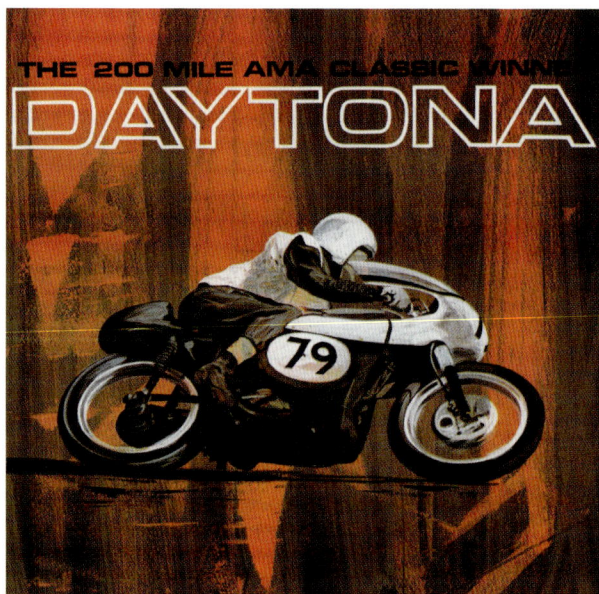

THE 200 MILE AMA CLASSIC WINNER
DAYTONA

improved frame, featuring additional support for the previously twisty swinging arm pivot. These improvements meant that Stan Brand's Hughes Daytona - most often ridden by Ray Knight - along with the private entries of Gary Green and Richard Guy regularly pinched podium places off Meriden's bigger twins. While Dave Nixon's Boyer prepared machine was capable of taking outright wins. Which was pretty good, as Boyer only started racing in 1966, when Stan Shenton decided it would be good for publicity. The first 650 Bonneville was prepared by veteran mechanic Lou Lancaster, assisted by Vic Lane, while workshop foreman Dave Nixon did the riding. He was joined later by Peter Butler, but Butler's machine was always prepared by George Hopwood, Shenton just helping with spares and entry fees. Nixon often took to the smaller, Tiger 100 machine however, as Boyer's version didn't take long to go extremely well.

Stan Shenton with one of his later creations, a Seeley Trident ridden by Mick Grant among others. Shenton went on to run the official Kawasaki race team and it all started from small, production, acorns

Rex Butcher hamming it up for the cameras on the Boyer's Bonneville at Brands Hatch

Stan Shenton: We started with a Triumph Bonneville, from stock, and fitted it with Triumph racing handlebars and rearsets and a small fairing. Dave kept saying that we needed this and that, but I said we'd have to wait and see how we got on. I was used to interpreting the small print on insurance policies, so I began to read the regulations very carefully indeed. There were a lot of rule-of-thumb tuners in those days, so using my friends in the car world I took an engine down to Piper Cams where Bob Gayler was a specialist in gas-flowing. This was a new thing at the time and Doug Hele at Meriden said that it was rubbish. But he soon changed his mind when he saw how well our Bonnie went. Another modification was dynamic balancing of the crankshaft, which made the engine much smoother. We balanced each rod individually, then paired them, together with piston, rings and gudgeon pin, then took everything down to the Brabham Racing Organisation, who prepared the Repco engines for Formula One. They would balance the crank dynamically. The result of all this work was that Dave won six races and finished third in three others between April and July. It was all down to gas flowing and Piper cams. Meriden had prepared a Tiger 100 for Percy Tait and this gave us the idea of preparing a 500cc for production racing. So I took a Tiger 100 engine down to Bob Gayler who pulled it to bits and studied it for a couple of days. According to him it had more potential as a racing engine than the Triumph Bonneville. When he had finished working on it and gas flowed the head we were getting 49hp, an increase of some 25%. The factory was most helpful once we started winning but we still had to buy our bikes.

The in-house Triumph set-up was well developed by this point, with the factory fully engaged – even if not officially – and the Experimental Department expanded by Doug Hele. Under Frank Baker, Les Williams and Harry Woolridge tested and built the engines, preparing the bikes too. But under Doug Hele, Arthur Jakeman, Bill Fannon and John Woodward were added, all doing their own engines, though these were only for the favoured few. The fifty two Thruxtons built in 1965 for instance were all assembled on the normal Meriden production line, merely being finished off by a small assembly team, fitting special parts. In comparison things were far less committed at stable-mate BSA.

Ron Smith: At Triumph Doug Hele would do all sorts of things on the side without Bert Hopwood knowing. When we'd go over there to the Triumph factory, to take something or pick something up, in the *Experimental* they'd be: '*Enemy's here!*' and if there was anything special on the bench they'd cover it up. They had loads of special parts, but our budget was so small we were always playing second fiddle to Triumph in that regard. If they wanted it, they got it. While our special parts list probably ran to one side of A4 paper! Against all these Triumphs it was just Tony Smith and maybe one other A65, and Hugh Evans out on his A50, in the 500s. So, it used to annoy them when Tony beat Percy and often he did. As our 650 was faster than theirs, even though with their 500 it was the other way around, as it had a lot more development than ours.

Ron Smith wheeling namesake Tony Smith's bike to scrutineering

Tony Smith on his works A65 in 1967

With the production racers we'd start by just pulling a production bike off the track, to get all the bits and pieces we needed, like cables, brackets and that. But it'd end up nothing like it came off the line. Everything was pretty standard, but ground and polished, and you could get a really good increase in power by just opening out the ports. Tony did his own of course, but everyone used to muck in on the others and none of the bikes we did were exactly the same.

We mainly trusted the frames, though some got checked in the tool room, and we'd then build the bike back up again, checking that everything was OK before taking them off to MIRA, the Motor Industry Research Association track, which was the main thing. This was to see that they handled, though Tony's frame was different of course: Reynolds there was just the one like that. I'm not sure if he had that from the very beginning, but he definitely had it later on. It was made of 531 tubing and if you put an ordinary A65 frame by the side of it, it was vastly different. For example we were grinding all the silencers away on the production bikes so had some big flats put on them, welded on. But Tony was still grinding them away, so what was done on that frame was the pillion foot rest loops, where they fastened on to the sub-frame, he cut those off and raised them up. Then when Clive Bennett got Alan Shepherd in to look after the production and the Daytona bikes it was even better, as Alan was a hands-on sort of chap. When *Shep* was there he had us trying all sorts of back suspension units to get them perfect and he was always playing round with the forks. The damping on the standard production bikes wasn't much good. We used to put thicker oil in, but that was about it. But Alan had mates at Girling and they did him some special parts, turned up in the tool room, which were proper hydraulic dampers. Just like a rear damper, but on the front and we ran those from then on. They were proper *Shep* jobs. But it was just Tony, me and Mick Boddice - who was an apprentice at the time - in there working on the twins as otherwise for parts it was just a case of Brian saying: '*Go up to the track and get your bits.*' We could take what we wanted off the production line, but there were very few special parts. There was a list of optional extra - close-ratio gears and that - but when most people tried to get them through the shops they said they simply couldn't get them.

Tony Smith: It was a good set up for me at BSA, as the deal was that I kept the prize money, start money and appearance money and would you believe, as I elected to use my own van, they even paid me mileage and all my expenses to all the race meetings. Even if they were unofficial, non-factory supported races. So every club race too. But when it came to the bikes you could still only build a bike with what was available on the shelf. For my race bikes I could go anywhere down the production line and pick off bits at that stage, then finish off the machining as I wanted it myself. It was far better like that and there was no money for special parts anyway. So while they had titanium frames for the motocross-ers we still ran cast iron barrels. We didn't have the budget for alloy which was a real shame, because if we'd had alloy barrels, Nikasiled bores like Jeff Smith's 500 single, we probably could have saved another 4 or 5kgs on weight. And if we'd done 180^0 cranks we could have got rid of 90% of the mass of that central flywheel, as we'd not have needed that big weight to counter-balance the pistons. We would have lost another 5kgs of weight instantly like that. So there were things which could have been done, but unfortunately that was never going to happen. We were on a budget and they tried to keep things as standard as possible, so they represented the bikes that they sold.

Clive Wall: There weren't many of Dick smiling. I think that must have been the day I bought half the bike off him?

Dave Nixon on the Boyer's Triumph. Once they went to full fairings they established their trade mark stripes. Blue for the 500s, red the 650s

That position was unlikely to change, as Shepherd was injured, when testing an A50 Daytona machine in February and once invalided out he was never replaced. BSA's road racing activities once more fell under Brian Martin and as such they became subservient to the demands of the off-road programme. Martin remained supportive and helpful though, to all the BSA privateers as well.

Clive Wall: I blew up the bike I was racing for RH Smith once. I dropped a valve at Brands, and I couldn't afford a cylinder-head, pistons, cranks and things. So, Dick Smith said to take the engine out, take it apart, go up to BSAs in the van and ask for the race department. I was very young and thought: *'Christ, I don't even know what I'm meant to say?'* But I walked out of there with virtually a new engine! I was on nodding terms with Tony Smith by then, but the guy running it was Brian Martin and when I went in he was sitting there, reading *Motor Cycle News* and I thought: *'Wow, he must be important – reading a newspaper at work!'* I always remember that. But he was such a nice bloke. He really was, and I got quite friendly with him subsequently. He said: *'If you ever want anything Clive, just give us a ring. And at the end of the year come up and we'll give you everything you need to rebuild it for the next season.'* It went along the lines of Brian saying: *'What do you need? Tony, give him what he wants.'* A cupboard would open and out would come a load of con-rods and the rest. I never had a complete engine, but I used to go up there and they used to re-bush the cases, line-bore them, new crank, barrels and pistons, con-rods, bolts, new oil pump, etc. and to get out the gates they'd say: *'Just throw a blanket over it.'*

There still weren't many proddie races at National meetings back then but there were big races at Snetterton and Lydden and I was ever so lucky at Lydden. It's a weird place, but I learnt a lot there, as you could ride in the Open races really close to very, very, quick people. It was such a short circuit that there was nowhere they could get away. There were no real 120mph corners, where good people would be 5mph faster, so if you could get away with them, at the Lord of Lydden meeting say, you could still finish 7th or 8th and it was a real eye opener. I remember following Steve Jolly there and when you went into the hairpin at the top, he would get half way round, pick the bike up again, squirt it at the bank, then drop it down again and pull four-foot away from you. Then I started doing the same and all of a sudden you'd find another ¼ of a second a lap. I just clicked at Lydden. I mean my Spitfire, with TT100s on it, round Chessons, I could drift it and have opposite lock on. 'Controlled with the throttle, to make it drive. In truth it wasn't the quickest way - if you kept it in line, you'd do a better time - but it looked spectacular! But it took me ages to get anywhere at Cadwell. Chris Hopes came down to Brands a lot and I could beat him easy, so he said: '*Ah you wanna come up to Cadwell Park. That's a real riders circuit.*' So, I went up there and it was like Brands on steroids. I'd been racing a few years by then, and I got lapped. Was I not happy. I hadn't been lapped for years and years, so he said: '*I'll show you the way round*' but I still couldn't keep up with him, as he was very good up there. I reckon I did a season of races before I found out what to do and then I did quite well. I'm pretty sure I never came off at Cadwell and I used to pass people all the time into the hairpin, where they just play follow the leader nowadays. I didn't make many friends mind, as you'd be bouncing into it, but I liked it up there.

Crystal Palace was actually the first place I ever won any money though. I think it was the first time I ever went there too. I just turned my eyes off to how dangerous it was, you know. As it was a beautiful circuit, lovely circuit, but it had a three-foot run-off, then 6-foot railways sleepers. I saw people fall off there, two or three times, who didn't get up. That sure focuses the mind!

That Crystal Palace payout was at the Metropolitan meeting, on Monday 28th August 1967 and it was noteworthy for being the first ever production event at the venue. Peter Butler won it, from Dave Nixon, Pete Davies, Harold Robinson and Wall and it wasn't the only new circuit in 1967. As mentioned by Wall, racers were now heading to Lydden where they held 1000cc events before production races proper started a year later. In August however, following the Metropolitan meeting, the *Hutch* came around again.

Hartle's *Hutch*

Journalist Dave Dixon noted there would be: '*John Cooper and Tony Smith on BSAs and a horde of Triumphs*'[17] at Brands Hatch and while it was actually Dave Degens, Dave Croxford and Pat Mahoney as BSA's hired-hands, there were indeed a lot of Triumphs. Fourteen, with the four factory bikes fitted with the new TLS front brakes which would appear on the 1968 road models. John Hartle took the win and Rod Gould was second, on the consecutively registered MAC 233E and MAC 232E respectively. In doing so John Hartle also won the Mellano Trophy, awarded to whichever rider, in any class, broke the existing lap record by the highest margin. It was the first time a production bike had achieved it and Hartle's name was added

Hartle in action

to the most recent solo winners - Redman, Fujii, Anderson and Hailwood. Exulted company. The Hutch was significant for other reasons too. A feature of the 1967 meeting was that it also held a two-leg 750cc race. In each, Hailwood's lap speeds, on his favourite and phenomenally quick, 297cc Honda four, were a couple of seconds quicker than Hartle's had been in the production race - Hartle's 83.87mph, to Hailwood's 85.65mph. But in each race Ray Pickrell brought the Dunstall 750 in second, ahead of the singles of Shorey, Cooper and Croxford. Pickrell's Dunstall was his full, no holds barred, race version, rather than his proddie bike which had come third in the Production race. But as Mick Woollett reported at the time:

> 'And if that was not enough for one day, after stripping off lights and mudguards, Hartle then turned out on the Bonneville for the second leg of the two-part 750cc Evening News International race – the major race of the day – when he actually led the race until he cornered a little too vigorously, ground a silencer and slid off unhurt!' [18]

This wasn't the first time road machinery had frightened the racers in 1967 either. Over Easter Rex Butcher had taken a couple of third places at the *King of Brands* meeting, while the following Monday Oulton Park had held the 750cc *Race of the North*. A 750cc race was unusual for the Cheshire circuit but the result was unusual too, as other than Dan Shorey's 540cc Manx, singles were nowhere, the result being Hartle (Triumph), Butcher (Norton), Shorey (Norton), Smith (BSA) and Tait (Triumph). Hartle's Triumph engine was in a Rickman frame, but the BSA and other Triumphs were all production racers. At the *Evening News* Brands International on 29th May Dave Degens took a 3rd on one of his Dresda Triumphs, behind Hailwood, but he went one better at the Mallory Park Post TT International, beating all the singles and only being bettered by Agostini on his MV four.

The Bill Chuck Bonneville was another machine which started to feature from 1967 onward, ridden by the likes of Graham Bailey, Clive Wall and John Blanchard

On 30th July Pickrell won the 1000cc race at Snetterton, and while there was no luck for the roadsters at Snetterton's *Race of Aces* on 27th August, the following day Peter Butler put in a sterling performance in the 1000cc event at Crystal Palace, to take 4th on his George Hopwood-tuned Bonneville against a gaggle of *'real'* racers. On 15th October at Snetterton Ray Pickrell took the 1000cc race on the Dunstall Norton again, and on 22nd at Brands Hatch it was also the big bikes winning. Pickrell could only manage 3rd place this time, but the Dunstall connection was still there as Derek Minter took the Curley Brothers Norton to the win, with

Dave Degens' Dresda Triton in 4th. This was just a snap shot of the results in the increasingly popular 750/1000cc class races, but they clearly showed the trajectory racing was on. In 1966 any of the top British racers could have turned up on their Grand Prix/British Championship Matchless G50 or Manx Norton to take a 1000cc class win. Engines nudging 600cc were there too, as a little bit of insurance, and they were needed by 1967 as the big bike races became more numerous, lucrative and competitive.

The big twins now taking the wins were not proddie bikes per se, as they often featured better brakes and some even had after-market frames, but the engines were the same as in the best production racers and in the case of Paul Dunstall's everything bar the number plate and tax disc was the same. In 1963 BSA, Norton and Triumph's biggest twin cylinder engines were hardly seen on the track. Four years later they were on the cusp of taking over.

Peter Butler on the Boyer's Bonneville. It was without doubt the best prepared non-factory bike on the circuit, meticulously prepared by George Hopwood and capable of beating Open class 750cc and 1000cc machines

TRIUMPH

T100T Daytona

Production	**1967-1973**
Predecessor	**T100A**
Bore	**69mm**
Stroke	**65.5mm**
Capacity	**490cc**
Compression	**9:1**
Front wheel	**3.25 x18**
Rear wheel	**3.50 x 18**
Front brake	**8" sls**
Rear brake	**7" sls**
Weight	**356lb**
Power	**39hp @ 7400rpm**
Top speed	**105mph**

Triumph's pre-unit 500 had been popular, but the unit version of 1958 was physically smaller and highly tune-able too. It was developed out of the diminutive 350cc Model 21 and while it lived in the shadow of the 650 Bonneville, as day to day transport it was probably better than both. Indeed 1967's, giant-killing, Daytona could live with the *Bonnie* at a push. Hyperbole? Perhaps, but the T100 effectively killed off British half-litre competition and could equal Japan's best. In later years its engine lived on, in spirit at least, through the stylish Adventurer off-roader, but it was abandoned by the Meriden Co-operative, in favour of the bigger twin.

The Baby Bonnie

Triumph liked a catchy name, especially if it had American connotations. The use of *Bonneville* was opportunistic – the 214.40mph achieved by Johnny Allen on the salt flats in 1956 was never officially ratified – but *Daytona* could not be questioned. A win at America's most important race in 1966, then again in 1967, cried out to be exploited and Triumph did it brilliantly with the T100T Daytona. It was executed better than the Bonneville too, as that took two bites at the cherry - first the engine, later the frame – while Doug Hele did it in one fell swoop with the Daytona, ditching the dodgy, whippy frame at the same time as adding twin-carburettors. The icing on the cake was 1969's

direct oil-feed to the main bearings, which added durability to speed, with the latter being controlled by fitting the same Group 8" tls brake to the Daytona, as on the 500lb Trident.

The Daytona road bike was not a copy of the Daytona racer, but the beauty was that the theory if not the detail of the tuning could be transferred across. And if Joe Public wanted to go racing the handling was there straight from the crate. Factory test rider Percy Tait showed what was possible by using his *'development'* racer to take numerous National and even Grand Prix podiums and many were tempted into thinking they could emulate him.

On the road the Daytona was outsold by the Bonneville through British and American obsession with big engines. But the Daytona was always popular and un-bust-able, as demonstrated by its endurance racing credentials. Ultimately its demise was an odd one, as in the chaos of the BSA-Triumph collapse, it died as much through neglect as obsolescence. The tooling for the T100 remained in the Coventry factory when NVT took over, but once the Meriden Co-operative took control the 500 twin was passed over for the 750cc T140. In the eyes of the buying public it seemed there really was no substitute for cubes.

Humble origins. Even Percy Tait's Grand Prix racer grew out of the 350cc Model 21

Percy Tait on his open class 500cc twin which was developed from the successful racers used by Triumph at Daytona. While the chassis increasingly deviated from standard much of the engine work was carried across to the Meriden-supported T100 proddie racers

1968 Shaking *all Over*

The Bonneville was a better bike if you looked it as an all round thing. I think the BSA might have had a little bit of extra grunt, but the Bonneville was easier to ride, it handled well and the Norton was even better. Clive Smithers, I raced him a lot and it was his bike, a Commando, which made me say to Dick Smith; *'We gotta have a Norton. It handles and it's like 10 mph quicker.'*

- Clive Wall

It was an odd year 1968. There were rumours of new bikes from a number of manufacturers – a new 350 Ducati, a Suzuki 500, Triumph and BSA triples, something new from Norton, a three cylinder bike from Kawasaki and a four cylinder one, a 750cc, from Honda - but little changed on the track. As in previous years there were a host of new names pestering the established order and as some bikes' performance peaked others were only just hitting their stride.

In the early season Triumph twins still predominated in the 750 and 500 classes while among the 250s the Suzukis and Ducatis went up a gear. They now had a couple of seasons tuning under their belts which soon became very apparent. With the season only just under way Mick Rogers delivered a shock to everyone when at the fast Snetterton circuit he took an outright win. He took it through virtue of the leader dropping out however and when the absentee, on a ubiquitous Thruxton Bonneville, made it back for race two Rogers' swift Ducati had to accept second place.

Ralph Ridley: I've got to admit I don't remember that win standing out particularly but another at Snetterton soon after I remember well. I can't remember the club, possibly Bemsee, but back in the day there was that long right-hander, Coram Curve, before the start and finish and there was a guy in front of me called Dave Vickers, on a Lightning. I don't think it was a factory bike, just the same as the rest of us, but a regular fast bike which was around. Anyway, he was going round Coram and of course we were all trying our hardest and he gets into this tank slapper and goes skittering off the side of the track. Off to the left-hand side and ends up in the grass, which from my point of view was sort of funny and also meant I was now in the lead. Until the Esses, when just as I was lining myself up Howy Robinson passes me on the inside, sending *me* skittering off to the outside of the track in turn. Pete Davies and a couple of other guys came by then as well, which dropped me down, to fifth or sixth position in the end, so I got my comeuppance for having snickered at Dave Vickers. But I had a right go at Howy back in the paddock, calling him an effing this and that, as I really thought I'd won that one.

Ralph Ridley was one of the most successful independent runners by the end of the decade. Having a Thruxton Bonneville helped

John Lancaster: Ralph actually started about '64 but I remember going to Snetterton, watching him, as Ralph had done a few High Speed Trials previously and had this bike, a road bike, a 500, but all stripped down, which he'd spent plenty of time on. I didn't know who Ray Knight was back then, but he was one of the ones up the front and I saw their production bikes and thought: '*Wow those Triumphs have got great big long silencers on them?*' I was fascinated and it was the first occasion that I thought: '*This looks really good. I wouldn't mind having a go at this?*' Then we all thought that we'd have a dabble. My original bike I bought as a sidecar outfit off a guy the other side of Nuneaton and I paid £12 for that I'll have you know. It was a '55 Thunderbird and I gradually took bits off and put on clip-ons, alloy guards, made a seat and it even started off with an SU carb, as that's what the Thunderbird had in those days. I had one or two competitive rides as with the standard gearbox it was quick out of the hairpin at Cadwell, even if changing down out of the Gooseneck the back end would zig zag. I remember we went over testing, for a relay race at Cadwell, to Lawford airfield over near Rugby. As there was like a triangle bit we used to practice on, with a little bit of an S-bend on it. I was on the Thunderbird and Ralph on the Thruxton he had by then. Then we swapped and he said: '*You go out on the*

John Lancaster negotiating an unidentified Norton at Snetterton in 1968

Thruxton and I'll go round on yours.' I was really chuffed to be on this Thruxton but he was in front of me and coming up to this left and right he just kept carrying straight on into the field. Well, when we stopped he said: *'How the bloody hell do you ride this thing? It's weaving all over the place!'* Well I'd got into the habit of leaning it over and putting the power on quite quickly as it kept it taut. As if you shut the throttle off the single down tube under the seat, it used to twist! But any road I gradually changed it. Put E3134 cams in, fitted a Bonneville head and it was quite quick, though it would never go over 6,000 revs. But I decided that as Ralph had got a Thruxton and got a 5th in class at the *500-miler* in '67, that I'd get one too, so what I did was buy a bike off Hughes, Stan Brand, advertised in London. Phil, Ralph's brother and I went down and I think the bike was outside, out front. I was saying: *'What do you reckon Phil?'* as it was a lot of money then, about £300. So we went off and had a coffee but I said *'I think I better have it.'* When I got it home, every night, I'd go down to the shed and sit on my little stool thinking how lovely it was. Thinking: *'I can't wait for the next year to come.'*

I'd never had a twin-leading-shoe brake before so I took the front wheel out and had the drum skimmed and new linings, AM4s fitted, and sent it off to Joe Dunphy to be done. Well, we went up to a practice day at Snetterton the start of 1968, March, very cold, and I went out on to the track, accelerated and the back wheel sort of came round, as I was leant over a bit. I thought: *'Blimey. I've never experienced anything like this on the power before!'* So I went round Riches, Sears, down the back straight and thought: *'Wow, it's so much smoother than my old Thunderbird.'* Under the bridge down towards the Esses and of course I've never gone so quickly and I'm approaching the lefthander thinking; *'Gosh I'm going a bit quickly here, I'll do exactly what I do with the old bike.'* I was laid over and just touched the brake, with a couple of fingers, but locked it on the very first lap, on a new bike and I went down and somersaulted. I got up and thought: *'What an idiot. I better not let anyone know'* so picked up the bike and thought I must get going. But I could only walk lopsided and of course I'd broken my collar bone and left ankle. So, many weeks went by - as six weeks for a collar bone, two months for a broken ankle was it? - but when I had the plaster off it was on a Thursday and I was riding that following weekend.

That was a couple of months into the season by which time even more new names had featured at or near the front. They were largely riding the usual mix of big twins with Tony Tucker and Bob Monnery doing well on 650 Triumphs, Graham Sanders and Les Mason on BSA A65s and Ron Wittich and Tony Smith - a different Tony Smith from the BSA version this time – on Nortons. Alan Walsh and Jeff Brett both got results on Velocettes however, while Dave Spruce took a win at Cadwell Park on May 11th on his Suzuki Super Six, against all the usual 650 opposition. It augured well for an interesting *500-miler* the following weekend and those looking for an upset weren't disappointed. The form book went out the window, the headlines reading *'Privateers' win stems foreign landslide.'* [19]

The Strangest of *500-Milers*

The three A65s of Bob Heath, Les Mason and Graham Horne get a grandstand seat as Tommy Robb takes his Suzuki T500 around the outside of Derek Minter's Ducati 250

Dave Nixon on the giant-killing Boyer's Triumph Daytona

The *500-miler* while not a game changer was certainly a head turner. As a rule of thumb the bookies looked among the Triumph Bonnevilles for a winner and in 1968 they were spoilt for choice. Pickrell and Croxford were also hot properties on the Dunstall Norton and there were six big BSA twins. But with fourteen Triumph T120s on the grid, most full Thruxtons, who was going to bet against one of them? Triumph was certainly confident, as for the very first time they stopped the pretence of their best bikes being dealer sponsored. The Triumph Engineering Co. Ltd name appeared alongside Tait/Gould and Uphill/Jolly, but any threat they'd offer was very short lived. After a couple of hours Uphill came in to replace his clutch, while Percy Tait was on his way to hospital by the 12th lap, after a bizarre accident.

> **Percy Tait:** I was wearing out boots at the rate of one pair, one race, so my wife Diane had them resoled with Stick-a-Soles, which also helped me with the push start. The problem was that when I touched the tarmac the rubber sole would grip on the tarmac and pull my foot back. When the pace became really hot I put my foot down firmly, the rubber dug in and I was thrown off the bike and into the trees. Luckily I didn't hurt myself, but the race was lost.

The speed trap figures indicated that the Dunstall and works Spitfires were the fastest on the track anyway, but the Pickrell/Croxford Dunstall threw its primary chain in the third hour then, just laps from the end the Mahoney/Smart Spitfire had to be withdrawn, after a steward saw that the swinging arm was broken after the luckless Pat Mahoney had brought it in for a stop. Surprises were on the cards then, with the first one being the speed of the smaller machines, the second their durability. Boyer had put their choice riders, Butler and Nixon on their 500 rather than the 650 and in the final hour they were leading from Gordon Keith and Brian Ball of the Suzuki Super Six entered by Reg Orpin of London Velocette dealers L Stevens. Just two laps behind were a gaggle of riders

Ray Knight handing over to Martin Carney, with Hughes Motorcycles Martin Love and Ron May (in beret) looking on

The Boyer's dream team. Dave Nixon, Stan Shenton and Peter Butler. Outright winners on a 500cc machine

fighting for third place, but again these were all on sub-500cc bikes. Chas Mortimer was on the latest Mach III Ducati, Chris Vincent was on the sole example of Suzuki's new T500 Cobra twin and Ray Knight was on his Triumph Daytona. It stayed like this to the close, Peter Butler cruising round with a safe lead to guarantee his finish and the outright win. The 500 class win therefore went to Ray Knight and co-rider Martin Carney, the 250 win to Chas Mortimer and Tom Dickie and the 750 class to a pair of relative unknowns.

Bob Harrington: I started racing because a bloke came to the company I was working at who it turned out had just done the Manx. I had a BSA A7 and he had a Goldie, so we both used to sort of race each other on the road, as we both worked in Luton but lived in Letchworth and he said: '*Why don't you go racing, you're pretty good?*' His name was Brian Owen and one day he comes into work with a letter and says: '*You're in at Brands, a Good Friday meeting, over Easter. I've entered you under my name!*' So I went up to the foreman at work and said: '*Bloody Brian's entered me in a race, can I have the day off?*' So I rode the bike down to Brands, as that's what you did then, raced, came 12th and thought: '*Hey I can do this*' and that was it, I'd got the bug. But the bike wasn't fast enough and it didn't handle like the Triumphs either.

At Silverstone, going round Maggotts, crikey it was all over the place. So that's when I got the Triumph 500 from Kings, who I rode that Bonnie for at Brands in '68. But in the 500 class by then there was Hugh Robertson, Colin Overy, John Wittman he was a lunatic, Colin Hope, Bob Prior and Ron

Bob Harrington and his original BSA A7. A fine road bike but no racer

The Harrington/Strijbis Kings Bonneville exiting Druids at Brands Hatch

Wittich, he was good until he killed himself, another Luton guy. John Judge and Ray Knight and most of them were on Triumphs, it was the only bike to be on at the time and while these guys were ever so good they were ever so helpful too. Dave Degens I remember one time at Snetterton, I'd done something on my Tiger 100 and it wasn't handling well, so he just said: 'Let me have a look at it' pulled on the forks a bit and said you need more damping. So I got some two way damper rods, the Eddie Dow type, and it was great after that. Dave Potter was another nice guy coming on to the scene around then, and I had quite a lot of success really after that.

It was the Midland Racing Club and Bemsee, just the two clubs really in those days and I got to know Jan Strijbis, as he worked at the Kings of Oxford shop, in Luton. He came over from Holland to learn English and to ride motorcycles, as he knew that being in England you could get a good bike and get a good ride, as proddie racing was getting really big back then. At the *500-miler* all the big dealers were there, as well as privateers, but even World Champions went proddie racing. You were dicing with these guys but normally it was the works guys who would win if they turned up, Rod Gould and the like. We had a lot to compete with and the only support we got off Kings was the loan of that 1968 Bonneville, as the 500 was always my own. Jan and I did the work on the bike - but then you always did in those days, if you wanted a bike you could rely on - and in the pits we

Fast company. Harrington pursued by Ray Pickrell and Rod Scivyer

only had the young kids who worked in the Kings of Oxford branch, from Luton. They were sort of apprentice mechanics. My wife was in the pits too, doing the teas and what not, but we didn't get proper pit signals. I don't think we even did lap scoring? As people would just come round with your laps done on a piece of paper. But in the race we had no problems other than Jan coming off. I remember he said: '*I didn't drop it. The bike slid away from under me*' a subtle difference! He dropped it up at Druids, when we were leading the race. The works Triumphs dropped out. Tait was out and the other had clutch problems. I noticed on them when they took them off they could take the whole clutch unit off as one, Uphill and the rest, and we certainly couldn't do that! But when Jan crashed I had to slacken everything off and straighten the bars, as he always seemed to come off in an awkward manner. So when I went out on it, it felt really strange. I think we ended up about four laps behind Peter Butler in the end and that was the time we spent straightening out the bike, after Jan dropped it. But once we did well in the *500-miler* we could get entries anywhere. The next race we entered after that I think was Zandvoort, then the Barcelona 24hr, but that was on my 500, as Kings only lent us the Bonneville for that one 500-mile race. We were on our own again after that.

It was the first time true privateers had *ever* won the premier class at the *500-miler* but it shouldn't have been that surprising. Harrington and Strijbis had come second in the 500 class the year previously so if the leading 500 had won overall that year, as Dave Nixon and Peter Butler had just done in 1968, they'd have been declared the 500 class winner. This was through the convention of the overall winner being excluded from the capacity class results and in 1968 Suzuki was the beneficiary of Butler and Nixon being excluded from the 500 category.

The Cobra Strikes

Of all the Japanese manufacturers Suzuki seemed to understand best the link between race success and sales. Suzuki won either 50cc or 125cc World Championships every year from 1962 to 1968 and while they never succeeded in the same way with their square-four 250, by the mid-1960s Yamaha and Honda were already engaged in an economically unsustainable arms race in the quarter litre class. It would cause both to withdraw from Grand Prix racing by the end of the decade, but Suzuki cashed their chips in early, to concentrate on racing their road bikes instead.

It was the old *'Race on Sunday sell on Monday'* mantra again which had worked for the Super Six and now, in the bigger bikes, Suzuki aimed for the same thing again. As while Honda were trading blows with MV Agusta around the 500cc Grand Prix circuits in 1967 no one was going to confuse Hailwood's four cylinder RC181 with Honda's road going CB450 twin.

The Suzuki T500 Cobra was similar in layout to the company's Super Six but a completely different and much larger machine. It would go on to even better things on the track in the 1970s though it was never as popular as the 250 model on the road

Suzuki also thought they'd aced the Black Bomber with their new machine, the 500cc, two-stroke, twin-cylinder Cobra. That's if you could find one, as they were rare as hen's teeth in early 1968, only just trickling into the UK from Japan. One arrived in time for Chris Vincent and Tommy Robb to ride it at Brands Hatch, with a badly fitting fairing and tank-seat unit being the only concessions to turning it in to a racing machine. One was all they needed to win, though the paucity of bikes and Suzuki's limited budget would shortly bite them back.

Chris Vincent: The 1965 Hutchinson 100, I came second to Toshio Fujii, on a 50cc for Suzuki GB. My sponsor Peter Chapman organised it all. There was an ex-BSA guy at Suzuki doing the bikes, Johny Harris, a motocross-er and I dare say he put the word in to Alan Kimber. He was the boss and the best bloke you could imagine. He had real understanding. They just supplied the bikes, I don't think I was even on a retainer, but this Alan Kimber he was simply a gentleman, for whom nothing was too much trouble. Suzuki was still quite small then, they used to have just this trailer behind the reps car, bringing bikes to dealers. They used to take a few sample bikes round and I had one of these 250s off the trailer originally. But they were getting bigger once they moved up to the Super Six. We provided him with two wins on the trot, they won the *MCN Machine of the Year* award and the Super Six really took off didn't it? Then they moved me on to the Cobra, with Tommy Robb this time and it was so different to things at BSA. Me and Tommy were equals, actually he struggled to match my times! But we were happy with each other on the bike, as physically we were about the same size too.

Alan Kimber with Stan Shenton, Shenton on one of his Boyer Triumphs at the *500-miler*

With Nixon and Butler being elevated to first place overall the Cobra was declared the *500-miler* 500cc class winner, with that making it a double for Suzuki, as Brian Ball and Gordon Keith won the 250 class with the Super Six for the second year running. Those were nice metrics for Suzuki, but statistically the 1968 running of the race was one of the

Assorted worthies gathered for the 1966 MCN Bike of the Year photo shoot. With, in the left hand photo, left to right, Barry Smith (Spa Motorcycles), Hugh Anderson (Suzuki GB), Martin Hodder of MCN, Alan Kimber of Suzuki GB, Chris Vincent (Suzuki GB) and Frank Whiteway (Crooks Suzuki)

The two men who were instrumental in raising the bar within production racing during the late 1960s. Stan Shenton of Triumph experts Boyer of Bromley and Vincent Davey of Norton specialists Gus Kuhn

oddest all round. A sub-650cc machine won overall for the first time since 1957, there were five 250s in the top nine - all Suzukis and Ducatis - the highest 650 was in sixth place, while the highest placed factory/dealer 650 could only make tenth – the Malcolm Uphill/Steve Jolly Meriden works Bonneville. Privateers won the premier class for the first time ever and there were just four laps separating the machines from third to eleventh place at the finish. With four of those bikes on the same lap, battling it out at the end of the race for fourth place, after nearly six and a half hours of racing. No other class could offer racing so close.

Those results probably acted as a wake-up call to the factories and bigger dealers, the links between which were becoming even stronger. Not just in terms of the factories supporting the dealers but the dealers providing valuable feedback in return. In this regard Syd Lawton was now largely out of the picture, having started importing Aermacchi racers from Italy, leaving Stand Brand's Hughes Motorcycles and Stan Shenton's Boyer of Bromley concern leading the way. Though soon they would be contending with new boy Vince Davey and his Norton franchise, Gus Kuhn.

MOTO DUCATI

250cc Mach I

Production	**1965-1969**
Predecessor	**Diana 250**
Bore	**74mm**
Stroke	**57.8mm**
Capacity	**248.5cc**
Compression	**10:1**
Front wheel	**2.50 x 18**
Rear wheel	**2.75 x 18**
Front brake	**180mm sls**
Rear brake	**160mm sls**
Weight	**255lb**
Power	**24hp @ 8,500rpm**
Top speed	**100mph**

Ducati's long-lived, overhead camshaft, bevel drive, singles started at 175cc. Great things were expected. But still being able to buy a Spanish version in the 1980s would have been beyond expectations in 1957, when the initial bikes were made. That was some shelf-life, and it was in part down to Fabio Taglioni's eye-catching *Desmo* of 1968.

Desmodromic valve operation would become a hallmark of Ducati's V-twins in the 1970s when, in essence, a pair of 450cc single cylinder top-ends were combined

First of the Italian Stallions

Ducati's singles were offered in many forms and capacities, but the UK-only 175 Silverstone started the ball rolling and 1964's 250cc Mach I cemented Ducati's place in the British market. *Cycle World* screwed the previous version, the Diana (Daytona in the UK), up to 104mph at Riverside Raceway in 1962, when fitted with the optional race kit. But the Mach I had these extras pretty much straight out of the box and a five-speed gearbox besides. And they weren't even that expensive. Dealer, later importer, Vic Camp actively raced what he sold – recruiting riders such as Paul Smart and Chas Mortimer – and plenty of budding *proddie* racers first sampled one at the Kirby/Camp race school he ran.

It was 1970 before a Ducati single actually won the *500-miler*, but by then devotees of the Bologna machines had already racked up numerous club championships, with Mick Rogers and Clive Thompsett probably pick of the bunch. They harassed 650s up and down the country, though it was Rogers who might have begrudged his lack of fame. Hardly acknowledged by Ducati

today, he took their first ever TT victory in 1969, with Chas Mortimer repeating the feat in 1970. With the Desmo in 1968 and the improved wide-case models in 1969, it was perfect marketing for Ducati, who then managed to blow it, by scoring a massive own goal. The new models coincided with a disastrous 1967 restyle which saw 3,500 'square' singles dumped on the UK market when the US importer refused to give the ugly ducklings a home. Liverpool dealer Bill Hannah pounced, banging them out at a discount, pricing Vic Camp's official imports out of the market as part of the very same deal. It did little for Ducati's reputation in the UK, but Hannah's fire-sale stock were a gold mine for production racers as the singles grew to 350cc then 450cc. These formed the basis of the company's V-twin roadsters which, in turn, would later write their own chapter in the production racing story.

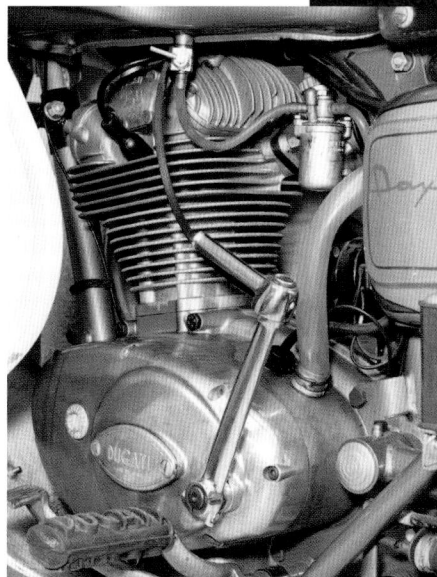

The Ducati single as most people got to know it. In definitive 250cc form

The 175 was a popular racer in other markets and in the UK too until the advent of the 250

Production bikes line up on the inside of the Mallory Park start-finish straight. Attempting rider changes, mid-race, was never going to be a good idea

Back on Track

The form book had gone out the window at the *500-miler,* but normality resumed thereafter. Peter Butler's Boyer Bonneville took club victories at Brands Hatch and Thruxton, while Paul Dunstall's bike hogged the limelight at two higher profile events. The second of these was an interesting, two-rider, 30-lap, mini endurance race at Mallory Park, where Ray Pickrell teamed up with Dave Croxford to win over the works BSA Spitfire of Tony Smith and Mick Andrew. The first race was the more impressive however as it was in front of 35,000 fans, at the Cadwell Park International. Hailwood, Ivy and Read were the big draw, but the reports had the production race as the finish of the day, in a battle between what might have been described as the haves and have nots.

Chris Hopes: I got a full racing bike in '69 but up to then it was always the Bonneville, bought from Cowie's which I made up to a Thruxton spec. It was really, really, good to ride, you got loads of feedback and I remember the International that year at Cadwell, the production race, as I led it. I had the whole length of Park Straight in the lead, then half way through the race the track started to dry out and Ray Pickrell was starting to catch me up. He didn't catch me up till the start finish at the flag. I led every corner, every lap, but I never won. David Dixon, who used to be a writer years ago, said in the papers that I'd shut it off, but I hadn't shut off at all. It was just that Pickrell's Norton, Dunstall Norton, was so much faster it looked like I was standing still. If it had kept raining he'd have been nowhere and the reason I had no screen on was that the previous week I'd binned it at Charlies and didn't have time to get a new one. The other reason was that we couldn't afford one as we didn't get any sponsorship up North. We thought we might get something off Triumph after our Barcelona ride. We contacted them for free bits basically, but nothing was forthcoming and if you look all the entrants for the *500-miler* they were all from down south. Our local dealer he wasn't interested. When we went to Barcelona he lent us some spares. He used it for publicity in the local Gazette but *charged* us for the clutch plates. So, we got nothing really at all.

Hopes leads Pickrell through Hall Bends, but not for long. Even at sinuous Cadwell Park the Dunstall's extra capacity told

But getting back to that Cadwell race Pickrell's Dunstall was so much faster. I used to lap at 1 minute 46 seconds on the full circuit, on the Triumph, that was the Jim Lee-framed racer I had from 1969, not the production bike. Then I rode Ken Redfern's 750 Norton in 1970 and I lapped at 1:45 and I wasn't riding anywhere near as good as I used to. It was just the fact that it was a full 750 that made the difference. Reg Curley's Norton back then was a 750 too, but you didn't realise just how much easier they were to ride, so much better the big bikes, until you had one too.

The Curley Nortons also acted as mobile advertising for the fibreglass components they made

Dunstall's Nortons had the advantage of disc brakes and tuning beyond what other 'factory' machines were allowed. Dunstall also had a secret weapon in the form of Ray Pickrell

The 750cc Norton Atlas engine had been slightly underwhelming when launched in 1962. It was in a much lower state of tune than the 650cc Dominator and was quoted as producing the same power. The increased capacity provided more torque than anything else and it wasn't really intended for racing. Over the years this handicap was slowly overcome, not least through the work of Paul Dunstall, with a small but increasing number of 750cc Norton's appearing on the track. Norton themselves had shied away from over tuning the 750, due to the harsh vibration this would provoke in a road machine, but in 1968 the gloves were off when they announced a brand new machine. The Norton Commando was a revelation as with its isolastic, rubber-mounted engine they could do virtually whatever they pleased with the Atlas engine. It was too new for any to actually be available for the TT but, as Chris Hopes had found out at the Cadwell Park International, there was still no substitute for cubes.

The peerless Ray Pickrell on his way to TT victory. Was his Dunstall a production bike? Well, they accepted it at the time

The TT – Everything Comes to he Who Waits

After the previous year's result the works Triumphs were favourites at the TT, particularly after their poor showings at the *500-miler* and Barcelona. The Triumph factory would pull all the stops out, and did, but again had no luck at all. Come race day Butcher and Hartle were both out and while Uphill finished it was a full eight minutes down on the leader due to one of those faults which it was impossible to predict. His kick-start broke on the line and with the lever wedged under his foot rest for the rest of the race the ratchet engaged permanently, creating excess heat which melted the solder off the clutch cable. The nipple therefore dropped off and Uphill was forced to continue without a clutch. How could you plan for that? It left Graham Bailey as best Triumph finisher, on his Bill Chuck-entered machine, but he too was over a minute behind Tony Smith on the works BSA. Smith took third place again, on only his second visit to the Island, but he could do nothing but chase home the two exceptionally fast 750 Nortons ahead. On the short circuits the smaller Triumph and BSA twins could live with even Paul Dunstall's machines, but over the Island's many climbs and altitude changes the bigger engines told. From Ramsey, through to the Gooseneck, then up on over the Mountain those extra ccs really counted. There were also the brakes to consider. The new TLS front brakes of the Triumphs and BSAs could handle the short circuits, as Mallory Park probably had three braking points on a production bike while Cadwell Park might have seven. They were no match for the

The café racers look on as Ray Knight takes his Hughes Triumph to TT victory, averaging over 90mph from a push start

two hundred-plus bends around the TT however as the brakes faded badly. Unlike those on Ray Pickrell's bike. The Dunstalls had courted controversy in '67 with their double discs, but they attracted more a year later with Pickrell taking the win. At two and a half minutes up the road the popular Londoner would probably have won without them though, and Triumph did at least have something to smile about. They'd just taken the 500 class win.

By his standards 1967 had been a quiet year for Ray Knight. There were mitigating circumstances though. He had been carrying out much more testing for *Motor Cyclist Illustrated* - including a Vic Camp Ducati and Colin Agate's Bonneville - while he was also helping to develop open class 350, 500 and 650 machines for Stan Brand at Hughes Motorcycles. In 1968 he was back on it however and for serious racing he was focusing exclusively on his 500 class machine, scoring twenty four top three places. Of these twelve were victories, including one very special one.

Ray Knight: For the 1968 season Stan obtained an ex-factory press road test Daytona model at a price that I couldn't refuse. It was the latest spec and turned out to be the source of many successes, usually running hard on the heels of the 650s. I spent the earlier part of the season dicing with or after the Nixon-Butler similar model and the Velocette Venom Clubman models, frequently with Tom Thorp aboard. Both hard chargers. I tried for many years on those Hughes Triumphs to lap the Manx GP course at 90mph, but the road holding just couldn't handle it. You got so close to it chucking you up the road, but as soon as they made a production version if you like, of the American race winning Daytona machine, what a difference. It was completely re-engineered 'cos they steered, they really did. And at the TT I actually didn't see a soul in that race and lapped at near 92mph.

I remember afterwards that sitting still in the saddle, as I tried to collect my thoughts, John Blanchard in words I'll never forget said: '*Did you win then?*' I nodded and he continued: '*You must be bloody mad.*' Well that was the greatest compliment ever paid to me, if you see what I mean.

Second placed John Blanchard (top) on the Dodkin Velocette was fast - Dodkin's bikes were always quick - but not fast enough to keep up with Ray Knight. The same went for Dave Nixon (below) who took third on the Boyer Daytona

Hugh Evans' fast starting BSA A50 actually got the holeshot from the Le Mans start, but once past him Ray Knight had a lonely, but trouble free ride out front, as he put in two extremely fast laps initially which gave him time to back it off on the third. He still won by a minute and a half though, from Blanchard on the prodigiously quick Dodkin Velocette. Dave Nixon brought the Boyer's Triumph in next, followed by Neil Kelly, on the Reg Orpin Velocette which had won the year previously. Knight lapped faster than Malcolm Uphill on a Bonneville and his race time would have placed fifth in the 750s. It was not too bad for the sport's elder statesman. He had no official factory support, though even those who had some often got less than others thought.

Chris Vincent: We'd won the 500cc class at Brands for Suzuki, but they'd still only got this one bloody bike. So at the Island they had me down to riding it in the production race, with standard exhausts, then they'd alter the spec and let Frank Perris out on it, for practice for the Senior. But, because Frank Perris was riding it all the time I only managed one lap in practice and to be honest it was all footpaths and hedgerows, wobbling itself around. Being a tester I could put up with most things, you had to at BSA, but it was a job to keep it on the tarmac as it was all over the place that day! Anyway, it didn't matter, as in the race the gearbox blew. I was on my way down off the Mountain, from the Creg and the thing was snatching its way down to Brandish, chattering, when I suppose all the teeth came off eventually. It was a shame because it was timed at 128mph and I was running third behind a Triumph and a Velo at the time. I don't know which ones they were, but I had so much power that coming out of Governor's Bridge on the last lap, with anybody, all I would have had to do was squirt it out to win. To be honest I was miffed. I'd been chucked down the road the previous year on Suzuki's 250, and this one, their 500, it nearly did for me again!

If Chris Vincent could have emulated his *500-miler* form at the TT he would have been a multiple TT winner. He was a win or bust sort of racer though - he was the same with his sidecars - and the big 500cc Suzuki Cobra called *'enough'* while he was pushing for the win in 1968

Harry Thompson with one of his road-going replicas. At the TT if he hadn't had bad luck he'd have had no luck at all

It was not Suzuki's year. Barry Smith won the 50cc TT on a Derbi and topped the 250cc production lap times on his Super Six, so it looked like a double was on the cards. But then, as a year previously, two Spanish bikes appeared fully race kitted on race day, when during practice they had carried road bike parts.

Barry Smith: Wednesday was the day for the 250 production race where both Harry and I were confident of getting another win. But as we started the bikes up in the warm up area I noticed that Trevor Burgess, who was riding a 250 Ossa, had fitted race kit parts, including an expansion chamber exhaust to his bike, while in practice he had ridden it as a standard road bike and as a consequence was well down on my times. It was quite obvious he had observed the antics of Bill Smith and Tommy Robb the previous year and pulled the same trick. And to rub salt into the wound George Leigh had done the same with his Bultaco Metralla. I pointed both of these bikes out to Harry who was warming up my T20 Suzuki. He was furious and went straight to the scrutineering bay to protest.

Trevor Burgess and his controversial Ossa. There was no way his expansion chamber was a genuine manufacturers road part

It was too late to affect the results as Trevor Burgess won, followed home by Leigh, with Smith just three seconds in arrears. Incredibly, the farce of 1967 was then re-run, with the scrutineers claiming that they were unable to uphold the protest. It had come in too late again Thompson was told, but the Yorkshire man proved he was made of sterner stuff. He pursued the matter and had his day, later in the year.

Barry Smith: The RAC has full control over all motor sport in the UK and has the final say on all protest matters, whether it be cars or bikes. We found ourselves in a huge boardroom facing a row of stern-faced elderly gentleman headed by their chairman Lord Shawcross. Then, after hearing what we had to say and viewing the evidence they upheld Harry's initial protest and disqualified both first and second places, but said they had no authority to elevate me to first place because that was up to the motorcycling governing body, the ACU. We were now back to square one and with no further course of action available to us. We walked out of the meeting bewildered and in a state of disbelief. So now we had a race with no official winner or second place, and to rub more salt in the wound the ACU never did amend the results of the race so history still shows these two disqualified riders as first and second in the 1968 250 production TT, with me in 3rd place. The only good thing that came out of this mess was that the ACU eventually changed the rules and allowed a protest to be put in after the race for all future events. I must be the only person in history to have won a TT but not be awarded first place!

Well, not quite, as while *MCN* confirmed that Smith was the winner, in an article on April 16th 1969, the whole episode was only brought to a conclusion five weeks later, when *MCN* devoted a whole page of their 21st May edition to cataloguing the whole saga, blow by blow, as things had changed again. They concluded by stating that 328 days after the original protest the RAC stewards had now *reinstated* the Ossa and Bultaco, the reasons for which were not entirely clear. The article also pointed out that both Leigh and

One under the radar. Bill Smith DNF'd on his CB250 but it legitimised countless 'replicas' decades later

Burgess would enter on the same Bultaco and Ossa machines in the following month's races, though neither bothered the podium. Burgess failed to finish and Leigh was a good 5mph slower than in 1968, through virtue of a far more standard – and legal – machine. It looked like the brief period of Spanish domination might be over sooner than 1969 however, as in 1968 the Spanish bikes were struggling even at home.

All smiles now? Ray Knight (centre) was a popular 500 winner and while Ray Pickrell (left) was popular his disc-braked 750 Dunstall was perhaps not. Trevor Burgess (right) was a different kettle of fish

Barcelona

He may have had no luck on the Island, but following the TT Peter Butler cleaned up at Brands Hatch and Cadwell Park over the two weekends before Barcelona. Here a Norton took the win and worse for Montesa, Bultaco and Ossa was the fact that the victorious Atlas was actually ridden by a pair of Spaniards! Ricardo Farga and Jose Antonio finished four laps ahead of the Bonneville ridden by Ken Buckmaster and Austin Kinsella. For the long term health of distance racing the bike in third place in the 750cc class – sixth overall - was perhaps the most interesting however, as it was the Mead & Tomkinson B44 ridden by Alan Peck and Mick Andrew. It had actually led the race after twelve hours but had stopped for over forty minutes with ignition trouble. Otherwise it would have undoubtedly won, since the Bultaco which took over was out with a broken crankshaft soon after leaving the BSA B44 in a long final battle with another Spanish machine.

Alan Peck: For the last two hours it was left to me to try and lap the Ossa, twice, to bag sixth place: *'you'll never do it Alan'* Richard had said. This made me even more determined and I set off for the last two-hour session flat on the tank, all tiredness and aches and pains forgotten. Half an hour later I had the satisfaction of passing them for the first time. The Ossa immediately came into the pit and a change was made to their quicker rider. They weren't giving up! At twenty three hours we were still three quarters of a lap behind. The Ossa was in sight now, he glanced behind and the dice was on. Down to the hairpin we went side by side: *'I'm not braking first, when's he going to brake?'* Leaving it very late, he sat up and braked. I waited until I was a length in front and clapped everything on, then concentrated on opening up a gap. I learned afterwards that the rider on the Ossa came past his pit after we had taken him and shrugged his shoulders, gesticulating that he couldn't go any faster. They seemed to give up after that and soon I got frantic slow-down signals. I'm against taking it too easily as one tends to lose concentration and make a mistake, so I just held 1,000 revs in hand and carried on scratching. We lapped him twice more before the end of the race. Paul Smart beat the other Ossa to secure third place. A wonderful ride.

Not something you got at Mallory Park. The awards being given out at Barcelona by the last living Fascist dictator in Europe.

Bob Harrington receiving the 500cc award off General Franco

It was by Smart as, paired with Reg Everett, he took the Vic Camp Mach III Ducati not only to third place overall, but first place in the 250 class which had previously been a Spanish monopoly. It further showed how the Ducati had come along as a racing machine, helped by the fact that it was now available in *'desmo'* form. Next British finishers were the Triumph 650 of Chris Hopes and Ken Redfern in 8th, followed by the 500 Triumph of Jan Strijbis and Bob Harrington in 9th place, showing that their *500-miler* result wasn't just a flash in the pan.

8th was a good result at Barcelona but at his 'home' track, Cadwell Park, Chris Hopes was always odds on for the win

Over the rest of the summer results were probably as unpredictable as they had ever been, with a host of new names even if they rode familiar machines. Les Mason won at Aintree, on the A65 he would soon become synonymous with, as boss of BSA specialists Devimead. While John Lancaster's Bonneville won at Silverstone and Don Jones version at Cadwell Park. Paddy Reid used a borrowed Norton Dominator to good effect at Cadwell Park, winning, repeatedly, while Butler, Hopes, Davies, Robinson and Bailey also took wins on Triumphs, all Thruxtons or, like Chris Hopes', built to Thruxton spec. Most ominous was Ray Pickrell however, as not having appeared on the Dunstall production bike very much recently he turned out for a Racing 67 Club meeting at Snetterton to take an easy win.

This was clearly a shakedown outing for the *Hutch* in a couple of weeks' time and the same probably went for Mick Andrew's last ride before the same event. He turned out at Lydden, on 4th August, to take third place in the Open 1,000cc event, behind the Seeley G50 of winner Dave Croxford and Oakley Quaife version of the G50 ridden by Pat Mahoney. Andrew, like Pickrell was on a Norton, but Andrew's was a very different beast.

Shenton was as good with the pen as he was with the spanners. His tuning manual became the standard text when it came to Triumphs

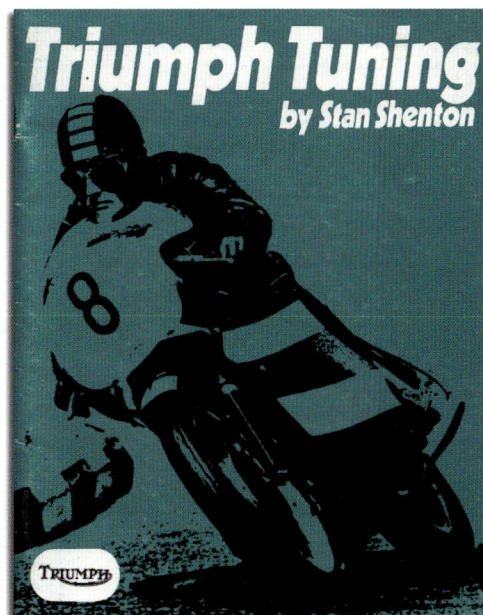

New Bikes at Last

In the premier class there hadn't really been a *'new'* machine since the BSA Lightning in 1965. The A65 line had actually been launched in 1962 so it was all upgrades and rehashes, not new bikes, before the 1968 *Hutch*. Then, without too much fanfare, Mick Andrew turned up at Brands Hatch on a Commando and was in the mix from the off, along with Pickrell on the Dunstall Norton, Smith on the works Spitfire, and Uphill, Gould and Butler all on Bonnevilles. The huge crowd had ostensibly come to see Britain's World Champions, Hailwood and Read, along with Renzo Pasolini on the four cylinder Benelli but as in 1967 the real sparks flew in the production race, where the handbags were out between Andrew and Uphill at half distance. It was all knees and elbows on lap eleven and a lap later Mick Andrew and the new Commando were down. Three laps further on Smith was forced to relinquish second place, sliding wildly with oil all over his back wheel, letting Uphill then Rod Gould through, with Gould piping Uphill a few laps later for second place. Ray Pickrell was long gone by this point however so while Gould broke the lap record in pursuit, it was all to no avail.

Mick Andrew's bike was the talking point however. With the arrival of the Commando and the Trident/Rocket Three in the wings, a wind of change was felt across British production racing. Which was perhaps the reason for the BSA Group's announcement, post-TT, that they were not going forward with a proposal to produce 100 racing twins of each make, BSA A65 and Triumph T120. The twins would be around for a good time yet, but as far as the factories were concerned, they'd soon be surplus stock.

Bob Heath at Darley Moor scrutineering. By 1968 he was unbeatable at the Derbyshire circuit

Stan Shenton: Later on they had to make two hundred sets of special parts for homologation and asked me how many Thruxton replicas I'd take if they went into production. I said 25 and so did Stan Brand of Hughes of Tooting, but Triumph never built them. We were already selling parts for tuning Triumphs and with their blessing I had written and published a book on Triumph tuning and in the end the factory asked me if I wanted all the Thruxton parts. When I asked how much they said not to worry. There were cams, tappets, cutaway oil tanks, carburettor extensions, special brake shoes and heaven knows what else and I never had a bill. I am 86 now and my memory is not so good as it was, but we built maybe two 500cc and at least six 650cc for the Team and maybe ten bikes to sell to the general public.

Rex Butcher, Stan Shenton and Dave Nixon outside Boyers

Mark Twain famously announced that news of his death was greatly exaggerated and so it was with the Bonneville. Just a week after the Hutch the Bantam Club held an anniversary meeting at Thruxton, with the likes of Pat Mahoney, Tom Dickie, Peter Butler and Ray Knight taking to Bantams against the regulars. It was ever-popular Dave Croxford who took the win, but in the production race it was business as usual, the top six all being on Bonnevilles in race one, and it being five Bonnevilles and Ray Knight's TT winning Daytona 500 in race two. It was Peter Butler and Pete Davies who took the wins, while two weeks later it was new name John Vincent. He was at the head of another Bonneville top six when the Southern 67 Club went to Brands Hatch, where a kid called Barry looked promising, scratching around on a Bultaco, provided by his dad, two-stroke tuner Frank Sheene.

There were other new names towards the end of the season too. Gerry Carter and Mike Pusey scored a number of wins on their Bonnevilles, though Peter Butler took Triumph's last on 19th October. It was his 9th win, out of 18 top three places and it probably made him the class of '68, given his *500-miler* win and victory at Snetterton's One Hour Enduro. Here he'd been hounded by Ray Hole who, putting his spannering duties for Pete Davies to one side, had brought his Vale-Onslow-supported A65 home in second place. He went

Proddie bikes in the assembly area for a Bantam Racing Club meeting at Snetterton in late 1968. Malcolm Button's 500 Dominator (35) and Len Read's BSA Lightning bracketing a pair of Triumphs

one better a week later, taking victory over Terry Haslam at the Midland Racing Club's Cadwell Park meeting, though it was partner in crime Pete Davies who won that club's championship. Hole's results demonstrated that a well prepared BSA could still run with the Bonnevilles and this was nowhere better demonstrated than at Darley Moor, where Bob Heath won the title easily on his Lightning. Indeed the Bemsee, Bantam Club, British Formula, Darley Moor, Aintree and Southern 67 Club championships were all won by Triumph or BSA twins and that would have set the pattern for 1969 too, were it not for the very last race of the season.

Bemsee had their final meeting, very late, on 20th October, at Snetterton. It can be cold and misty at the fenland circuit by this time of year but all the top production racers turned out, as it would be their last chance to turn a wheel before March. Len Phelps and John Hedger won the open races on their non-production compliant Triumphs, but Peter Butler, Roger Bowring and new find Gerry Carter all came to the line alongside Phelps in the production race. Peter Butler was the hot favourite but it was a Norton taking the win.

Mick Andrew had turned up with his Commando again and now better sorted went out and took the win. 'Commando scores win at Snetterton'[20] was an uninspired headline, but it told the readers of the weekly bike papers all they needed to know. The press had been full of the Commando for months, but now it had racing credibility too. A month later *Motor Cycle News* all important poll was launched and by Christmas the votes were in. He who laughs last, laughs loudest, as the Norton Commando was the 1968 *MCN* 'Machine of the Year' and the orders started to roll in.

```
EVENT 4 - PRODUCTION

1    34   M. Andrew          Norton Commando     18.31.2    87.79   1st 1000
2    10   P.A. Butler        Triumph T120        18.31.4    87.78   2nd 1000
3    38   L. Phelps          Triumph T120        18.44.0    86.79   3rd 1000
4    32   R.V. Bowring       Triumph T120        19.02.8    85.37   4th 1000
5    5    J. Pinckney        Triumph T120        19.24.6    83.76
6    36   G. Carter          Triumph T120        19.29.2    83.44
7    37   M. Pusey           Triumph T120        19.29.6    83.41
8    41   G.F. Green         Triumph T100T       19.29.8    83.40   1st 500
9    30   J. Kanka           Triumph T120        19.36.4    82.93
10   22   R.L. Knight        Triumph T100T       20.12.2    80.48   2nd 500
11   15   J. Davey           Triumph T120        20.12.6    80.45
12   16   K.G. Buckmaster    Triumph T120        20.13.8    80.37
13   46   R. Harrington      Triumph T100        20.17.6    80.13   3rd 500
14   42   R.P. Hole          BSA A.65L           20.18.6    80.06
15   40   K. Buckmaster      Triumph T100T       20.19.0    80.04   4th 500
16   43   D. Campion         Triumph T120        20.21.0    79.91
17   28   M.E. Button        Norton 88SS         18.39.2    9 Laps
18   23   J. Judge           Triumph T100T       18.41.0
19   27   C.P. Thompsett     Ducati Mach 1       18.52.2            1st 250
20   12   D. Woolley         Triumph T120        19.07.8
21   18   D.E.V. Clark       Velocette Thruxton  19.25.2
22   1    P. Wyncoll         Dunstall Atlas      19.26.6
23   26   S.L. Fry           Ducati Mach 3       19.37.4            2nd 250
24   21   M.W. Love          Triumph T100T       19.38.2
25   20   M.V. Warrington    Triumph T100T       19.46.8
26   31   M. Christian       Triumph T120        19.58.6
27   14   G. Haffenden       Triumph T120        19.58.8
28   24   A.G. Dell          Ducati Mach 1       26.02.4            3rd 250

Fastest Lap: M. Andrew in 1m.49.6s. at 89.01mph.
```

There were twelve Triumphs in the top thirteen on 20th October, but Mick Andrew's Kuhn Commando took the win, giving a taste of what was to come

Norton
MOTORCYCLES

Commando 750

Production	**1967-1973**
Predecessor	**Atlas 750**
Bore	**73mm**
Stroke	**89mm**
Capacity	**745cc**
Compression	**8.9:1**
Front wheel	**3.00 x19**
Rear wheel	**3.50 x 19**
Front brake	**8" tls/disc**
Rear brake	**7" sls**
Weight	**398lb**
Power	**56hp @ 6,500rpm**
Top speed	**116mph**

In the great British tradition the Commando was a rehash, but a brilliant one at that. Norton's 500cc Model 7 of 1948 grew in stages through the Dominator to the 745cc Atlas, with the genius of the Commando coming through its isolation of the rider from vibration, using just a bit of rubber and a lot of thought. It shouldn't have worked, but it did, making 829cc possible in 1973, by which time a disc brake was fitted. An electric start soon followed and in this guise the Commando soldiered on until 1977

Good Vibrations

While the BSA-Triumph Group's 1971 re-launch was an unmitigated disaster, Norton's punt three years previously, was inspired. Norton's attempt at a new engine, the P10, had tanked. So, the design team of Dr Stefan Bauer, Bob Trigg and Bernard Hooper concentrated on the chassis and produced a radical gem. This isolated the engine, swinging arm and rear wheel from the front forks and main frame, through bonded rubber *isolastic* mountings, which damped down the vibration endemic in any large capacity twin. Suddenly the performance of the featherbed-framed Atlas engine could be used in comfort and its power was progressively increased in a 40lb lighter machine. It peaked at around 65hp on the *Combat* version – hot poop in the early 1970s - and while this proved unreliable on the road it could be devastating on the track.

Here Commando successes drew the attention of John Player cigarettes, whose red, white and blue No10. branding soon bank-rolled Norton's return. Inspired F750

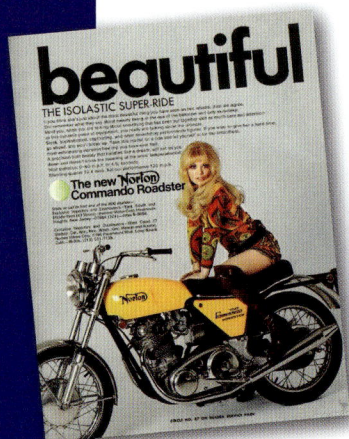

machines came from the fertile mind of talented development engineer/rider Peter Williams, while crowd pleasing team mate Dave *'Crasher'* Croxford earned every penny, through the publicity he generated both on and off the track. There was a dedicated 750 production racer too, dubbed the Yellow Peril, using the 77mm bore of the 850cc engine with a shorter-stroke crank and it contributed to the Commando winning the *MCN 'Machine of the Year'* title an incredible five years running, between 1968 and 1972. Sales were fantastic and marked by the John Player Special, a twin head-lamped, race-replica, built purely for the road.

The problem was that the Commando was only ever envisaged as a stop gap. The 1947 engine was staring down the barrel of increasingly stringent noise and emissions regulations, but it brazened it out in a last ditch, rearguard effort, before new, world-beating models came along. Unfortunately, the seventh cavalry never arrived. A water-cooled twin-cylinder engine developed by Cosworth flopped, while the rotary Wankel engine championed by BSA needed several years more development. The Commando was brilliant in its day however and a monument to what could be done through lateral thinking and ingenuity when guided by creative minds.

The drum braked Roadster followed the Fastback and accounted for the bulk of Commando sales. Dealers could not get enough

1969 The Shape of *Things to Come*

I had so much go wrong at the end of '68 I thought, bugger it. Then Ray Knight turned up at Snetterton, with a bog-standard Trident and vanished. I mean, that was the future. I knew I was staring at what are now *Super Bikes*, as the first 750 Honda had just appeared too and I thought we're looking at new bikes and loads of money and I simply couldn't see it

– Chris Lodge

There'd been a few red herrings in 1968. It was true, new machines were all around, but they were largely on the front covers of magazines or in dealer's windows. The Honda CB 750 was shown at the Tokyo Show in November 1968 and was trickling into showrooms, but a damp mid-March paddock saw just the usual suspects gathered, for the Cadwell Park season opener. There were no Honda 750s, nor Kawasaki triples. There were no Suzuki 500s either, though it was a 500, an aged and less fancied one, making the early running.

Hugh Evans: I did a while with the A50 as a proddie bike, doing club races and I was sort of midfield. Then some idiot bought me a book, the whole theme of which was the will to win. I thought: *'It can't be as simple as that?'* but read the book three times over the winter. The first meeting following was at Cadwell. I looked round the paddock and all the usual quick guys were there. But I thought: *'Nah, I can beat this lot.'* They were on 650s and 750s, but I thought sod it, the flag went down, I went off like a scalded cat, and finished second. That was when I started racing as opposed to just riding racing bikes

Some race reports had Hugh Evans' A50 second behind Ray Hole, while others had him finishing third, pipped for second by Graham Bailey. But what was perhaps most revealing was the support going into those respective 650s. Bailey was on the Chuck Components Bonneville he'd run at the TT, which was a well-developed dealer entry, highly tuned and with *'funny'* cams. While Hole was back on a home-tuned BSA twin, albeit a different version than the one he'd started out on, almost a decade before.

Ray Hole: Given the choice you'd have bought a Bonneville wouldn't you? Something which was pretty good to start with. But at the time I was working at Vale-Onslow's and while they used to sell Triumphs as well they were more BSA than Triumph, being a Birmingham dealer. They gave me basically what was a standard A65, I can't remember what year it was, but it started off as just a standard old single-carb bike. But then, over the winter, once I'd done it up it had twin-carbs and high compression pistons that I got off Len Vale-Onslow in spares. I took the cylinder head out by hand as Lenny had this little lathe in the workshop and I put a reamer on it, pushed the cylinder head on and took out the inlet ports like that. But they were right on the limit, as it smoked a lot after that, as there was a little hole between the inlet port and where the springs sat where it had actually broken through. That sounds a bit Heath-Robinson but it was all rule of thumb, as you have to remember in those days lots of the blokes still rode their bikes to the circuits and cobbled the race numbers on once they were there.

Where'd they go? Ray Hole looks back at Cadwell's club circuit hairpin in a vain attempt to locate his pursuers

Though they were only round the corner from Vale-Onslows there was no help from the BSA factory, but as that bike ended up with twin GP carbs on it and modified exhausts it really did fly when it was chiming at its best. You'd be going down the straights passing people like they were going the other way, as ultimately a good A65 was faster than a Triumph, though people won't have it these days. I remember at Snetterton, you were talking about a mile straight and you could pass anything down there, as it really was that quick.

Ray Knight: Yes, there weren't many Triumphs that could live with Tony Smith's example, as frequently it would turn up at a meeting and be the fastest bike out there. That was in its heyday, turn up, break the lap record, but then sometimes have to drive away 'cos the bike had broken down. But I'm not saying they didn't know what they were doing because boy, when they were on song, did they go.

A prime example was Graham Sanders' self-tuned A65 which would win fourteen races over the course of 1969. It made him, rather than Tony Smith, the most successful A65 runner, but there were extenuating circumstances in Smith's seeming lack of form. And it wasn't due to breakdowns.

Smith leads Tait at Mallory Park. By 1969 both had formidable Open class racers which could beat any Manx or G50

John Hedger: In 1969 Ivor decided to quit production racing and move up in to unlimited class with a Rickman Métisse frame and a Bonneville engine fitted with Weslake barrels, eight-valve head with a Quaife 5-speed gearbox and Gardner carbs. It was with this bike that, at the Cadwell Park International in September 1969, I finished 5th behind Agostini, Read, etc. and later that month, at the Evening News International at Brands Hatch, I finished 4th, behind Agostini.

As he said, Hedger's bike wasn't a production bike. But it was based on one and had it carried Dunstall stickers, who knows, perhaps it could have passed as one too? Others were in a similar position as dealers realised that with just small modifications their production bikes could become highly competitive open class machines. It was becoming an important factor. John Brown's Paddock Gossip in *MCN* was *the* chat room of the wider British racing scene and his introduction to the 1969 season was damning of the: *'British Championships which have sunk to a complicated and uninteresting position in recent seasons with a definite lack of spectator, and in cases, rider interest'.* He went on to point out that: *'It is disappointing that the ACU did not see fit to include a 750cc or even 1000cc championship, to cater for the big twins that seem increasing favourites with riders and spectators.'*[21]

He wasn't wrong, as at the first National of the season it was the non-championship 1000cc race which was the talking point. Where Ray Pickrell's Dunstall Norton snatched victory from Tony Smith's BSA. As with Hedger's bike, Smith's and Pickrell's machines were not production machines, but they were sufficiently close to demonstrate which way racing would go. From now on a Manx Norton or G50, even a *'big un'* of around 630cc – which a G50 could be stretched to – now struggled to match a 750cc twin and as a result factory employees Tony Smith and Percy Tait increasingly directed their energies towards these higher profile, open class races, with dealer entrants and even privateers following suit. Chris Hopes' was typical of the latter, getting Jim Lee - sponsor and frame builder to Mick Grant - to build him a special Triumph frame. This left *'space'* in the production ranks, as dealers' favoured riders - the likes of Nixon and Butler - were increasingly racing in open classes. As such there were new dealers and riders winning. On Triumphs Len Phelps riding for Elite Motorcycles and Gerry Carter on the Deeprose Bros Bonneville both stepped up as did Paul Vincent, brother of John, on another ex-Peter Butler machine. For BSA Graham Sanders was the rising star, while for the Norton fans it really was a whole new ball game.

Graham Sanders in action. Lots of style and very little run-off

Gus Kuhn

Since the Syd Lawton years genuinely competitive Nortons had been thin on the ground, outside of Paul Dunstall's specials. The launch of the Commando changed all that and unlike other machines, where there was a slow and sometimes painful transition from road bike to racer, the Commando was bang on the money, straight from the crate. Not least through a new dealer and sponsor. By rights Gus Kuhn should have been called Vincent Davey. As it was when 'Dave' took over the company in 1967 that things really took off. The Kuhn name appeared from nowhere as while the firm had previously held multiple franchises Davey decided early on to go exclusively with Norton, backed up with a race programme to promote the new Commando. Davey had spells at BSA and Norton before Kuhn and within a few years that experience showed. Gus Kuhn became the biggest Norton dealer globally and was highly regarded by the company.

Mike Jackson: I first met Vincent through Bob Manns soon after I'd joined Norton Villiers in 1969; from the outset it was clear he was a cut above the average motorcycle dealer. Unlike the majority of shop owners his concentration was primarily on spares and service. He'd regularly give us a hard time if we failed to fulfil his spares orders and, whilst capable of solving 99% of the mechanical malfunctions suffered by his Norton customers, he was constantly in touch with Norton's service personnel in his endeavours to ensure the factory were fully aware of his current techno deficiencies! Vincent's view was that if our machines performed satisfactorily in the customer's hands additional sales would automatically follow. Given the healthy market at that time his assumption was 100% correct.

Barry Sheene on the Seeley-Kuhn Commando. Riders this good only signed-up through Davey's reputation for meticulous machine preparation

Another of his many good points was that he did not subscribe to the blatant discount culture operated by so many of his contemporaries. Gus Kuhn Motors in fact were well known for unashamedly charging full price. Following the introduction of VAT one witty trader suggested that as far as South London was concerned the acronym stood for *Vincent's Added Tax!* Vincent, quite correctly, claimed that a price-cutting dealer was incapable of holding a sufficient stock of spare parts, and that his workshop facilities were often suspect.

From a factory perspective, he was utterly straightforward to deal with, and it was always a pleasure to meet him at a race or exhibition, and particularly one-to-one when he visited. He was a man who raised the standard.

Graham Bailey became a regular rider for Gus Kuhn.

Seen here taking the Commando for a push down the Glencrutchery Road in 1969 after his points closed-up over the Mountain on lap two

Vincent Davey did and with the Commando the impact was immediate. Following a visit to the Barcelona 24 hour race with Stan Shenton of Boyer Motorcycles he met and recruited Mick Andrew, not just as a rider but as a workshop mechanic too. The early machines he raced were all remarkably standard however, as while the Gus Kuhn catalogue was soon full of parts, these were initially cosmetic. The Norton factory was far too busy sorting out teething problems with the early road bikes for any tinkering and when they did get round to modifications, capable of turning the roadsters into production racers, the alterations were actually quite extreme.

> **Norman White**: We moved the whole engine/cradle assembly ⅜" to the right, pivoting the cradle assembly around the rear isolastic position, repositioned the front mounting lugs to suit, then chamfered off a flat in the chaincase just below the generator, plus welding a plate and polishing it back. It gave the required ground clearance though even that did not completely solve the grounding problems when professionals rode in International competition. The first Production racer had been built in the experimental shop at Woolwich in 1967/8 by John McLaren and the late Eric Goodfellow. It wasn't yellow either, but candy apple red, with Atlas-type silencers and a fastback-type oil tank and battery cover. Two more were built, one green, one yellow and these were loaned to Gus Kuhn and ridden by John Blanchard and others. This was when I stepped into my first position in the company which was as development test rider.

Those bikes came later though and in 1968/9 the Commando benefitted from none of the alterations, which made Gus Kuhn all the more remarkable, for being able to put a shot across Triumph's bows. It was Graham Bailey who took their first win in 1969, on 12th March, at Brands Hatch, in an open 1000cc race over Barry Ditchburn. But he went on to further production wins at Cadwell, Snetterton and Brands Hatch again, before the end of June. Over the same period Ron Wittich took multiple wins at Snetterton, on his privately entered Commando, before the bike's first big one.

The promoters were always looking for gimmicks - relays, team races, handicaps, etc – many of which would make current competitors' toes curl. The previous year it had been a 30-lap, two-rider race at Mallory Park with a full, Le Mans-style, running start. Logistically Mallory wasn't really suited. It was actually bloody dangerous as the race had seen machines pulling in to switch riders parallel to the start-finish line while others were screaming round the Devil's Elbow, flat on the tank, tucked in behind the screen. It was a recipe for disaster, so it was switched to just a one-rider race on May 25th. The 30 laps was kept however, which perhaps excused Dave Croxford sauntering over to his machine, while others ran, claiming: *'I'll never get this thing started.'* He did, first kick, before roaring ahead of Ray Pickrell's Dunstall, to take a memorable win. It looked like the Commando had arrived, but so too had another machine, as while Pete Davies' Bonneville was in third place there was a far more intriguing machine behind. On possibly its first privateer mainland outing Dave Browning brought a Suzuki 500 Cobra home in fourth.

Spoilt For Choice

Like the Honda 450, the Cobra was a bit of a slow burner and luckily for Suzuki it hadn't been talked up as much as the Honda. On the street the big 500cc two-stroke twin would never really recover from its plain Jane styling, but on the race track its performance would take it as far as the Grand Prix circuits. Like most two-strokes it would take time to unleash that performance reliably, but the company's smaller Super Six had already been punching above its weight for some time. This was to the extent that Roger Cope and Brian House achieved a unique result at Cadwell Park, on April 12th, when their 250s beat all the 750s to take an outright production win a piece. The Cobra wasn't quite at this stage yet and to prove the old guard weren't going anywhere Martin Russell was able to take a 1000cc class win on his 500 Velocette, while Alan Walsh and Jeff Brett similarly made a nuisance of themselves on their own black and gold Venoms. Such new winners were possible due to the availability of well proven or competitive off-the-peg, machinery - such as the Super Six - but also due to the huge increase in meetings, circuits and clubs running production races.

The Dave Browning/Grant Gibson Cobra as later used at the *500-miler*

Races for which production bikes were eligible, such as 750cc or *Open* events, were being offered within National championship meetings and by clubs including the British Formula Racing, Midland Motor Cycle Racing, Bantam Racing, Louth & District, Derby Phoenix, Grantham Pegasus, Batley, Lincoln Motor Cycle and Car, Nottingham & District, the Vincent Owners, Formula 5, Racing 50, Skegness & District *and those were just the ones at Cadwell Park*. Nationally the racing scene was burgeoning. Every circuit with the exception of Oulton Park and Castle Combe now ran 1000cc events and there were new circuits appearing too. Staverton and Elvington were the latest additions in 1969.

In terms of races exclusively for production bikes these were now run by the circuit owners them-selves at Brands Hatch, Lydden Hill, Darley Moor, Mallory Park, Crystal Palace and Cadwell Park. While clubs running their own race meetings and championships had grown from just four a few years previously - the Bantam Racing Club, British Formula Racing Club, Midland Motor Cycle Racing Club and Bemsee – to nine by 1969, with the addition of the Newmarket Club, Southern 67, Waterloo & District, Formula Five and Cardiff Eagles clubs. These in turn brought in Aintree, Thruxton and Llandow as additional circuits at which proddie races were held, meaning ten circuits in total. This was discounting Scotland and Northern Ireland, both of which had multiple clubs and

Clive Wall (above) receives the British Formula Racing Club Production Championship award from Paul Smart at the Café Royal in London's swanky Mayfair

Len Vale-Onslow (below) hands out the tinware to 250cc winner, Graham Horne, at the annual Midland Racing Motor Cycle Club awards. The Midland club alone had over 800 active members in the 1960s

circuits of their own hosting production races through which, as an example, BSA recruit Brian Steenson came, having run a Norton 650SS in the Kirkistown races in 1967.

Just three years previously it was the same machines and riders that had crossed paths at nearly every meeting, as racers had scoured the race calendars in *Motor Cycle News* and *Motor Cycling* for the limited number of meetings at which production races were held. Now, it was highly unlikely that the same riders would cross swords more than a couple of times a season, unless tied to a particular club. It made for a dynamic, unpredictable racing scene which was heavily oversubscribed. There were always reserves and while the British Formula Racing Club might run three production races a day, riders might only get an entry in one. Darley Moor started to run heats to deal with their large number of entries and this backdrop, of ever rising popularity meant that only the biggest names got an entry at the race on 11th May. Not least since the *500-miler* was back at Thruxton, its spiritual home, after a four year absence.

Hampshire's Wide Open Spaces

At the beginning of the season there was speculation about all sorts of large capacity, multi-cylinder machines at Thruxton, but it didn't quite work out that way. The Honda 750 was a no-show and ultimately only a solitary Triumph Trident appeared. Colin Dixon and veteran Rex Avery circulating solidly on it, without fuss, for a respectable if relatively pedestrian 7th place, fourteen laps down on the winners. It was actually the 500cc class which showcased the new stuff, with 350cc models from Yamaha and Ducati, three Suzuki Cobras and an example of the jaw-dropping Kawasaki triple, ridden by Tony Dunnell and Graham Penny. The Kawasaki couldn't fail to draw a crowd but for patriots there were also the surprisingly quick BSA B44 singles, entered by Mead & Tomkinson.

Following a sprint across the track the first couple of riders get their machines away at the '69 Thruxton 500-miler

Older heads prevailed though, as while Dave Browning and Grant Gibson got their T500 Suzuki Cobra up in to second place it was three laps down on the Triumph Daytona of Martin Carney and Ray Knight, which they had brought home in second place the year previously. As such Ray Knight was able to add the *500-miler* title to his TT replica, in his bulging trophy cabinet.

In terms of the 250s while there was a solitary BSA Starfire on track – the latest rehash of the C15 - the market for L-plate racers had long since been abandoned by the British, making it an entirely foreign affair. Frank Whiteway and Stan Woods brought the Eddie Crooks machine under the winner's flag for the first of many Crooks Suzuki victories, but what was interesting were the number of Ducatis in the mix, as they weren't so far behind. While the British manufacturers had been content to launch a good product - such as the Ariel Arrow or Royal Enfield Super 5 - then leave it down to the privateers to develop it, Ducati did not sit on their laurels. They updated their bevel drive singles constantly and the performance rose annually, partly due to their highly competitive domestic racing scene. A multitude of Italian manufacturers – Aermacchi, Moto Morini, Motobi, etc - competed to top the race results, as in their home market 250s had taken over from 175s as the most popular sized road machine.

Ducati never forgot the link between success in the sales room and victory on the track and while the Italians had bigger bikes coming, they weren't around yet. It meant there was a familiar Bonneville podium at Thruxton, though it wasn't all plain sailing for Meriden. The results inevitably only told half the tale. Percy Tait won again, this time with Malcolm Uphill, but the third placed Len Phelps/Chris Carr bike was from Elite Motorcycles and far less special than the factory entries, particularly the winning machine.

Tait's bike had W&S valve springs retained by titanium collets at the top-end of the engine and dripped with more special parts as you worked your way down. It wouldn't have stood a scrutineer's strip-down, yet it had also been harassed by the Rex Butcher/Ray Pickrell Bonneville throughout. This was actually a Paul Dunstall machine and the reason Dunstall was not racing his more familiar featherbed Norton was because of all the other Nortons around. Commandos were everywhere.

Percy Tait (above) took 1st with Malcolm Uphill, while John Cooper (below) was 2nd with Steve Jolly. A perfect finish for the works Triumphs

Percy Tait taking the flag and looking over John Cooper's machine

The Ron Wittich/Tony Melody Commando had led early on and Dave Croxford and Mick Andrew had been up to 4th on the Gus Kuhn version before a rod cap went walkabout and the luckless engine got trashed. Peter Williams had then made it in to third place, on the Arter Bros Commando he shared with Tony Godfrey, before dropping it. The Wittich Commando was by then the highest placed private machine, but it too went out shortly after when it lost its final drive chain. It looked like an odd failure but it was a result of a driveline issue already known at Gus Kuhn's.

> **Frank Kateley:** The one thing I tried to do was to convince Vincent Davey, 'Dave', to change the clutch, to not run the Commando clutch, as I'd already done that trick on another bike. The Commando was a diaphragm clutch, with no shock absorber in it, while the old Norton one was like the Triumph, BSA and all the rest, with a shock absorber in it. I'd already twigged that. I had a friend, Roy Simmons, an also ran at the TT, but a great engineer. We'd put a Panther rear hub on his, which was what Nortons pretty much adopted later. A cush-drive in the rear hub. We used a Commando clutch then, with a cush-drive hub, but Norton were well lucky that no one got hurt with the original set-up, as the gearbox is the worst thing to go. Later, at Barcelona, we smashed one and the other was ready to go. While at Montlhéry they both went. At Barcelona we'd just fitted 5-speed gearboxes from Rod Quaife, and of course Dave was angry with them for breaking, blaming Quaife, though of course he later realised the error of his ways. As it was the clutch. Though I sort of understood Dave as he was tied up with Nortons, he was their biggest dealer by then and he said: 'No, we've got to use the standard bits' as they were just brand new bikes that we got in at Gus Kuhn and that we raced, we got nothing special. But what happened was that the engines came out and went to Jim Boughen. Jim Boughen had worked in the race shop at AMC, but that had all died by then and he lived local to us in south London.

So he did all the engines for Gus Kuhn, the G50s, 7Rs and the Norton twins, as he was good. Very good. They went so bloody quick because of those Jim Boughen engines, though the one thing which we did on the chassis was I made a head-steady out of front engine mounts, the Commando isolastic front engine mounts. We took off the steady they'd made at the factory, a silly thing with exhaust pipe rubbers on it, and made one which you could shim up and adjust like the other two. Later on you could buy 'em, as people were making them, but we made our own first.

I'd worked before at Harold Daniells', a great place to work, as it was learning from the master if you like and 1967 I think we had the very first one in the shop, a Commando, at Harold's on the Dartmouth Road. An awful thing it was! It was all funny colours and we took it up to the Connaught Rooms when they did the launch for it. But I don't think it came back as it was orange, a nasty thing and we'd put it in a side window at the shop, as it was a bit embarrassing really, with the green spot instruments and that. But I was at Gus Kuhn for about two years after that and looked after Dave Croxford. I remember the first time I met him it was really funny. Vince Davey says to me: '*Go and pick Dave up, because he's lost his licence again.*' He had a yellow E-type Jaguar, but he couldn't drive it as he'd lost his licence, so I knocked on the door and his missus says; '*Come in, Dave's just fixing the gas meter.*' God alone knows what he was doing, but we had a good time, as me and Mick Andrew worked in the workshop together, in what they called the race-shop, at the end of the workshop, a bit sort of partitioned off, where I looked after Dave's bikes and Mick looked after his own. Though, when it came to race meetings, I'd knuckle in with all of them.

29th June, at the Thruxton International, Mick Andrew's Kuhn Commando rounds Brian Kemp's Curley example

Dunstall initially didn't have a Commando in 1969, but he'd beat Norton to an enlarged engine, with his 810cc kit

The writing was clearly on the wall. The Commando might not have won at Thruxton but it was the coming thing, as none of the bikes currently racing had undergone much serious modification. This sounds odd for *production* bikes, but it had been many years since the front runners were genuine dealer-fresh, untouched examples. Plenty of tuning could be carried out on the Commando and both Triumph and Dunstall were on notice, BSA already having dropped the Spitfire from their range twelve months previously.

The new Norton wasn't of too much interest to the privateers however, for whom BSA and Triumph twins would remain the go-to bikes, particularly if they had a degree of factory support.

The 750 Fastback engine. It was as old as the hills, but as fast as the wind. With the Commando's isolastic engine mounting greater performance could also be extracted without terminal damage to the cycle parts. . . . . . or rider

Graham Horne: I'd ridden the 500-miler previously on my own bike, a 650SS, and rode it to work the following Monday. I could keep it in the Comp Shop and when he saw it Brian Martin said; *'That bike is not to move until you've put a new tyre on it.'* Because it was down to the canvas, as that's how we finished. Brian Martin was good to me like that and I remember the first year I rode the Manx he just gave me a works 350 Gold Star engine to use, as they were sort of done by then for factory purposes. I got it not on merit, but just as I was a good lad and I did the hours sort of thing. But come '69 Tony Rutter was down to ride with Norman Hanks but said: *'I ain't riding that'* and that was it. So, Norman said: *'How'd you fancy it?'* 'Cos we were good friends back then. I said; *'OK'* as 1969 had been a bad year for me. I'd been running a DMW Hornet up to then and if you look at the results, 9 times out of 10 in the Nationals, I was the first British 250 home. I'd beat the Cottons and Greeves and things and won the Midland Championship, and 'thought: *'If I get myself a Yamaha TD1C I'll move up. I won't have to ride any better, I'll just move up.'* 'Didn't happen, 'didn't finish a race, it was so unreliable. The crank went and all sort of things and the only decent ride I had on it was at Aintree when the gearbox went. It wouldn't stay in third. I was leading and was absolutely livid. I'd had a season of it so put the bike straight back in the van and drove back to Dugdales, the Yamaha dealers I'd got it off. I'd paid 500 quid for it in 1968, which was a lot of money, but they said: *'OK, we'll buy it'* and got £475 back.

At the time I said: *'That's it. I'm finished'* but as I'd never finished in the Manx I thought I'd keep doing that till I did, and had one or two other rides, so when Norman offered I said: *'OK, but I'm going out to finish, that's it. I'm not going to blow it up or throw it away. I'm going out to finish.'* But I remember at Thruxton there's some big bends and a long straight, then a hairpin towards the pits. Well as you come down that straight there's a part where another old runway crosses it, and there's a hump, well I just couldn't keep it flat out through there. Every time I thought: *'I'll do it'* but couldn't. I got behind Percy Tait and as we went over that hump there were two puffs of smoke from his silencers and I thought: *'Well, if Percy is shutting off too, I'm not doing too bad'* but shortly after I caught a friend of mine who'd worked at BSA, but moved to Triumph, John Woodward, on a Bonneville. I followed him, got next to him, but then he went down like it was an aeroplane crash. Bits of bike everywhere. So that slowed me down a bit and I think we were 12th overall. Which is pretty much as I finished previously, on my Norton, which I wasn't going to push too hard, as it was still on hire purchase at the time!

Graham Horne, Norman Hanks and Spitfire. 'Corporate' livery was care of Bell helmets, as the jackets came free with the new American full-face helmets which were slowly appearing on the domestic scene

Woodward's machine wasn't on hire purchase, but his Thruxton crash ended in what would have been a similar scenario. Down on his luck and heavily out of pocket.

John Woodward: The one good thing about Meriden was Doug Hele. He was good, he would listen to you. A good guy, not that he could get any more sense out of the top people I think and the racing was done on the cheap. It's very difficult to get a handle on it now, but I was racing then and I had a 350 and 500 Manx, and when we were doing the last bikes for Daytona I had this beat-up old Thames van. So, when we wanted to test the works racers we got the Triumph Ford Transit and my Thames, loaded five bikes in and off we went to MIRA, with Percy, Doug Hele, Arthur Jakeman and Jack Shemans all crammed inside, freezing cold, 'cos we were always preparing them in February. Percy did all the riding and it was a case of: *'OK, that's all good, no oil leaks everything's right, good speed, 120 mph.'* 123mph I think they were doing, though the timing straight was limited as it had a sort of egg-timer bend at each end of it, so you couldn't build up speed. So anyway, afterward Jack Shemans and myself got in my van, they took off in the Transit and of course ours wouldn't start. Flat battery, as I was penniless, always. Well luckily they'd seen it so came back and gave us a push. So there was the works team, Doug Hele, Percy and Arthur all pushing, as that's how it was. There was no reference to insurance and that, as it was all so amateurish back then with, can you believe, the works team pushing the van!

Anyway, I bought this Triumph and then decided to race it, but I'd only been to a couple of club meetings by then, as Thruxton was quite early in the season. Doug was good to me, as this was a works bike, as good as, and it had the short exhaust system which came up and over the timing cover so you had to have your foot-rests up in the air about 2" which was uncomfortable as I was too tall to be a racer really. In conjunction with that the K81 tyre, the TT100, they only did in the 4.10 size initially. Well, when I raced the bike first at Cadwell it had racing tyres on it, but when it came to Thruxton they said: *'Racing tyres? No good, they won't do it. They won't last.'* So I ended up putting a K81 on, a big front tyre, though all the works bikes were exactly the same. As to all intents and purposes my bike *was* a works bike, in every respect, as what I bought was an ex-Experimental bike, bought from Triumph themselves, and it was quick, bloody quick it really was, and it handled really well.

But around Thruxton that big front wheel, the gyroscopic effect round those great long corners made it hard work. *Jock* (Alistair) Copeland went out on it and I think he was fourth or fifth and then I went out I followed Percy for three laps, but then it started to rain. That's what done for me. After that bit of a complex, you are going out towards the fast bits, but the road isn't actually straight, it has a slight curve to it, before going into a left hander. I suppose you were doing 90mph there because as I said it was a quick bike. Well I got into a big broadside on it, sideways across the track, on to the grass, held it, but up in front there was a bloody marshal's box, corrugated iron, dug right into the ground. I thought: *'I can't go straight in to that!'* as while it was a long way away admittedly the grass was wet and you know you can't do anything on that. So I tried to ease it off and went down. Well the bike hit the bloody barrier and bounced across the track and I thought: *'Well it's me next!'* I'd sat up and slowly turned but hit the barrier on my hip, broke the bones in my wrist and shattered my pelvis, so I was in traction for three months and that accident's what Graham Horne saw! I was in hospital a week when Neville Goss from the Southampton & District Club phoned and said: *'We've moved that barrier!'* as he could see the point. It came at a bad time for me though, as my Triumph was wrecked, my Manxes were worth nought as out of date and if I wanted to keep on doing production racing in a meaningful way I probably needed to get a Trident, and I couldn't face the thought.

I was broke as I never got paid while I was in hospital, as that's how it was back then. So decided: *'That's it, I'm not good enough, it's finished.'* But Daryl Pendlebury, a tester, used my engine that I'd built for Thruxton, put it in his bike for the TT, used it, and came third!

Woodward's misfortune would be Pendlebury's bit of luck. Woodward was a top engine builder at Meriden and his handiwork would tell in June

TRIUMPH

T150 Trident

Production	1968-1975
Predecessor	N/A
Bore	67mm
Stroke	70mm
Capacity	740cc
Compression	9.5:1
Front wheel	3.25 x 19
Rear wheel	4.10 x 19
Front brake	8" tls/disc
Rear brake	7" sls
Weight	468lb
Power	58hp @ 7,250rpm
Top speed	122mph

The prototype Trident was up and running in 1965. Internal politics kept it on the back-burner however while full production was further delayed through the decision to launch a very similar, but different, sloping BSA version, the Rocket Three.

It was innovative, but when bikes finally trickled on to the market in 1969 customers baulked at the boxy styling and Dan Dare silencers. They were bloody expensive too, but gained greater popularity in the 1970s once re-styled. The final T160 was a visual masterpiece and there was an 850cc in the offing too, the T180, but it all came a decade too late

Too Late To The Party

Bert Hopwood and Doug Hele both had a long standing interest in a three cylinder design. Work started on the triple concept not long after Hele joined Triumph in October 1962 and strapped for both time and cash they worked from the dimensions of the 63x80mm 500cc pre-unit twin, since the bike was a rush job and effectively 1½ 500s bolted together as one. Management indecision ensured it was a rush job which took *years* and when the result, the much delayed Trident – with revised bore and stroke - finally hit the showroom everyone was underwhelmed.

Sure, it had a funky crank and was fast, but the BSA version was ugly and the Triumph even worse. Kicking a man when he was down, Honda announced their *cheaper* 750 almost simultaneously offering four cylinders, another gear, disc brake and an electric start. Slow T150 sales in America stuttered then stalled, what could Triumph do?

Go racing! In 1970 BSA and Triumph versions were prepared for the Daytona races, giving birth to the iconic Rob North triples. These totally dominated the American AMA Grand National series, the budding F750 formula class and the Transatlantic races too.

Developments forged in the heat of competition fed back into the Triumph road machines - the BSA version being dropped in 1972 – with the most obvious beneficiary being *Slippery Sam*, the legendary, if rule bending, works production racer. *Sam* won five consecutive production TTs before being banned for being *too old*, but by this time the final T160 was out with the 5-gears, disc brakes, electric start and the fabulous, classic, Triumph looks that the Trident should have flaunted from the start.

The BSA and Triumph engine variants had subtle differences and each had to be bench tested before fitting. It all came at a cost

Poor ground clearance was always the killer though, in terms of using the triple at speed. School bus queues might have been impressed by sparks from the outlandish Ray Gun silencers, but grinding frame rails were scary if you raced. This was solved when Triumph sneaked in their 'short' production frame in 1970, which raised the swinging arm pivot point and lifted the engine cradle to give 1⅜ greater ground clearance. But this frame never made it on to the road bikes and, if Triumph were honest, the Trident never quite cracked it on the street.

Malcolm Uphill en route to a 100.37mph second lap and victory

99.99mph

Daryl Pendlebury's third place at the TT should have been a bigger story than it was. He was just a Triumph road tester after all and he didn't even get a bike from the factory, just a loan of John Woodward's engine and the rolling chassis of Dave Jones machine. Jones' being a good one, the Welsh rider regularly popping up in the top three on the club scene. But with Malcolm Uphill posting the first 100mph lap – 100.37mph - by a production machine, averaging 99.99mph from a push start, Pendlebury was bound to have his thunder stolen.

Over its 115 year history there have been many standout TT races. Hailwood and Agostini's nail biting 1967 Senior, or Steve Hislop and Carl Fogarty's epic 1992 duel, resulting in Hislop's Norton taking the first British win in the Senior since 1961. There's also Stanley Woods and Jimmie Guthries' 1935 master class, or Hailwood's legendary return in 1978, to win on a Ducati after an eleven year absence. The magnitude of some of those races has only been fully realised over time however, which was not the case with Uphill's. By today's standards 100mph doesn't sound that fast, but for anyone who has ridden the Mountain course, or indeed ridden a standard 1969 Bonneville, the speed really was astounding. In practice Rod Gould's works Bonneville was timed at 140.1mph through the Highlander, a speed only bettered by Agostini's MV Agusta. Indeed the race speeds of Uphill and second place man Paul Smart were only bettered by Agostini and would have put them second and third respectively behind him in the Senior race. 100mph was a hell of a speed. Compared to the standards of today the tarmac was worse, the corners tighter, the brakes non-existent and the tyres laughable. They were indeed just road tyres, Roadmaster K81s. Everyone was soon talking about 'the 100mph TT tyre' however and Dunlop went with it. The moulds for the K81 soon had the TT100 suffix added and the TT100 swiftly became the only tyre any self-respecting road rider would countenance. Sales were astounding – you can still buy the same tyre today – which showed the impact racing success could have on sales. Lucas, Champion, Castrol, you name it, they all wanted a piece of the action, as while it was nice for a spark plug or oil company to be associated with Agostini, they knew customers were more likely to buy their products if they were used on a motorcycle similar to their own. The win was

Rod Gould was timed at over 140mph in practice but his works Bonneville broke its crankshaft on lap two while in second place

Paul Smart's all-action style took him to second place and a 99.37mph average speed on the Arter Bros. Commando built by Norton backroom boy John McLaren. It was originally earmarked for Peter Williams so it wasn't too bad for a stand in!

pretty good advertising for Triumph too. Eight years later only Ray Pickrell on a triple had gone faster and fifty further on there's still a pub which commemorates Malcolm Uphill's name. Even Joey Dunlop had to buy his own. The Bonneville victory also obscured the fact that there were two Commando's in the top four, with Mick Andrew's fourth place a real stand out, as he'd never even ridden at the TT before. The Commando was of course totally new to the TT, but it wasn't the only new 750 knocking on the door. Triumph weren't prepared to risk fielding a Trident of their own over the Mountain - though they did prepare a couple of marshal's bikes - but one of their top dealers had other ideas.

Martin Carney: It was my brother, who is six years older than me, who brought motorbikes into our house as he read me all the magazines of the day, from 1956 onwards. He took me to my first race at Brands Hatch on the back of his Velo 500 Clubman and one of the highlights of the year was the Thruxton 500-miler, as *all* the stars raced the production machines. The likes of McIntyre, Hailwood and Shorey, and the crowds were huge that went to watch. It was a big deal back in the day and it gave me my inspiration to start racing. In 1967 I'd won the 125 British Championship and was top five in the 250s, on Bultacos. I lived in Wallington, Surrey, where the Hughes Triumph satellite shop was and my sponsor at the time, Reg Thomas, had a friend who worked at the main Hughes shop in Tooting. He mentioned to Stan Brand that he should get this local boy out on his proddie bikes so Stan called and asked if I would be interested in racing their 500, with Ray Knight and Ray and I did very well. I think we finished 2nd or 3rd in class and I liked riding the 500, as it was nimble, quite quick, but Stan then asked me if I would like to race his Thruxton Bonneville at the TT. I told Stan I would be concentrating on my 125, 250 and new 350, before going out on the Bonnie and as the week went on I was having breakdowns and couldn't always get back to go out on other bikes. Stan was very upset as the week went on, as I hadn't ridden a 650 before, but we managed to get in two laps and I qualified on the last day.

In the race I got a good start and was going quite well, getting used to the bike then coming up the Mountain, it's thick fog, Hartle and Gould crash out at Windy Corner and I go into the next lap in 5th. At Glen Helen the bike dies, a condenser wire breaks, but I loved the bike and lapped at 90 mph. So after the TT Stan asked if I would like to race the Bonnie at the Hutchinson 100, at Brands, and again I did quite well and finished 5th. In 1969 Ray and I rode the *500-miler* at Brands on the 500 again and won, after which I get a call from Stan, asking me to come down to the shop and ride this *new* bike. It was a 750 Trident and I thrashed it around Wallington for half an hour before Stan says: '*I want to enter it at the TT. Would you like to ride it?*' Now at the time I was 5ft 7in and 9st 6lbs but it was such an exciting and dynamic bike, how could I refuse? I had 125, 250 and 350 bikes so once again I asked Stan to be patient and after

Martin Carney's Hughes Trident leads Roger Bowring on the Chuck Bonneville

a few days I managed to get two laps in on the Trident to barely qualify. Everyone I spoke to, Percy Tait, Rodney Gould, Malcolm Uphill, Tony Jefferies and the rest of them, they all said I must be mad. But I found it great to ride, except for the lack of ground clearance and the useless front brake, which was actually the same as on the 500. Stan mounted a top fairing, which made it very comfortable and in the race I got a good start and was getting more confident as the race went on. I did 130mph past the Highlander and caught and passed Tony Jefferies on the works Bonnie for 6th place. After the race he said: '*Thanks Mart, you woke me up there!*' as he re-passed me afterwards and as I chased him coming out of the Ramsey hairpin the clutch started slipping, so I had to back it off to just get a finish. But that Trident, the first ever three cylinder around the Island, bog standard, I had a lap of over 96mph. Magic, and for 1970 Ray and I got 5th place at the Thruxton *500-miler* and Stan got hold of a Low-Boy frame, Fontana front brake and a Quaife 5-speed gearbox for the TT.

That footnote actually told the tale. As while Carney took a highly creditable 7th place the Triumph factory had no intention of racing the machine themselves, until brake improvements and frame alterations - illegal frame alterations - provided the chassis to win. Meriden stuck with the Bonneville for 1969 and with seventeen entered at the TT, one nominally a Saint, it was always going to be a case of who was going to win, not which machine. It wasn't so predictable in the 500s.

Bomber!

Suzuki, Honda and Kawasaki all had real contenders in the race, though with Kelly and Heckles on their very rapid Velocettes Venom again – both consistently timed as the fastest 500s - and a number of Triumph Daytonas, including those of Knight, Chatterton and Nixon, the money was still on a British win. How wrong could they be?

Ray Knight: While I was favourite for the proddie race, Stan's replacement motor was never quite equal to the previous year's performance. Following the customary Le Mans run across the road in the 500cc production race I never did catch sight of Tony Dunnell on the Kawasaki Mach I triple, but then neither did anyone else. Eventually, miles in the lead and bounding into the

Fast but not fastest. If Knight had matched his 1968 speed he would have won again, easily

Tony Dunnell fell victim to the Kawasaki's legendary evil handling. A few miles from the flag he thought he was on his way to victory, but instead found himself on his way to Nobles Hospital

33rd Milestone the unruly handling of the Kawasaki won the argument over navigation and Tony and the triple-stroker detoured rapidly down the side of the Mountain. He was certainly *'shaken and stirred.'* Meanwhile, by Kirkmichael, I'd caught Graham Penny who had his Honda CB450 in 2nd place at the time and while I could sneak by in several places, the Honda had enough horses under the tank to get back in front every time. By the Gooseneck the Triumph was still carrying me in the Honda's slipstream but as soon as we commenced the climb up the Mountain I was left for dead, as at each gear change the higher revving Honda held on to each of its five gears, to draw away and I lost the tow. Graham eventually cleared off to win and I grabbed a lonely 2nd place, which could hardly be bad.

From the start Tony Dunnell led on the new Kawasaki and surely would have won had the *flying hinge* not lived up to its reputation. Dunnell got tied in knots and was off, meaning Honda finally took their CB450 win. It should have been a great achievement but was overshadowed by Uphill's and in truth it was four years too late. Honda would keep updating the CB450 annually, but with a raft of four cylinder models in the wings the twins were really dead meat. You could still make two cylinders fly in the 500cc class though and third fastest on Monday's practice boards had been a remarkably unlikely machine. *No one* raced a BSA A50.

Hugh Evans riding to 5th place with little more than an 8″ single-sided, single leading shoe, front brake to stop him. He liked a challenge though, riding the A50 in the Senior too

An Obsession Observed

Hugh Evans: Yeah I was about the only person out there campaigning one. I was very lucky though that I had brilliant workshop facilities that I could use any time. Because I, singular, was the *'Research & Development Department'* at Biggin Hill airfield, for Decca Navigator and the workshop had some pretty good machinery. I could do all sorts of things. Dick Rainbow and I had a reasonable relationship for a long time and through Dick I got to know Tony Smith. So, I then got an *'in'* to the factory from Tony when he went to work there. We had a rapport, and I think the factory liked the fact that I was getting reasonable results on an A50. I was the only one publicising it for them to be honest and I certainly didn't ride the fact that I was getting support. I think they appreciated that too. The strange thing was though that the first time I entered it at the TT, in the proddie race, '67, the ACU came back and said: *'It's not homologated. You can't ride it.'* So, I got in touch with Brian Martin, who I knew by then, and he said: *'Well, have you got any nice pictures of your bike you could send? Do that and we will homologate your bike as 'the' Cyclone Clubman.'*

I only ever got on to them when I really needed something and around that time, '69, a guy called Paul Coombs did the *500-miler* with me. At Thruxton, just before the TT, and threw it up the road. The forks and frame and all sorts of things were bent, so I rang the factory and they said: *'Well, OK, put a list together of what you need. But how are you gonna pick it up?'* At the time I was working at Biggin Hill, the AA had their spotter plane on the airfield and I happened to know the pilot quite well. So I said: *'Are you going anywhere near Birmingham over the next few days?'* And he said: *'Yeah, this afternoon.'* He told me where he was going to be, and at what times he was going to be there, so I rang the factory and spoke to Micky Boddice, to ask if he could get these bits to the airport? *'No problem.'* I literally got them the same day. Then later, on the

Island, I had an early 5 gallon tank on the bike and it split in practice. I went up to Tony and the BSA guys and they said: '*Well we've got a tank, one of the long slim works alloy ones, with a seat, you can borrow that.*' OK, fine, I thought: '*I'll bring it back to you after the race.*' I happened to finish 5th and afterwards I went back to the guys, with the intention of giving it back. They just laughed and said: '*No, that's OK, you can keep all that.*' A lot of things came down to me like that, so I was always very appreciative of what BSAs did for me at the time. It was great actually, a real friendly association with the factory over the years. So I hope I did some good for them, as I never ever parted with any money.

5th was pretty good on a road model which would struggle to top 90mph. Evans averaged 85.16mph from a standing start, just 3mph down on the winning Honda. He in turn only beat the winning 250 machine by a similar margin however and this race was a real landmark affair. The rise of the two strokes had looked inexorable in the smallest production class but it was stopped by three Ducatis in the top six, all completing the three laps from a push start at over 80mph.

Ray Knight on Clive Thompsett's Ducati Mach I (top) and Vic Camp (below) the 1960s Ducati guru. Camp was a stalwart supporter of production racing, firmly believing that success on the track was the key to success in the sales room

Before the race it had looked like Suzuki might finally get their win, as Barry Smith was fastest qualifier at over 85mph, way quicker than Chas Mortimer's Ducati at 82mph. As usual though Suzuki was at the heart of another good story. Harry Thompson was a huge flag-waver for Suzuki, and as he marketed a range of tuning and cycle parts for the Super Six he entered his machines as '*Thompson Suzukis*'. In 1969 though he fell foul of

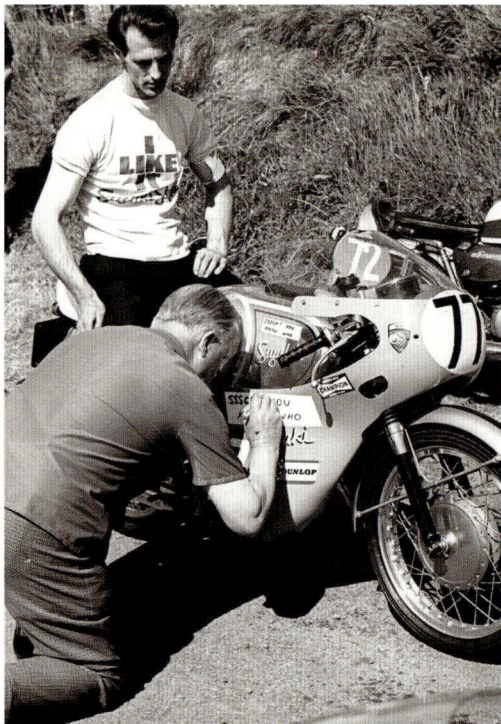

Harry Thompson applies the ACU required alterations to his 'Thompson' Suzukis

the TT's rules on sponsorship and advertising. These would soon change, dramatically, but in 1969 Thompson's bikes were deemed Suzukis, not *Thompson* Suzukis, as unlike Dunstall, Thompson was not registered as a manufacturer. This was patently ridiculous as the Suzukis had *'Thompson Suzuki'* written on them in 1967 and 1968 but ever with an eye to publicity Thompson snatched victory from the jaws of defeat. Everyone knew the Schweppes soft drinks adverts at the time, so the Thompson name was over laid by stickers with their *'Sssch you know who!'* catch phrase and photos appeared of the bikes in every motor-cycling magazine and newspaper. They got more publicity than they could have ever hoped for but it ended quickly as Barry Smith seized on the first lap after a spark plug electrode broke down, Dave Spruce coasted in on lap two and Trevor Holdsworth could only make seventh place as a late stand in for Derek Woodman.

As such Chas Mortimer led from Trevor Burgess' dreaded Ossa, but the Spanish bike was out after a lap leaving it a three-way fight between Mortimer, Frank Whiteway on the Eddie Crooks Suzuki and Alastair Rogers on his older Mach I Ducati, which was probably the most well-used 250 around. He had managed only eighth place the previous year but he was a regular winner on the club scene and upped his pace on lap two as Mortimer slowed. He was seven, twelve then seventeen seconds faster than Whiteway's Suzuki as the three laps unfolded, so that while Mortimer put in the fastest lap of the race as he closed in on the finishing flag, Rogers won by an easy thirty seconds.

The one that everyone forgets. Alastair Rogers (above) took Ducati's first TT win on his Mach I Ducati in 1969

While scarcely acknowledged today Rogers' win was actually a momentous achievement, as it was Ducati's first ever TT victory. It was against stiff opposition too. As a sign of the times there wasn't a single British machine in the race and while GP regular Jim Curry was also missing, there were Honda twins - the new, vertical, CB250-type - two-strokes from Ossa, Montesa, Bultaco, Yamaha and Suzuki and a gaggle of Ducatis similar to Rogers. Ducati had arrived.

Stiff opposition? Frank Whiteway on the Crooks Suzuki (top right), John Williams on the Skellern Honda CB250 (middle) and Chas Mortimer on the Vic Camp Ducati Mach III (bottom). They'd go on to accumulate thirteen TT wins between them from thirty two podium finishes

Home Soil

Back on the mainland Knight got over his TT second place by establishing yet another landmark. Having taken the first ever win on an officially designated Thruxton Bonneville he did the same on a Triumph Trident, taking the machine's first ever win - first and second victories actually - at Thruxton on Sunday 29th June. They were perhaps Pyrrhic victories however as being the font of knowledge on all the rules and regulations he was promptly excluded from the results.

Rod Scivyer wasn't racing, but acting as the chief scrutineer that day, at the Southern 67 meeting and he deemed the bike's top fairing illegal. It was the same as Martin Carney had used at the TT, as it was the very same Hughes machine, but it meant that while Knight was allowed to ride and race, his result would be excluded from the production championship results. It was duly printed that any result would have been *'obtained through the use of illegal parts'* leaving Knight hoisted by his own petard!

It was also a new machine winning the following Saturday, after a ding-dong battle with a BSA rider, with Knight soon riding the machine too, since he had a bit of 'history' with the manufacturer in question.

Rising star Dave Potter looks on as mechanics Dave Gardner and Vic Lane work on the new Boyer production Tridents. They would be firing on all six by 1970, but it was still Bonnevilles for 1969

Gerry Millward's was a typical privateers production machine, prepared in a normal family garage and funded through a pay packet. On its day, it was still more than capable of challenging the best

Gerry Millward; I rode an A65 as that's what I'd got, a Lightning Clubman and it was a fair looking piece of kit. I wanted to race, but to begin with it was more like having a few beers and having some fun and when I first got the bike it wasn't right actually, so kept going backwards and forwards to Glanfield Baldet, where Mick Hemmings used to work as a mechanic. It had a habit of breaking cranks, well mine did, so I got another from BSA and had to pay a fair amount for it. But after a year that was going too, so I got another free, as it was a recon, though obviously I didn't tell them that by now I was racing it!

Then I had a third one go and put an A50 crank in it from Tony Clark Motorcycles in Northampton and it was better with that in it, smoother, it went really well. I put a Spitfire head on it, with the bigger valves and carbs and when I got it I didn't know it was going to have a close ratio gearbox as standard. But it did, being a Clubman. So, once I'd sorted it all out it was as fast as a Bonneville, as with the Spitfire head on it was really quite quick. I didn't have a problem with the handling either, though then again, I wasn't quite John Cooper! But that one in '69 was my first race win and I won it quite easily. But the second time out he was up my arse, it was a works bike after all and I fell off at the Gooseneck.

(Top) Richard Stevens with the 'works' MkII Interceptor. Interestingly it carries the number plate from the 800cc development prototype

(Below) The factory team of Richard Stevens, unknown (possibly Steve Hobbs), Chris Ludgate on the earlier MkI Interceptor racer, Reg Thomas and Roger Shuttleworth

Richard Stevens: The guy on the Bonneville, Paul Chambers was it? He was my main rival in the Bantam Club, and a friend of Gerry Millward. He was a handy rider too, but I remember Gerry falling off at Cadwell, as I've still got the trophy in the lounge! For me the racing started when I finished my apprenticeship in a garage and one of the guys who was in our little gang he was on the assembly line at Enfield and says there's a job coming up as development engineer and road tester. There were four of us on development, me, Reg Thomas the Chief Designer, his assistant David Brierley and Chris Ludgate, who was the Chief Development Engineer who I learned a lot off. I was mainly on the road and we were doing the 750 twins, the Series I Interceptor, which was very similar to the Constellation engine. But then the Series II, which was an entirely new engine. It had a timing cover more like the Triumph, triangular, rather than the great big one the Constellation had. I'd started off racing with an iron head Triumph 110, I started on the same day as Barry Sheene actually and prior to the factory job I had a Suzuki Super Six, which as you know was really competitive back then. But most of the factory guys were on trials bikes or motocross, nothing to do with road racing and as I was spending a lot of time on the road at work I thought a way to possibly be competitive without spending loads of money, on Yamahas and the like, was to talk Reg Thomas into allowing me to use a road bike in production racing. So we could carry out some development with parts under racing conditions.

It was agreed we had to do the bike in our own time, me and Chris Ludgate, so we used to stay on after work preparing it, getting it ready, lightening things, and getting it a bit more racey like. Though we never got a van or anything like that off the company. We just got the bike and I paid my own entry fees and petrol, though one of the guys on assembly, Steve Hobbs, used to come as a mechanic and we all had those lancer-front overalls, so it looked sort of official! We fitted a close-ratio box in it and in the end it was pretty competitive.

The Royal Enfield Interceptor MkI (top) and MkII (bottom) were superficially similar but different

Performance was close to a Bonneville, as it had the Norton forks by then as we were connected to Norton Villiers and it had the twin leading shoe brake, which stopped really well, as Joe Dunphy did the brakes. AM4 Ferodo linings, which I used on the back as well as the front. Joe said not many used them on the back, as they were too vicious, but it was only a 6" brake on the Enfield. '68 Butler and Nixon were on Boyer Triumphs, the ones to beat in production, but Ron Wittich was about then too and super quick when he got a Commando. Lenny Phelps from Elite Motors he was quick and in the mix, while *PK* Davies was fast on the old Bonneville as was John Hedger. He was very quick. But 1969 was the only year we really raced the Interceptor. I did a couple early on in 1970 but then the factory decided they'd pull the plug, which was a shame, as I was on the 800 by then.

I had six months on that, but about June-July '70 they decided there'd be no more development, even though it was really quick. That bike, the 800, went to Barcelona and back, two up, faultlessly, 80mph the whole time on the French roads though there was originally just one bike and two engines, that was our whole development programme! But I remember Percy Tait from Triumph and Peter Brown from BSA were up at MIRA when we went one day. We were doing carburetion on the 800, while they were doing tests on the speed trap. So we went over and asked if we could put the Enfield through. I rode that through at 128mph, 1969 that was, and I can tell you it raised a few eyebrows.

It makes you think. Had Enfield hurried the development along the Series II Interceptor could have made for a formidable production racer. Which Ray Knight tended to agree with, when he got the chance to race Steven's bike, in his role as *MCI* tester.

Ray Knight: As a last hurrah I was offered a race test and was quite impressed. It was near equal to the Bonnevilles of the day and with its new Norton front-end it showed much promise. Where I would have changed down twice on a Thruxton Bonneville, once would suffice on the Interceptor. The road holding was good, surprisingly good, not better than a Thruxton – I don't think there was one better in that respect - but nearly as good and Reg Thomas confessed that there was still a little more work to be done to improve the navigation. One could use a little more front brake, but then I suppose one always could on a production racing bike, unless you have discs. But this too was saying that it was not quite as good as the very best and the motor was certainly a good one, with so much middle-range power and spread of torque that you didn't have to scream it to get anywhere. What's more, after our hard races there was not a trace of oil on the outside. The *'Oilfield'* was dead.

When not racing other people's bikes Ray Knight kept to his own Triumph Daytona. Though later in the year he was so impressed when testing Peter Butler's Boyer Bonneville, he actually bought it

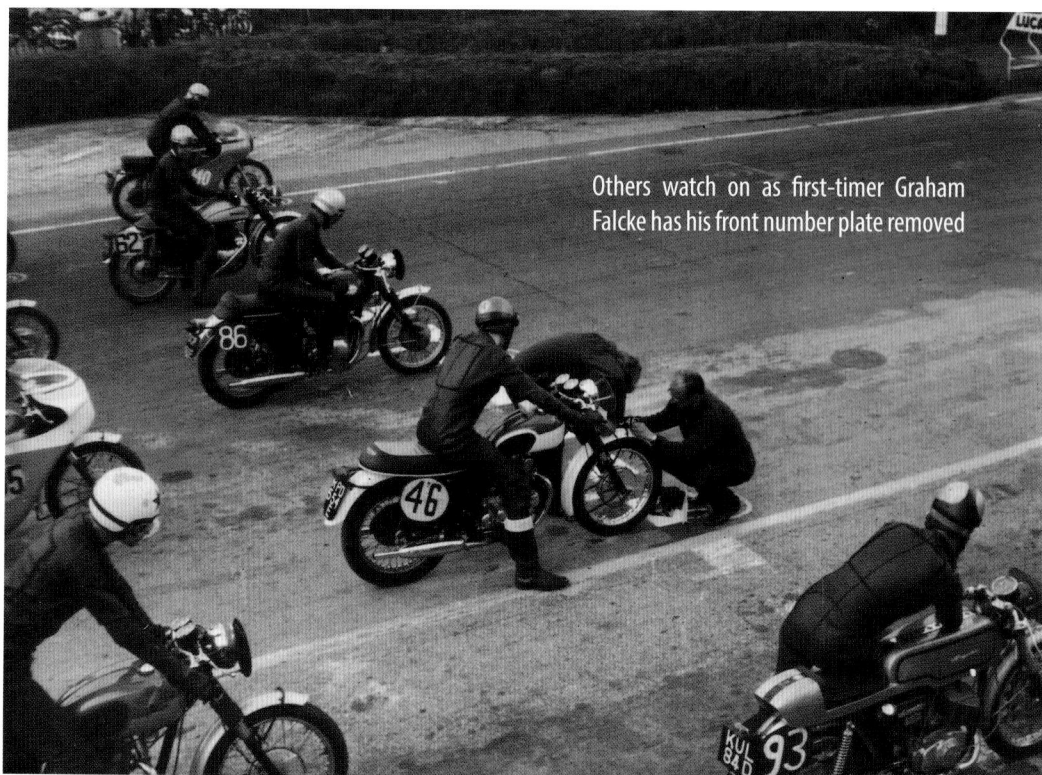

Others watch on as first-timer Graham Falcke has his front number plate removed

The test bike held third place and for good measure Richard took it to another third in another race to conclude a good day. The bike was a good one, showing real potential in only its first few months of racing. As a postscript, that winter, I had a letter from Jack Booker, who was Enfield's Development Manager, offering me a job as a development rider on the bike for the following season. But the axe fell over the winter and the company was run down and closed in June 1970. So my works ride was stillborn. Oh well!

It was a great shame. The remaining 750cc MkII engines ultimately made their way into Rickman chassis which would have made an ever better racer. The Rickmans remained on the road though, as did the Honda 750s. The Trident remained elusive too and there were no racing Rocket Threes, the BSA equivalent. Among the 500s no one seemed brave enough to try a Kawasaki after Tony Dunnell's experience at the TT, though there were a small number of Suzuki 500s. Les Trotter's pair of third places at Snetterton in July were probably the machine's standout results, but it meant that Triumph's 500 was still the one to have, particularly if it had a bit of *previous*.

Graham Falcke: I got into it as a friend built a Triton and when matey boy wanted it raced he chose me. As I was reasonably quick as a road rider, wore the footrests down all the time, left and right, that sort of thing, and was up for it. But while we all thought he was a fantastic engineer of course we had no real technical knowledge and it fell apart as most bikes would if you thrashed them flat out down the Norwich Straight. With the vibration and that things broke and fell off and I don't think it finished at all the first three races that day, but I was smitten. I had a Daytona road bike at the time so the obvious conclusion was to go racing on that, so I did.

I never actually rode my bike down, though others did, as I had an Anglia van. We took the front wheel out and pushed it in backwards in such a way that we could drive it all the way down to Lydden, with the bike hanging out the back, as that was how it was back then. In my very first production race, nobody told me to take my front number plate off, so I pulled up for the start and two guys ran out and took it off, on the grid and one of the blokes behind complained: '*Oi, you should have done that before you came!*' Well, I said: '*I asked for regs but no one sent me any.*' It was British Formula, BFRC, and I was on the front row as the draw was out of a ballot. I got 4th, 3rd and 2nd that day, in the three races I entered, so was quite pleased with that, not really having done it before. I raced that for a year and then *MCN* did a feature on Daytonas. I sent them some info and I remember them saying '*lucky 19 year old Graham Falcke is racing one.*' Then *MCN* did it again, with a road test and a feature on the bike that had won the *500-miler*. Clearly there was a non-standard steering damper, so I wrote in to the letters page and said: '*Well

Graham Falcke (No.31) gridded-up on the ex-Boyer 500-miler/Barcelona machine. Now with two con-rods

clearly that's not standard, one wonders what else isn't?' My comments caused quite a controversy and a good number of letters of support came in over the next couple of weeks, agreeing with me. But it was quite embarrassing too, as I ended up buying the bike! At the end of the season, the year Boyer won the *500-miler* with the 500, it was up for sale. I'd realised by then that these things were probably non-standard bikes and when they sold it to me the implication certainly was that it wasn't!

Falcke in pursuit of Gary Green at Snetterton. Both on Daytonas with Thruxton spec. silencers

There were two different cylinder head gaskets, for different degrees of reliability, different thicknesses, and that kind of thing. It was nothing serious by modern standards, in terms of cheating, but it amazed me that anything went on like that as I was naive enough, innocent enough, to believe that the bikes genuinely came out of the factory and on to the track as they were, which was never the case. Mine had finished with just one con rod at Barcelona, as they'd sawn one off, Dave Nixon and Peter Butler, to get to the finish. But they were honest enough to admit that and I remember Boyer's mechanic telling me that it would rev cleanly well past 9,000, which was amazing in those days. I never did, as I was aware the wear if you got above 8k, may be 8,500, but Hugh Robertson was another Daytona guy and he reckoned he revved over 9,000 too.

The Boyer's bike was the same model as mine, but because of two years' development and its pedigree the handling was incredible. They didn't tell me anything about that but I presume it had alterations. It handled extremely well and while I don't think they did anything to the frame at all it had stiffer forks and I think they played around with spring rates too. Basically it had a bit of know-how put into it, because they were experienced pros which we weren't. I'd never even attempted to drain or refill the fork oil! It was well sorted and I remember Gary Green had quite a reputation at the time. He was something a bit special, but he passed me at Snetterton and I hung on to him quite comfortably. He looked around after a bit and then took a second look you know, like a comedian on TV, as he couldn't believe I was still there and he really started trying and got a bit ragged after that. Maybe he just had a bad day but I honestly never really remember getting beaten after that. Though I could only afford to race five or six times a year. I couldn't afford more than that as I was only earning £7.50 a week, though of course one pair of tyres lasted all season. It was only club racing but I did the *500-miler* two years running, the first year with John Vincent and the following year with Dick Hunter, both Bantam Club guys, as everybody was incredibly helpful and friendly back then and it was the classic case that while you'd be knocking spots off each other on the track you were then all mates in the evening. Brilliant, as they were a really good crowd and everyone got on.

John Lancaster with top-fairing at Silverstone

By 1969 that crowd included many names which would become prominent in the 1970s. Gary Green would become a rider in demand, by the works supported Japauto Honda team in particular, while Mick Grant popped up at Cadwell Park British Formula Club meetings on his Velocette. Dave Railton and Mick Hemmings would become stars of an even more prominent production racing scene in the 1970s while Dave Potter would progress from his production Commando to harrying Barry Sheene on Ted Broad-sponsored Yamahas. The Haslam name would also loom large, and it was middle brother Phil being tipped for the top at the time, on the National and International scene.

John Lancaster: '69 I did a race up at Snetterton, 17th May. It was pouring with rain and this Phil Haslam chap got in front. But when we came to Sears he had his back end out, he literally went sort of sideways, so I got past, leading him. But then on the last corner there were a bunch of back markers, we were lapping them and Phil got past and I didn't, so he crossed the line before me. Anyway I don't know how old I was

Back to a naked set-up over the cracks at Staverton airfield.

When the popularity of road racing went stratospheric in the 1970s a lot more venues such as Staverton would be used so great was the demand for new circuits

in '69? In my 20s anyway, and Phil was just a youngster as far as I was concerned and he came over to me afterwards and said: '*You rode really well!*' I said: '*Oh, thank you!*' but in my head I was thinking: '*You cheeky young bugger.*' And then when I was heading home I was in my TR4 with my Thruxton on the back, and as I went through the paddock the Haslams were all there waving back. Anyway, just before I sold the Thruxton I went up to Cadwell and Phil was there with his production Kuhn Commando by then and I did something I'd never done before. Normally I'd put on standard gearing, but it was still slightly over geared like that, as you had to go up that hill on the back straight. The standard Triumph sprocket was 46 teeth, or you could have a 43 tooth, so 43 would give 120mph at 7,000rpm while the 46 was I think about 112mph. What I did was get a drum and machined the teeth off, but left a flange. I'd bought a Vincent 1000 sprocket and machined the OD of the drum so that this sprocket would just slide over the top, 'drilled it, put six bolts through and suddenly I'd got a 52 tooth sprocket, which was something like 104mph at 7000rpm.

I tried it in practice and found that on the back straight, at the bottom of the dip I was bang on 7,000, and up the other side it was still holding it. It seemed OK and in the first race the flag went down and I got straight into the lead. I came over the top of the hill, Charlies, to go down to the straight, 'was putting the power on when the back-end comes round and the next thing I know I'm standing on the footrests. Heading for the Gooseneck and the back-end's round again. The gearing was good, but the next thing I'm coming out of the Hairpin and the revs soar as it jumps out of gear. I carried on and was OK 'till next time at the hairpin when it jumps out of gear again and fortunately Haslam comes round the outside of me, instead of running into me, which he could. I got it back into gear and by the end of the straight I'm three or four lengths behind him, able to stick with him, but he won and I was second.

Liverpool's Tony Carlton at Darley Moor in 1969. Privateers now had Commandos too

(Left) The Boyer's team of George Hopwood, Peter Butler and Dave Nixon. (Right) The Triumph works team in Holland of Percy Tait (no.5) who was second, Rod Gould (no.6) who won and Malcolm Uphill (no.4) who was third

The next race the flag goes down and I'm lying about 6th or 7th coming down the back straight stuck behind a whole load of guys thinking: *'these are all going pretty well!'* but on the next lap when we came over the top, down the hill, I gained on them, then up the hill I pass these guys. Alan Walsh was in the lead on his Bonneville so as we came towards the end I left my braking really late and did something a bit naughty, which was I shot past him, braked late, then went round beside him with my back end sliding. We were talking afterwards and I said: *'I thought you braked a bit early there Alan!'* but of course I was just being a bit silly. Anyway I didn't know where Haslam was at the time but I won the race and Phil got second. It was still jumping out of gear though and sliding around so I packed up then, 'didn't go out for the third race, but went home happy as I thought: *'Beat you, you little bugger!'*

The Triumph riders were probably thinking the same in the distance events as they were making these their own. Over the summer there were two continental races counting towards the *Coupe d'Endurance*, but due to a clash of dates with the TT, only Ken Buckmaster went to a new event at Jarama, though it was certainly worth the time.

Ken Buckmaster: I remember that race very well. There were only three of us in the van George Collis, Peter Male and myself. It took approximately twenty hours to drive there and it was the first time we had seen the circuit. In practice we realised that we had got the gearing completely wrong, the last corner was a fast downhill right-hander, on the finishing line the bike was already reaching full revs. I phoned to Frank Baker at Meriden for advice; *'Look away and hope for the best!'* So we did, won and when we got back home and stripped the engine it was still within factory tolerances.

It was a ringing endorsement of the Bonneville's stamina which was confirmed at Montjuïc Park a month later. While a 360cc Bultaco prototype won overall, Malcom Uphill and Steve Jolly came second and won the production class, on the machine Jolly had ridden to 5th place at the TT. Buckmaster and Collis finished 4th and the Commando of

It was all Commandos at the 500-miler

Ron Wittich and Tony Melody was 5th. The Commando's finish was a great result for a new machine and the Norton would have done better had it not run over a dog – supporting Chris Lodge's previous observations on animal welfare around Barcelona – then lost its battery while leading the race by eight laps on the Sunday. The Kuhn Commando was similar, fast while running and up at the front, but as explained by Frank Kateley previously it went out when the lack of a cush-drive in the clutch broke the gearbox main-shaft. The best two results out of three – *Thruxton, Jarama and Barcelona* – decided the championship so Uphill took the title, with Jolly in second and George Collis and Ken Buckmaster equal third. It was a huge coup for Triumph, as they had entered as a factory team and the Bonnie's dominance continued on 24th August when Triumph machines took the first three places at the non-championship race at Anderstorp, Sweden.

> **Percy Tait:** After practice we realised that our works Bonnevilles were faster than the other riders, the only competitors we were worried about were the Boyer's bikes ridden by Peter Butler and Dave Nixon, so Rod Gould and I plus Malcolm Uphill agreed to put up a show for the benefit of the public and share the prize money. But during the lining-up lap I had carburetion problems and the bike would not run correctly. On the starting line Arthur Jakeman found that the Metalastic support of the remote float of my Amal GP had broken, so he rushed to a near-by fence and returned with a piece of barbed wire, with which he wired the float bowl as best as he could. Of

course the float level was not correct and when I closed the throttle the engine tended to cut out. So off we went and Rod Gould, aware of my problems, did not do as we had agreed and the last laps were a real ding-dong battle. Before the last hairpin before the finishing straight there was a very fast right-hander, I normally took it in third gear, but tried and managed to take it in fourth. So next time round Rod tried the same manoeuvre, which resulted in a great tank-slapper so I thought: *'that will keep him quiet for a bit'* but on the last lap he passed me on the straight, his bike was faster than mine, but I went past him on the last corner. He kept the inside line while cornering for the last corner, but when I came round him and accelerated my engine hiccuped and I ended outside the course and up the banking, but I managed to re-gain the tarmac and finished second. The organisers were so happy for the battle we put up that they gave me a special prize!

The race was interesting as Percy Tait was actually running an American 750cc kit on his Bonneville, which was borderline legal. The American East Coast distributor was bolting these Sonny Routt kits on, in-country, to produce enough T120RT machines to meet AMA flat track eligibility rules, so perhaps it was fine? Every cc mattered, as big bikes were taking over in endurance racing and the good news for the British contingent was that a new round would be added in 1970. It would be run as part of the North West 200, with sponsorship from Wills, who put up cash and *'a casket of cigarettes'* for the winners in the three capacity classes. A crate of fags might not go down so well nowadays, but non-trade support was coming in and, for sponsors, production bikes had a lot of appeal. This was equally true for the last big race of the 1960s domestic scene, as the 37th running of the Hutchinson 100, on 10th August, was sponsored by *The Evening News*.

In With the New

By late in the year insiders knew that 1969 would be the Bonneville's swan song. For the *Hutch* Triumph had riders of the calibre of John Cooper, Malcolm Uphill, Rod Gould, Dave Degens, Peter Butler, Pete Davies, Ray Knight….well it went on and on actually. There were no less than twenty two Triumphs on the track but as Uphill had crashed his bike, Tait gave him his. Having won the *500-miler*, TT and *Coupe d'Endurance* it was probably felt Uphill was capable of a clean

Tony Smith's super fast works A65. Bob Heath stepped in to take his place in 1970 after which it was largely triples in the production class for BSA

A Suzuki Super Six, Thruxton Bonneville and BSA Spitfire negotiate the Cadwell Park hairpin. By 1969 many bikes were fitted with full fairings but they still carried road legal mudguards, clocks, horns and lights which were expected to work

sweep in the blue riband events, but it didn't happen. While Gould was ultimately able to take 3rd ahead of Ray Pickrell's Dunstall and Peter Williams' Commando, the bike in 6th place was the critical one to watch. Percy Tait appeared on a Triumph T150 Trident which was pretty standard apart from some generic racing cosmetics, but was also very swift. The writing was on the wall for the Bonneville, but not just because of the Trident. Both were outpaced by others around Brands Hatch.

Having won the race's first two runnings, with Mike Hailwood in 1965 and John Cooper in 1966, BSA had fallen behind in the production racing arms race. They had always been massively outnumbered by Triumphs on the track, but since 1967 development rider Tony Smith had been having considerable success with his open class A65. Much as Triumph's Percy Tait had been having with his own open class 500cc T100 machine. This fed back into his production racer and on Sunday August 10th it showed. Smith had the Triumph's easily beaten, along with Pickrell's Dunstall Norton. There was just one spanner in the works, the Kuhn Commando, which was also blindingly fast. In 1965 Smith and Andrew had been young team mates, riding for Dick Rainbow Motorcycles, but over the 20 laps around Brands Hatch, run as ever in reverse, they fought tooth and nail for the lead. Mick Andrew had the advantage for most of the race, but Smith harried him on every corner, breaking the lap record on the last lap, on the way to a head to head dash for the line.

Tony Smith: The thing about Mick was that he always made brilliant starts, while I was the opposite. I could never get anything started. When they brought in clutch starts, later, I would have been in heaven, but at the *Hutch* I actually managed to get away second behind Mick and I was genuinely just sitting there behind him. Brian Martin, I mean he was desperate for me to win the *Hutch* for him and I just followed Mick on the Kuhn Commando knowing I could take it at any time. We were half a lap ahead of everyone else with three laps to go and by chance we came across Hugh Evans, lapping him, and Mick went underneath him, touched him, knocked him across the road in to me, and took me off the circuit. I was going down the grass and lost a good ten yards but only lost the race by inches, to a photo finish on the line. Well, if they'd *had* such a thing as photo finishes back then. I broke the lap record trying to do it and some people thought I'd won it and some thought he had. My mechanics thought I'd won it, it was that close. I wasn't sure but Mick was ecstatic as he crossed the line and that might have swung the decision, as I was never exuberant after winning a race, I just sort of acknowledge it with a quick wave of my hand. I was desperate to win too, but just didn't show it. But anyway it was Mick who got given the result and the terrible thing was I had three chances to win the *Hutch*, but never won any of them and that really hurt.

Tony Smith in pursuit of Mick Andrew. Ultimately the Kuhn Commando would prove just too fast

Mick Andrew leads the 350cc Grand Prix Yamahas of Rod Gould (2) and Phil Read (1), along with John Blanchard's Matchless G50. In the two leg Championship race at the *Hutch* his Commando was twice beaten by Rod Gould, but each time Andrew came second, finishing ahead of Grand Prix regulars Phil Read (Yamaha), Karl Hoppe (4 cylinder URS), Franta Stastny (Jawa), Jack Findlay' (Linto), Bo Granath (Husqvarna) and Santiago Herrero (Ossa), as well as all the British stars

It would have been a great sign-off for the A65, as everyone knew the Rocket Three was coming in for 1970 to replace it, the same as the Trident would replace the Bonneville. But the same held true for Smith. After four years at BSA he'd be off to pastures new. It was probably good timing too, as while Smith's Spitfire was acknowledged as one of the fastest machines on the scene and at the pinnacle of its development, it was also at the end of the road. The Commando on the other hand was entirely new. There was loads which could be done to it, as the Kuhn version was largely just a cosmetic update, and not a very good one at that.

Frank Kateley: I was looking after Mick Andrew's bike that day and the bloody thing was falling apart. When he came in afterwards it had only just about managed it, though Mick could just about ride anything. For some riders it had to be perfect, but some blokes – *Crockett*, Dave Croxford, was another one – they just got on it and rode it as it was and when Mick won that bike was only just hanging together. The body work mostly. The motor ran lovely, no problem at all, but it was plastic tanks and plastic seats and this, that and the other which was nearly the downfall of it actually. As Gus Kuhn had got all these extras, of which there were a load and to be fair they weren't very good in reality. They didn't look very nice and didn't perform much better. But that's what they were trying to market and sell at the time, so that's what we fitted. With the success we had the yellow thing came out soon after, the works *Yellow Peril* Commando production racer and I actually went down to Thruxton to get one. I don't know if it was the very first one which they sold to Kuhns, but I went down to collect it and they said: *'Have a few laps on it before you load it in the van.'*

But getting back to the *Hutch* there was a funny end to the story, as there was quite big prize money for the production race by then. So when we won, Mick, they gave him the cash there and then. We went down to the prizegiving sort of thing and there was this big wad of cash and it was all still bound up in the bank wrappers. Anyway we were going for a drink afterwards and Mick says: *'Hey can you buy the drinks 'cos I don't want to break this wrapper.'* I don't know whether it was the first big one he'd won or what, but he wouldn't break open this wad of cash and it was all a bit of a laugh at the time.

It may have been a laugh but the 1969 Hutchinson 100 was also a watershed in the changing racing scene. While Bonnevilles and Spitfires could still hold their own you needed a good 'un to stay on the pace and a works bike if you expected to win. Critically new entrants, such as Gus Kuhn, had upped the ante as production racers climbed the paddock pecking order. Three or four years previously a production race might have bulked out a National meeting, adding a bit of variety, an interlude between the *'real'* racing. By 1969 a production race could challenge a 500cc National Championship race for top event of the day and pay out a wad of cash. Mick Andrew walked away with £120 in total prize money on 10th August, as the biggest winner of the day. It was the same at other meetings too. When Dave Croxford won the proddie race at the Mallory Park Carreras National on May 25th he got £50 which, while not a lot for the effort put in, was £10 more than was on offer for winning the Senior race, which he also happened to win that day.

Giacomo Agostini and his MV Agusta won the Race of the South on October 15th but he couldn't help admiring the size of Mick Andrew's pay cheque for second place, taken on the far more humble Kuhn Commando

In 1968 he and Ray Pickrell had picked up £75 each for their production win at the Mallory Park 2,000 Guineas races, which again was the top cash on offer in any class that day. It is always difficult to quantify these things but the average weekly wage in 1969 was £23 18s 3d[22] meaning nearly a month's wages could be picked up in a day. It wasn't huge money, but it all stacked up for riders who might ride in three or four different classes at a meeting and be on start money too if they were bigger names. It also changed how riders prioritised those rides, when the production race might be the biggest payer of the day. Who was going to risk their neck in a British Championship race if the proddie race paid more?

This swinging pendulum wasn't lost on the biggest names either and the *new bikes-new priorities-new cash* scenario was nicely encapsulated by events over at Andover the Monday following the *Hutch*. Giacomo Agostini hadn't raced at Brand Hatch that day, but flew in to Thruxton by private plane. He was met by Norton officials, but spent as much time with Vincent Davey and Mick Andrew, who had brought the winning Kuhn Commando down from London specifically for him to see. The World Champion declined the opportunity of a ride but his interest was piqued and it wasn't at all surprising. As a play thing Agostini had picked up a Triumph Trident in July, at exactly the same time that Barry Sheene was competing in the Barcelona 24hr race on a Kuhn Commando. That was on the full race version but it wasn't a million miles away from the bike *Ago* was currently mulling over. It showed quite how much the landscape was changing and it was changing even faster on the continent

Agostini's latest play thing was a Triumph Trident fitted with drop bars and rear-set footrest. He took it for a spin at Cadwell Park on delivery, but much to the regret of fans, ultimately he wasn't tempted to race it

Earlier in the year Tommy Robb and Bill Smith had gone to France to race their *'works'* CB750 Honda at Montlhéry. This was presumably a low profile, under the radar test, to assess the suitability of the machine for future race use in the UK. The Bol d'Or 24hr race was still just a National race in France at the time and Smith and Robb had taken out French licences to comply.

A 1971 Brands Hatch Anglo-American 750cc grid embodying quite how far production bikes had come. Barry Sheene's Kuhn Commando (23) and Bob Heath's ex-Tony Smith works BSA twin (20) only used production engines, but Brian Edwards Bonneville (15) was a 100% box-stock, road legal, production machine

They were stopped from entering however, perhaps for breaking the spirit if not letter of the law. For test purposes it didn't matter too much however as they handed the machine over to two local teenagers, Michel Rougerie and Daniel Urdich, who promptly went out and won. What was remarkable about the race was not the result of the Honda itself though, but the machines throughout the field. In France there was a whole new look to the racing. A couple of years previously it had been all smoking two-stroke tiddlers, Italian lightweights and aged British twins. Now, while a Triumph Trident came ninth, the rest of the entrants were almost completely unrecognisable. Two Honda 750s, three Kawasaki 500s, an Aermacchi 350, two Kawasaki 250s, and two of the new Moto Guzzi 750s made up the top ten. While 750 Laverdas and 750 BMWs also featured among the thirty three finishers, only two of which were British besides the Trident. It was clear the 1970s were going to be a whole new thing.

The pre-unit Triumphs and Vincent V-twins would still be there in 1970, but so to would the Tridents, Laverda twins and so much more besides

Vive la différence!

Ten years previously a new breed of racer had appeared. They raced the bikes they rode on the street and the performance of those bikes rose annually. Within a decade the ripples those first make-do-and-mend racers sent across the calm waters of the British National scene had turned into international waves.

America had always been more market orientated. They pushed road bike-based racing far harder than anywhere else and disregarding staunch patriotism did so even if it was at the expense of Indian and Harley-Davidson. From 1969 American Class C rules allowed modified 750cc overhead valve production machines to compete on American dirt tracks against Harley's side-valves, the move which allowed Percy Tait's 750cc barrels and the A65 to eventually be developed into the 750cc A70. This ruling was extended to road racing machines from 1970. It was a huge change which brought in the legendary Rob North three-cylinder racers from BSA and Triumph. These American road races, of which the Daytona 100 is the best known became incredibly important to the manufacturers and laid the foundations of Formula 750, the big brother of *Superbike*, which was just around the corner. The Isle of Man was ahead of the game in this regard however – as it had been with the production TT – by holding the first Formula 750 TT in 1971, the same year that the Ontario Speedway hosted the richest race on the planet, the Champion Spark Plug 250. John Cooper won it on his BSA Rocket Three, landing the lion's share of the colossal $100,000 purse. It's impossible to conceive of a £500,000 prize event in 2022, but a year later it was Imola's turn, where Paul Smart took his 750SS, Ducati's latest V-twin road bike, to victory in front of 70,000 screaming Italian fans at *'The Daytona of Europe.'*

1971 also saw the first running of the Transatlantic Match Races, with the opening round at Brands Hatch laying the blueprint for what would become the decade's most popular spectator draw in the UK. On Friday 9th April 1971 the Match Races, of which there were two, were between American and British teams racing exclusively on BSA/Triumph Rob North triples. What was telling however was that five of the other eight solo races that day were open to production or production-based machines. There *was* a 500cc event, just one, open to Grand Prix class machinery, but that was not what the crowds were paying to see. In 1959 they watched Manx Nortons and AJS 7Rs circulating around Britain's most famous circuit and in 1971 the sad truth was that they got offered exactly the same. Technically the 500 class had stagnated, while over the same period the production scene had evolved beyond all recognition. You would no more have ridden the 1960 *500-miler* winning Matchless 650 in 1965, than the 1966 250 class winning Cotton Conquest in 1969. Racing *did* improve the breed and the manufacturers who understood and engaged with the racing reaped the benefit.

The 500cc Grand Prix scene would regain its sparkle, through Kenny Roberts and above all Barry Sheene. But the bikes they rode had no road-going equivalents and that was uncomfortable in a period of unprecedented road bike sales. It was one reason Honda stood aside, as they no longer saw any benefit in Grand Prix racing for the road bikes that they sold. One side of the paddock went two-stroke while the other went in an entirely different direction. By promoting classes based on big, booming, four-stroke road bikes they democratised the sport, opening it up to yet another new generation of racers and bringing in sponsorship from some of the biggest names in the sport.

Dave Croxford and Bob Heath (behind) were big national stars by 1969. They had production races firmly in their sights however, as big money was increasingly on offer

At the end of October 1969 Secretary Ken Shierson highlighted the ACU's seeming volte face by saying: '*Anything which encourages production-machine racing is fine as far as I'm concerned, I think that this is racing of the future. I'm all in favour of it.*' Bemsee's Jim Swift adding: '*Some organisers need to be jolted into running more production events. This could do the trick. What's more a national championship might attract a worth-while sponsor.*'[23] The ACU initially baulked at a national championship and while some of the classes which *were* established failed the test of time – F750 and Formula One, Two and Three ultimately all fell by the way side – *Superbike* started to take shape in their shadow. Critically, Centurion Helmets then Avon tyres must have heard Jim Swift's comments as they were behind a move to establish a national production racing series which would go on to transform the sport. Triumphs, Nortons and BSAs were replaced by metalflake entries from Ducati, Laverda, Suzuki and Kawasaki, ensuring that while the 1960s had been largely in black and white, production racing in the 1970s would be in glorious Technicolor.

Mick Andrew and the Kuhn Commando. They marked both the end of a decade and the start of a new era

Summary of *Production Racing* Results 1960 - 1969

1960

Saturday 21st May   **Oulton Park**   ACU Cheshire Centre   The *Clubmans Trophy*

Production 400-700 - 1st **A Dugdale** (Tri 650) / 2nd **M Brookes** (Velocette 499) / 3rd **K Douglas** (Velocette 500) / 4th **R Knight** (Royal Enfield 692) / 5th **B Potter** (BSA 650) / 6th **J Williams** (Tri 650)

Saturday 25th June   **Thruxton**   Southampton & District   The *500 Miler*

Production Over 500 (multi-cylinder) - 1st **R Langston/D Chapman** (AJS 650) 220 laps / 2nd **D Shorey/J Payne** (Tri 650) 217 laps / 3rd **J Holder/P Webb** (Tri 650) 215 laps / 4th **R Minto/J Simmonds** (Tri 650) 213 laps / 5th **V Cottle/R Blanning** (Matchless 650) 211 laps / 6th **C Hubbard/B Denehy** (Tri 650) 210 laps **Production 500** - 1st **D Greenfield/F Swift** (Nor 500) 212 laps / 2nd **P James/V Willoughby** (Velocette 500) 206 laps / 3rd **W Siddles/D Williams** (BSA 500) 190 laps / 4th **M Brookes/P Dunphy** (Velocette 500) 189 laps / 5th **P Bennett/D Ellis** (BSA 500) 186 laps / 6th **E Washer/C Edwards** (BSA 500) 185 laps **Production 250** - 1st **R Prowting/M Munday** (Royal Enfield 250) 197 laps / 2nd **C Sandford/S Miller** (Ariel 250) 196 laps / 3rd **R Good/B Fortescue** (Ariel 250) 193 laps / 4th **R Dowty/B Potter** (Royal Enfield 250) 192 laps / 5th **R Difazio/A Mustard** (Ariel 250) 189 laps / 6th **A Morris/G Dunn** (BSA 250) 188 laps

Saturday 2nd July   **Silverstone**   Bemsee   The *Speed Trial*

Production Unlimited Race 1 (5 laps) - 1st **G Breach** (Vincent 1000) / 2nd **D Cray** (Nor 597) / 3rd **R Knight** (Royal Enfield 692) **Unlimited Race 2 (10 laps)** - 1st **B Potter** (BSA 646) / 2nd **G Breach** (Vincent 1000) / 3rd **P Carrana** (Tri 498) **Production Handicap (5 laps)** - 1st **P Carrana** (Tri 498) / 2nd **E Hurley** (BSA 499) / 3rd **J Brett** (BSA 499)

Saturday/Sunday 6th-7th July   **Barcelona**   Penya Motorista   *24 Horas de Montjuïc*

Production General Classification - 1st **F Villa/A Balboni** (Ducati 175) 603 laps / 2nd **B Daniels/P Darvill** (BMW 600) 600 laps / 3rd **R Fargas/E Rippa** (Ducati 175) 570 laps / 4th **G Lattini/Gozza** (Ducati 175) 570 laps / 5th **A Dagan/J-C Bargetzi** (BMW 500) 539 laps / 6th **J Balasch/J Arenas** (Ducati 175) 536 laps

Saturday 20th August   **Silverstone**   Bemsee   *Trophy Day*

Production (12 laps) - 1st **G Breach** (Vincent 1000) / 2nd **R Knight** (Royal Enfield 692) / 3rd **P Carrana** (Tri 500) / 4th **M Bennett** (Vincent 1000) / 5th **B Bennett** (Tri 649) / 6th **M Gunyon** (AJS 650)

Saturday 8th October   **Silverstone**   Bemsee   *Club Day*

Production 1000 (10 laps) - 1st **C Mills** (Vincent 1000) / 2nd **G Breach** (Vincent 1000) / 3rd **P Carrana** (Tri 500) / 4th **D Degens** (BSA 500) **Production Single** - 1st **C Hunt** (Nor 500)

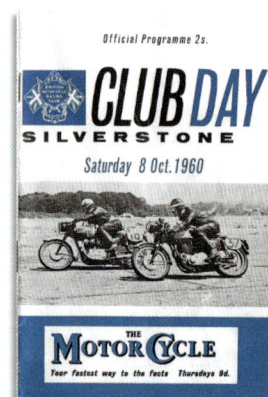

1961

Saturday 20th May   **Silverstone**   Bemsee   *1000 Kilometre*

Production 1000 - 1st **B Daniels/P Darvill** (BMW 600) 215 laps / 2nd **P Tait/W Smith** (Tri 650) 209 laps / 3rd **J Payne/D Shorey** (Tri 650) 207 laps / 4th **R Ingrm/L Carr** (Tri 650) 206 laps / 5th **F Warr/B Morle** (Harley-Davidson 883) **Production 500** - 1st **H German/I Goddard** (Velocette 500) 203 laps / 2nd **D Greenfield/F Swift** (Nor 500) 180 laps / 3rd **S Brand/R May** (Tri 500) 179 laps **Production 350** - 1st **C Edwards/J Tanswell** (BSA 500) 177 laps / 2nd **M O'Rourke/R Rowe** (Nor 350) 152 laps **Production 250** - **C Peck/J Somers** (Honda 250) 185 laps / 2nd **R Good/P Inchley** (Ariel 250) 184 laps / 3rd **J Murgatroyd/P Jordan** (NSU 250) 179 laps

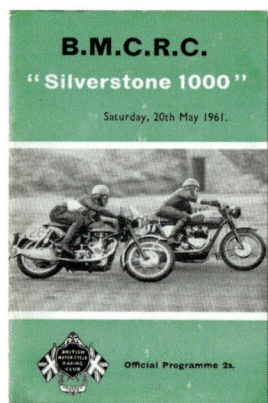

Monday 22nd May   **Oulton Park**   Cheshire Centre ACU   *Clubmans Trophy*

Production 251- 750 (10 laps) - 1st **R Wittich** (Tri 500) / 2nd **J Williams** (Tri 650) / 3rd **A Sweetman** (Nor 500) **Production 250** - 1st **P Padgett** (Royal Enfield 250) / 2nd **P Malloy** (Royal Enfield 250) / 3rd **S Graham** (125 Honda)

Sunday 28th May   **Prees Heath**   Cheshire Motor Cycle Road Racing Club

Production 700 (8 laps) - 1st **A Dugdale** (Tri 649) / 2nd **J Williams** (Tri 649) / 3rd **R Oliver** (BSA 497)

Saturday/Sunday 1st-2nd July   **Barcelona**   Penya Motorista   *24 Horas de Montjuïc*

Production General Classification - 1st **N Price/P Darvill** (BMW 600) / 2nd **R Fargas/E Rippa** (Ducati 175) / 3rd **P Inchley/R Good** (Ariel 250) / 4th **P Vasseur/C Guillotin** (BMW 600) / 5th **J Bordoy/R M Travers** (Bultaco 175) / 6th **C Gracia/J Busques** (Montesa 125)

Saturday 8th July   **Thruxton**   Southampton & District   The *500 Miler*

Production 1000 - 1st **T Godfrey/J Holder** (Tri 650) 220 laps / 2nd **P Tait/R Fay** (Tri 650) 219 laps / 3rd **F Neville/F Rutherford** (AJS 650) 219 laps / 4th **C Erskine/A Burton** (Tri 650) 211 laps / 5th **J Dugdale/J Buxton** (Tri 650) 208 laps / 6th **J Baughn/J Russell** (Tri 650) 205 laps

Production 500 - 1ˢᵗ **D Greenfield/F Swift** (Nor 500) 219 laps **/** 2ⁿᵈ **T Thorp/R Mayhew** (Velocette 500) 219 laps **/** 3ʳᵈ **R Grant/K Payne** (Velocette 500) 216 laps **/** 4ᵗʰ **I Goddard/G Downes** (Velocette 500) 211 laps **/** 5ᵗʰ **E Washer/G Murphy** (Nor 500) 210 laps **/** 6ᵗʰ **P Middleton/R Dawson** (Velocette 500) 210 laps **Production 250** - 1ˢᵗ **W Smith/J Hartle** (Honda 250) 209 laps **/** 2ⁿᵈ **R Good/P Inchley** (Ariel 250) 207 laps **/** 3ʳᵈ **N Surtees/F Hardy** (Royal Enfield 250) 207 laps **/** 4ᵗʰ **K James/A Scott** (Ariel 250) 198 laps **/** 5ᵗʰ **J Dunn/C Peck** (Honda 250) 195 laps **/** 6ᵗʰ **R Harrison/A Sheffield** (Royal Enfield 250) 193 laps

Saturday 19ᵗʰ August   **Silverstone**   Bemsee   *Trophy Day*

Production 1000 (8 laps) -1ˢᵗ **M Bennett** (Vincent 1000) **/** 2ⁿᵈ **C Jones** (Tri 500) **/** 3ʳᵈ **R Knight** (Royal Enfield 692) **Production 250** - **B Lawton** (Honda 250)

Sunday 20ᵗʰ August   **Prees Heath**   Cheshire Centre ACU

Production - 1ˢᵗ **A Dugdale** (Tri 649) **/** 2ⁿᵈ **W Purnell** (Tri 649) **/** 3ʳᵈ **S Murray** (Honda 249)

30ᵗʰ September   **Silverstone**   Bemsee   *Club Day*

Production 171-1000 (7 laps) - 1ˢᵗ **C Mills** (Vincent) **/** 2ⁿᵈ **M Bennett** (Vincent) **/** 3ʳᵈ **R Knight** (Royal Enfield 692) **Production 250 (7 laps)** - 1ˢᵗ **J Heale** (Honda) **Production 351-500 Single (7 laps)** - 1ˢᵗ **P Jones** (Velo) **Production 351-500 Twin (7 laps)** - 1ˢᵗ **T White** (Tri 500)

1962

Saturday 28ᵗʰ April   **Prees Heath**   Midland Motor Cycle Racing Club

Production 201 - 1000 - 1ˢᵗ **J Williams** (Tri 650) **/** 2ⁿᵈ **T Smith** (BSA 500) **/** 3ʳᵈ **R Blondell** (BSA 650)

Saturday 12ᵗʰ May   **Snetterton**   Bantam Racing Club

Production 1000 - 1ˢᵗ **J Bowman** (Tri 650) **/** 2ⁿᵈ **R Knight** (Royal Enfield 692) **/** 3ʳᵈ **C Thompsett** (Matchless 646)

Saturday 19ᵗʰ May   **Silverstone**   Bemsee   The *1,000 Kilo*

Production 1000 - 1ˢᵗ **P Read/B Setchell** (Nor 650) 215 laps **/** 2ⁿᵈ **E Minihan/C Conn** (Tri 650) 213 laps **/** 3ʳᵈ **B Denehy/J Stracey** (Tri 650) 213 laps **Production 500** - 1ˢᵗ **D Greenfield/E Swift** (Nor 500) 206 laps **/** 2ⁿᵈ **B James/I Goddard** (Velocette 500) 206 laps **/** 3ʳᵈ **J Tanswell/W Scott** (Tri 500) 194 laps **Production 350** - 1ˢᵗ **M Hayward/S Robinson** (Nor 350) 182 laps **/** 2ⁿᵈ **E Denyer/E Phelps** (BSA 350) 174 laps **Production 250** - 1ˢᵗ **G Leigh/F Stevens** (Honda 250) 192 laps **/** 2ⁿᵈ **P Inchley/R Good** (Ariel 250) 190 laps **/** 3ʳᵈ **C Peck/J Somers** (Honda 250) 188 laps

Sunday17ᵗʰ June   **Snetterton**   Bemsee The *Norwich Trophy*

Production 1000 (6 laps) - 1ˢᵗ **J Bowman** (Tri 650) **/** 2ⁿᵈ **M Bennett** (Vincent 1000) **Production 500** - 1ˢᵗ **P Carrana** (Tri 500) **Production 350** - 1ˢᵗ **P Walker** (Velocette 350) **Production 250** - 1ˢᵗ **M Rawnsley** (205 Ducati)

Saturday 23ʳᵈ June   **Thruxton**   Southampton & District   The *500 Miler*

Production 1000 - 1ˢᵗ **P Read/B Setchell** (Nor 650) 228 laps **/** 2ⁿᵈ **S Manns/M Gunyon** (AJS 650) 219 laps **/** 3ʳᵈ **R Langston/B Main-Smith** (Nor 650) 218 laps **/** 4ᵗʰ **F Rutherford/J Lewis** (Matchless 650) 217 laps **/** 5ᵗʰ **B Denehy/J Stracey** (Tri 650) 217 laps **/** 6ᵗʰ **D Powell/D Williams** (BSA 650) 213 laps **Production 500** - 1ˢᵗ **R Ingram/F Swift** (Nor 500) 221 laps **/** 2ⁿᵈ **E Boyce/T Phillips** (Velocette 500) 220 laps **/** 3ʳᵈ **H German/G Downes** (Velocette 500) 205 laps **/** 4ᵗʰ **P Carrana/D Dicker** (Tri 500) 204 laps **/** 5ᵗʰ **J Oliver/M Hancock** (Nor 500) 181 laps **/** 6ᵗʰ **E Phelps/E Denyer** (BSA 500) 166 laps **Production 250** - 1ˢᵗ **D Minter/W Smith** (Honda 250) 212 laps **/** 2ⁿᵈ **P Inchley/R Good** (Ariel 250) 209 laps **/** 3ʳᵈ **C Sandford/M O'Rourke** (Ariel 250) 207 laps **/** 4ᵗʰ **D Lee/D Woodman** (BSA 250) 202 laps **/** 5ᵗʰ **D Ellis/J Somers** (Honda 250) 201 laps **/** 6ᵗʰ **G Leigh/F Stevens** (Honda 250) 201 laps

Saturday 21ˢᵗ July   **Snetterton**   Bantam Racing Club

Production 1000 - 1ˢᵗ **J Bowman** (Tri 650) **/** 2ⁿᵈ **R Knight** (Royal Enfield 692) **/** 3ʳᵈ **D Littelwood** (Tri 650)

Sunday 29ᵗʰ July   **Prees Heath**   Cheshire Motor Cycle Road Racing Club

Production 700 (6 laps) - 1ˢᵗ **J Williams** (Nor 650) **/** 2ⁿᵈ **W Purnell** (Tri 650) **/** 3ʳᵈ **B Warmsley** (Tri 650)

Saturday 18ᵗʰ August   **Silverstone**   Bemsee   *Trophy Day*

Production (8 laps) - 1ˢᵗ **B Lawton** (Nor 650) **/** 2ⁿᵈ **M Bennett** (Vincent 1000) **/** 3ʳᵈ **P Bettisson** (Nor 500) **/** 4ᵗʰ **R Knight** (Enfield 700) **/** 5ᵗʰ **D Menzies** (Nor 650) **/** 6ᵗʰ **B Bennett** (Tri 650)

Saturday 22ⁿᵈ September   **Silverstone**   Bemsee   *Baragwanath Trophy*

Production 1000 (8 laps) - 1ˢᵗ **M Bennett** (Vincent 1000) **/** 2ⁿᵈ **W Graves** (Nor 646) **/** 3ʳᵈ **J Bowman** (Tri 649) **/** 4ᵗʰ **R Pepper** (Nor 650) **/** 5ᵗʰ **R Smith** (Matchless 650) **/** 6ᵗʰ **D Doyle** (AJS 650) **Production 500 (8 laps)** - 1ˢᵗ **D Kidd** (Velocette 499) **/** 2ⁿᵈ **C Atkinson** (Velocette 499) **/** 3ʳᵈ **E Bradwell** (Tri 500) **Production 250 (8 laps)** - 1ˢᵗ **T Rawnsley** (Ducati 204) **/** 2ⁿᵈ **M Bailey** (Ariel 247) **/** 3ʳᵈ **L Gillbanks** (Ariel 247)

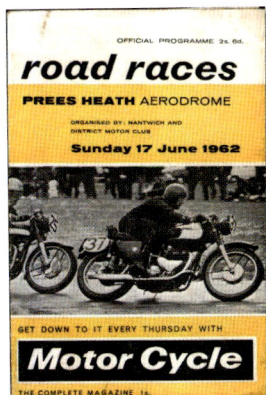

Sunday 7th October **Snetterton** Bemsee The *Guinness Trophy*

Production 1000 (6 laps) - 1st **J Bowman** (Tri 650) **/** 2nd **W Griffiths** (Nor 650) **/** 3rd **J Pepper** (Nor 650) **Production 500** - 1st **E Bardwell** (Tri 500) **Production 350** - 1st **R Ford** (BSA 350) **Production 250** - 1st **W Ottewell** (Honda 250) **/** 2nd **T Rawnsley** (Ducati 204)

1963

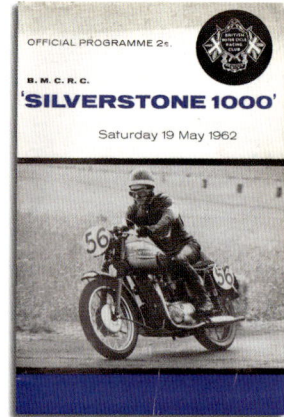

March 23rd **Snetterton** Bantam Racing Club

Production - 1st **J Bowman** (Tri 650) **/** 2nd **B Lawton** (Nor 650) **/** 3rd **P Butler** (AJS 650)

Friday April 12th **Prees Heath** Cheshire MCRRC

Production 1000 Race 1 - 1st **J Bowman** (Tri 650) **/** 2nd **P Butler** (AJS 650) **/** 3rd **B Bennett** (Tri 650) **Race 2** - 1st **P Butler** (AJS 650) **/** 2nd **D Littlewood** (TBC) **/** 3rd **J Hill** (TBC) **Production 250 Race 1** - 1st **S Rawnsley** (Ducati 205) **/** 2nd **M Scott-Coomber** (TBC) **/** 3rd **R Faull** (TBC) **Race 2** - S **Rawnsley** (Ducati 205) **/** 2nd **R Faull** (TBC) **/** 3rd **G Bonney** (TBC)

Saturday 28th April **Prees Heath** Midland Motor Cycle Racing Club

Production Race 1 - 1st **W Purnell** (Tri 650) **/** 2nd **O Dixon** (Nor 650) **/** 3rd **D Roberts** (Tri 650) **/** 4th **A Pearce** (BSA 500) **/** 5th **R Mackay** (Vincent 1000) **/** 6th **R Blundell** (Nor 600) **Race 2** - 1st **W Purnell** (Tri 650) **/** 2nd **O Dixon** (Nor 650) **/** 3rd **D Roberts** (Tri 650) **/** 4th **B Bennett** (Tri 650) **/** 5th **R Mackay** (Vincent 1000) **/** 6th **R Blundell** (Nor 600)

Saturday 18th May **Oulton Park** Bemsee The *1,000 Kilometre* Race

Production over 500cc - 1st **E Driver/P Dunphy** (Matchless 650) 226 laps **/** 2nd **P Read/B Setchell** (Nor 650) 223 laps **/** 3rd **R Langston/B Main-Smith** (Nor 650) 220 laps **/** 4th **B Bennett** (Tri 650) 208 laps **Production 500** - 1st **J Oliver/G Barnacle** (Nor 500) 205 laps **/** 2nd **H German/P Darvill** (Velocette 500) 198 laps **/** 3rd **P Bettison/D Watson** (Nor 500) 195 laps **Production 350** - 1st **M Low/D Peacock** (Tri 350) 193 laps **/** 2nd **A Dugdale/T Fearns** (Tri 350) 193 laps **/** 3rd **K Buckmaster/A Jackson** (Nor 350) 191 laps **Production 250** - 1st **G Leigh/F Stevens** (Honda 250) 205 laps **/** 2nd **P Preston/D Warren** (Honda 250) 200 laps **/** 3rd **G Collis/A Morris** (Yamaha 250) 192 laps

Sunday 19th May **Prees Heath** Cheshire Motor Cycle Road Racing Club

Production - 1st **W Purnell** (650 Tri) **/** 2nd **O Dixon** (650 Nor) **/** 3rd **B Nadin** (650 Tri) **/** 4th **M Brogdale** (500 BSA)

Saturday 22nd June **Thruxton** Southampton & District The *500 Miler*

Production 500 mile 1000 Race - 1st **P Read/B Setchell** (Nor 650) 228 laps **/** 2nd **W Mizen/J Holder** (Tri 650) 228 laps **/** 3rd **J Bowman/R Chandler** (Tri 650) 227 laps **/** 4th **M Duff/W Smith** (AJS 650) 225 laps **/** 5th **B Main-Smith/J Kidson** (Nor 650) 222 laps **/** 6th **R Langston/D Williams** (BSA 650) 222 laps **Production 500** - 1st **B Davis/W Scott** (Tri 500) 224 laps **/** 2nd **T Phillips/T Thorpe** (Velocette 500) 224 laps **/** 3rd **D Chapman/D Peacock** (Tri 500) 219 laps **/** 4th **J Oliver/G Barnacle** (Nor 500) 212 laps **/** 5th **J Baughn/E Bardwell** (Tri 500) 208 laps **/** 6th **K Buckmaster/A Jackson** (Tri 500) 207 laps **Production 250** - 1st **K Martin /F Gonzales** (Bultaco 196) 215 laps **/** 2nd **J Hartle/J Buxton** (Royal Enfield 250) 215 Laps **/** 3rd **J Arenas/O Regas** (Montesa 175) 205 laps **/** 4th **T Payner/P Stacey** (Honda 250) 192 laps **/** 5th **B Winstanley/M Sheehan** (Ariel 250) 186 laps **/** 6th **E Meyer/M Rahn** (DKW 197) 186 laps

Sunday 23rd June **Prees Heath** Midland Motor Cycle Racing Club

Production 201-1000 - 1st **O Dixon** (Nor 650) **/** 2nd **W Purnell** (Tri 650) **/** 3rd **A Pearce** (BSA 499) **/** 4th **R Blundell** (Nor 600)

Sunday 30th June **Snetterton** Bemsee The *Members Meeting*

Production - 1st **W Bowman** (Tri 650) **/** 2nd **D Menzies** (Nor 650) **/** 3rd **B Davis** (Tri 500) **/** 4th **P Butler** (AJS 650) **/** 5th **W Graves** (Nor 650) **/** 6th **D Littlewood** (Tri 650)

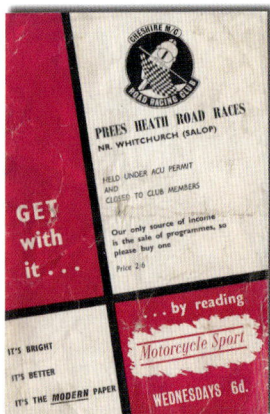

Sunday 21st July **Snetterton** Bantam Racing Club

Production Race 1 - 1st **W Bowman** (Tri 650) **/** 2nd **R Herring** (Nor 650) **/** 3rd **T Smith** (Tri 650) **/** 4th **O Dixon** (Nor 650) **/** 5th **W Buckle** (Nor 600) **/** 6th **M Bool** (Tri 650) **Race 2** - 1st **W Bowman** (Tri 650) **/** 2nd **R Herring** (Nor 650) **/** 3rd **O Dixon** (Nor 650) **/** 4th **M Bool** (Tri 650) **/** 5th **R Wittich** (Nor 650) **/** 6th **D Wood** (Nor 600)

Sunday 28th July **Prees Heath** Cheshire Motor Cycle Road Racing Club

Production (6 laps) - 1st **W Purnell** (Tri 650) **/** 2nd **M Brogdale** (BSA 500) **/** 3rd **J Sumner** (Nor 650) **/** 4th **T Fearns** (Tri 650) **/** 5th **A Dovall** (Tri 650) **/** 6th **T Swindlehurst** (Tri 500)

Sunday 4th August **Little Rissington** Cheltenham Motor Club

Production 175-500 - 1st **K Hawkes** (Tri 500) **Production 500-1000** - 1st **D Vallis** (Tri 650)

Saturday 10th August **Cadwell Park** Bantam Racing Club

Production Race 1 (10 laps) - 1st **T Smith** (Tri 650) **/** 2nd **A Riches** (Nor 600) **/** 3rd **D Older** (Vincent 1000) **/** 4th **M Bool** (Tri 650) **/** 5th **C Lodge** (Tri 650) **/** 6th **E Pearson** (Royal Enfield 692) **Race 2** - 1st **A Smith** (Tri 650) **/** 2nd **D Older** (Vincent 1000) **/** 3rd **A Carlton** (Nor 650) **/** 4th **E Webb** (Tri 650) **/** 5th **H Aldous** (BSA 500) **/** 6th **D Hill** (Tri 650)

Saturday 17th August **Silverstone** Bemsee *Trophy Day*

Production 1000 - 1st **J Bowman** (Tri 650) / 2nd **B Lawton** (Nor 650) / 3rd **O Dixon** (Nor 650) / 4th **M Bennett** (Vincent 1000) / 5th **R Cockrell** (AJS 650) / 6th **G Smith** (BSA 650) **Production 500** - 1st **E Bardwell** (Tri 490) / 2nd **H Cope** (Velo 500) **Production 350** - 1st **M Charles** (Velo 350) **Production 250** - 1st **T Rawnsley** (Ducati 205) / 2nd **D Foxley** (Aermacchi 250)

Sunday 25th August **Brands Hatch** The *Redex Trophy* meeting

Production 350-1000 - 1st **J Bowman** (Tri 650) / 2nd **D Menzies** (Nor 650) / 3rd **P Carrana** (Tri 500) / 4th **M Gunyon** (AJS 650) / 5th **R Warren** (Tri 650) / 6th **D Bayle** (Nor 650)

Sunday 1st September **Snetterton** Bantam Racing Club

Production (8 laps) Race 1 - 1st **J Bowman** (Tri 650) / 2nd **B Lawton** (Tri 650) / 3rd **A Smith** (Tri 650) / 4th **D Older** (Vincent 1000) / 5th **E Bardwell** (Tri 500) **Race 2** – 1st **B Lawton** (Tri 650) / 2nd **J Bowman** (Tri 650) / 3rd **A Smith** (Tri 650) / 4th **T Sheaff** (Nor 650) / 5th **A Carlton** (Nor 650) / 6th **D Wood** (Nor 600)

Saturday 7th September **Prees Heath** Midland Motor Cycle Racing Club

Production Race 1 - 1st **O Dixon** (Nor 650) / 2nd **R Brundell** (600 Nor) / 3rd **G Horne** (650 Nor) **Race 2** - 1st **O Dixon** (Nor 650) / 2nd **R Brundell** (600 Nor) / 3rd **G Horne** (650 Nor)

Saturday 21st September **Silverstone** The *Baragwanath Trophy*

Production - 1st **O Dixon** (Nor 650) / 2nd **M Bennett** (Vincent 1000) / 3rd **P Older** (Vincent 1000)

Sunday 22nd September **Prees Heath** Cheshire Motor Cycle Road Racing Club

Production - 1st **O Dixon** (Nor 650) / 2nd **J Evans** (Nor 650) / 3rd **W Purnell** (Tri 650) / 4th **J Summer** (Nor 650) / 5th **A Duvall** (BSA 650)

Sunday 6th October **Snetterton** Bemsee The *Guinness Trophy*

Production - 1st **O Dixon** (Nor 650) / 2nd **J Evans** (Nor 650) / 3rd **W Purnell** (Tri 650)

Sunday 13th October **Brands Hatch** The Brands Racing Committee

Production 1000 (10 laps) - 1st **B Lawton** (Nor 650) / 2nd **D Bayle** (Nor 650) / 3rd **A Smith** (Tri 650) / 4th **W Purnell** (Tri 650) / 5th **P Butler** (Tri 650) / 6th **D J Else** (AJS 650) **Production 500** - 1st **B Davis** (Tri 500) / 2nd **R Knight** (Tri 500) / 3rd **W Hookway** (Nor 500). **Production 350** - 1st **W Scott** (Honda 305) **Production 250** - **W Ottenewell** (Honda) 250

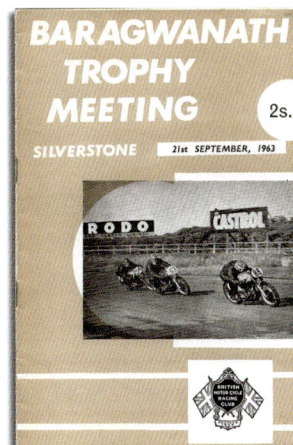

1964

Friday 27th March **Snetterton** Bantam Racing Club

Production (8 laps) - 1st **P Butler** (AJS 650) / 2nd **R Knight** (Tri 650) / 3rd **C Hopes** (Tri 650) / 4th **R Chambers** (Tri 650) / 5th **M Warrington** (Tri 500) / 6th **G W Wallis** (Tri 500)

Saturday 28th March **Perton** Midland Motor Cycle Racing Club

Production 201- 1000 - 1st **O Dixon** (Nor 650) / 2nd **R Blundell** (Nor 600) / 3rd **J Conoly** (AJS 650)

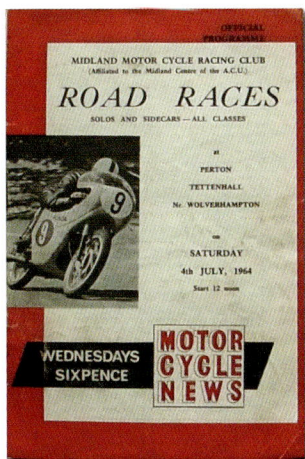

Saturday 18th April **Cadwell Park** British Formula Racing Club

Production 1000 Race 1 - 1st **G Wallace** (Tri 490) / 2nd **O Dixon** (Nor 650) / 3rd **D Hill** (Tri 649) **Race 2** - 1st **O Dixon** (Nor 650) / 2nd **G Wallace** (Tri 490) / 3rd **D Hill** (Tri 649) **Production 350 Race 1** - 1st **D Foxley** (Aermacchi 250) / 2nd **C Macey** (Honda 250) / 3rd **T Smith** (Velocette 350) **Race 2** – **C Macey** (Honda 250) / 2nd **D Foxley** (Aermacchi 250) / 3rd **T Smith** (Velocette 350)

Sunday 19th April **Brands Hatch** The Brands Racing Committee

Production 1000 (5 laps) - 1st **P Butler** (AJS 650) / 2nd **G Bunyan** (Nor 650) / 3rd **A Smith** (Tri 650) / 4th **R Knight** (Tri 650) / 5th **D Else** (AJS 650) / 6th **M Nevill** (Tri 650)

Saturday 25th April **Snetterton** Bantam Racing Club *One Hour Enduro*

Production Race 1 (8 laps) - 1st **A Smith** (Tri 650) / 2nd **P Butler** (AJS 650) / 3rd **M Neville** (Tri 650) / 4th **P Carrana** (Tri 500) / 5th **N Ling** (Tri 650) / 6th **A Carlton** (Nor 650) **Race 2** - 1st **P Butler** (AJS 650) / 2nd **D Bayle** (Tri 650) / 3rd **P Carrana** (Tri 500) / 4th **R Chambers** (Tri 650) / 5th **N Ling** (Tri 650) / 6th **G Wallace** (Tri 500)

Saturday 25th April **Perton** Midland Motor Cycle Racing Club

Production 201- 1000 Race 1 - 1st **O Dixon** (Nor 650) / 2nd **P Davis** (Nor 600) / 3rd **R Blundell** (Nor 600) / 4th **A Longdon** (Tri 650) / 5th **J Dallow** (Nor 500) **Race 2** – 1st **O Dixon** (Nor 650) / 2nd **A Longdon** (Tri 650) / 3rd **R Hole** (Tri 650) / 4th **J Dallow** (Nor 500) / 5th **R Mackay** (Vincent 1000)

Sunday 26th April   **Snetterton**   Bemsee   *Senior Service Tipped* Trophy
Production 175 – 1000 (6 laps) - 1st **B Lawton** (Nor 650) / 2nd **B Davis** (Tri 500) / 3rd **D Bayle** (Tri 650) / 4th **P A Butler** (AJS 650) / 5th **R Avery** (Tri 650) / 6th **R Massey** (Tri)

Saturday 9th May   **Oulton Park**   Cheshire Motor Cycle Road Racing Club
Production 1000 - 1st **O Dixon** (Nor 650) / 2nd **T Swindelhurst** (Nor 650) / 3rd **W Hughes** (BSA 650) / 4th **A Carlton** (Nor 650) / 5th **A Duvall** (BSA 650) **Race 2** - 1st **O Dixon** (Nor 650) / 2nd **A Duvall** (BSA 650) / 3rd **T Swindelhurst** (Nor 650) / 4th **A Carlton** (Nor 650) / 5th **W Hughes** (BSA 650)

Saturday 30th May   **Cadwell Park**   Bantam Racing Club
Production Race 1 (10 laps) - 1st **R Knight** (Tri 649) / 2nd **G Wallace** (Tri 500) / 3rd **C Lodge** (Tri 650) / 4th **P Butler** (AJS 646) / 5th **C Dixon** (Nor 500) / 6th **M Warrington** (Tri 490) **Race 2 (8 Laps)** - 1st **R Knight** (Tri 649) / 2nd **G Wallace** (Tri 500) / 3rd **P Butler** (AJS 650) / 4th **C Lodge** (Tri 650) / 5th **C Dixon** (Nor 500) / 6th **W Buckle** (Nor 597)

Saturday 20th June   **Thruxton**   Southampton & District Motorcycle Club   **The *500 Miler***
Production 1000 - 1st **D Woodman/B Setchell** (Nor 650) 228 laps / 2nd **P Tait/F Smith** (Tri 650) 228 laps / 3rd **J Holder/J Payne** (BMW R69S) 218 laps / 4th **P Butler/A Smith** (Tri 650) 217 laps / 5th **D Else/A Frost** (AJS 650) 216 laps / 6th **A Copeland/D Greenfield** (Tri 650) 213 laps
Production 500 - 1st **A Harris/H German** (Velocette 500) 226 laps / 2nd **R Avery/B James** (Velocette 500) 217 laps / 3rd **G Jenkins/C Conn** (Velocette 500) 213 laps / 4th **G Barnacle/G Wallace** (Tri 500) 213 laps / 5th **R King/R Richie** (Tri 500) 209 laps / 6th **D Warren/T Grotefeld** (Honda 305) 202 laps **Production 250** - 1st **P Williams/T Wood** (AJS 250) 202 laps / 2nd **W Ottewell/M Bailey** (Honda 250) 193 laps / 3rd **F Meyer/M Rahm** (Montesa 175) 191 laps / 4th **G Leigh/J Evans** (Honda 250)190 laps / 5th **R May/C Thompsett** (Royal Enfield 250) 174 laps / 6th **P Brooks/B Hoare** (Royal Enfield 250) 174 laps

Sunday 21st June   **Brands Hatch**   The Brands Racing Committee
Production 1000 (10 laps) - 1st **W Penny** (Tri 650) / 2nd **G Allcock** (Nor 650) / 3rd **L Lovell** (Tri 650) / 4th **R Chambers** (Tri 650) / 5th **W Buckle** (Nor 600) / 6th **C Bennett** (Honda 305)

Saturday 27th June   **Silverstone**   15th MCC High Speed Trials
Production 1000 - 1st **O Dixon** (Nor 650) / 2nd **R McKay** (Vincent 1000) / 3rd **M Gunyon** (AJS 650) / 4th **R Knight** (Tri 650)

Sunday 28th June   **Snetterton**   Bemsee   *Norwich Trophy*
Production - 1st **O Dixon** (Nor 650) / 2nd **R Knight** (Tri 650) / 3rd **P Butler** (Tri 650) / 4th **R Rippingdale** (Nor 650) / 5th **R Lovell** (Tri 650) / 6th **W Buckie** (Nor 650)

Saturday   4th July   **Cadwell Park**   Bantam Racing Club
Production Race 1 (8 laps) - 1st **R Knight** (Tri 650) / 2nd **C Dixon** (Nor 500) / 3rd **N Ling** (Tri 650) / 4th **A Riches** (Nor 650) / 5th **E Webb** (Tri 650) / 6th **A Carlton** (Nor 650) **Race 2** – 1st **W Penny** (Tri 650) / 2nd **R Knight** (Tri 650) / 3rd **C Lodge** (Tri 650) / 4th **C Dixon** (Nor 500) / 5th **P Butler** (AJS 646) / 6th **W Buckle** (Nor 650)

Saturday 4th July   **Perton**   Midland Motor Cycle Racing Club
Production 201- 1000 Race 1 - 1st **O Dixon** (Nor 650) / 2nd **P Davies** (BSA 650) / 3rd **A Langdon** (Tri 650) / 4th **J Connolly** (AJS 650) / 5th **R Hole** (BSA 650) / 6th **K Matthews** (BSA 650) **Race 2** – 1st **O Dixon** (Nor 650) / 2nd **R Hole** (BSA 650) / 3rd **A Langdon** (Tri 650) / 4th **B Bennett** (Tri 500) / 5th **J Dallow** (Nor 500) / 6th **A Kendrick** (Nor 500)

Saturday 11th July   **Aintree**   Waterloo & District Motor Club
Production 125-1000 (6 Laps) - 1st **O Dixon** (Nor 650) / 2nd **A Carlton** (Nor 650) / 3rd **M Brogdale** (BSA 500) / 4th **M Baines** (Nor 500) / 5th **A Langdon** (Tri 650) / 6th **T Barclay** (Nor 650)

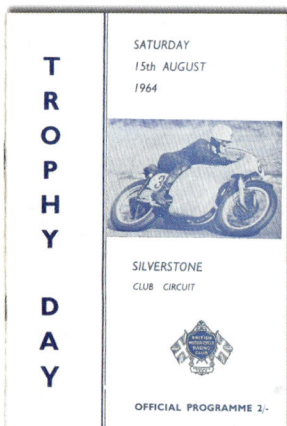

11th /12th July   **Barcelona**   24 Horas de Montjuïc
Overall 24hr Production - 1st **B Spaggiari/G Mandolini** (Ducati 285) 635 laps / 2nd **P Darvill/N Price** (BMW R69S) 630 laps / 3rd **C Sicar/P Millet** (Montesa 175) **Other 250+ Category Finishers** - 8th **G Collis/R Herring** (Tri 500) / 11th **C Conn/E Boyce** (Velocette 500) / 20th **K Buckmaster/A Jackson** (Tri 500)

Saturday 18th July   **Silverstone**   Bemsee   *Club Day*
Production (20 Lap) - 1st **R Watmore** (Tri 650) / 2nd **O Dixon** (Nor 650) / 3rd **R Knight** (Tri 500) / 4th **C Lightfoot** (Nor 500) / 5th **W Ottewell** (Honda 250) / 6th **M Warrington** (Tri 500)

Saturday 1st August   **Snetterton**   Watton & District Motor Cycle & Car Club
Production - 1st **W Penny** (Tri 650) / 2nd **B Davis** (Nor 750) / 3rd **W Buckle** (Nor 650) / 4th **P Butler** (AJS 650) / 5th **R Chambers** (Tri 650) / 6th **N Ling** (Tri 650)

Saturday 8th August   **Cadwell Park**   Bantam Racing Club
Production Race 1 - 1st **C Dixon** (Nor 500) / 2nd **A Carlton** (Nor 500) / 3rd **M Brogdale** (BSA 500) / 4th **W Buckle** (Nor 650) / 5th **C Lodge** (Tri 650) / 6th **G Wallace** (Tri 500) **Race 2** – 1st **C Lodge** (Tri 650) / 2nd **C Dixon** (Nor 500) / 3rd **G Wallace** (Tri 500) / 4th **W Buckle** (Nor 650) / 5th **A Riches** (Nor 600) / 6th **M Brogdale** (BSA 500) **Race 3** – 1st **C Dixon** (Nor 500) / 2nd **W Buckle**

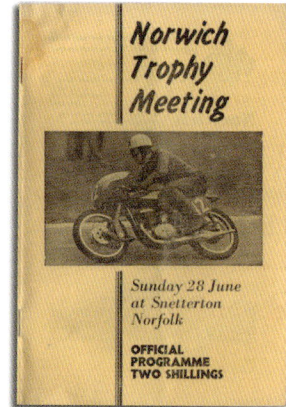

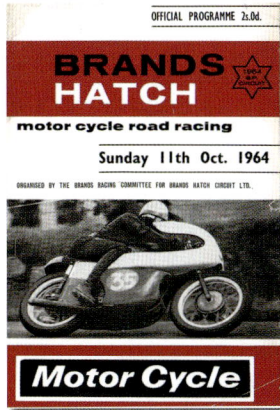

OFFICIAL PROGRAMME 2s.0d.

BRANDS HATCH

motor cycle road racing

Sunday 11th Oct. 1964

ORGANISED BY THE BRANDS RACING COMMITTEE FOR BRANDS HATCH CIRCUIT LTD.

Motor Cycle

(Nor 650) / 3rd **C Lodge** (Tri 650) / 4th **A Riches** (Nor 600) / 5th **N Ling** (Tri 650) / 6th **W Penny** (BSA 500)

Saturday 15th August   **Silverstone**   Bemsee   *Trophy Day*
Production 176-1000 (20 Laps) - 1st **O Dixon** (Nor 650) / 2nd **R Watmore** (Tri 650) /3rd **D Doyle** (AJS 650) / 4th **K Buckmaster** (Tri 500) / 5th **R Knight** (Tri 500) / 6th **D Warren** (Honda 305)

Saturday 5th September   **Snetterton**   Bantam Racing Club
Production Race 1 (8 Lap) - 1st **D Nixon** (Tri 500) / 2nd **D Bayle** (Tri 650) / 3rd **W Buckle** (Nor 650) / 4th **C Dixon** (Nor 500) / 5th **A Carlton** (Nor 650) / 6th **C Hopes** (Tri 650) **Race 2** – 1st **D Nixon** (Tri 500) / 2nd **C Dixon** (Nor 500) / 3rd **E Warburton** (Tri 650) / 4th **W Buckle** (Nor 650) / 5th **A Carlton** (Nor 650) / 6th **D Bayle** (Tri 650) **Race 3** – 1st **P Butler** (AJS 650) / 2nd **C Hopes** (Tri 650) / 3rd **A Carlton** (Nor 650) / 4th **R Lovell** (Tri 650) / 5th **D Nixon** (Tri 500) / 6th **D Doyle** (AJS 646)

Saturday September 5th   **Perton**   Midland Motor Cycle Racing Club
Production Race 1 (5 Laps) - 1st **O Dixon** (Nor 650) / 2nd **R Hole** (BSA 650) / 3rd **A Longdon** (Tri 650) / 4th **J Dallow** (Nor 500) / 5th **M Baines** (Nor 500) / 6th **M Scruby** (Ariel 250) **Race 2** – 1st **O Dixon** (Nor 650) / 2nd **R Hole** (BSA 650) / 3rd **A Longdon** (Tri 650) / 4th **J Dallow** (Nor 500) / 5th **W Davis** (BSA 650) / 6th **M Baines** (Nor 500)

Saturday 12th September   **Oulton Park**   Cheshire Motor Cycle Road Racing Club
Production Race 1 (5 laps) - 1st **A Carlton** (Nor 650) / 2nd **M Brogdale** (BSA 500) / 3rd **B Nadin** (Tri 650) / 4th **A Hendry** (Tri 650) / 5th **M Moffat** (BSA 500) / 6th **E Bailey** (Tri 650) **Race 2** – 1st **A Carlton** (Nor 650) / 2nd **M Brogdale** (BSA 500) / 3rd **B Nadin** (Tri 650) / 4th **M Hughes** (BSA 650) / 5th **M Moffat** (BSA 500) / 6th **E Bailey** (Tri 650)

Sunday 20th September   **Brands Hatch**   The Brands Racing Committee   The *Redex Trophy*
Production (10 laps) - 1st **W Penny** (Tri 650) / 2nd **P Butler** (AJS 650) / 3 rd **C Allcock** (Nor 650) / 4th **C Dixon** (Nor 500) / 5th **D Nixon** (Tri 500) / 6th **D Cooper** (Tri 650)

Sunday 4th October   **Snetterton**   Bemsee   The *Guinness Trophy*
Production 175 – 1000 (5 laps) - 1st **R D Watmore** (Tri 650) / 2nd **G Hunter** (Nor 750) / 3rd **P Butler** (Tri 650) / 4th **R Knight** (Tri 650) / 5th **D Nixon** (Tri 500) / 6th **W G Penny** (Tri 650)

Sunday 11th October   **Brands Hatch**   The Brands Racing Committee
Production (10 laps) - 1st **P Butler** (Tri 650) / 2nd **G Allcock** (Nor 650) / 3rd **J Jackson** (Nor 750) / 4th **R Roberts** (BSA 650) / 5th **R White** (AJS 650) / 6th **D Doyle** (AJS 650)

1965

Sunday 21st March   **Brands Hatch**   The Brands Racing Committee   *Redex Trophy*
Unlimited Production (5 laps) - 1st **A Smith** (BSA 654) / 2nd **W Penny** (Tri 650) / 3rd **P Butler** (Tri 650) / 4th **D Doyle** (Nor 650) / 5th **P Carrana** (Tri 500) / 6th **P Russell** (BSA 500) **350 Production (5 Laps)** - 1st **I Plumridge** (Yam 250) / 2nd **B Jeffries** (Ducati 250) / 3rd **R Prior** (Honda 250) / 4th **L Fox** (Ducati 250) / 5th **P Rogers** (Honda 305) / 6th **J McColllum** (Honda 305)

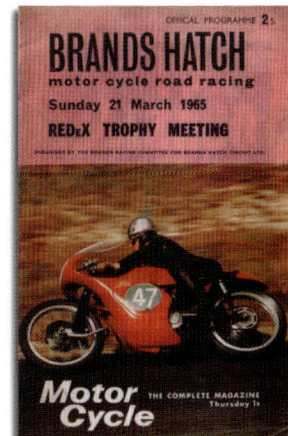

OFFICIAL PROGRAMME 2s.

BRANDS HATCH
motor cycle road racing
Sunday 21 March 1965
REDEX TROPHY MEETING

PRODUCED BY THE BRANDS RACING COMMITTEE FOR BRANDS HATCH CIRCUIT LTD.

Motor Cycle THE COMPLETE MAGAZINE Thursday 1s

Saturday 23rd March   **Cadwell Park**   Bantam Racing Club
Race 1 - 1st **A Smith** (BSA 654) / 2nd **W Davies** (BSA 650) / 3rd **P Butler** (AJS 650) / 4th **R Lovell** (Tri 650) / 5th **C Hopes** (Tri 650) / 6th **D Nixon** (Tri 500) **Race 2** - 1st **R Lovell** (Tri 650) / 2nd **C Hopes** (Tri 650) / 3rd **W Davies** (BSA 650) / 4th **D Nixon** (Tri 500) / 5th **P Butler** (AJS 650) / 6th **N Ling** (Tri 650)

Saturday 10th April   **Silverstone**   Bemsee   *Club Day*
Production (15 laps) - 1st **J Hedger** (Tri 650) / 2nd **P Butler** (Tri 650) / 3rd **R MacKay** (Vincent 998) / 4th **R Lovell** (Tri 650) / 5th **K Buckmaster** (Tri 650) / 6th **R Roberts** (BSA 650) **500 Class** - 1st **M Button** (Nor 500) / 2nd **M Warrington** (Tri 490) / 3rd **J Dallow** (Nor 500) **250 Class** - 1st **A Rogers** (Ducati 250) / 2nd **D Williams** (TBC) / 3rd **R Denny** (Yamaha 250)

Friday 16th April   **Darley Moor**   Darley Moor MCRRC
Production (8 laps) - 1st **B Nadin** (Tri 650) / 2nd **O Dixon** (Nor 650) / 3rd **G Boase** (BSA 500) / 4th **J Dallow** (Nor 500) / 5th **J Bean** (Nor 600) / 6th **J Pearson** (Aermacchi 250)

Saturday 24th April   **Snetterton**   Bantam Racing Club   The *One Hour Enduro*
Production Race 1 - 1st **R Lovell** (Tri 650) / 2nd **D Nixon** (Tri 500) / 3rd **P Butler** (Tri 650) / 4th **C Hopes** (Tri 650) / 5th **M Rice** (Tri 650) / 6th **P Carrana** (Tri 500) **Production Race 2** - 1st **D Nixon** (Tri 500) / 2nd **A Smith** (BSA 654) / 3rd **P Butler** (Tri 650) / 4th **C Hopes** (Tri 650) / 5th **A Carlton** (Nor 650) / 6th **M Andrew** (Tri 650)

Sunday 2nd May **Snetterton** British Formula Racing Club

Production 1000 Race 1 - 1st **D Doyle** (Nor 650) / 2nd **D Nixon** (Tri 500) / 3rd **G Smith** (Tri 650) / 4th **R Roberts** (BSA 650) **Production 1000 Race 2** - 1st **D Doyle** (Nor 650) / 2nd **D Nixon** (Tri 650) / 3rd **D Vallis** (Nor 650) / 4th **G Smith** (Tri 650) **Production 350 Race 1** - 1st **A Rogers** (Ducati 250) / 2nd **B Jeffries** (Ducati 250) / 3rd **C Thompsett** (Ducati 250) / 4th **P Brightman** (BSA 350) **Production 350 Race 2** - 1st **T Jeffries** (Ducati 250) / 2nd **A Rogers** (Ducati 250) / 3rd **A Coulson** (TBC) / 4th **R McGladdery** (TBC)

Sunday 9th May **Brands Hatch** The Brands Racing Committee The *Golden Laps* Meeting

Production (8 laps) - 1st **P Butler** (Tri 650) / 2nd **D Dixon** (Tri 500) / 3rd **G Allcock** (Nor 650) / 4th **R Roberts** (BSA 650) / 5th **D Kelly** (Nor 650) / 6th **B Davison** (Nor 650)

Saturday 8th May **Perton** Midland Motor Cycle Racing Club

Production Race 1 - 1st **R Hole** (BSA 650) / 2nd **G Horne** (BSA 650) 3rd / **D Doyle** (Nor 650) / 4th **J Dallow** (Nor 500) / 5th **P Davies** (BSA 650) **Production Race 2** - 1st **K Matthews** (BSA 650) / 2nd **D Doyle** (Nor 650) / 3rd **R Hole** (BSA 650) / 4th **J Dallow** (Nor 500) / 5th **M Baines** (Nor 500)

Sunday 16th May **Darley Moor** Darley Motor Motor Cycle Road Race Club

Production (6 laps) - 1st **W Bate** (Nor 650) / 2nd **A Carlton** (Nor 650) / 3rd **A Giles** (BSA 500) / 4th **G Boase** (BSA 650) / 5th **B Nadin** (Tri 650) / 6th **P Welfare** (Nor 600)

Sunday 23rd May **Snetterton** Bemsee The *Norwich Trophy*

Production - 1st **R Watmore** (Tri 650) / 2nd **P Butler** (Tri 650) / 3rd **D Doyle** (Nor 650)

Saturday 29th May **Cadwell Park** The Bantam Racing Club

Production Race 1 - 1st **D Nixon** (Tri 500) / 2nd **D Doyle** (Nor 650) / 3rd **C Hopes** (Tri 650) / 4th **M Rice** (Tri 650) / 5th **M Andrew** (BSA 654) / 6th **R Knight** (Tri 500) **Production Race 2** –1st **D Doyle** (Nor 650) / 2nd **M Rice** (Tri 650) / 3rd **M Andrew** (BSA 654) / 4th **C Lodge** (Tri 650) / 5th **E Webb** (Tri 500) / 6th **R Knight** (Tri 500)

Sunday 30th May **Cadwell Park** British Formula Racing Club

Production 351-1000 Race 1 - 1st **D Nixon** (Tri 500) / 2nd **A Smith** (BSA 654) / 3rd **R Guy** (Tri 500) **Race 2** - 1st **D Nixon** (Tri 500) / 2nd **G Smith** (BSA 650) / 3rd **M Andrew** (BSA 654) **Race 3** - 1st **A Smith** (BSA 654) / 2nd **R Hilgate** (Nor 500) / 3rd **D Nixon** (Tri 500) **Production 350** - 1st **A Rogers** (Ducati 250) / 2nd **Pickett** / 3rd **M Wordsal**l (Yamaha 250)

Saturday 12th June **Silverstone** Bemsee *Trophy Day*

Production (14 laps) - 1st **R Mackay** (Vincent 1000) / 2nd **D Doyle** (Nor 650) / 3rd **R Roberts** (BSA 650) / 4th **B Davidson** (Nor 650) / 5th **E W Webb** (Tri 650)

Sunday 27th June **Brands Hatch** Brands Racing Committee The *Golden Sash* meeting

Production 175-1000 10 lap - 1st **P Butler** (Tri 650) / 2nd **D Nixon** (Tri 490) / 3rd **G Allcock** (Nor 650) / 4th **R Roberts** (BSA 650) / 5th **B Davidson** (Nor 650) / 6th **M Rice** (Tri 650)

Saturday 3rd July **Snetterton** The Bantam Racing Club

Production - 1st **R Knight** (Tri 650) / 2nd **M Rice** (Tri 650) / 3rd **M Andrew** (BSA 654) / 4th **R Lovell** (BSA 650) / 5th **D Doyle** (Nor 650) / 6th **C Hopes** (Tri 650)

Saturday 10th July **Aintree** Waterloo & District Motor Club

Production (6 laps) - 1st **D Vallis** (Nor 650 Nor) / 2nd **K Dickinson** (Nor 650) / 3rd **C Hopes** (Tri 650 Tri) / 4th **A Carlton** (Nor 650) / 5th **C Hutton** (650 Matchless) / 6th **G Mahoney** (BSA 650)

Sunday 11th July **Darley Moor** Darley Moor MCRRC

Production (6 laps) - 1st **B Boase** (BSA 500) / 2nd **A Giles** (BSA 500) / 3rd **M Brogdale** (BSA 500) / 4th **P Welfare** (Nor 650) / 5th **C Foy** (Nor 350) 6th / **T Robbins** (Tri 650)

Sat/Sun10th/11th July **Montjuïc Park** Barcelona *24 Horas de Montjuïc*

Production 24hr Overall - 1st **D Degens/R Butcher** (Triton 650) / 2nd **C Rocamora/J Carné** (Montesa 250) / 3rd **E Boyce/T Phillips** (Velocette 500) / 4th **J Busquets/E Gracia** (Montesa 250) / 5th **J Sirera/E Sirera** (Montesa 250) / 6th **L Yglesias/E Millet** (Ossa 175) **Production over 250cc** -1st **D Degens/R Butcher** (Triton 650) / 2nd **E Boyce/T Phillips** (Velocette 500) / 3rd **W Purnell/D Cooper** (Tri 650) / 4th **R Schick/G Zander** (Honda 350) / 5th **P Menichelli/Caliciotti** (BMW 600)

Sunday 18th July **Cadwell Park** British Formula Racing Club

Production 1000 Race 1 (6 laps) - 1st **M Andrew** (BSA 654) / 2nd **A Smith** (BSA 654) / 3rd **B Booth** (Nor 650) / 4th **R Lovell** (BSA 650) / 5th **G Green** (Tri 500) / 6th **M Baines** (Nor 500) **Race 2** – 1st **A Smith** (BSA 654) / 2nd **M Andrew** (BSA 654) / 3rd **G Smith** (Tri 650) / 4th **R Lovell** (BSA A654) / 5th **G Green** (Tri 500) **Race 3** – 1st **M Andrew** (BSA 654) / 2nd **R Lovell** (BSA 654) / 3rd **A Smith** (BSA 654) / 4th **G Green** (Tri 500) / 5th **G Smith** (Tri 650) / 6th **M Baines** (Nor 500) **Production 350** - 1st **G Simon** (BSA 350) / 2nd **C Curtis** (Honda 250) / 3rd **P Brightman** (BSA 350) / 4th **B Hart** (Yamaha 250) / 5th **A Rogers** (Ducati 250) / 6th **R Gorman** (BSA 350)

Saturday 24th July **Castle Combe** **The 500 Miler**

Production 1000 - 1st **D Degens/B Lawton** (Tri 650) 272 laps / 2nd **A Smith/N Ling** (BSA 654) 262 laps / 3rd **W Purnell/D Cooper** (Tri 650) 254 laps / 4th **P Williams/B Smith** (Matchless 650) 248 laps / 5th **C Lodge/E Webb** (Tri 650) 244 laps / 6th **A Gardiner/M Andrew** (BSA 654) 239 laps Production 500 - 1st **J Dunphy/D Dixon** (Velocette 500) 230 laps / 2nd **C Vance/C Larkin** (Nor 500) 228 laps Production 250 - **D Minter/P Inchley** (Cotton 250) 259 laps / 2nd **J Busequets/C Rocamura** (Montesa 175) 257 laps / 3rd **B Davis/W Scott** (Honda 250) 247 laps / 4th **G Keith/J Rudge** (Royal Enfield 250) 246 laps / 5th **J Carne/E Siera** (Montesa 175) 241 laps / 6th **P Millet/L Yglesias** (Ossa 175) 238 laps

Saturday 31st July **Snetterton** Bemsee

Production Race 1 (6 laps) - 1st **M Rice** (Tri 650) / 2nd **P Butler** (AJS 650) / 3rd **A Smith** (BSA 654) / 4th **C Lodge** (Tri 650) / 5th **N Ling** (Tri 650) / 6th **E Webb** (Tri 650) Race 2 – 1st **P Butler** (Tri 650) / 2nd **A Smith** (BSA 654) / 3rd **N Ling** (Tri 650) / 4th **E Webb** (Tri 650) / 5th **C Lodge** (Tri 650) / 6th **B Booth** (Nor 650)

Saturday 7th August **Perton** Midland Motor Cycle Racing Club

Production Race 1 - 1st **P Davies** (BSA 650) / 2nd **J Dallow** (Nor 650) / 3rd **W Davis** (BSA 650) / 4th **K Matthews** (BSA 650) / 5th **J Macklen** (Tri 650) Race 2 – 1st **P Davies** (BSA 650) / 2nd **W Davis** (BSA 650) / 3rd **P West** (BSA 650) / 4th **J Dallow** (Nor 650) / 5th **A Langton** (BSA 500)

Sunday 8th August **Cadwell Park** Bantam Racing Club

Production Race 1 - 1st **M Rice** (Tri 650) / 2nd **A Smith** (BSA 654) / 3rd **D Nixon** (Tri 500) / 4th **C Lodge** (Tri 650) / 5th **C Hopes** (Tri 650) / 6th **D Doyle** (Nor 650) Race 2 – 1st **A Smith** (BSA 654) / 2nd **M Rice** (Tri 650) / 3rd **D Nixon** (Tri 500) / 4th **R Lovell** (654 BSA) / 5th **C Hopes** (Tri 650) / 6th **C Lodge** (Tri 650)

Saturday 14th August **Silverstone** **Hutchinson 100**

Production 175-1000 (15 laps) - 1st **M Hailwood** (BSA 654) / 2nd **P Read** (Tri 649) / 3rd **P Tait** (Tri 649) / 4th **R Gould** (BSA 654) / 5th **E Driver** (Matchless 747) / 6th **T Phillips** (Velocette 500)

Saturday 21st August **Darley Moor** Darley Moor MCRRC

Production (8 laps) - 1st **K Fulstow** (Nor 600) / 2nd **M Brogdale** (Tri 650) / 3rd **A Carlton** (Nor 650) / 4th **G Boase** (BSA 650) / 5th **B Boase** (BSA 500) / 6th **W Bate** (Nor 600)

Saturday 11th September **Oulton Park** Cheshire Motor Cycle Road Racing Club

Production - 1st **C Hopes** (Tri 650) / 2nd **M Brogdale** (BSA 650) / 3rd **T Jones** (BSA 650) / 4th **D Tucker** (Nor 650) / 5th **B James** (Tri 650) / 6th **A Carlton** (Nor 650)

Sunday 19th September **Snetterton** Bantam Racing Club

Production Race 1 - 1st **C Hopes** (Tri 650) / 2nd **A Smith** (BSA 654) / 3rd **C Lodge** (Tri 650) / 4th **B Wymer** (Nor 600) / 5th **E Webb** (Tri 650) / 6th **M Warrington** (Tri 500) Race 2 – 1st **C Hopes** (Tri 650) / 2nd **A Smith** (BSA 654) / 3rd **M Rice** (Tri 650) / 4th **C Lodge** (Tri 650) / 5th **E Webb** (Tri 650) / 6th **B Wymer** (Nor 600)

Sunday 19th September **Brands Hatch** **The Brands Hatch Shield**

Production (10 lap) - 1st **R Knight** (Tri 650) / 2nd **D Nixon** (Tri 500) / 3rd **R Mackay** (Vincent 1000) / 4th **B Vallis** (Tri 650) / 5th **M Andrew** (BSA 654) / 6th **B Davidson** (Nor 650)

Sunday 19th September **Darley Moor** Darley Moor Motor Cycle Road Race Club

Production (8 laps) -1st **M Brogdale** (BSA 650) / 2nd **K Fulstow** (Nor 650) / 3rd **A Carlton** (Nor 650) / 4th **B Nadin** (Tri 650) / 5th **A Giles** (Velocette 500) / 6th **D Hollinshead** (Tri 500)

Saturday 18th September **Perton** Midland Motor Cycle Racing Club

Production (8 laps) - 1st **R Hole** (BSA 650) / 2nd **W Bate** (Nor 650) / 3rd **M Lunde** (Honda 305) / 4th **P West** (BSA 650) / 5th **J Dallow** (Nor 600) / 6th **J Matthews** (BSA 650)

Saturday 25th September **Silverstone** Bemsee **The Ace of Clubs**

Production - 1st **R Mackay** (Vincent 1000) / 2nd **P Butler** (Tri 650) / 3rd **D Vallis** (Nor 650) / 4th **R Guy** (Tri 500) / 5th **E Webb** (Tri 650) / 6th **D Doyle** (Nor 650)

Sunday 3rd October **Snetterton** Bemsee **The Guinness Trophy**

Production - 1st **D Degens** (Triton 650) / 2nd **P Butler** (Tri 650) / 3rd **D Vallis** (Nor 650) / 4th **B Davidson** (Nor 650) / 5th **A Smith** (BSA 654) / 6th **P Newman** (Nor 650)

Sunday 10th October **Darley Moor** Darley Moor Motor Cycle Road Race Club

Production (8 laps) - 1st **A Carlton** (Tri 650) / 2nd **W Bate** (Nor 600) / 3rd **M Brogdale** (BSA 650) / 4th **B Nadin** (Tri 650) / 5th **M Trapess** (Nor 650) / 6th **B Boase** (BSA 500)

Saturday 16th October   **Snetterton**   Bantam Racing Club

Production Race 1 - 1st **P Butler** (Tri 650) / 2nd **A McGlashen** (Tri 650) / 3rd **M Rice** (Tri 650) / 4th **M Andrew** (BSA 654) / 5th **B Davidson** (Nor 650) / 6th **C Hopes** (Tri 650)   **Race 2** – 1st **A Smith** (BSA 654) / 2nd **A McGlashen** (Tri 650) / 3rd **M Rice** (Tri 650) / 4th **M Andrew** (BSA 654) / 5th **B Davidson** (Nor 650) / 6th **C Lodge** (Tri 650)

Sunday 17th October   **Snetterton**   British Formula Racing Club

Production Race 1 - 1st **P Butler** (Tri 650) / 2nd **R Knight** (Tri 650) / 3rd **D Nixon** (Tri 650) / 4th **B Booth** (Nor 650) / 5th **G Smith** (Tri 650) / 6th **E Webb** (Tri 650) **Race 2** - 1st **P Butler** (Tri 650) / 2nd **R Knight** (Tri 650) / 3rd **B Davidson** (Nor 650) / 4th **A Smith** (BSA 654) / 5th **G Smith** (Tri 650) / 6th **B Booth** (Nor 650)

1966

Saturday 12th March   **Snetterton**   Bantam Racing Club
Production Race 1 (8 laps) - 1st **R Knight** (Tri 650) / 2nd **B Davidson** (Nor 646) / 3rd **J Hedger** (Tri 650) / 4th **A Smith** (BSA 654) / 5th **D Doyle** (998 Vincent) / 6th **E Webb** (Tri 649)

Sunday 27th March   **Darley Moor**   Darley Moor Motor Cycle Road Race Club
Production (8 laps) - 1st **W Bate** (Nor 600) / 2nd **A Carlton** (Nor 650) / 3rd **J Allen** (Tri 650) / 4th **D Williams** (BSA 650)

Saturday 2nd April   **Silverstone**   Bemsee   *Club Day*
Production 175-1000 (10 laps) - 1st **J Hedger** (Tri 650) / 2nd **P Newman** (Nor 650) / 3rd **D Vallis** (Tri 650) / 4th **B Davidson** (Nor 650) / 5th **C Hopes** (Tri 650) / 6th **R Mackay** (Vincent 1000)

Friday 8th April   **Darley Moor**   Darley Moor Motor Cycle Road Race Club
Production (8 laps) - 1st **M Brogdale** (BSA 650) / 2nd **B Bate** (Nor 600) / 3rd **D Williams** (BSA 650) / 4th **J Allen** (Tri 650) / 5th **B Nadin** (Tri 650) / 6th **E Bushell** (Velocette 500)

Saturday 23rd April   **Snetterton**   Bantam Racing Club   *One Hour Enduro*
Production 1 hour - 1st **P Butler** (Tri 650) / 2nd **R Knight** (Tri 650) / 3rd **J Hedger** (Tri 650) / 4th **A Smith** (BSA 654) / 5th **D Nixon** (Tri 650) / 6th **B Davidson** (BSA 650)

Saturday 23rd April   **Oulton Park**   Cheshire Motor Cycle Road Racing Club
Production (7 laps) - 1st **M Brogdale** (BSA 650) / 2nd **R Heath** (BSA 654) / 3rd **D Vallis** (Nor 600) / 4th **J Allen** (Tri 650)

Saturday 30th April   **Cadwell Park**   Midland Motor Cycle Racing Club
Production 250-1000 (8 laps) - 1st **J Hedger** (Tri 650) / 2nd **D Nixon** (Tri 650) / 3rd **W Davies** (BSA 650) / 4th **J Stephenson** (Velocette 500) / 5th **S Williams** (BSA 650) / 6th **J Macklen** (Tri 650)

Sunday 1st May   **Darley Moor**   Darley Moor Motor Cycle Road Race Club
Production (7 laps) - 1st **B Smith** (Honda 450) / 2nd **M Brogdale** (BSA 650) / 3rd **J Allen** (Tri 650) / 4th **R Heath** (BSA 654) / 5th **A Carlton** (Nor 650)

Sunday 8th May   **Snetterton**   British Formula Racing Club
Production 1000 Race 1 (6 laps) - 1st **P Bulter** (Tri 650) / 2nd **A Smith** (BSA 654) / 3rd **C Hopes** (Tri 650) / 4th **G Smith** (Tri 650) / 5th **J Hedger** (Tri 650) / 6th **B Davidson** (Nor 650) **Race 2** - 1st **J Hedger** (Tri 650) / 2nd **P Butler** (Tri 650) / 3rd **M Shoesmith** (Nor 650) / 4th **A Smith** (BSA 654) / 5th **G Smith** (Tri 650) / 6th **M Andrew** (BSA 654) **Production 250 Race 1** - 1st **A Rogers** (Ducati 250) / 2nd **S Woods** (Ducati 250) / 3rd **E Bryant** (Honda 250) / 4th **M Wordsall** (Yamaha) / 5th **D Savory** (Bultaco) / 6th **D Pickett** (Yamaha) **Race 2** - 1st **A Rogers** (Ducati 250) / 2nd **E Bryant** (Honda 250) / 3rd **C Thompsett** (Ducati 250) / 4th **D Pickett** (Yamaha) / 5th **M Wordsall** (Yamaha) / 6th **R Christie** (Tri 200) **Race 3** - 1st **E Bryant** (Honda 250) / 2nd **M Wordsall** (Yamaha 246) / 3rd **R Christie** (Tri 200) / 4th **J Parkin** (TBC) / 5th **S Newman** (Honda 250) / 6th **R Wimpress** (BSA 175)

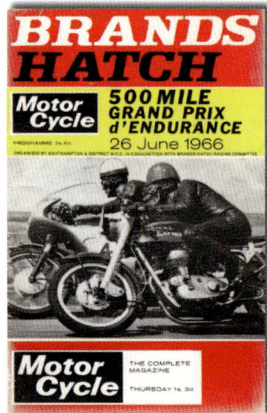

Saturday 14th May   **Cadwell Park**   The Bantam Racing Club
Production Race 1 - 1st **D Nixon** (Tri 650) / 2nd **P Butler** (Tri 650) / 3rd **R Knight** (Tri 650) / 4th **G Green** (Tri 500) / 5th **M Rice** (Tri 650) / 6th **R Guy** (Tri 500) **Race 2** - 1st **P Butler** (Tri 650) / 2nd **D Nixon** (Tri 650) / 3rd **R Knight** (Tri 650) / 4th **G Green** (Tri 500) / 5th **M Rice** (Tri 650) / 6th **R Guy** (Tri 500)

Sunday 15th May   **Crimond**   Bon-Accord Motorcycle Club
Production - 1st **W Dey** (Honda 450) / 2nd **J Moncrieff** (BSA 650) / 3rd **B Mercer** (BSA 650) / 4th **G Dowie** (Enfield 500)

Saturday 21st May   **Perton**   Midland Motor Cycle Racing Club
Production Race 1 - 1st **D Nixon** (Tri 650) / 2nd **J Hedger** (Tri 650) / 3rd **W Bate** (Nor 600) / 4th **P Davies** (BSA 650) / 5th **P West** (BSA 650) / 6th **J Macklen** (Tri 650) **Race 2** - 1st **J Hedger** (Tri 650) / 2nd **D Nixon** (Tri 650) / 3rd **W Bate** (Nor 600) / 4th **P Davies** (BSA 650) / 5th **K Matthews** (BSA 650) / 6th **P West** (BSA 650)

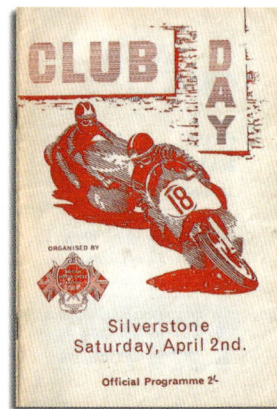

Saturday 4th June   **Imola**   6 Hours of Imola   Coupe d'Endurance
General Classification - 1st **Cere/Giovenardi** (Ducati 250) / 2nd **Polenghi/Orsenigo** (Ducati 250) / 3rd **Bertarelli/Mognoni** (Morini 175) / 4th **Rocamura/Carne** (Bultaco 250) / 5th **Farne/Garagnani** (Ducati 350) / 6th **Collis/Chatterton** (Nor 750) / 7th **Burlando/Casagrande** (Morini 175) / 8th **Smith/Butler** (BSA 654) / 9th **(TBC)** / 10th **Buckmaster/Jackson** (Tri 650)

Saturday 4th June   **Cadwell Park**   Midland Motor Cycle Racing Club
Production 250-1000 (8 laps) - 1st **D Nixon** (Tri 650) / 2nd **P Davies** (BSA 650) / 3rd **D Williams** (BSA 650) / 4th **T Haslam** (Nor 750)

Sunday 5th June   **Cadwell Park**   British Formula Racing Club
Production 350-1000 Race 1 - 1st **J Hedger** (Tri 650) / 2nd **C Hopes** (Tri 650) / 3rd **R Bowler** (Nor 500) / 4th **E Smith** (Tri 650) / 5th **K Moyes** (BSA 650) / 6th **B Booth** (Nor 650) **Race 2** - 1st **J Hedger** (Tri 650) / 2nd **C Hopes** (Tri 650) / 3rd **M Shoesmith** (Nor 650) / 4th **B Booth** (Nor 650) / 5th **R Bowler** (Nor 500) / 6th **E Smith** (Tri 650) **Race 3** - 1st **J Hedger** (Tri 650) / 2nd **M Andrew** (Tri 500) / 3rd **B Booth** (Nor 650) / 4th **K Moyes** (BSA 654) / 5th **H Aldous** (TBC) / 6th **M Wordsall** (Yamaha 250)

Saturday 11th June   **Silverstone**   Bemsee   *Trophy Day*
Production 1000 - 1st **R Knight** (Tri 650) / 2nd **B Davis** (Tri 650) / 3rd **M Andew** (BSA 654) / 4th **D Doyle** (Nor 500) / 5th **K Buckmaster** (Tri 650) / 6th **C Wall** (BSA 500)

Sunday 26th June   **Darley Moor**   Darley Moor Motor Cycle Road Race Club
Production 6 lap - 1st **W Bate** (Nor 650) / 2nd **M Brogdale** (BSA 650) / 3rd **D Williams** (BSA 650) / 4th **J Allen** (Tri 650) / 5th **A Carlton** (Nor 650) / 6th **B Boase** (BSA 500)

Sunday 26th June   **Brands Hatch**   Southampton & District Motorcycle Club   *Brands 500 Marathon*
Production 1000 - 1st **D Degens/R Butcher** (Tri 650) 189 laps / 2nd **P Tait/P Read** (Tri 650) 189 laps / 3rd **G Jenkins/D Dixon** (Norton 750) 184 laps / 4th **D Chapman/R Avery** (Tri 650) 184 laps / 5th **J Dunphy/R Pickrell** (Tri 650) 184 laps / 6th **C Burton/M Rice** (BSA 654) 179 laps. **Production 500** - 1st **T Phillips/D Croxford** (Velocette 500) 181 laps / 2nd **R Knight/M Love** (Tri 500) 171 laps / 3rd **I Duffel/W Bowsher** (Nor 500) 160 laps / 4th **B Bennett/J Oliver** (Tri 500) 160 laps / 5th **R Guy/G Green** (Tri 500) 158 laps / 6th **J Stephenson/E Bushell** (Velo 500) 156 laps. **Production 250** - 1st **R Everett/P Inchley** (Cotton 250) 180 laps / 2nd **T Robb/C Vincent** (Suzuki 250) 179 laps / 3rd **C Mora/J Carne** (Bultaco) 173 laps / 4th **O Regas/R Marsans** (Montesa) 172 laps / 5th **D Simmonds/C Mates** (Royal Enfield 250) 172 laps / 6th **W Smith/S Adams** (Honda 250) 165 laps

Saturday 2nd July   **Snetterton**   The Bantam Racing Club
Production Race 1 - 1st **P Butler** (Tri 650) / 2nd **D Nixon** (Tri 650) / 3rd **D Doyle** (Nor 750) / 4th **C Hopes** (Tri 650) / 5th **E Webb** (Tri 650) / 6th **C Lodge** (Tri 650) **Race 2** - 1st **P Butler** (Tri 650) / 2nd **D Nixon** (Tri 650) / 3rd **D Doyle** (Nor 750) / 4th **E Webb** (Tri 650) / 5th **A Smith** (BSA 654) / 6th **C Lodge** (Tri 650)

Saturday 9th July   **Cadwell Park**   Lincoln & District Motor Cycle & Light Car Club
Production 500-1000 - 1st **C Hopes** (Tri 650) / 2nd **T Jones** (BSA 500) **Production 175-350** - 1st **E Bryant** (Honda 250) / 2nd **D Curtis** (BSA)

Sat/Sun 9th/10th July   **Montjuïc Park**   Barcelona 24hr
Production 24hr - 1st **Busquets/Villa** (Montesa 250) 646 laps / 2nd **Sirere/Sirera** (Montesa 250) 637 Laps / 3rd **Phillips/Croxford** (Velocette 500) 624 laps / 4th **Degens/Butcher** (Tri 650) 616 laps / 5th **Yglesias/Petrus** (Ossa 250) 608 laps / 6th **Lawton/Carr** (Tri 650) 607 laps / 7th **Botella/Castellanos** (Montesa 250) 585 laps / 8th **Menichelli/Trabalzini** (BMW 600) 584 laps / 9th **Other British Riders** - 14th **Smith/Butler** (BSA 654) 552 laps / 15th **Evans/Lodge** (BSA 654) 541 laps / 18th **Guy/Aim** (Tri 500) 527 laps / 20th **Buckmaster/Jackson** (Tri 650) 511 laps / 24th **Fulton/J Evans** (Velocette 500) 495 laps

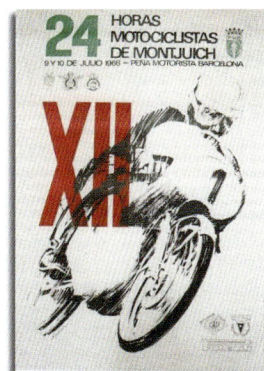

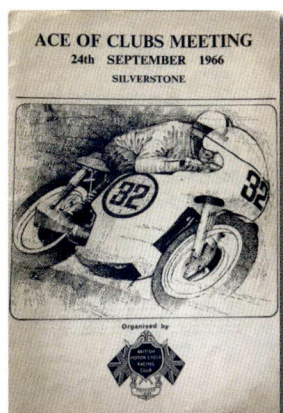

Sunday 24th July   **Snetterton**   Bemsee
Production - 1st **P Butler** (Tri 650) / 2nd **M Andrew** (Tri 650) / 3rd **R Knight** (Tri 650) / 4th **J Hedger** (Tri 650) / 5th **C Hopes** (Tri 650) / 6th **R Mackay** (Tri 650)

Saturday 30th July   **Cadwell Park**   Bantam Racing Club
Production Race 1 - 1st **C Hopes** (Tri 650) / 2nd **J Hedger** (Tri 650) / 3rd **P Butler** (Tri 650) / 4th **A Carlton** (Nor 650) / 5th **E Webb** (Tri 650) / 6th **D Nixon** (Tri 650) **Race 2** - 1st **P Butler** (Tri 650) / 2nd **J Hedger** (Tri 650) / 3rd **C Hopes** (Tri 650) / 4th **E Webb** (Tri 650) / 5th **G Green** (Tri 500) / 6th **C Lodge** (Tri 650)

Sunday 31st July   **Darley Moor**   Darley Moor Motor Cycle Road Race Club
Production (7 laps) - 1st **D Williams** (BSA 650) / 2nd **B Smith** (Honda 450) / 3rd **R Heath** (BSA 654) / 4th **J Allen** (Tri 650) / 5th **B Bate** (Nor 600) / 6th **A Carlton** (Nor 650)

Sunday 31st July   **Crimond**   Bon Accord Motorcycle Club
Production - 1st **W Dey** (Honda 450) / 2nd **D Davidson** (Nor 650) / 3rd **M Fraswer** (Nor 650) / 4th **D Wright** (BSA 650) / 5th **F Troup** (Nor 600)

Saturday 6th August **Perton** Midland Motor Cycle Racing Club
Production Race 1 - 1st **J Hedger** (Tri 650) / 2nd **D Nixon** (Tri 650) / 3rd **W Bate** (Nor 600) / 4th **K Jordan** (Nor 500) / 5th **R Tuner** (Honda 450) / 6th **I Jukes** (Tri 500) **Race 2** - 1st **J Hedger** (Tri 650) / 2nd **D Nixon** (Tri 650) / 3rd **W Bate** (Nor 600) / 4th **C Wilkinson** (Nor 500) / 5th **K Jordan** (Nor 500) / 6th **I Jukes** (Tri 500)

Sunday 14th August **Brands Hatch** *Hutchinson 100*
Production - 1st **J Cooper** (BSA 654) / 2nd **P Tait** (Tri 650) / 3rd **M Andrew** (Tri 650) / 4th **R Gould** (BSA 654) / 5th **P Butler** (Tri 650) / 6th **P Carrana** (Tri 650) / 7th **J Hedger** (Tri 650) / 8th **D Nixon** (Tri 650) **500 Class** - 1st **T Phillips** (Velo 500) **250 Class** - 1st **D Browning** (Cotton 250)

Sunday 28th August **Darley Moor** Darley Moor Motor Cycle Road Race Club
Production - 1st **R Heath** (BSA 654) / 2nd **W Bate** (Nor 600) / 3rd **A Carlton** (Nor 650) / 4th **B Boase** (BSA 500)

Monday 29th August **Cadwell Park** Louth & District *Conqueror of Cadwell*
Production 175-1000 (8 laps) - 1st **R Gould** (BSA 654) / 2nd **S Spencer** (Tri 650) / 3rd **J Hedger** (Tri 650) / 4th **A Smith** (BSA 654) / 5th **C Hopes** (Tri 650) / 6th **D Vickers** (Tri 650)

Saturday 3rd September **Cadwell Park** British Formula Racing Club
Production Race 1 - 1st **J Hedger** (Tri 650) / 2nd **C Lodge** (Tri 650) / 3rd **C Hopes** (Tri 650) / 4th **J Kanka** (Tri 650) / 5th **P Hitchcox** (BSA 650) / 6th **R Ridley** (Tri 500) **Race 2** - 1st **J Hedger** (Tri 650) / 2nd **C Hopes** (Tri 650) / 3rd **E Webb** (Tri 650) / 4th **H Robinson** (BSA 650) / 5th **C Lodge** (Tri 650) / 6th **R Roley** (Tri 500) **Race 3** - 1st **J Hedger** (Tri 650) / 2nd **E Webb** (Tri 650) / 3rd **C Lodge** (Tri 650) / 4th **P Hitchcox** (BSA 650) / 5th **D Magill** (Aermacchi 250) / 6th **J McCollum** (Honda 305)

Sunday 4th September **Cadwell Park** Midland Motor Cycle Racing Club
Production (8 laps) - 1st **J Hedger** (Tri 650) / 2nd **D Nixon** (Tri 650) / 3rd **C Hopes** (Tri 650) / 4th **T Haslam** (Nor 750) / 5th **D Jones** (Tri 650)

Sunday 18th September **Snetterton** The Bantam Racing Club
Production Race 1 - 1st **D Nixon** (Tri 650) / 2nd **M Andrew** (Tri 650) / 3rd **P Butler** (Tri 650) / 4th **J Hedger** (Tri 650) / 5th **C Wall** (BSA 654) / 6th **C Lodge** (Tri 650) **Race 2** - 1st **D Nixon** (Tri 650) / 2nd **P Butler** (Tri 650) / 3rd **M Andrew** (Tri 650) / 4th **J Hedger** (Tri 650) / 5th **E Webb** (Tri 650) / 6th **C Lodge** (Tri 650)

Saturday 24th September **Perton** Midland Motor Cycle Racing Club
Production Race 1 - 1st **D Nixon** (Tri 650) / 2nd **C Hopes** (Tri 650) / 3rd **R Heath** (BSA 654) / 4th **P Jones** (Tri 650) / 5th **R Tuner** (Honda 450) / 6th **I Jukes** (Tri 650) **Race 2** - **D Nixon** (Tri 650) / 2nd **C Hopes** (Tri 650) / 3rd **P West** (Tri 500) / 4th **T Haslam** (Nor 750)

Saturday 24th September **Silverstone** Bemsee
Production (14 laps) - 1st **J Hedger** (Tri 650) / 2nd **P Butler** (Tri 650) / 3rd **A Smith** (BSA 654) / 4th **C Wall** (BSA 654) / 5th **H Robinson** (Tri 650) / 6th **K Buckmaster** (Tri 650)

Saturday 1st October **Cadwell Park** British Formula Racing Club
Production 1000 Race 1 - 1st **C Hopes** (Tri 650) / 2nd **C Lodge** (Tri 650) / 3rd **E Webb** (Tri 650) / 4th **H Robinson** (Tri 650) / 5th **P Hitchcox** (Tri 650) / 6th **H Evans** (BSA 500) **Race 2** - 1st **C Hopes** (Tri 650) / 2nd **A Smith** (BSA 654) / 3rd **J Hedger** (Tri 650) / 4th **E Webb** (Tri 650) / 5th **C Lodge** (Tri 650) / 6th **P Hitchcox** (Tri 650) **Race 3** - 1st **C Hopes** (Tri 650) / 2nd **A Smith** (BSA 654) / 3rd **J Hedger** (Tri 650) / 4th **H Evans** (BSA 500) / 5th **C Lodge** (Tri 650) / 6th **E Webb** (Tri 650)

Saturday 1st October **Llandow** Cardiff Eagles Motor Cycle & Car Club
Production - 1st **G Mahoney** (BSA 650) / 2nd **P Fisher** (Tri 650) / 3rd **J Allen** (AJS 650)

Sunday 2nd October **Snetterton** Bemsee *Guinness Trophy*
Production 1000 - 1st **J Hedger** (Tri 650) / 2nd **D Nixon** (Tri 650) / 3rd **R Knight** (Tri 650) / 4th **B Davis** (Tri 650) / 5th **C Hopes** (Tri 650) / 6th **P Bailey** (Nor 600)

Saturday 15th October **Snetterton** The Bantam Racing Club
Production Race 1 - 1st **A Smith** (BSA 654) / 2nd **P Butler** (Tri 650) / 3rd **D Nixon** (Tri 650) / 4th **E Webb** (Tri 650) / 5th **M Rice** (Tri 650) / 6th **R Knight** (Tri 650) **Race 2** - 1st **A Smith** (BSA 654) / 2nd **D Nixon** (Tri 650) / 3rd **J Hedger** (Tri 650) / 4th **R Knight** (Tri 650) / 5th **E Webb** (Tri 650) / 6th **M Rice** (Tri 650)

Saturday 22nd October **Silverstone** Bemsee
Production - 1st **J Hedger** (Tri 650) / 2nd **P Butler** (Tri 650) / 3rd **A Smith** (BSA 654) / 4th **C Wall** (BSA 654) / 5th **H Robinson** (Tri 650) / 6th **K Buckmaster** (Tri 650)

Sunday 30th October **Snetterton** Bemsee *Autumn Road Races*
Production Race 1 - 1st **A Smith** (BSA 654) / 2nd **P Butler** (Tri 650) / 3rd **D Nixon** (Tri 650) / 4th **C Hopes** (Tri 650) / 5th **W Penny** (Honda 450) / 6th **K Buckmaster** (Tri 650) **Race 2** - 1st **A Smith** (BSA 654) / 2nd **P Butler** (Tri 650) / 3rd **C Hopes** (Tri 650) / 4th **W Penny** (Honda 450) / 5th **K Buckmaster** (Tri 650) / 6th **R Maskell** (BSA 650)

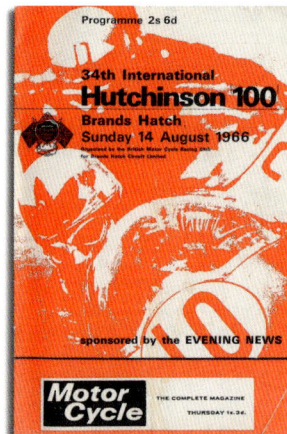

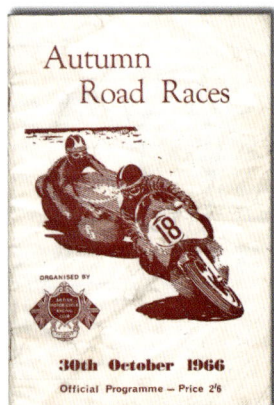

Saturday 18th March   **Snetterton**   The Bantam Racing Club

Production Race 1 - 1st **A Smith** (BSA 654) **/** 2nd **P Butler** (Tri 650) **/** 3rd **J Hedger** (Tri 650) **/** 4th **M Andrew** (Tri 650) **/** 5th **D Nixon** (Tri 500) **/** 6th **M Rice** (BSA 654) **Race 2 -** 1st **A Smith** (BSA 654) **/** 2nd **J Hedger** (Tri 650) **/** 3rd **P Butler** (Tri 650) **/** 4th **M Andrew** (Tri 650) **/** 5th **D Nixon** (Tri 500) **/** 6th **H Robinson** (Tri 650)

Sunday 19th March   **Snetterton**   British Formula Racing Club

Production Race 1 - 1st **A Smith** (BSA 654) **/** 2nd **C Hopes** (Tri 650) **/** 3rd **H Robinson** (Tri 650) **/** 4th **G P Smith** (Tri 650) **/** 5th **C Wall** (BSA 654) **/** 6th **R Ridley** (Tri 650) **Race 2 -** 1st **A Smith** (BSA 654) **/** 2nd **C Hopes** (Tri 650) **/** 3rd **M Rice** (BSA 654) **/** 4th **C Wall** (BSA 654) **/** 5th **R Ridley** (Tri 650) **/** 6th **H Robinson** (Tri 650) **Race 3 -** 1st **M Rice** (BSA 654) **/** 2nd **C Wall** (BSA 654) **/** 3rd **G Smith** (Tri 650) **/** 4th **R Ridley** (Tri 650) **/** 5th **R Innes** (Montesa 250)

Monday 27th March   **Snetterton**   ***Easter Trophy***

Production 1000 - 1st **J Hedger** (Tri 650) **/** 2nd **C Hopes** (Tri 650) **/** 3rd **P Butler** (Tri 650) **/** 4th **D Nixon** (Tri 650) **/** 5th **H Robinson** (Tri 650) **/** 6th **K Buckmaster** (Tri 650)

Monday 27th March   **Kirkistown**

Production Handicap - 1st **B Steenson** (Nor 650) **/** 2nd **C Agnew** (Nor 600) **/** 3rd **R Gray** (Nor 650) **/** 4th **S Davis** (Tri 500)

Saturday 1st April   **Cadwell Park**   Midland Motor Cycle Racing Club

Production Race 1 (4 laps)- 1st **C Hopes** (Tri 650) **/** 2nd **J Hedger** (Tri 650) **/** 3rd **P Davies** (Tri 650) **/** 4th **D Jones** (Tri 650) **/** 5th **J Wilson** (Tri 650) **/** 6th **R Heath** (BSA 654) **Race 2 -** 1st **J Hedger** (Tri 650) **/** 2nd **C Hopes** (Tri 650) **/** 3rd **R Heath** (BSA 654) **/** 4th **T Haslam** (Nor 650) **/** 5th **D Jones** (Tri 650)

Sunday 2nd April   **Darley Moor**   Darley Moor Motor Cycle Road Race Club

Production (6 laps) - 1st **R Heath** (BSA 654) **/** 2nd **D Jones** (Tri 650) **/** 3rd **A Carlton** (Nor 650) **/** 4th **G Mahoney** (BSA 650) **/** 5th **D Vickers** (BSA 654) **/** 6th **R Turner** (Honda 350)

Saturday 8th April   **Llandow**   Cardiff Eagles Motor Cycle & Car Club

Production Race 1 (10 laps) - 1st **D Jones** (Tri 650) **/** 2nd **G Mahoney** (BSA 650) **/** 3rd **A Rogers** (Ducati 250) **/** 4th **J Allen** (AJS 650) **Race 2 (5 laps)-** 1st **J Allen** (AJS 650) **/** 2nd **A Rogers** (Ducati 250) **/** 3rd **A Foster** (BSA 650) **/** 4th **C Bishop** (Tri 650) **/** 5th **J Davis** (BSA 650) **/** 6th **D Rogers** (Ducati 250)

Saturday 15th April   **Snetterton**   Newmarket Club

Production Race 1 - 1st **P Butler** (Tri 650) **/** 2nd **J Hedger** (Tri 650) **/** 3rd **C Wall** (BSA 654) **Race 2 -** 1st **P Butler** (Tri 650) **/** 2nd **D Nixon** (Tri 650) **/** 3rd **K Buckmaster** (Tri 650)

Sunday 16th April   **Snetterton**   Midland Motor Cycle Racing Club

Production 250-1000 - 1st **C Hopes** (Tri 650) **/** 2nd **P Butler** (Tri 650) **/** 3rd **D Nixon** (Tri 650) **/** 4th **R Heath** (BSA 654) **/** 4th **M Clarke** (Tri 650) **/** 5th **T Haslam** (Nor 750)

Saturday 22nd April   **Snetterton**   The Bantam Racing Club

Production Race 1 - 1st **G Bailey** (Tri 650) **/** 2nd **H Robinson** (Tri 650) **/** 3rd **C Wall** (BSA 654) **/** 4th **E Webb** (Tri 650) **/** 5th **B M Smith** (BSA 650) **/** 6th **M Clarke** (Tri 650) **Race 2 -** 1st **C Wall** (BSA 654) **/** 2nd **G Bailey** (Tri 650) **/** 3rd **H Robinson** (Tri 650) **/** 4th **B Smith** (BSA 650) **/** 5th **M Clarke** (Tri 650) **/** 6th **G Carter** (Tri 650)

Saturday 22nd April   **Cadwell Park**   British Formula Racing Club

Production Race 1 - 1st **D Vickers** (BSA 654) **/** 2nd **T Haslam** (Nor 750) **/** 3rd **H Robertson** (Tri 500) **/** 4th **D Spruce** (Suzuki 250) **/** 5th **S Billingham** (Tri 650) **/** 6th **E Bryant** (Honda 250) **Race 2 -** 1st **D Vickers** (BSA 654) **/** 2nd **T Haslam** (Nor 750) **/** 3rd **S Billingham** (Tri 650) **/** 4th **H Robertson** (Tri 500) **/** 5th **P Russell** (Aermacchi 250) **/** 6th **M Snell** (Aermacchi 250) **Race 3 -** 1st **D Vickers** (BSA 654) **/** 2nd **T Haslam** (Nor 750) **/** 3rd **S Billingham** (Tri 650) **/** 4th **H Robertson** (Tri 500) **/** 5th **E Bryant** (Honda 250) **/** 6th **C Wilkinson** (Nor 500)

Sunday 23rd April   **Brands Hatch**   Brands Grand Prix d'Endurance   ***500 Miler***

Production 750 - 1st **P Tait/R Gould** (Tri 650) 189 laps **/** 2nd **J Dunphy/R Pickrell** (Tri 650) 188 laps **/** 3rd **R Knight/M Andrew** (Tri 650) 171 laps **/** 4th **A Baker/D Dixon** (Tri 650) **/** 5th **B Davidson/C Vance** (Nor 650) 166 laps **/** 6th **C Horton/A Sutton** (Tri 650) **Production 500 -** 1st **G Penny/T Dunnell** (Honda 350) 173 laps **/** 2nd **J Strijbis/R Harrington** (Tri 500) 168 laps **/** 3rd **B Bennett/G Barnacle** (Tri 500) 165 laps **/** 4th **T Phillips/R Everett** (Velo 500) 164 laps **/** 5th **R May/M Love** (Tri 500) 159 laps **/** 6th **G Green/R Guy** (Tri 500) 158 laps **Production 250 -** 1st **C Vincent/K Cass** (Suzuki 250) 176 laps **/** 2nd **C Thompsett/R Baylie** (Ducati 250) 171

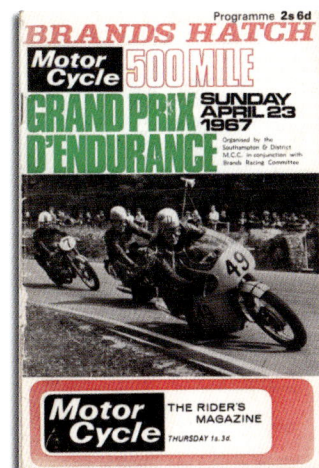

laps / 3rd **K Watson/C Sanby** (Ducati 250) 170 laps / 4th **M Chatterton/C Ward** (Yamaha 250) 167 laps / 5th **H Crowder/T Burgess** (Suzuki 250) 165 laps / 6th **C Mortimer/J Blanchard** (Royal Enfield 250) 162 laps

Sunday 30th April   **Snetterton**   British Formula Racing Club
Production 125-1000 Race 1 - 1st **H Robinson** (Tri 650) / 2nd **H Robertson** (Tri 500) / 3rd **T Kingham** (Vincent 1000) / 4th **M Moyne** (Honda 350) / 5th **R Ridley** (Tri 650) / 6th **E Bryant** (Honda 250) **Race 2** - 1st **H Robinson** (Tri 650) / 2nd **T Kingham** (Vincent 1000) / 3rd **H Robertson** (Tri 500) / 4th **M Moyne** (Honda 350) / 5th **R Ridley** (Tri 650) / 6th **P Kilner** (Ducati 250) **Race 3** - 1st **H Robinson** (Tri 650) / 2nd **H Robertson** (Tri 500) / 3rd **P Kilner** (Ducati 250) / 4th **T Ryan** (Nor 600)

Saturday 6th May   **Aintree**   Waterloo & District
Production (7 laps) - 1st **P Butler** (Tri 650) / 2nd **C Hopes** (Tri 650) / 3rd **A Carlton** (Nor 650) / 4th **K Dixon** (Nor 650) / 5th **J Allen** (Tri 650) / 6th **P Molloy** (Royal Enfield 700)

Sunday 21st May   **Snetterton**   Bemsee
Production (7 laps) - 1st **J Hedger** (Tri 650) / 2nd **P Butler** (Tri 650) / 3rd **R Knight** (Tri 650)

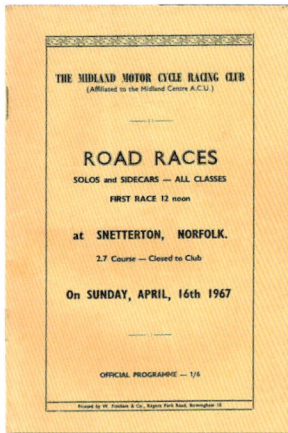

Sunday 21st May   **Cadwell Park**   British Formula Racing Club
Production Race 1 - 1st **P Davies** (Tri 650) / 2nd **D Vickers** (BSA 654) / 3rd **C Lodge** (Tri 650) / 4th **P Kilner** (Ducati 250) / 5th **S Billingham** (Tri 650) / 6th **I Hesketh** (BSA 654) **Race 2** - 1st **C Lodge** (Tri 650) / 2nd **P Davies** (Tri 650) / 3rd **D Vickers** (BSA 654) / 4th **H Robertson** (Tri 500) / 5th **P Kilner** (Ducati 250) / 6th **S Billingham** (Tri 650) **Race 3** - 1st **C Lodge** (Tri 650) / 2nd **D Vickers** (BSA 654) / 3rd **R Ridley** (Tri 650) / 4th **J White** (DMW 250) / 5th **P Kilner** (Ducati 250) / 6th **A Clatworthy** (Tri 500)

Saturday 27th May   **Cadwell Park**   The Bantam Racing Club
Production Race 1 - 1st **J Hedger** (Tri 650) / 2nd **P Butler** (Tri 650) / 3rd **H Robinson** (Tri 650) / 4th **P Davis** (Tri 650) / 5th **C Lodge** (Tri 650) / 6th **B James** (Tri 650) **Race 2** - 1st **J Hedger** (Tri 650) / 2nd **P Butler** (Tri 650) / 3rd **P Davies** (Tri 650) / 4th **C Hopes** (Tri 650) / 5th **H Robinson** (Tri 650) / 6th **G Green** (Tri 500)

Sunday 28th May   **Snetterton**   Midland Motor Cycle Racing Club
Production - 1st **C Hopes** (Tri 650) / 2nd **P Butler** (Tri 650) / 3rd **H Robinson** (Tri 650)

Saturday 3rd June   **Brands Hatch**   Bemsee   Trophy Day
Production - 1st **J Hedger** (Tri 650) / 2nd **P Davies** (Tri 650) / 3rd **C Hopes** (Tri 650) / 4th **K Buckmaster** (Tri 650) / 5th **H Robinson** (Tri 650) / 6th **C Wall** (BSA 654)

Saturday 3rd June   **Kirkistown**   Belfast & District Motor Club
Production Handicap - 1st **D Wood** (Honda 250) / 2nd **J McCartney** (Honda 125) / 3rd **B Steenson** (Nor 650) / 4th **A Alexander** (Nor 650) / 5th **S Davis** (BSA 650) / 6th **C Coulter** (Tri 350)

Sunday 4th June   **Darley Moor**   Darley Moor Motor Cycle Road Race Club
Production (6 laps) - 1st **B Bate** (Tri 650) / 2nd **D Vickers** (BSA 654) / 3rd **A Carlton** (Nor 650) / 4th **D Jones** (Tri 650) / 5th **P Hagan** (Tri 650) / 6th **J Woolley** (Nor 650)

Saturday 10th June   **Isle of Man**   The **1st Production TT**
Production 750 (3 lap) - 1st **J Hartle** (Tri 650) 1hr 09min 56.8sec - 97.1mph / 2nd **P Smart** (Dunstall/Nor) 1hr 11min 48 sec - 94.6mph / 3rd **A Smith** (BSA 654) 1hr 15min 42sec - 89.73mph / 4th **L Weil** (Tri 650) 1hr 15min 45.8 sec - 89.66mph / 5th **P Butler** (Tri 650) 1hr 16min 28sec - 88.83mph / 6th **T Godfrey** (Nor 750) 1hr 17min 22sec - 87.79mph / 7th **G Bailey** (Tri 650)1hr 20min 11.8sec - 84.7mph / 8th **M Rice** (BSA 654) 1hr 23min 55.8sec - 80.93mph / 9th **T McGurk** (Tri 650) 1hr 24min 16.6sec - 80.6mph / 10th **J Strijbis** (Tri 650) 1hr 24min 22.2sec - 80.51mph **Production 500 (3 lap)** - 1st **N Kelly** (Velocette 500)1hr 15min 33.8sec - 89.89mph / 2nd **K Heckles** (Velocette 500) 1hr 16min 11.6sec- 89.15mph / 3rd **D Nixon** (Tri 500) 1hr 19min 48sec - 85.11mph / 4th **G Penny** (Honda 450) 1hr 20min 26sec - 84.45mph / 5th **N Hanks** (BSA 500) 1hr 22min 56.2sec - 81.9mph / 6th **A Peck** (Tri 500) 1hr 22min 56.2sec - 81.9mph / 7th **T Dunnell** (Honda 305) 1hr 23min 40.2sec - 81.18mph / 8th **R Baylie** (Tri 500) 1hr 23min 42.4sec - 81.15mph / 9th **D Doyle** (Nor 500) 1hr 23min 46sec - 81.08mph / 10th **B Biscardine** (Velocette 500) 1hr 25min11.2sec - 79.74mph **Production 250 3 lap** - 1st **W Smith** (Bultaco 250) 1hr 16min 38.2sec- 88.63mph / 2nd **T Robb** (Bultaco 250) 1hr 16min 38.6sec - 88.62mph /3rd **B Smith** (Suzuki 250) 1hr 18min 43.2sec - 86.29mph /4th **F Whiteway** (Suzuki 250)1hr 19min 08.6sec - 85.82mph /5th **K Carruthers** (Suzuki 250) 1hr 19min 53.4sec - 85.03mph / 6th **K Cass** (Bultaco 250)1hr 22min 36.8sec - 82.22mph / 7th **D Simmonds** (Kawasaki 250) 1hr 23min 43.6sec - 81.13mph / 8th **C Vincent** (Suzuki 250) 1hr 24min14.6sec - 80.63mph / 9th **E Crooks** (Suzuki 250) 1hr 25min 00.2sec - 79.91mph / 10th **C Thompsett** (Ducati 250) 1hr 26.min1.6sec - 78.96mph

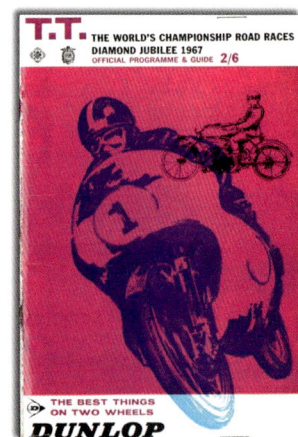

Sunday 11th June   **Cadwell Park**   British Formula Racing Club
Production 125-1000 Race 1 - 1st **P Davies** (Tri 650) / 2nd **H Robinson** (Tri 650) / 3rd **T Smith** (Nor 650) / 4th **E Booth** (Tri 650) / 5th **H Robertson** (Ti 500) / 6th **P Hagan** (Tri 650) **Race 2** - 1st **H Robinson** (Tri 650) / 2nd **D Vickers** (BSA 654) / 3rd **E Booth** (Tri 650) / 4th **D Spruce** (Suzuki 250) / 5th **C O'Callaghan** (Tri 650) / 6th **T Smith** (Nor 650) **Race 3** - 1st **P Davies** (Tri 650) / 2nd **H Robinson** (Tri 650) / 3rd **T Haslam** (Nor 750) / 4th **T Smith** (Nor 650) / 5th **H Robertson** (Tri 500) / 6th **O'Callaghan** (Tri 650)

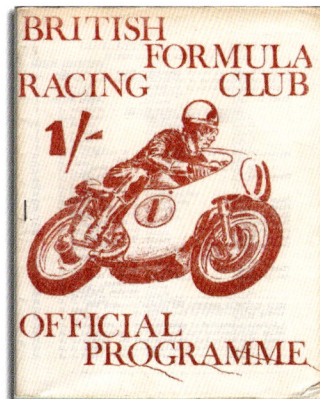

Saturday 17th June   **Brands Hatch**   Bemsee
Production - 1st **J Hedger** (Tri 650) / 2nd **P Butler** (Tri 650) / 3rd **D Nixon** (Tri 500) / 4th **P Davies** (Tri 650) / 5th **C Wall** (BSA 654) / 6th **H Robinson** (Tri 650)

Saturday 1st July   **Cadwell Park**   Midland Motor Cycle Racing Club
Production 225 - 1000 (10 laps) - 1st **J Hedger** (Tri 650) / 2nd **P Davies** (Tri 650) / 3rd **C Hopes** (Tri 650) / 4th **R Hole** (Tri 650) / 5th **D Jones** (Tri 650) / 6th **M Orange** (Tri 650)

July 8th 9th   **Barcelona**   24 Horas de Montjuïc
General Classification - 1st **Luis Yglesias/Carlos Giró** (Ossa 230) 663 laps / 2nd **Dixon/Andrew** (Tri 500) 628 laps / 3rd **Pedro Millet/José Maria Palomo** (Ossa 250) 621 laps / 4th **S Trias/R Blanch** (Montesa 250) 600 laps / 5th **José Luis Aguilar/Jacques Roca** (Ducati 250) 591 laps / 6th **B Smith/C Goosens** (Suzuki 250) 591 laps / 7th **D Tucker/C Hornby** (Norton) 582 laps / 8th **R Guy/G Green** (Tri 500) 569 laps / 9th **S Yago/J M Torres** (Montesa 250) 569 laps / 10th **K Buckmaster/A Kinsella** (Tri 650) 562 laps / 11th **F Meyer/H Lautrich** (Montesa 175) 556 laps / 12th **C Lodge/C Hopes** (BSA 650) 550 laps / 13th **B Fulton/J Evans** (Norton 650) 537 laps / 14th **G Barnacle/J Oliver** (Tri 500) 532 laps / 15th **P Hogervorst/T Lablans** (Suzuki 250) 529 laps / 16th **P Butler/ D Nixon** (Tri 500) 526 laps (4th placed **S. Trias/R. Blanch** later disqualified)

Saturday 8th July   **Aintree**   Waterloo & District Motor Club
Production (7 laps) - 1st **A Carlton** (Nor 650) / 2nd **J Allen** (Tri 650) / 3rd **K Dixon** (Nor 650) / 4th **G Leigh** (Honda 250) / 5th **N Overend** (Nor 650) / 6th **A Ralspon** (Nor 750)

Saturday 8th July   **Snetterton**   Bantam Racing Club
Production Race 1 - 1st **A Smith** (BSA 654) / 2nd **J Hedger** (Tri 650) / 3rd **H Robinson** (Tri 650) / 4th **P Davies** (Tri 650) / 5th **G Bailey** (Tri 650) / 6th **J Kanka** (Tri 650) **Race 2** - 1st **J Hedger** (Tri 650) / 2nd **A Smith** (BSA 654) / 3rd **P Davies** (Tri 650) / 4th **H Robinson** (Tri 650) / 5th **C Agate** (Tri 650) / 6th **G Bailey** (Tri 650)

Sunday 9th July   **Llandow**   Cardiff Eagles Motor Cycle & Car Club
Production - 1st **R Heath** (BSA 654) / 2nd **D Jones** (Tri 650) / 3rd **S Shanon** (Nor 600) / 4th **A Tucker** (Tri 650) / 5th **M Clarke** (Tri 650) / 6th **D Watson** (Matchless 600)

Sunday 16th July   **Darley Moor**   Darley Moor Motor Cycle Road Race Club
Production (6 laps) - 1st **J Allen** (Tri 650) / 2nd **B Bate** (Tri 650) / 3rd **A Carlton** (Nor 650) / 4th **J Woolley** (Nor 650) / 5th **E Bushell** (Velocette 500) / 6th **M Thomas** (Nor 500)

Sunday 23rd July   **Snetterton**   Bemsee
Production 175-1000 - 1st **P Butler** (Tri 650) / 2nd **D Nixon** (Tri 650) / 3rd **C Hopes** (Tri 650) / 4th **C Wall** (BSA 654) / 5th **H Robinson (**Tri 650) / 6th **M Bailey** (Nor 650)

Saturday 29th July   **Cadwell Park**   The British Formula Racing Club
Production Race 1 - 1st **C Hopes** (Tri 650) / 2nd **D Vickers** (BSA 654) / 3rd **C Wall** (BSA 654) / 4th **H Robinson** (Tri 650) / 5th **R Guy** (Tri 500) / 6th **P Davies** (Tri 650) **Race 2** - 1st **C Hopes** (Tri 650) / 2nd **D Vickers** (BSA 654) / 3rd **P Hagan** (Tri 650) / 4th **D Spruce** (Suzuki 250) / 5th **R Guy** (Tri 500) / 6th **P Kilner** (Ducati 250)

Sunday 30th July   **Crimond**   Bon-Accord Motorcycle Club
Production - 1st **W Dey** (Honda 450) / 2nd **K Dingwall** (BSA650) / 3rd **A Llan** (BSA 650) / 4th **E Donnelly** (BSA 650) / 5th **A Roxton** (Nor 600) / 6th **M McIntosh** (Tri 650)

Saturday 5th August   **Cadwell Park**   Midland Motor Cycle Racing Club
Production - 1st **C Hopes** (Tri 650) / 2nd **P Davies** (Tri 650) / 3rd **R Heath** (BSA 654) / 4th **R Hole** (Tri 650) / 5th **G Horne** (BSA 650) / 6th **M Clarke** (Tri 650)

Saturday 5th August   **Brands Hatch**   Bemsee   *Ace of Clubs*
Production 175-1000 (10 laps) - 1st **J Hedger** (Tri 650) / 2nd **P Butler** (Tri 650) / 3rd **D Nixon** (Tri 500) / 4th **R Knight** (Tri 650) / 5th **H Robinson** (Tri 650) / 6th **K Buckmaster** (Tri 650)

Sunday 6th August   **Snetterton**   Bantam Racing Club
Production 125-1000 Race 1 - 1st **A Smith** (BSA 654) / 2nd **P Davies** (Tri 650) / 3rd **H Robinson** (Tri 650) / 4th **D Vickers** (BSA 654) / 5th **R Hole** (Tri 650) / 6th **R Ridley** (Tri 650) **Race 2** - 1st **P Davies** (Tri 650) / 2nd **H Robinson** (Tri 650) / 3rd **R Ridley** (Tri 650) / 4th **R Hole** (Tri 650) / 5th **D Vickers** (BSA 654) / 6th **R Guy** (Tri 500) **Race 3** - 1st **H Robinson** (Tri 650) / 2nd **P Davies** (Tri 650) / 3rd **R Hole** (Tri 650) / 4th **R Guy** (Tri 500) / 5th **G Falcke** (Tri 500) / 6th **S Howe** (Vincent 1000)

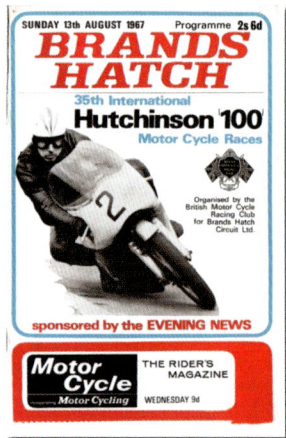

Saturday 12th August **Darley Moor** Darley Moor MCRRC
Production (6 laps) - 1st **R Heath** (BSA 654) / 2nd **B Bate** (Tri 650) / 3rd **A Carlton** (Nor 650) / 4th **G Mahoney** (BSA 650) / 5th **D Jones** (Tri 650) / 6th **J Allen** (Tri 650)

Sunday 13th August **Brands Hatch** Bemsee *Hutchinson 100*
Production (20 laps) - 1st **J Hartle** (Tri 650) / 2nd **R Gould** (Tri 650) / 3rd **R Pickrell** (Dunstall 750) / 4th **P Smart** (Dunstall 750) / 5th **M Andrew** (Tri 650) / 6th **A Smith** (BSA 654)

Saturday 19th August **Cadwell Park** Bantam Racing Club
Production Race 1 - 1st **A Smith** (BSA 654) / 2nd **J Hedger** (Tri 650) / 3rd **P Butler** (Tri 650) / 4th **R Knight** (Tri 650) / 5th **G Green** (Tri 500) / 6th **C Lodge** (Tri 650) **Race 2** - 1st **A Smith** (BSA 654) / 2nd **P Butler** (Tri 650) / 3rd **R Knight** (Tri 650) / 4th **P Davies** (Tri 650) / 5th **G Green** (Tri 500) / 6th **M Clarke** (Tri 650).

Monday 28th August **Crystal Palace** Bemsee *Metropolitan* meeting
Production (6 laps)- 1st **P Butler** (Tri 650) / 2nd **D Nixon** (Tri 500) / 3rd **P Davies** (Tri 650) / 4th **H Robinson** (Tri 650) / 5th **C Wall** (BSA 654) / 6th **R Guy** (Tri 500)

Sunday 3rd September **Cadwell Park** Midland Motor Cycle Racing Club
Production 225-1000 - 1st **P Davies** (Tri 650) / 2nd **R Heath** (BSA 654) / 3rd **G Luck** (Tri 650) / 4th **R Hole** (Tri 650) / 5th **W Davies** (BSA 650) / 6th **M Russell** (Velocette 500)

Sunday 3rd September **Snetterton** Bemsee Guinness Trophy
Production - 1st **D Nixon** (Tri 650) / 2nd **H Robinson** (Tri 650) / 3rd **G Carter** (Tri 650) / 4th **J Allen** (Tri 650) / 5th **K Buckmaster** (Tri 650) / 6th **R Mackay** (Vincent 1000)

Saturday 23rd September **Maghaberry** Road Racing Club of Ireland
Production (8 lap) - 1st **T Bossell** (Nor 600) / 2nd **J Wilkinson** (Tri 500) / 3rd **B Mann** (Bultaco 250) / 4th **C Agnew** (Nor 600) / 5th **K Ferguson** (Tri 650) / 6th **E Coates** (Nor 500)

Sunday 24th September **Darley Moor** Darley Moor Motor Cycle Road Race Club
Production (6 laps) - 1st **R Heath** (BSA 654) / 2nd **B Bate** (Tri 650) / 3rd **J Allen** (Tri 650) / 4th **J Woolley** (Nor 650) / 5th **P Hagan** (Tri 650) / 6th **J Allen** (Tri 650)

Saturday 14th October **Brands Hatch** Berks, Oxon and Bucks Club
Production - 1st **J Hedger** (Tri 650) / 2nd **I With** (Tri 650) / 3rd **E Wallace** (Matchless 650) / 4th **B Barrington** (Velocette 500) / 5th **R Timms** (Montesa 250) / 6th **A Ayers** (Velocette 500)

Sunday 15th October **Darley Moor** Darley Moor Motor Cycle Road Race Club
Production (6 laps) - 1st **R Heath** (BSA 654) / 2nd **J Allen** (Tri 650) / 3rd **B Bate** (Tri 650) / 4th **D Jones** (Tri 650) / 5th **A Carlton** (Nor 650) / 6th **P Allen** (AJS 650)

Sunday 15th October **Cadwell Park** The British Formula Racing Club
Production 125-1000 Race 1 - 1st **P Davies** (Tri 650) / 2nd **H Robinson** (Tri 650) / 3rd **M Grant** (Velo 500) / 4th **S Howe** (Vincent 1000) / 5th **R Guy** (Tri 500) / 6th **A Ayres** (Velocette 500) **Race 2** - 1st **H Robinson** (Tri 650) / 2nd **P Davies** (Tri 650) / 3rd **R Guy** (Tri 500) / 4th **M Brooksbank** (Tri 650) / 5th **P Kilner** (Ducati 250) / 6th **P Reid** (Cotton 250) **Race 3** - 1st **H Robinson** (Tri 650) / 2nd **M Grant** (Velocette 500) / 3rd **R Guy** (Tri 500) / 4th **M Baines** (Nor 500) / 5th **T Ryan** (Nor 600) / 6th **P Kilner** (Ducati 250)

Sunday 22nd October **Brands Hatch**
Production 1000 - 1st **A Rogers** (Nor 650) / 2nd **P Butler** (Tri 650) / 3rd **B Rodwell** (Tri 650) / 4th **J Hedger** (Tri 650)

Sunday 22nd October **Snetterton** Bemsee
Production - 1st **H Robinson** (Tri 650) / 2nd **R Heath** (BSA 654) / 3rd **M Bailey** (Nor 650) / 4th **G Green** (Tri 650) / 5th **K Buckmaster** (Tri 650) / 6th **R Guy** (Tri 500)

Sunday 29th October **Snetterton** Bantam Racing Club
Production Race 1 (8 laps)- 1st **P Butler** (Tri 650) / 2nd **A Smith** (BSA 654) / 3rd **J Hedger** (Tri 650) / 4th **C Hopes** (Tri 650) / 5th **H Robinson** (Tri 650) / 6th **C Wall** (BSA 654) **Race 2** - 1st **P Butler** (Tri 650) / 2nd **J Hedger** (Tri 650) / 3rd **H Robinson** (Tri 650) / 4th **C Wall** (BSA 654) / 5th **R Knight** (Tri 500) / 6th **G Bailey** (Tri 650)

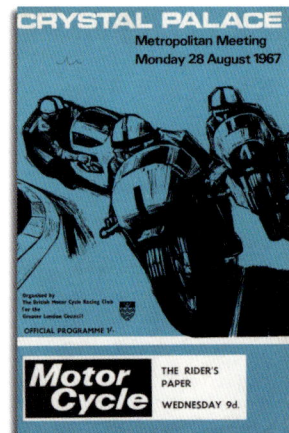

Saturday 9th March **Snetterton** Racing 50 Motor Cycle Club
Production (8 laps) - 1st **R Heath** (BSA 654) **/** 2nd **A Walsh** (Velo 500) **/** 3rd **P Reid** (Cotton 250) **/** 4th **J Thompson** (Tri 650) **/** 5th **M Moyne** (Tri 650) **/** 6th S Brown (BSA 654)

Sunday 10th March **Snetterton** Bemsee *Norwich Trophy Meeting*
Production (7 laps) - 1st **H Robinson** (Tri 650) **/** 2nd **R Heath** (BSA 654) **/** 3rd **D Nixon** (Tri 500) **/** 4th **R Knight** (Tri 500) **/** 5th **J Pinkney** (Tri 650) **/** 6th **T Smith** (Nor 750)

Sunday 10th March **Cadwell Park** National
Production (8 laps) - 1st **C Hopes** (Tri 650) **/** 2nd **T Jones** (BSA 500) **/** 3rd **L Porter** (Tri 650) **/** 4th **D Vickers** (BSA 654) **/** 5th **G Green** (Tri 500) **/** 6th **P Hagan** (Tri 650)

Saturday 23rd March **Snetterton** Bantam Racing Club
Production Race 1 - 1st **H Robinson** (Tri 650) **/** 2nd **P Butler** (Tri 650) **/** 3rd **P Davies** (Tri 650) **/** 4th **G Green** (Tri 500) **/** 5th **J Graham** (Honda 350) **/** 6th **G Bailey** (Tri 650) **Race 2** -1st **H Robinson** (Tri 650) **/** 2nd **P Butler** (Tri 650) **/** 3rd **P Davies** (Tri 650) **/** 4th **D Jones** (Tri 650) **/** 5th **J Graham** (Honda 350) **/** 6th **G Bailey** (Tri 650)

Saturday 30th March **Cadwell Park** Midland Motor Cycle Racing Club
Production - 1st **C Hopes** (Tri 650) **/** 2nd **P Davies** (Tri 650) **/** 3rd **R Heath** (BSA 654) **/** 4th **L Mason** (BSA **/** 5th **D Jones** (Tri 650) **/** 6th **P Reid** (Cotton 250)

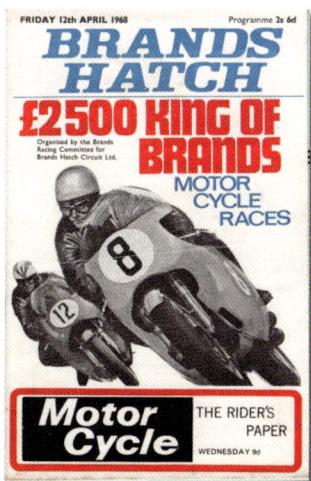

Saturday 30th March **Brands Hatch** Bemsee Trophy Meeting
Production 175-1000 - 1st **J Hedger** (Tri 650) **/** 2nd **D Nixon** (Tri 500) **/** 3rd **H Robinson** (Tri 650) **/** 4th **E Wallace** (Tri 650) **/** 5th **G Bailey** (Tri 650) **/** 6th **R Ridley** (Tri 650)

Sunday 31st March **Snetterton** British Formula Racing Club
Production 125-1000. Race 1 - 1st **A Rogers** (Ducati 250) **/** 2nd **R Wittich** (Nor 750) **/** 3rd **J Lancaster** (Tri 650) **/** 4th **H Robertson** (Tri 500) **/** 5th **C Wilkin** (Nor 500) **Race 2** - 1st **R Ridley** (Tri 650) **/** 2nd **A Rogers** (Ducati 250) **/** 3rd **R Wittich** (Nor 750) **/** 4th **J Lancaster** (Tri 650) **/** 5th **C Wilkin** (Nor 500) **/** 6th **J Brett** (Velocette 500)

Friday 12th April **Darley Moor** Darley Moor Motor Cycle Road Race Club
Production Heat 1 - 1st **R Heath** (BSA 654) **/** 2nd **G Sanders** (BSA 654) **/** 3rd **K Guy** (Nor 650) 4th **K Little** (Tri 650) **/** 5th **F Rutter** (Nor 650) **/** 6th **A Carlton** (Nor 650) **Heat 2** - 1st **P Davies** (Tri 650) **/** 2nd **T Haslam** (Tri 650) **/** 3rd **W Bate** (BSA 650) **/** 4th **W Davies** (BSA 650) **/** 5th **R Bean** (BSA 650) **/** 6th **B Lloyd** (BSA 650) **Final** - 1st **R Heath** (BSA 654) **/** 2nd **P Davies** (Tri 650) **/** 3rd **A Carlton** (Nor 650) **/** 4th **F Rutter** (Nor 650) **/** 5th **G Sanders** (BSA 654) **/** 6th **K Guy** (Nor 650)

Friday 12th April **Brands Hatch** Brands Racing Committee *King of Brands*
Production 1000 (10 laps) - 1st **C Dixon** (Tri 650) **/** 2nd **J Hedger** (Tri 650) **/** 3rd **P Butler** (Tri 650) **/** 4th **H Robinson** (Tri 650) **/** 5th **G Bailey** (Tri 650) **/** 6th **R Knight** (Tri 500) **Production 350** - 1st **C Thompsett** (Ducati 250) **/** 2nd **C Crookes** (Ducati 250) **/** 3rd **J Blanchard** (BSA 350) **/** 4th **M Stirk** (Suzuki 250) **/** 5th **S Snow** (Ducati 250) **/** 6th **M Button** (TBC)

Saturday 13th April **Snetterton** Newmarket Motor Cycle & Light Car Club
Production (6 laps) - 1st **P Butler** (Tri 650) **/** 2nd **J Hedger** (Tri 650) **/** 3rd **P Davies** (Tri 650) **/** 4th **R Heath** (BSA654) **/** 5th **K Buckmaster** (Tri 650) **/** 6th **C Lodge** (Tri 650) **Race 2** - 1st **J Hedge**r (Tri 650)

Sunday 14th April **Snetterton** Bemsee
Production - 1st **H Robinson** (Tri 650) **/** 2nd **P Butler** (Tri 650) **/** 3rd **P Davies** (Tri 650) **/** 4th **K Buckmaster** (Tri 650) **/** 5th **J Pinkney** (Tri 650) **/** 6th **J Kanka** (Tri 650)

Saturday 20th April **Llandow** Bantam Racing Club
Production Race 1 - 1st **C Bishop** (Tri 650) **/** 2nd **P Fisher** (Suzuki 250) **/** 3rd **D Pickering** (Tri 650) **/** 4th **H Frost** (Tri 650) **/** 5th **G Green** (Tri 500) **/** 6th **K Griffiths** (Bultaco 250) **Race 2** - 1st **D Jones** (Tri 650) **/** 2nd **C Bishop** (Tri 650) **/** 3rd **H Frost** (Tri 650) **/** 4th **P Fisher** (Suzuki 250) **/** 5th **D Pickering** (Tri 650) **/** 6th **K Griffiths** (Bultaco 250)

Saturday 27th April **Snetterton** The British Formula Racing Club
Production Race 1 - 1st **A Barr** (Nor 650) **/** 2nd **J White** (Nor 650) **/** 3rd **J Thompson** (Tri 650) **/** 4th **G Millward** (BSA 654) **/** 5th **R Wittich** (Nor 650) **/** 6th **D Simpson** (Nor 600) **Race 2** - 1st **J Thompson** (Tri 650) **/** 2nd **R Wittich** (Nor 650) **/** 3rd **T Haslam** (Nor 750) **/** 4th **J Vincent** (Tri 650) **/** 5th **A Rogers** (Ducati 250) **/** 6th **H Robertson** (Tri 500)

Saturday 27th April   **Brands Hatch**   Southern 67

Production - 1st **A Tucker** (Tri 650) / 2nd **P Davies** (Tri 650) / 3rd **R Monnery** (Tri 650) / 4th **P Smith** (BSA 654) / 5th **A Green** (Suzuki 250) / 6th **R Knight** (Tri 500)

Sunday 28th April   **Snetterton**   Midland Motor Cycle Racing Club

Production Race 1 - 1st **P Davies** (Tri 650) / 2nd **R Heath** (BSA 654) / 3rd **G Sanders** (BSA 654) **Race 2** - 1st **P Davies** (Tri 650) / 2nd **D Rae** (DRS) / 3rd **H Porter** (Nor 750) **Race 3** - 1st **P Davies** (Tri 650) / 2nd **G Sanders** (BSA 654) / 3rd **R Wyatt** (Tri 650)

Saturday 4th May   **Brands Hatch**   Bemsee   *Club Day*

Production 175- 1000 (10 laps) - 1st **P Butler** (Tri 650) / 2nd **G Bailey** (Tri 650) / 3rd **J Kanka** (Tri 650) / 4th **A Monnery** (Tri 650) / 5th **K Buckmaster** (Tri 650) / 6th **E Wallace** (Tri 650)

Saturday 4th May   **Aintree**   Waterloo & District Motor Club

Production (7 laps) - 1st **R Heath** (BSA 654) / 2nd **L Mason** (BSA 654) / 3rd **R Ridley** (Tri 650) / 4th **A Carlton** (Nor 650) / 5th **R Gittins** (Bultaco 250) / 6th **J Baker** (Nor 650)

Saturday 4th May   **Thruxton**   Southern 67

Production - 1st **R Moreau** (Dunstall 650) / 2nd **P Davies** (Tri 650) / 3rd **B Barrington** (Velo 500) / 4th **B Smith** (BSA 650) / 5th **A Ayers** (Velo 500) / 6th **P Rowe** (Velo 500)

Saturday 11th May   **Lydden Hill**   The British Formula Racing Club

Production Race 1 - 1st **E Wallis** (Tri 650) / 2nd **J Vincent** (Tri 650) / 3rd **G Falcke** (Tri 500) / 4th **P Kilner** (Ducati 250) / 5th **C Fox** (Tri 650) / 6th **C Odlin** (Nor 650) **Race 2** - 1st **E Wallis** (Tri 650) / 2nd **J Vincent** (Tri 650) / 3rd **G Falcke** (Tri 500) / 4th **P Kilner** (Ducati 250) / 5th **C Odlin** (Nor 650) / 6th **Nicholas** (BSA 654)

Saturday 11th May   **Cadwell Park**   Bantam Racing Club

Production Race 1 (8 laps) - 1st **D Spruce** (Suzuki 250) / 2nd **B Davies** (Tri 650) / 3rd **J Thompson** (Tri 650) / 4th **C Wall** (BSA 654) / 5th **T Seaman** (Nor 650) / 6th **M Moyne** (Honda 350) **Race 2** - 1st **B Davies** (Tri 650) / 2nd **D Spruce** (Suzuki 250) / 3rd **C Wall** (BA 654) / 4th **J Thompson** (Tri 650) / 5th **T Seaman** (Nor 650) / 6th **M Moyne** (Honda 350)

Sunday 12th May   **Llandow**   Cardiff Eagles Motor Cycle & car Club

Production Race 1 (7 laps) - 1st **D Jones** (Tri 650) / 2nd **D Pickering** (Tri 650) / 3rd **J Jones** (Tri 650) / 4th **D Lewis** (Tri 650) / 5th **J Poulson** (Tri 500) / 6th **G Lucas** (Tri 650) **Race 2** - 1st **D Jones** (Tri 650) / 2nd **D Pickering** (Tri 650) / 3rd **J Jones** (Tri 650) / 4th **D Lewis** (Tri 650) / 5th **J Poulson** (Tri 500) / 6th **G Lucas** (Tri 650)

Sunday 12th May   **Crimond**   Bon-Accord Motorcycle Club

Production (8 laps) - 1st **B Mercer** (BSA 654) / 2nd **K Dingwall** (BSA 654) / 3rd **I Thompson** (BSA 654) / 4th **R Niven** (Tri 650) / 5th **K Birch** (Nor 600) / 6th **P Miller** (Honda 450)

Sunday 12th May   **Brands Hatch**   *500 Miler*

Production 750 - 1st **J Strijbis/R Harrington** (Tri 650)185 laps / 2nd **M Uphill/S Jolly** (Tri 650) 183 laps / 3rd **L Weil/M Ashwood** (Tri 650) 183 laps / 4th **T Smith/M Andrew** (BSA 654) 180 laps / 5th **B Kemp/C Brown** (Tri 650) 178 laps **Production 500** - 1st **D Nixon/P Butler** (Tri 500) 189 laps / 2nd **T Robb/C Vincent** (Suzuki 500) 185 laps / 3rd **R Knight/M Carney** (Tri 500) 185 laps / 4th **H Evans/P Coombs** 176 laps / 5th **D Minter/R Everett** (Ducati 340) 175 laps **Production 250** - 1st **G Keith/B Ball** (Suzuki 250) 187 laps / 2nd **T Dickie/C Mortimer** (Ducati 250) 186 laps / 3rd **B Smith/S Graham** (Suzuki 250) 185 laps / 4th **T Burgess/ H Crowder** (Suzuki 250) 184 laps / 5th **C Thompsett/R Baylie** (Ducati 250) 184 laps / 6th **E Jonson/J Lishman** (Suzuki 250) 180 laps

Saturday 18th May   **Brands Hatch**   Bemsee   Kent Cup

Production 175-1000 - 1st **P Butler** (Tri 650) / 2nd **D Nixon** (Tri 500) / 3rd **T Smith** (Nor 750) / 4th **J Pickney** (Tri 650) / 5th **J Kanka** (Tri 650) / 6th **J Vincent** (Tri 650)

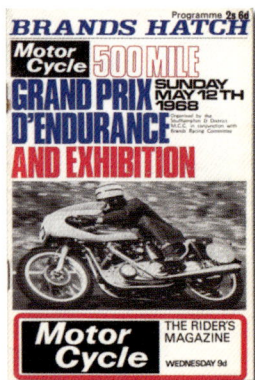

Sunday 19th May   **Darley Moor**   Darley Moor Motor Cycle Road Race Club

Production (8 laps) - 1st **R Heath** (BSA 654) / 2nd **F Rutter** (Nor 650) / 3rd **A Carlton** (Nor 650) / 4th **E Wallace** (Tri 650) / 5th **K Guy** (Nor 650) / 6th **F Jones** (Tri 650)

Sunday 19th May   **Cadwell Park**   Louth & District   *Cadwell International*

Production 1000 (8 laps) - 1st **R Pickrell** (Dunstal 750) / 2nd **C Hopes** (Tri 650) / 3rd **S Spencer** (Tri 650) / 4th **P Davies** (Tri 650) / 5th **B Richards** (Bultaco 250) / 6th **L Porter** (BSA 654)

Saturday 25th May   **Brands Hatch**   Southern 67

Production (10 laps) - 1st **R More** (Dunstall 650) / 2nd **A Tucker** (Tri 650) / 3rd **N Wallace** (Tri 650) / 4th **A Ayers** (Velocette 500) / 5th **C Bolton** (Nor 500) / 6th **M Kenny** (Tri 650)

Saturday 25th May   **Thruxton**   Bantam Racing Club

Production Race 1 - 1st **P Butler** (Tri 650) / 2nd **P Davies** (Tri 650) / 3rd **H Robinson** (Tri 650) / 4th **R Knight** (Tri 500) / 5th **B Smith** (BSA 654) / 6th **R Ridley** (Tri 650) **Race 2** - 1st **P Butler** (Tri 650) / 2nd **P Davies** (Tri 650) / 3rd **J Pinkney** (Tri 650) / 4th **R Ridley** (Tri 650) / 5th **R Knight** (Tri 500) / 6th **G Green** (Tri 500)

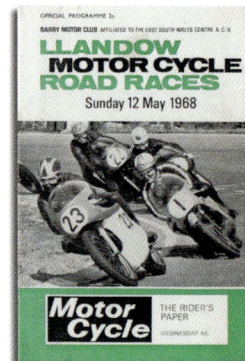

Monday 3rd June **Darley Moor** Darley Moor Motor Cycle Road Race Club
Production 8 lap - 1st **J Allen** (Tri 650) / 2nd **E Wallace** (Tri 650) / 3rd **A Carlton** (Nor 650) / 4th **J Barrow** (BSA 650) / 5th **M Orange** (Tri 650) / 6th **F Rutter** (Nor 650)

Saturday 1st June **Cadwell Park** The British Formula Racing Club
Production 1000 Race 1 - 1st **P Reid** (Nor 600) / 2nd **E Wallace** (Tri 650) / 3rd **D Jones** (Tri 650) / 4th **T Haslam** (Nor 750) / 5th **A Barr** (Nor 650) / 6th **A Walsh** (Velo 500) **Race 2** - 1st **P Reid** (Nor 600) / 2nd **E Wallace** (Tri 650) / 3rd **A Walsh** (Velo 500) / 4th **A Barr** (Nor 650) / 5th **D Jones** (Tri 650) / 6th **G Millward** (BSA 654) **Race 3** - 1st **P Reid** (Nor 600) / 2nd **E Wallace** (Tri 650) / 3rd **T Haslam** (Nor 750) / 4th **D Jones** (Tri 650) / 6th **G Millward** (BSA 654)

Sunday 2nd June **Mallory Park** Motor Circuit Developments
Production (30 laps) - 1st **R Pickrell/D Croxford** (Dunstall 750) / 2nd **A Smith/M Andrew** (BSA 654) / 3rd **M Ashwood/J Dunphy** (Tri 650) / 4th **G Green/R Guy** (Tri 500) / 5th **A Giles/G Smith** (Tri 650) / 6th **P Butler/D Nixon** (Tri 650)

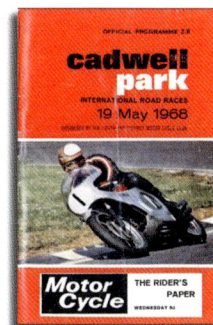

Wednesday 12th June **Isle of Man** Production TT
Production 750 (3 laps) -1st **R Pickrell** (Dunstall Norton)1hr 09min 13.2sec - 98.13mph / 2nd **B Nelson** (Norton 750)1hr 11min 47.2 sec - 94.62mph / 3rd **A Smith** (BSA 654) 1hr 12min 23.8 sec - 93.82mph / 4th **G Bailey** (Tri 650) 1hr 13min 21.6 sec - 92.59mph / 5th **M Uphill** (Tri 650) 1hr 17min 7 sec - 88.08mph / 6th **T Godfrey** (Dunstall Norton) 1hr 19 min 3.2 sec - 85.92mph **Production 500** - 1st **R Knight** (Tri 500)1hr 15 min 23.6 sec - 90.09mph / 2nd **J Blanchard** (Velocette 500) 1 hr16 min 41.2 sec - 88.58mph / 3rd **D Nixon** (Tri 500) 1hr 16 min 44.4 sec - 88.52mph / 4th **N Kelly** (Velocette 500) 1hr 18 min 33 sec - 86.47mph / 5th **G Robinson** (Honda 450) 1hr 19min 24.2 sec - 85.54 mph / 6th **G Barnacle** (Tri 500) 1hr 20 min 38.6 sec - 84.23mph **Production 250** - 1st **T Burgess** (Ossa)1hr 17 min 53.4 sec - 87.21mph / 2nd **G Leigh** (Bultaco) 1 hr 19min 41.8 sec - 85.23 mph / 3rd **B Smith** (Suzuki 250) 1 hr 19 min 45 sec - 85.17mph / 4th **B Richards** (Bultaco) 1 hr 21 min 14 sec - 83.61mph / 5th **G Keith** (Suzuki 250) 1 hr 21min 35.2 Sec - 83.26mph / 6th **T Robb** (Suzuki 250) 1 hr 21 min 48.0 sec - 83.03mph

Saturday 22nd June **Brands Hatch** Bemsee *Trophy Day*
Production (10 laps) - 1st **P Butler** (Tri 650) / 2nd **P Davies** (Tri 650) / 3rd **J Davey** (Tri 650) / 4th **J Vincent** (Tri 650) / 5th **G Bailey** (Tri 650) / 6th **C Bolton** (Nor 650)

Saturday 29th June **Cadwell Park** Bantam Racing Club
Production Race 1 - 1st **P Butler** (Tri 650) / 2nd **P Davies** (Tri 650) / 3rd **H Robinson** (Tri 650) / 4th **C Wall** (BSA 654) / 5th **M Pusey** (Tri 650) / 6th **R Hole** (Tri 650) **Race 2** - 1st **P Butler** (Tri 650) / 2nd **P Davies** (Tri 650) / 3rd **H Robinson** (Tri 650) / 4th **C Wall** (BSA 654) / 5th **G Carter** (Tri 650)

Sunday 30th June **Brands Hatch**
Production (10 laps) - 1st **R Pickrell** (Dunstall 750) / 2nd **P Butler** (Tri 650) / 3rd **A Smith** (BSA 654) / 4th **D Dixon** (Tri 650) / 5th **B Kemp** (Tri 650) / 6th **J Blanchard** (Velocette 500)

July 6th 7th **Barcelona** *24 Horas de Montjuïc*
Production 24hr - 1st **J A Rodés/R Fargas** (Norton 750) 635 laps / 2nd **K Buckmaster/A Kinsella** (Tri 650) 631 laps / 3rd **R Everett/P Smart** (Ducati 250) 623 laps / 4th **P Juliá/J Mañer** (Ossa 230) 622 laps / 5th **S Néstor/A Sala** (Ossa 230) 618 laps / 6th **A Peck/M Andrew** (BSA 441) 608 laps / 7th **Pitin/M Millet** (Ossa 230) / 8th **C Hopes/K Redfern** (Tri 650) / 9th **J Strijbis/R Harrington** (Tri 500) / 10th **P Castellvi/J Alguersuari** (Bultaco 250) / 11th **H Glück/D Döhmann** (Yamaha 350) / 12th **A Julien/B Grau** (Bultaco 250)

Saturday 6th July **Aintree** Waterloo & District Motor Club
Production - 1st **L Mason** (BSA 654) / 2nd **A Carlton** (Nor 650) / 3rd **K Dixon** (Nor 650) / 4th **R Heath** (BSA 654) / 5th **J Barber** (Nor 650) / 6th **J Allen** (Tri 650)

Saturday 6th July **Cadwell Park** Midland Motor Cycle Racing Club
Production 1000 (8 laps) - 1st **P Davies** (Tri 650) / 2nd **R Hole** (BSA 654) / 3rd **P Reid** (Nor 650) / 4th **D Jones** (Tri 650) / 5th **T Waterer** (BSA 654) / 6th **M Scott** (Tri 650)

Saturday 6th July **Brands Hatch** Southern 67
Production - 1st **H Robinson** (Tri 650) / 2nd **E Wallace** (Tri 650) / 3rd **R Bowring** (Tri 650) / 4th **J Pinkney** (Tri 650) / 5th **G Marks** (Tri 650) / 6th **R Knight** (Tri 500)

Saturday 13th July **Snetterton** Bemsee *Baragwanath Trophy*
Production (7 laps) - 1st **P Davies** (Tri 650) / 2nd **J Pinkney** (Tri 650) / 3rd **T Smith** (Nor 750) / 4th **C Wall** (BSA 654) / 5th **M Pusey** (Tri 650) / 6th **J Kanka** (Tri 650)

Saturday 13th July **Cadwell Park** The British Formula Racing Club
Production Race 1 - 1st **D Jones** (Tri 650) / 2nd **G Millward** (BSA 654) / 3rd **P Reid** (Nor 650) / 4th **G Smith** (Tri 650) / 5th **T Seaman** (Nor 650) / 6th **P Kilner** (Ducati 250) **Race 2** - 1st **P Reid** (Nor 650) / 2nd **M Rice** (BSA 654) / 3rd **G Smith** (Tri 650) / 4th **P Kilner** (Ducati 250) / 5th **D Jones** (Tri 650) / 6th **J**

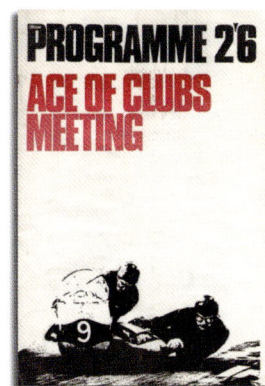

Bassingdale (Nor 750) **Race 3** - 1ˢᵗ **P Reid** (Nor 650) **/** 2ⁿᵈ **G Smith** (Tri 650) **/** 3ʳᵈ **T Seaman** (Nor 650) **/** 4ᵗʰ **P Kilner** (Ducati 250) **/** 5ᵗʰ **D Jones** (Tri 650) **/** 6ᵗʰ **J Brett** (Velocette 500)

Sunday 21ˢᵗ July   **Snetterton**   Newmarket Club
Production Race 1 - 1ˢᵗ **P Davies** (Tri 650) **/** 2ⁿᵈ **T Smith** (Nor 750) **/** 3ʳᵈ **R Heath** (BSA 654) **/** 4ᵗʰ **M Pusey** (Tri 650) **/** 5ᵗʰ **A Tucker** (Tri 650) **/** 6ᵗʰ **R Wittich** (Nor 750) **Race 2** - 1ˢᵗ **P Davies** (Tri 650) **/** 2ⁿᵈ **T Smith** (Nor 750) **/** 3ʳᵈ **R Heath** (BSA 654) **/** 4ᵗʰ **M Pusey** (Tri 650) **/** 5ᵗʰ **A Tucker** (Tri 650) **/** 6ᵗʰ **R Wittich** (Nor 750)

Sunday 21ˢᵗ July   **Llandow**   Cardiff Eagles MC&CC
Production Race 1 - 1ˢᵗ **D Jones** (Tri 650) **/** 2ⁿᵈ **D Pickering** (Tri 650) **/** 3ʳᵈ **C Crookes** (Ducati 250) **/** 4ᵗʰ **J Ellis** (BSA 654) **/** 5ᵗʰ **G Lucas** (Tri 500) **/** 6ᵗʰ **M Gordon** (Tri 650) **Race 2** - 1ˢᵗ **D Jones** (Tri 650) **/** 2ⁿᵈ **D Pickering** (Tri 650) **/** 3ʳᵈ **C Crookes** (Ducati 250) **/** 4ᵗʰ **C Bishop** (Tri 650) **/** 5ᵗʰ **G Lucas** (Tri 500) **/** 6ᵗʰ **M Gordon** (Tri 650)

Saturday 27ᵗʰ July   **Snetterton**   Southern 67
Production - 1ˢᵗ **R Pickrell** (Dunstall 750) **/** 2ⁿᵈ **P Davies** (Tri 650) **/** 3ʳᵈ **J Pinkney** (Tri 650) **/** 4ᵗʰ **E Wallace** (Tri 650) **/** 5ᵗʰ **A Tucker** (Tri 650) **/** 6ᵗʰ **J Vincent** (Tri 650)

Sunday 28ᵗʰ July   **Crimond**   Bon Accord Motorcycle Club   *Players No.6*
Production (8 laps) - 1ˢᵗ **C Hopes** (Tri 650) **/** 2ⁿᵈ **I Thomson** (BSA 654) **/** 3ʳᵈ **M Spiler** (BSA 654) **/** 4ᵗʰ **E Donnelly** (BSA 654) **/** 5ᵗʰ **K Birch** (Nor 650) **/** 6ᵗʰ **J Smith** (Tri 650)

Saturday 3ʳᵈ August   **Brands Hatch**   Bemsee   *Ace of Clubs*
Production 1000 - 1ˢᵗ **G Bailey** (Tri 650) **/** 2ⁿᵈ **E Wallace** (Tri 650) **/** 3ʳᵈ **J Vincent** (Tri 650) **/** 4ᵗʰ **M Pusey** (Tri 650) **/** 5ᵗʰ **J Kanka** (Tri 650) **/** 6ᵗʰ **J Overy** (Tri 650)

Sunday 4ᵗʰ August   **Cadwell Park**   Bantam Racing Club
Production Race 1 - 1ˢᵗ **P Butler** (Tri 650) **/** 2ⁿᵈ **P Davies** (Tri 650) **/** 3ʳᵈ **G Green** (Tri 500) **/** 4ᵗʰ **T Reed** (Cotton 250) **/** 5ᵗʰ **T Seaman** (Nor 650) **/** 6ᵗʰ **H Evans** (BSA 500) **Race 2** - 1ˢᵗ **P Butler** (Tri 650) **/** 2ⁿᵈ **G Green** (Tri 500) **/** 3ʳᵈ **H Robinson** (Tri 650) **/** 4ᵗʰ **T Seaman** (Nor 650) **/** 5ᵗʰ **P Davies** (Tri 650) **/** 6ᵗʰ **G Millward** (BSA 654)

Sunday 11ᵗʰ August   **Brands Hatch**   Bemsee   *Hutchinson 100*
Production (20 laps) - 1ˢᵗ **R Pickrell** (Dunstall 750) **/** 2ⁿᵈ **R Gould** (Tri 650) **/** 3ʳᵈ **M Uphill** (Tri 650) **/** 4ᵗʰ **A Smith** (BSA 654) **/** 5ᵗʰ **P Tait** (Tri 650) **/** 6ᵗʰ **P Butler** (Tri 650)

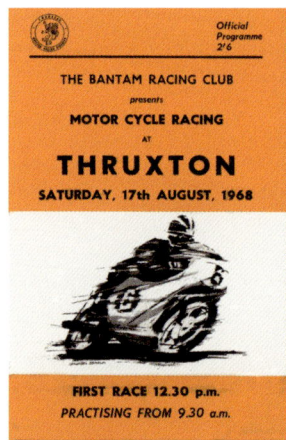

Saturday 17ᵗʰ August   **Thruxton**   Bantam Racing Club
Production Race 1 - 1ˢᵗ **P Butler** (Tri 650) **/** 2ⁿᵈ **P Davies** (Tri 650) **/** 3ʳᵈ **R Ridley** (Tri 650) **/** 4ᵗʰ **J Pinkney** (Tri 650) **/** 5ᵗʰ **G Bailey** (Tri 650) **/** 6ᵗʰ **J Lancaster** (Tri 650) **Race 2** - 1ˢᵗ **P Davies** (Tri 650) **/** 2ⁿᵈ **G Bailey** (Tri 650) **/** 3ʳᵈ **J Pinkney** (Tri 650) **/** 4ᵗʰ **R Ridley** (Tri 650) **/** 5ᵗʰ **R Knight** (Tri 500) **/** 6ᵗʰ **L Phelps** (Tri 650)

Sunday 18ᵗʰ August   **Darley Moor**   Darley Moor Motor Cycle Road Race Club
Production Heat 1 (8 laps) - 1ˢᵗ **R Heath** (BSA 654) **/** 2ⁿᵈ **G Sanders** (BSA 654) **/** 3ʳᵈ **L Mason** (BSA 654) **/** 4ᵗʰ **A Carlton** (Nor 650) **/** 5ᵗʰ **A Giles** (Tri 650) **/** 6ᵗʰ **A Brooks** (Tri 650) **Heat 2** - 1ˢᵗ **W Bate** (Nor 650) **/** 2ⁿᵈ **M Orange** (Tri 650) **/** 3ʳᵈ **R Howe** (Nor 650) **/** 4ᵗʰ **B Boase** (BSA 500) **/** 5ᵗʰ **P Haslam** (Tri 650) **/** 6ᵗʰ **R Campbell** (Velocette 500) **Final** - 1ˢᵗ **R Heath** (BSA 654) **/** 2ⁿᵈ **G Sanders** (BSA 654) **/** 3ʳᵈ **A Carlton** (Nor 650) **/** 4ᵗʰ **A Giles** (Tri 650) **/** 5ᵗʰ **W Bate** (Nor 650) **/** 6ᵗʰ **M Orange** (Tri 650)

Saturday 24ᵗʰ August   **Brands Hatch**   Southern 67
Production 200-1000 (10 laps) - 1ˢᵗ **J Vincent** (Tri 650) **/** 2ⁿᵈ **J Kanka** (Tri 650) **/** 3ʳᵈ **P Davies** (Tri 650) **/** 4ᵗʰ **J Pinkney** (Tri 650) **/** 5ᵗʰ **L Phelps** (Tri 650) **/** 6ᵗʰ **H Robinson** (Tri 650)

Saturday 31ˢᵗ August   **Cadwell Park**   Midland Motor Cycle Racing Club
Production - 1ˢᵗ **P Davies** (Tri 650) **/** 2ⁿᵈ **R Hole** (BSA 654) **/** 3ʳᵈ **D Jones** (Tri 650) **/** 4ᵗʰ **G Sanders** (BSA 654) **/** 5ᵗʰ **D Murfin** (Honda 250) **/** 6ᵗʰ **E Archer** (Tri 650)

Monday 2ⁿᵈ September   **Darley Moor**   Darley Moor Motor Cycle Road Race Club
Production (8 laps) Race 1 - 1ˢᵗ **R Heath** (BSA 654) **/** 2ⁿᵈ **G Sanders** (BSA 654) **/** 3ʳᵈ **W Bate** (Nor 650) **/** 4ᵗʰ **F Rutter** (Nor 650) **/** 5ᵗʰ **R Howe** (Nor 650) **/** 6ᵗʰ **M Orange** (Tri 650) **Race 2** - 1ˢᵗ **R Heath** (BSA 654) **/** 2ⁿᵈ **A Carlton** (Nor 650) **/** 3ʳᵈ **W Bate** (Nor 650) **/** 4ᵗʰ **G Sanders** (BSA 654) **/** 5ᵗʰ **M Orange** (Tri 650) **/** 6ᵗʰ **D Jones** (Tri 650)

Monday 2ⁿᵈ September   **Crystal Palace**   *Players No.6*
Production 175-1000 (8 laps) - 1ˢᵗ **R Pickrell** (Dunstall 750) **/** 2ⁿᵈ **M Ashwood** (Tri 650) **/** 3ʳᵈ **P Butler** (Tri 650) **/** 4ᵗʰ **D Nixon** (Tri 650) **/** 5ᵗʰ **M Andrew** (Nor 750) **/** 6ᵗʰ **P Davies** (Tri 650)

Sunday 8th September — **Cadwell Park** — The British Formula Racing Club
Production Race 1 - 1st **G Carter** (Tri 650) / 2nd **J Thompson** (Tri 650) / 3rd **A Walsh** (Velocette 500) / 4th **J Bassindale** (Nor 750) / 5th **T Haslam** (Nor 750) / 6th **J Brett** (Velocette 500) **Race 2** - 1st **J Thompson** (Tri 650) / 2nd **G Carter** (Tri 650) / 3rd **J Bassindale** (Nor 750) / 4th **G Millward** (BSA 654) / 5th **J Brett** (Velo 500) / 6th **A Walsh** (Velo 500) **Race 3** - 1st **G Carter** (Tri 650) / 2nd **J Thompson** (Tri 650) / 3rd **J Bassindale** (Nor 750) / 4th **J Brett** (Velo 500) / 5th **A Walsh** (Velo 500) 6th **P Reid** (Cotton 250)

Saturday 14th September — **Lydden Hill** — The British Formula Racing Club
Production Race 1 - 1st **G Carter** (Tri 650) / 2nd **J Vincent** (Tri 650) / 3rd **J Bassindale** (Nor 750) / 4th **J Glazebrook** (Suzuki 250) / 5th **G Falke** (Tri 500) / 6th **J Brett** (Velo 500) **Race 2** - 1st **J Vincent** (Tri 650) / 2nd **J Bassindale** (Nor 750) / 3rd **P Kilner** (Ducati 250) / 4th **J Glazebrook** (Suzuki 250) / 5th **D Jarvis** (BSA 654) / 6th **G Carter** (Tri 650) **Race 3** - 1st **J Vincent** (Tri 650) / 2nd **J Brett** (Velo 500) / 3rd **J Bassindale** (Nor 750) / 4th **D Jarvis** (BSA 654) / 5th **P Kilner** (Ducati 250) / 6th **G Falke** (Tri 500) **Race 4** - 1st **J Bassindale** (Nor 750) / 2nd **P Kilner** (Ducati 250) / 3rd **G Falke** (Tri 500) / 4th **Fox** (Montesa 250) / 5th **T Doe** (Ducati 250)

Saturday 14th September — **Brands Hatch** — Bemsee *Silver Trophy*
Production (10 laps) - 1st **D Nixon** (Tri 650) / 2nd **P Butler** (Tri 650) / 3rd **P Davies** (Tri 650) / 4th **K Buckmaster** (Tri 650) / 5th **J Pinkney** (Tri 650)

Sunday 15th September — **Snetterton** — Racing Club — *One Hour Enduro*
Production 1hr - 1st **P Butler** (Tri 650) / 2nd **R Hole** (BSA 654) / 3rd **H Robinson** (Tri 650) / 4th **G Green** (Tri 500) / 5th **J Vincent** (Tri 650) / 6th **C Lodge** (Tri 650)

Saturday 21st September — **Maghaberry** — Motor Cycle Road Racing Club of Ireland
Production (8 laps) - 1st **A Alexander** (Nor 650) / 2nd **E Coates** (Tri 650) / 3rd **C Gorman** (Tri 650) / 4th **J Pyper** (Tri 650)

Saturday 21st September — **Cadwell Park** — Midland Motor Cycle Racing Club
Production 1000 - 1st **R Hole** (BSA 654) / 2nd **E Archer** (Tri 650) / 3rd **T Haslam** (Nor 750) / 4th **G Sanders** (BSA 654) / 5th **B Bassindale** (Nor 750) / 6th **E Wilson** (Tri 650)

Sunday 29th September — **Darley Moor** — Darley Moor Motor Cycle Road Race Club
Production (8 laps) -1st **R Heath** (BSA 654) / 2nd **G Sanders** (BSA 654) / 3rd **A Carlton** (Nor 650) / 4th **E Wallace** (Tri 650) / 5th **D Jones** (Tri 650) / 6th **P McLaughlin** (Tri 650)

Sunday 29th September — **Snetterton** — Bemsee — *Guinness Trophy* Meeting
Production 1000 - 1st **P Butler** (Tri 650) / 2nd **D Nixon** (Tri 650) / 3rd **J Pinkney** (Tri 650) / 4th **L Phelps** (Tri 650) / 5th **R Corbett** (Nor 650) / 6th **J Vincent** (Tri 650)

Saturday 12th October — **Cadwell Park** — The British Formula Racing Club
Production 1000 Race 1 - 1st **G Carter** (Tri 650) / 2nd **P Reid** (Cotton 250) / 3rd **J Vincent** (Tri 650) / 4th **J Bassingdale** (Nor 750) / 5th **P Haslam** (Tri 650) / 6th **A Glazebrook** (Suzuki 247) **Race 2** - 1st **G Carter** (Tri 650) / 2nd **M Pusey** (Tri 650) / 3rd **J Vincent** (Tri 650) / 4th **M McClelland** (Nor 750) / 5th **P Haslam** (Tri 650) **Race 3** - 1st **M Pusey** (Tri 650) / 2nd **J Vincent** (Tri 650) / 3rd **G Carter** (Tri 650) / 4th **J g** (Nor 750) / 5th **T Odlin** (Nor 650) / 6th **G Millward** (BSA 654)

Saturday 12th October — **Kirkistown**
Production - 1st **C Gorman** (Tri 650) / 2nd **J Bankhead** (Tri 650) / 3rd **K McAtamney** (Nor 650) / 4th **A Alexander** (Nor 650)

Sunday 13th October — **Darley Moor** — Darley Moor Motor Cycle Road Race Club
Production (8 laps) - 1st **R Heath** (BSA 654) / 2nd **G Sanders** (BSA 654) / 3rd **L Mason** (BSA 654) / 4th **A Carlton** (Nor 650) / 5th **T Haslam** (Nor 750) / 6th **M Orange** (Tri 650)

Saturday 19th October — **Snetterton** — Bantam Racing Club
Production Race 1 (8 laps) - 1st **P Butler** (Tri 650) / 2nd **L Phelps** (Tri 650) / 3rd **G Bailey** (Tri 650) / 4th **J Pinney** (Tri 650) / 5th **H Robinson** (Tri 650) / 6th **R Hole** (BSA 654) **Race 2** - 1st **P Butler** (Tri 650) / 2nd **G Bailey** (Tri 650) / 3rd **L Phelps** (Tri 650) / 4th **J Pinney** (Tri 650) / 5th **H Robinson** (Tri 650) / 6th **J Allen** (Tri 650)

Sunday 20th October — **Snetterton** — Bemsee
Production - 1st **M Andrew** (Nor 750) / 2nd **P Butler** (Tri 650) / 3rd **L Phelps** (Tri 650) / 4th **R Bowring** (Tri 650) / 5th **J Pinkney** (Tri 650) / 6th **G Carter** (Tri 650)

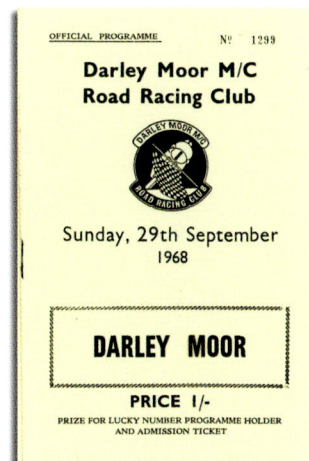

OFFICIAL PROGRAMME   Nº 1299

**Darley Moor M/C
Road Racing Club**

Sunday, 29th September
1968

DARLEY MOOR

PRICE 1/-
PRIZE FOR LUCKY NUMBER PROGRAMME HOLDER
AND ADMISSION TICKET

Sunday 15th March **Cadwell Park** Bantam Racing Club
Production Race 1 - 1st **R Hole** (BSA 654) / 2nd **G Bailey** (Tri 650) / 3rd **H Evans** (BSA 499) / 4th **D Chambers** (Tri 650) / 5th **P Davies** (Tri 650) / 6th **S Howe** (Vincent 998) **Race 2** - 1st **R Hole** (BSA 654) / 2nd **G Bailey** (Tri 650) / 3rd **P Davies** (Tri 650) / 4th **D Chambers** (Tri 650) / 5th **G Bassingdale** (Nor 750) / 6th **R House** (Suzuki 250)

Sunday 16th March **Snetterton** Bemsee
Production (7 laps) - 1st **D Nixon** (Tri 650) / 2nd **L Phelps** (Tri 650) / 3rd **G Smith** (Nor 750) / 4th **J Vincent** (Tri 650) / 5th **D Wooley** (Tri 650) / 6th **P Davies** (Tri 650)

Saturday 22nd March **Cadwell Park** Midland Motor Cycle Racing Club
Production (6 laps) - 1st **G Bailey** (Nor 650) / 2nd **J Bassingdale** (Tri 650) / 3rd **S Brown** (BSA 654) / 4th **T Haslam** (Tri 650) / 5th **J Baker** (Tri 650) / 6th **R Hole** (BSA 654)

Saturday 23rd March **Darley Moor** Darley Moor Motor Cycle Road Race Club
Production (8 laps) - 1st **T Haslam** (Tri 650) / 2nd **P Haslam** (Tri 650) / 3rd **M Orange** (Tri 650) / 4th **F Jones** (Tri 650) / 5th **M Cranmer** (BSA 670)

Sunday 30th March **Snetterton** Bantam Racing Club
Production Race 1 - 1st **P Davies** (Tri 650) / 2nd **C Wall** (Tri 650) / 3rd **D Chambers** (Tri 650) / 4th **C Agate** (Tri 650) / 5th **R Hole** (BSA 654) / 6th **H Frost** (Tri 650) **Race 2** - 1st **P Davies** (Tri 650) / 2nd **R Hole** (BSA 654) / 3rd **C Agate** (Tri 650) / 4th **W Penny** (Honda 450) / 5th **G Millward** (BSA 654) / 6th **D Chambers** (Tri 650)

Sunday 30th March **Brands Hatch** Bemsee *Trophy Day*
Production 175-1000 (10 laps) - 1st **P Butler** (Tri 650) / 2nd **L Phelps** (Tri 650) / 3rd **D Nixon** (Tri 650) / 4th **C Wall** (BSA 654) / 5th **M Pusey** (Tri 650) / 6th **H Robertson** (Tri 500)

Friday 4th April **Darley Moor** Darley Moor Motor Cycle Road Race Club
Production (8 laps) - 1st **G Sanders** (BSA654) / 2nd **T Haslam** (Tri 650) / 3rd **P Haslam** (Tri 650) / 4th **M Orange** (Tri 650) / 5th **M Cranmer** (BSA 670) / 6th **J Howe** (Vincent 100)

Sunday 6th April **Snetterton** Bemsee *Easter Cup*
Production 175-1000 (7 laps) - 1st **R Wittich** (Nor 750) / 2nd **P Butler** (Tri 650) / 3rd **E Wallace** (Tri 650) / 4th **K Buckmaster** (Tri 650) / 5th **P Vincent** (Tri 650) / 6th **G Carter** (Tri 650)

Monday 7th April **Kirkistown**
Production (6 laps) - 1st **A Alexander** (Nor 650) / 2nd **K Ferguson** (Tri 650) / 3rd **J Bankhead** (Tri 650) / 4th **J Millican** (Tri 650) / 5th **K McAttammey** (Nor 650) / 6th **W Wilson** (Tri 650)

Saturday 12th April **Cadwell Park** Bantam Racing Club
Production Race 1 - 1st **R Cope** (Suzuki 250) / 2nd **D Chambers** (Tri 650) / 3rd **J Bassingdale** (Tri 650) / 4th **R House** (Suzuki 250) / 5th **D Spruce** (Suzuki 250) / 6th **S Howe** (Vincent 998) **Race 2** - 1st **R House** (Suzuki 250) / 2nd **L Knott** (Nor 750) / 3rd **R Cope** (Suzuki 250) / 4th **J Bassingdale** (Tri 650) / 5th **S Howe** (Vincent 998) / 6th **G Millward** (BSA 654)

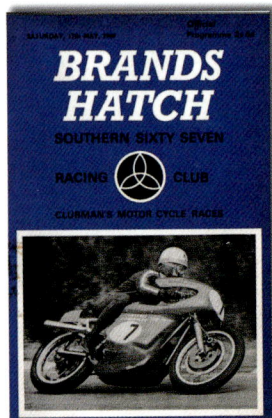

Sunday April 13th **Lydden Hill** British Formula Racing Club
Production Race 1 - 1st **G Carter** (Tri 650) / 2nd **E Wallis** (Tri 650) / 3rd **R Knight** (Tri 500) / 4th **C Thompsett** (Ducati 250) / 5th **M Lawrence** (TBC) / 6th **P Vincent** (Tri 650) **Race 2** - 1st **G Carter** (Tri 650) / 2nd **E Wallis** (Tri 650) / 3rd **R Knight** (Tri 500) / 4th **P Vincent** (Tri 650) / 5th **J Brett** (Velocette 500) / 6th **C Thompsett** (Ducati 250) **Race 3** - 1st **E Wallis** (Tri 650) / 2nd **P Vincent** (Tri 650) / 3rd **G Carter** (Tri 650) / 4th **A Rogers** (Ducati 250) / 5th **P Kilner** (Ducati 250) / 6th **J Evans** (Montesa 250)

Sunday 20th April **Snetterton** Newmarket Club
Production Race 1 - 1st **T Smith** (Nor 750) / 2nd **R Wittich** (Nor 750) / 3rd **R Browning** (Tri 650) / 4th **P Davies** (Tri 650) / 5th **K Buckmaster** (Tri 650) / 6th **D Jones** (Tri 650) **Race 2** - 1st **T Smith** (Nor 750) / 2nd **R Wittich** (Nor 750) / 3rd **P Davies** (Tri 650) / 4th **D Thomas** (BSA 654) / 5th **K Buckmaster** (Tri 650) / 6th **D Jones** (Tri 650).

Saturday 26th April **Snetterton** British Formula Racing Club
Production Race 1 - 1st **G Bailey** (Nor 750) / 2nd **G Carter** (Tri 650) / 3rd **C Agate** (Tri 650) / 4th **J Judge** (Tri 500) / 5th **J Vincent** (Tri 650) / 6th **P Wincoll** (Nor 750) **Race 2** - 1st **G Bailey** (Nor 750) / 2nd **G Carter** (Tri 650) / 3rd **C Agate** (Tri 650) / 4th **J Judge** (Tri 500) / 5th **G Millward** (BSA 654) / 6th **E Monahan** (Nor 750) **Race 3** - 1st **G Bailey** (Nor 750) / 2nd **J Vincent** (Tri 650) / 3rd **G Carter** (Tri 650) / 4th **J Judge** (Tri 500) / 5th **D Chambers** (Tri 650) / 6th **G Millward** (BSA 654)

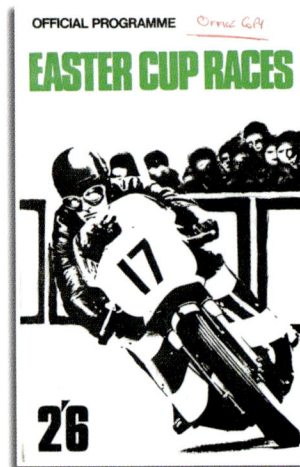

Saturday 26th April   **Maghaberry**
Production (8 laps) - 1st **K Furguson** (Tri 650) **/** 2nd **A Alexander** (Nor 650) **/** 3rd **E Coates** (Tri 650)

Saturday 26th April   **Brands Hatch**   Racing 67
Production (10 laps) - 1st **L Phelps** (Tri 650) **/** 2nd **E Wallace** (Tri 650) **/** 3rd **A Monnery** (Tri 650) **/** 4th **R Knight** (Tri 500) **/** 5th **C Thompsett** (Ducati 250) **/** 6th **G Baraham** (Suzuki 250)

Saturday 3rd May   **Aintree**   Waterloo & District Motor Club
Production 1000 - 1st **K Buckmaster** (Tri 650) **/** 2nd **J Lancaster** (Tri 650) **/** 3rd **D Carlton** (Nor 750) **/** 4th **J Bassingdale** (Tri 650) **/** 5th **K Dixon** (Nor 650) **/** 6th **M Cranmer** (BSA 654)

Saturday 3rd May   **Brands Hatch**   Bemsee   Club Day
Production 175-1000 (10 laps) - 1st **P Butler** (Tri 650) **/** 2nd **G Bailey** (Nor 750) **/** 3rd **T Smith** (Nor 750) **/** 4th **L Phelps** (Tri 650) **/** 5th **R Knight** (Tri 500) **/** 6th **K Rawlinson** (Nor 650)

Sunday 11th May   **Brands Hatch**   Southampton & District   *500 Miler*
Production 750 - 1st **P Tait/M Uphill** (Tri 650) 212 laps **/** 2nd **J Cooper/S Jolly** (Tri 650) 203 laps **/** 3rd **L Phelps/C Carr** (Tri 650) 207 laps **/** 4th **A Smith/P Mahoney** 202 laps **/** 5th **K Buckmaster/G Collis** (Tri 650) 199 laps **/** 6th **R Avery/C Dixon** (Tri 750) 198 laps
Production 500 - 1st **R Knight/M Carney** (Tri 500) 199 laps **/** 2nd **D Browning/G Gibson** (Suzuki 500) 196 laps **/** 3rd **P Butler/D Nixon** (Tri 500) 188 laps **/** 4th **G Green/R Guy** (Tri 500) 187 laps **/** 5th **P Smart/T Dickie** (Ducati 350) 187 laps **/** 6th **C Williams/A Peck** (BSA 440)
Production 250 - 1st **F Whiteway/ Woods** (Suzuki 250) 191 laps **/** 2nd **K Watson/C Mortimer** (Ducati 250) 187 laps **/** 3rd **P Walsh/T Loughridge** (Suzuki 250) 174 Laps **/** 4th **H Kist/T Lablans** (Honda 250) 173 Laps **/** 5th **C Bond/E Pitt** (Yamaha 250) 173 Laps **/** 6th **G Dickson/N Kelly** (Suzuki 250) 172 Laps

Saturday 17th May   **Brands Hatch**   Southern 67
Production - 1st **L Phelps** (Tri 650) **/** 2nd **A Monnery** (Tri 650) **/** 3rd **B Barrington** (Velocette 500) **/** 4th **R Knight** (Tri 500) **/** 5th **G Barham** (Suzuki 250) **/** 6th **D Simpson** (Nor 600)

Saturday 17th May   **Snetterton**   British Formula Racing Club
Production Race 1 - 1st **R Wittich** (Nor 750) **/** 2nd **D Jones** (Tri 650) **/** 3rd **P Haslam** (Tri 650) **/** 4th **S Brown** (BSA 654) **/** 5th **J Bassingdale** (Tri 650) **/** 6th **S Howe** (Vincent 998) **Race 2** - 1st **P Haslam** (Tri 650) **/** 2nd **J Lancaster** (Tri 650) **/** 3rd **G Millward** (BSA 654) **/** 4th **S Howe** (Vincent 988) **/** 5th **A Rogers** (Ducati 250) **/** 6th **J Judge** (Tri 500)

Saturday 17th May   **Cadwell Park**   Formula 5 Motorcylce Racing Club
Production - 1st **J Browning** (BSA 654) **/** 2nd **M Evans** (Suzuki 250) **/** 3rd **D Smith** (BSA654) **/** 4th **M James** (Tri 650)

Saturday 17th May   **Llandow**   Bantam Racing Club
Production - 1st **P Fisher** (Tri 650) **/** 2nd **R Stevens** (Royal Enfield 750) **/** 3rd **H Rees** (Nor 750) **/** 4th **R House** (Suzuki 250) **/** 5th **P Reynolds** (BSA 500) **/** 6th **L Knott** (Nor 750)

Sunday 18th May   **Llandow**   Cardiff Eagles Motor Cycle & Car Club
Production unlimited (10 laps) - 1st **J Allen** (Tri 650) **/** 2nd **P Fisher** (Tri 650) **/** 3rd **L Knott** (Nor 750) **/** 4th **P Reynolds** (BSA 654) **/** 5th **C Bishop** (Tri 650) **/** 6th **M Russell** (Velocette 500)

Sunday 25th May   **Mallory Park**   Carreras National
Production (30 laps) - 1st **D Croxford** (Nor 750) **/** 2nd **R Pickrell** (Dunstall 750) **/** 3rd **P Davies** (Tri 650) **/** 4th **D Browning** (Suzuki 500) **/** 5th **J Judge** (Tri 500) **/** 6th **H Robinson** (Tri 650)

Monday 26th May   **Darley Moor**   Darley Moor Motor Cycle Road Race Club
Production (8 laps) - 1st **G Sanders** (BSA 654)

Saturday 31st May   **Brands Hatch**   Bemsee   *Kent Cup*
Production - 1st **E Wallace** (Tri 650) **/** 2nd **T Smith** (Nor 750) **/** 3rd **G Green** (Tri 500) **/** 4th **P Wyncoll** (Dunstall 750) **/** 5th **P Vincent** (Tri 650) **/** 6th **D Woolley** (Tri 650)

Saturday May 31st   **Cadwell Park**   Midland Motor Cycle Racing Club
Production - 1st **D Jones** (Tri 650) **/** 2nd **C Hughes** (Tri 650) **/** 3rd **J Wilson** (Tri 650) **/** 4th **M Redfern** (BSA 654) **/** 5th **S Brown** (BSA 654) **/** 6th **D Draper** (Nor 650)

Wednesday 11th June   **Isle of Man**   *Production TT*
Production 750 (3 laps) - 1st **M Uphill** (Tri 650) 1 hr 7 min 55.4 sec - 99.99mph **/** 2nd **P Smart** (Nor 750) 1 hr 8 min 21.2 sec - 99.37mph **/** 3rd **D Pendlebury** (Tri 650) 1 hr 10 min 16.2 sec - 96.66mph **/** 4th **M Andrew** (Nor 750) 1 hr 11 min 21.8 sec - 95.18 mph **/** 5th **S Jolly** (Tri 650) 1 hr 12 min 53 sec - 93.19 mph **/** 6th **T Jefferies** (Tri 650) 1 hr 12min 56.2 sec - 93.13mph
Production 500 (3 laps) - 1st **G Penny** (Honda 450) 1 hr 17 min 1.6 sec - 88.18 mph **/** 2nd **R Knight** (Tri 500) 1 hr 17 min 30.4 sec - 87.64 mph **/** 3rd **R Baylie** (Tri 500) 1 hr 19 min 4 sec - 85.9 mph **/** 4th **A Cooper** (Suzuki 500) 1 hr 19 min 45.4 sec - 85.17mph **/** 5th **H Evans** (BSA 499) 1 hr 19 min 45.6 sec - 85.16 mph **/** 6th **M Chatterton** (Tri 500) 1 hr 20 min 53.6 sec - 83.97 mph

THE BEST THINGS ON TWO WHEELS
DUNLOP

Production 250 (3 laps) - 1st **A Rogers** (Ducati 250) 1 hr 21 min 3.8 sec - 83.79 mph / 2nd **F Whiteway** (Suzuki 250) 1 hr 21 min 33.4 sec - 83.29mph / 3rd **C Mortimer** (Ducati 250) 1 hr 22 min 49.6 sec - 82.01 mph / 4th **G Leigh** (Bultaco 250) 1 hr 23 min 35.2 sec - 81.26 mph / 5th **C Thompsett** (Ducati 250) 1 hr 24 min 43.2 sec - 80.18 mph / 6th **W Benson** (Suzuki 250) 1 hr 25 min 45.4 sec - 79.21mph

Saturday 14th June **Maghaberry**
Production - 1st **R Spence** (Tri 650) / 2nd **S Davies** (BSA 654) / 3rd **E Coates** (Tri 650) / 4th **A Alexander** (Nor 650) / 5th **B Taggart** (Tri 650) / 6th **M McGeown** (Nor 650)

Saturday 21st June **Cadwell Park** British Formula Racing Club
Production 1000 Race 1 - 1st **D Jones** (Tri 650) / 2nd **M McClelland** (Nor 750) / 3rd **J Bassingdale** (Nor 750) / 4th **D Chambers** (Tri 650) **Race 2** - 1st **G Sanders** (BSA 654) / 2nd **D Jones** (Tri 650) / 3rd **H Muxloe** (Tri 650) / 4th **D Chambers** (Tri 650) / 5th **G Millward** (BSA 654) / 6th **J Bassingdale** (Nor 750) **Race 3** - 1st **G Sanders** (BSA 654) / 2nd **D Jones** (Tri 650) / 3rd **G Millward** (BSA 654) / 4th **J Bassingdale** (Nor 750) / 5th **J Brett** (Velocette 500) / 6th **T Plumridge** (Nor 500)

Sunday 22nd June **Darley Moor** Darley Moor Motor Cycle Road Race Club
Production (6 laps) - 1st **G Sanders** (BSA 654) / 2nd **A Carlton** (Nor 650) / 3rd **M Cranmer** (BSA 670) / 4th **F Jones** (Tri 650) / 5th **P Pardo** (Nor 650) / 6th **D Thomas** (BSA 650)

Saturday 28th June **Lydden Hill** The British Formula Racing Club
Production race 1 - 1st **P Vincent** (Tri 650) / 2nd **J Brett** (Velocette 500) / 3rd **C Thompsett** (Ducati 250) / 4th **R Knight** (Tri 500) / 5th **A Walsh** (Velo 500) / 6th **A Rogers** (Ducati 250) **Race 2** - 1st **R Knight** (Tri 500) / 2nd **C Thompsett** (Ducati 250) / 3rd **A Walsh** (Velocette 500) / 4th **P Vincent** (Tri 650) / 5th **A Rogers** (Ducati 250) / 6th **M Lawrence** (Bridgestone 350) **Race 3** - 1st **R Knight** (Tri 500) / 2nd **A Walsh** (Velo 500) / 3rd **M Lawrence** (Bridgestone 350) / 4th **J Brett** (Velo 500) / 5th **A Rogers** (Ducati 250) / 6th **J Bassingdale** (Tri 650)

Saturday 28th June **Brands Hatch** Bemsee Trophy Day
Production - 1st **G Bailey** (Nor 750) / 2nd **G Carter** (Tri 650) / 3rd **P Wyncoll** (Dunstall 750) / 4th **D Stannard** (Tri 650) / 5th **R Rudling** (Tri 500) / 6th **D Clark** (Velocette 500)

Sunday 29th June **Thruxton** Southern 67
Production Race 1 - 1st **R Knight** (Tri 750) / 2nd **B Barrington** (Velocette 500) / 3rd **R Stevens** (Royal Enfield 750) / 4th **C Agate** (Tri 650) / 5th **C Thompsett** (Ducati 250) / 6th **M Bennett** (Yamaha 250) **Race 2** - 1st **R Knight** (Tri 750) / 2nd **A Monnery** (Tri 650) / 3rd **C Agate** (Tri 650) / 4th **R Stephens** (Royal Enfield 750) / 5th **N Swaffer** (Tri 500) / 6th **S Brown** (BSA 654)

Saturday 5th July **Cadwell Park** Bantam Racing Club
Production Race 1- 1st **G Millward** (BSA 654) / 2nd **R Stevens** (Royal Enfield 750) / 3rd **I Bezes** (Tri 650) / 4th **J Bassingdale** (Tri 650) / 5th **D Woolley** (Tri 650) / 6th **M Christian** (Tri 650) **Race 2** - 1st **R Stevens** (Royal Enfield 750) / 2nd **D Chambers** (Tri 65) / 3rd **J Bassingdale** (Tri 650) / 4th **M Christian** (Tri 650) / 5th**D Woolley** (Tri 650) / 6th **R Kent** (Tri 650)

Saturday 5th July **Aintree** Waterloo & District Motor Club
Production - 1st **J Allen** (Tri 650) / 2nd **L Mason** (BSA 654) / 3rd **K Dixon** (Nor 650) / 4th **P Pilling** (Rickman Triumph) / 5th **A Carlton** (Nor 750) / 6th **M Cranmer** (BSA 654)

5th / 6th July **Barcelona** *24 H'Oras de Montjuïc*
General Classification 24hr - 1st **S Canellas/C Rocamora** (Bultaco 360) 684 laps / 2nd **M Uphill/S Jolly** (Tri 650) 662 laps / 3rd **P Pares/B Grau** (Ossa 250) 658 laps / 4th **K Buckmaster/G Collis** (Tri 650) 638 laps / 5th **R Wittich/T Melody** (Nor 750) 637 laps / 6th **J Bordons/A Martin** (Bultaco 250) 628 laps / 7th **C Horton/A Sutton** (Tri 650) 624 laps / 8th **P Julia/A Julien** (Ossa 250) 624 laps / 9th **D Degens/I Goddard** (Dresda 650) 623 laps / 10th **M Millet/P Torres** (Ossa 250) 610 laps

Saturday 12th July **Brands Hatch** Southern 67
Production (10 laps) - 1st **E Wallace** (Tri 650) / 2nd **T Monnery** (Tri 650) / 3rd **R Knight** (Tri 500) / 4th **D Chalmers** (Tri 650) / 5th **D Simpson** (Nor 600) / 6th **C Thompsett** (Ducati 250)

Saturday 12th July **Snetterton** Bemsee *Baragwanath Trophy*
Production 175-1000 Race 1 - 1st **T Smith** (Nor 750) / 2nd **D Woolley** (Tri 650) / 3rd **P Wyncoll** (Dunstall 750) / 4th **M Warrington** (Tri 500) / 5th **R Faulks** (Tri 650) / 6th **R Peacock** (BSA 654) **Race 2** - 1st **T Smith** (Nor 750) / 2nd **D Woolley** (Tri 650) / 3rd **G Carter** (Tri 650) V 4th **G Bailey** (Nor 750) / 5th **R Peacock** (BSA 654) / 6th **M Christian** (Tri 650)

Sunday 13th July **Llandow** Cardiff Eagles MC&CC
Production Race 1 - 1st **J Allen** (Tri 650) / 2nd **R Stevens** (Royal Enfield 750) / 3rd **M Hunt** (Tri 500) / 4th **D Jones** (Tri 650) / 5th **D Lewis** (Tri 650) / 6th **I Bezer** (Tri 650) **Race 2** - 1st **R Stevens** (Royal Enfield 750) / 2nd **M Hunt** (Tri 500) / 3rd **J Allen** (Tri 650) / 4th **D Jones** (Tri 650) / 5th **I Bezer** (Tri 650) / 6th **D Aitken** (Tri 650)

Sunday 13th July   **Darley Moor**   Darley Moor Motor Cycle Road Race Club
Production (8 laps) - 1st **G Sanders** (BSA 654) / 2nd **A Carlton** (Nor 650) / 3rd **T Haslam** (Tri 650) / 4th **M Orange** (Tri 650) / 5th **F Jones** (Tri 650) / 6th **N Overend** (Nor 650)

Saturday 19th July   **Cadwell Park**   British Formula Racing Club
Production Race 1 - 1st **T Haslam** (Nor 750) / 2nd **J Brett** (Velocette 500) / 3rd **A Walsh** (Velocette 500) / 4th **P Vincent** (Tri 650) / 5th **D Gilling** (BSA 654) / 6th **J Vincent** (Tri 650) **Race 2** - 1st **G Millward** (BSA 654) / 2nd **T Haslam** (Nor 750) / 3rd **J Vincent** (Tri 650) / 4th **P Vincent** (Tri 650) / 5th **J Brett** (Velocette 500) / 6th **A Walsh** (Velocette 500) **Race 3** - 1st **P Vincent** (Tri 650) / 2nd **J Vincent** (Tri 650) / 3rd **T Haslam** (Nor 750) / 4th **G Millward** (BSA 654) / 5th **A Walsh** (Velocette 500) / 6th **R Guy** (Tri 500)

Saturday 19th July   **Snetterton**   Racing 50 Club
Production Race 1 - 1st **G Sanders** (BSA 654) / 2nd **D Jones** (Tri 650) / 3rd **L Trotter** (Suzuki 500) / 4th **M Orange** (Tri 650) / 5th **P Pardo** (Nor 650) / 6th **K Little** (Tri 650) **Race 2** - 1st **G Sanders** (BSA 654) / 2nd **D Jones** (Tri 650) / 3rd **L Trotter** (Suzuki 500) / 4th **D Draper** (Nor 650) / 5th **M Orange** (Tri 650) / 6th **K Little** (Tri 650)

Sunday 20th July   **Snetterton**   Newmarket Motor Cycle & Light Car Club
Production Race 1 - 1st **R Wittich** (Nor 750) / 2nd **T Smith** (Nor 750) / 3rd **M Newjamb** (Tri 650) / 4th **R Bowring** (Tri 650) / 5th **P Vincent** (Tri 650) / 6th **G Carter** (Tri 650) **Race 2** - 1st **R Wittich** (Nor 750) / 2nd **T Smith** (Nor 750) / 3rd **M Newjamb** (Tri 650) / 4th **R Bowring** (Tri 650) / 5th **K Buckmaster** (Tri 650) / 6th **G Carter** (Tri 650) .

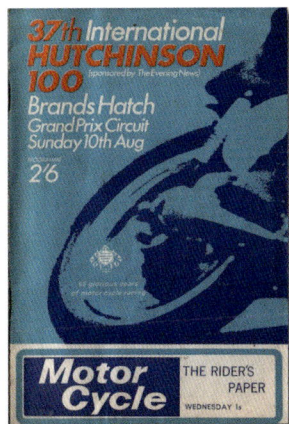

Saturday 26th July   **Brands Hatch**   Bemsee   *Trophy Day*
Production - 1st **D Nixon** (Tri 650) / 2nd **P Butler** (Tri 650) / 3rd **E Wallace** (Tri 650) / 4th **A Monnery** (Tri 650) / 5th **L Phelps** (Tri 650) / 6th **G Carter** (Tri 650)

Saturday 2nd August   **Brands Hatch**   Bemsee   *Ace of Clubs*
Production 175-1000 - 1st **E Wallace** (Tri 650) / 2nd **J Kanka** (Tri 650) / 3rd **J Vincent** (Tri 650) / 4th **P Vincent** (Tri 650) / 5th **R Knight** (Tri 500) / 6th **D Thomson** (Tri 650)

Sunday 3rd August   **Darley Moor**   Darley Moor Motor Cycle Road Race Club
Production (8 laps) - 1st **G Sanders** (BSA 654) / 2nd **A Carlton** (Nor 650) / 3rd **K Little** (Tri 650) / 4th **A Butler** (Nor 750) / 5th **P Pardo** (Nor 650) / 6th **D Walker** (Nor 650)

Sunday 10th August   **Brands Hatch**   Bemsee   *Hutchinson 100*
Production (20 laps) - 1st **M Andrew** (Nor 750) / 2nd **A Smith** (BSA 654) / 3rd **R Gould** (Tri 650) / 4th **R Pickrell** (Dunstall 750) / 5th **P Williams** (Nor 750) / 6th **P Tait** (Tri 750)

Sunday 17th August   **Snetterton**   British Formula Racing Club
Production Race 1 - 1st **G Sanders** (BSA 654) / 2nd **P Vincent** (Tri 650) **Race 2** - 1st **P Vincent** (Tri 650) / 2nd **G Sanders** (BSA 654)

Saturday 23rd August   **Cadwell Park**   Bantam Racing Club
Production Race 1 (8 laps) - 1st **R Stevens** (Royal Enfield 750) / 2nd **H Evans** (BSA 499) / 3rd **A Jones** (Suzuki 250) / 4th **D Arnold** (Ducati 250) / 5th **T Seaman** (Nor 650) **Race 2** - 1st **R Stevens** (Royal Enfield 750) / 2nd **D Chambers** (Tri 650) / 3rd **H Evans** (BSA 499) / 4th **J Bassingdale** (Tri 650) / 5th **T Odlin** (Nor 650) / 6th **T Seaman** (Nor 650)

Saturday 23rd August   **Brands Hatch**   Southern 67
Production - 1st **J Kanka** (Tri 650) / 2nd **P Wilkins** (Nor 650) / 3rd **S Baldwin** (Tri 650) / 4th **P Vincent** (Tri 650) / 5th **R Knight** (Tri 500) / 6th **A Monnery** (Tri 650)

Saturday 30th August   **Lurgan Park**   Armagh Motor Club
Production - 1st **K McAttamney** (Nor 650) / 2nd **T Fraser** (Montesa 250) / 3rd **A Alexander** (Nor 650)

Saturday 30th August   **Cadwell Park**   Midland Motor Cycle Racing Club
Production (8 laps) - 1st **G Sanders** (BSA 654) / 2nd **L Mason** (BSA 654) / 3rd **F Peier** (Tri 650) / 4th **D Jones** (Tri 650) / 5th **P Pardo** (Nor 650) / 6th **K Little** (Tri 650)

Monday 1st September   **Darley Moor**   Darley Moor Motor Cycle Road Race Club
Production (8 laps) - 1st **G Sanders** (BSA A654) / 2nd **T Haslam** (Tri 650) / 3rd **M Orange** (Tri 650) / 4th **K Little** (Tri 650) / 5th **N Overend** (Nor 750) / 6th **F Jones** (Tri 650)

Monday 1st September   **Crystal Palace**
Production Race 1 (10 laps) - 1st **P Butler** (Tri 650) / 2nd **C Sanby** (Tri 650) / 3rd **L Phelps** (Tri 650) / 4th **G Sharpe** (Tri 650) / 5th **G Carter** (Tri 650) / 6th **K Buckmaster** (Tri 650) **Race 2** - 1st **C Sanby** (Tri 650) / 2nd **P Butler** (Tri 650) / 3rd **D Nixon** (Tri 650) / 4th **L Phelps** (Tri 650) / 5th **G Carter** (Tri 650) / 6th **J Kanka** (Tri 650)

Saturday 6th September   **Cadwell Park**   British Formula Racing Club
Production Race 1 - 1st **J Vincent** (Tri 650) / 2nd **L Mason** (BSA 654) / 3rd **A Walsh** (Velo 500) / 4th **H Evans** (BSA 499) / 5th **J Brett** (Velocette 500) / 6th **P Pardo** (Nor 650) **Race 2** - 1st **J Vincent** (Tri 650) / 2nd **L Mason** (BSA 654) / 3rd **T Haslam** (Tri 650) / 4th **H Evans** (BSA 499) / 5th **P**

Pardo (Nor 650) / 6th **T Odlin** (Tri 650) **Race 3** - 1st **J Vincent** (Tri 650) / 2nd **L Mason** (BSA 654) / 3rd **T Haslam** (Tri 650) / 4th **P Pardo** (Nor 650) / 5th **H Evans** (BSA 499) / 6th **A Walsh** (Velo 500)

Sunday 7th September   **Snetterton**   Newmarket Motor Cycle & Light Car Club
Production Race 1 - 1st **R Wittich** (Nor 750) / 2nd **T Smith** (Nor 750) / 3rd **K Buckmaster** (Tri 650) / 4th **J Vincent** (Tri 650) / 5th **G Carter** (Tri 650) / 6th **D Jones** (Tri 650) **Race 2** - 1st **T Smith** (Nor 750) / 2nd **S Baldwin** (Tri 650) / 3rd **K Buckmaster** (Tri 650) / 4th **Monahan** (Nor 750) / 5th **G Carter** (Tri 650) / 6th **J Vincent** (Tri 650)

Saturday 13th September   **Lydden Hill**
Production Race 1 - 1st **J Vincent** (Tri 650) / 2nd **J Brett** (Velo 500) / 3rd **P Vincent** (Tri 650) / 4th **A Walsh** (Velo 500) / 5th **C Thompsett** (Ducati 250) / 6th **R Knight** (Tri 500) **Race 2**- 1st **J Vincent** (Tri 650) / 2nd **P Vincent** (Tri 650) / 3rd **J Brett** (Velo 500) / 4th **R Knight** (Tri 500) / 5th **C Thompsett** (Ducati 250) / 6th **A Walsh** (Velo 500) **Race 3** - 1st **J Vincent** (Tri 650) / 2nd **P Vincent** (Tri 650) / 3rd **J Brett** (Velocette 500) / 4th **R Knight** (Tri 500) / 5th **H Evans** (BSA 499) / 6th **J Bassingdale** (Tri 650)

Sunday 14th September   **Snetterton**   *One Hour Enduro*
Production 1hr - 1st **R Knight** (Tri 750) / 2nd **J Vincent** (Tri 650) / 3rd **D Jones** (Tri 650) / 4th **C Agate** (Tri 650) / 5th **L Knott** (Nor 750) / 6th **M Warrington** (Tri 500)

Sunday 14th September   **Llandow**   Cardiff Eagles MC&CC
Production Race 1 - 1st **M Russell** (Velo 500) / 2nd **K Little** (Tri 650) / 3rd **M Strutt** (Suzuki 250) / 4th **A Woollon** (Velocette 500) / 5th **G Marley** (Suzuki 250) / 6th **R Medcraft** (Nor 500) **Race 2** - 1st **B Walker** (Tri 650) / 2nd **C Crookes** (Ducati 250) / 3rd **M Russell** (Velocette 500) / 4th **K Little** (Tri 650) / 5th **A Woollon** (Velocette 500) / 6th **M Strutt** (Suzuki 250)

Saturday 20th September   **Cadwell Park**   Midland Motor Cycle Racing Club
Production (8 laps) - 1st **G Sanders** (BSA 654) / 2nd **L Mason** (BSA 654) / 3rd **T Odlin** (Tri 650) / 4th **P Pardo** (Nor 650) / 5th **P Lovell** (Nor 750) / 6th **J Bassingdale** (Tri 650)

Saturday 20th September   **Aintree**   Waterloo & District Motor Club
Production (7 laps) - 1st **J Allen** (Tri 650) / 2nd **K Buckmaster** (Tri 650) / 3rd **A Carlton** (Nor 650) / 4th **H Robertson** (Tri 500) / 5th **N Overend** (Nor 650) / 6th **S Howe** (Vincent 998)

Sunday 28th September   **Snetterton**   Bemsee   Guinness Trophy
Production 175-1000 - 1st **P Butler** (Tri 650) / 2nd **E Wallace** (Tri 650) / 3rd **J Carter** (Tri 650) / 4th **J Vincent** (Tri 650) / 5th **P Davies** (Tri 650) / 6th **K Buckmaster** (Tri 650)

Sunday 5th October   **Darley Moor**   Darley Moor Motor Cycle Road Race Club
Production (8 laps) - 1st **G Sanders** (BSA 654) / 2nd **M Orange** (Tri 650) / 3rd **A Butler** (Nor 650) / 4th **K Little** (Tri 650) / 5th **F Jones** (Tri 650) / 6th **D Arnold** (Ducati 250)

Sunday 12th October   **Cadwell Park**   British Formula Racing Club
Production Race 1 (4 laps) - 1st **P Haslam** (Tri 650) / 2nd **J Bassingdale** (Nor 750) / 3rd **M James** (Tri 650) / 4th **J Brett** (Velocette 500) / 5th **T Odlin** (Tri 650) / 6th **D Armold** (Ducati 250) **Race 2** - 1st **P Haslam** (Tri 650) / 2nd **M James** (Tri 650) / 3rd **A Walsh** (Velocette 500) / 4th **J Bassingdale** (Nor 750) / 5th **P Vincent** (Tri 650) / 6th **D Arnold** (Ducati 250)

Saturday 18th October   **Snetterton**   Bantam Racing Club
Production Race 1 - 1st **R Knight** (Tri 650) / 2nd **P Butler** (Tri 650) / 3rd **G Bailey** (Nor 750) / 4th **J Vincent** (Tri 650) / 5th **D Bick** (BSA 654) / 6th **J Kanka** (Tri 650) **Race 2** - 1st **G Bailey** (Nor 750) / 2nd **P Butler** (Tri 650) / 3rd **R Knight** (Tri 650) / 4th **J Vincent** (Tri 650) / 5th **J Kanka** (Tri 650)

Sunday 19th October   **Snetterton**   Bemsee
Production 175-1000 - 1st **P Davies** (Tri 650) / 2nd **G Carter** (Tri 650) / 3rd **J Vincent** (Tri 650) / 4th **J Kanka** (Tri 650) / 5th **P Butler** (Tri 650) / 6th **K Buckmaster** (Tri 650)

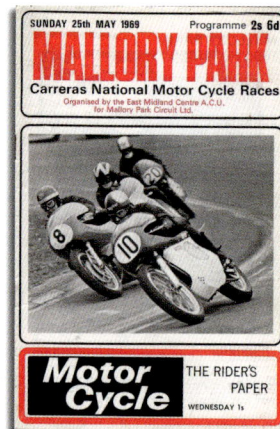

Notes on Results - The above results are not comprehensive, as those of many clubs were not published during the period. They are a representative summary of the major races however, based on the results published in *Motor Cycle News*, *Motor Cycling* and *Motor Cyclist illustrated*, along with those issued by the clubs and circuits themselves. They also come from the records of many of the riders quoted.

References & Bibliography

1. Page ii - Section 2.1.1, page 74, *FIM Superbike, Supersport & Supersport 300 World Championships Regulations 2021*. Fédération Internationale de Motocyclisme
2. Page 18 - Guy Tremlett, page 95, the *Bemsee Journal*. Vol 16, No.6, June 1963
3. Page 22 - *MCN* Wednesday 26th December 1962
4. Page 32 - ACU proposal late January 1947, published in *The Motor Cycle* quoted in *The History of the Cubman's TT races 1947-1956*, Pidcock/Snelling, page 16
5. Page 33 - Pages 1 & 2 of the *Supplementary Regulation for the 1968 National Restricted Standard Production Machine Race* – TT, 12th June 1968, ACU
6. Page 34 - Page 3 of the *Supplementary Regulation for the 1968 National Restricted Standard Production Machine Race* – TT, 12th June 1968, ACU
7. Page 35 - Page 3 of the *Programme for the 1962 Thruxton 500 Miler*. The 1961 programme quoted similarly stating *'....which must have been manufactured after 1st September 1957'* rather than 1958
8. Page 36 - *Regulations of the Southampton & District 500-miler* as published for clarification in all Brands Hatch and Thruxton 500-miler programmes between 1966 to 1969
9. Page 37 - *Isle of Man Examiner, TT Special supplement*, page 17, Wednesday 14th June 1967
10. Page 37 - Clause (d), Page 2, of the *Supplementary Regulation for the 1968 National Restricted Standard Production Machine Race* – TT 12th June 1968
11. Page 45 - Page 7, *Isle of Man Examiner TT Special supplement*, Monday 12th June, 1967,
12. Page 49 - Page 2, of the *Supplementary Regulation for the 1968 National Restricted Standard Production Machine Race* – TT, 12th June 1968, ACU
13. Page 78 - *MCN* 28th April 1965
14. Page 89 - *MCN* 18th August 1965
15. Page 89 - *Motor Cycling* 21st August 1965
16. Page 95 - Page 1, Editorial, *Bemsee Journal*, January 1966
17. Page 157 - *Motor Cycle* 5th August 1967
18. Page 158 - *Motor Cycle* 16th August 1967
19. Page 165 - *MCN* 15th May 1968
20. Page 191 - *MCN* 23rd October 1968
21. Page 197 - *MCN* Season Summary February 1969
22. Page 238 - *Hansard* - Volume 792: Friday 28 November 1969
23. Page 241 - David Dixon column, *Motor Cycle* 8th October 1969

Bibliography

The History of the Clubman's TT races 1947-1956. Fred Pidcock & Bill Snelling. Amulree. 2007. ISBN 978-1-901508109
Road Racing History of the Triumph 500 Unit Twin. Claudio Sintich. Panther. 2010. ISBN 978-0-9564975-0-5
Triumph Thruxton Bonneville 1959-1969. Claudio Sintich. Panther. 2015. ISBN 978-1-909213-20-3
Ever More Speed: the autobiography of a TT racer. Ray Knight. Lily Publications. 2013. ISBN 978-1-907945-35-9
One Man's Mountain. Graham Bailey. The Conrad Press 2021. ISBN 978-1-914913-37-2
Whispering Smith. Barry Smith. ISBN 978-0-646-95515-5
Hailwood to Vincent. Peter Crawford. WIDELINE. ISBN 9781838133627
Racing Line. Bob Guntrip. Veloce ISBN 978-1-845847-93-7
Triumph Experimental - Doug Hele and his development team 1962-1975. Mick Duckworth. Oracle Publishing
Darley Moor M/C Club 1965-1974. John Dowson. Dowson 20. ISBN 978 1678 163969

Index

Castle Combe - 31, 73, 79, 81, 201
Chandler Ron - 31, 45
Chubb John - 81, 88
Chuck Bill (dealer) - 158, 179, 195, 215
Clubman TT - 4, 5, 7, 8, 16, 26, 32, 33, 34, 35, 36,
127, 133,
Collis George - 231, 232
Comerfords (dealer) - 53, 68, 128
Cooper John - 84, 88, 97, 109, 112, 115, 117, 132,
157, 158, 203, 204, 223, 233, 234, 240
Cotton - 32, 34, 38, 39, 42, 70, 81, 82, 83, 101, 112,
117, 241
Cox Bruce - 40, 71, 89,
Croft - 61, 118,
Crooks Eddie - 2, 121, 139, 140, 203, 220, 221
Croxford Dave - 29, 54, 106, 111, 113, 114, 130,
157, 158, 166, 167, 176, 187, 193, 200, 204, 205,
236, 237, 241
Curley Bros - 158, 178, 205
Curley Norman - 43, 44, 45
Crystal Palace - 44, 98, 157, 158, 201

D

Daniels Harold - 66, 205
Darley Moor - 35, 49, 76, 77, 78, 93, 109, 115, 118,
126, 188, 190, 201, 202, 230
Darvill Peter - 99, 100, 148
Davey Vincent - 173, 198, 204, 205, 238
Davies Pete *PK* - 20, 21, 45, 46, 109, 122, 127, 157,
163, 187, 189, 190, 200, 224, 233
Davies Clive - 34
Davis Brian - 27, 28, 45, 69, 70
Deeprose (dealer) - 197
Degens Dave - 42, 77, 79, 80, 82, 94, 95, 98, 99,
100, 103, 104, 105, 106, 107, 112, 114, 117, 130,
157, 158, 159, 169, 233
Denley Monty - 38, 82
Devimead - 165, 187
Dickie Tom - 168, 189
Dixon Colin - 55, 150, 202
Dixon Dave - 34, 45, 70, 81, 110, 112, 114, 157,
177
Dixon Oscar - 20, 21, 24, 64, 77,
Dodkin Geoff - 29, 111, 113 (114), 117, 143, 181,
182
Dow Eddie - 7, 33, 79, 81, 88, 117, 118, 126, 169
Doyle Declan - 23, 25, 61, 78, 109,
Dresda - 42, 94, 95, 158, 159
Driver Paddy - 31, 56, 87, 88,

Ducati - 57, 94, 95, 97, 98, 100, 113, 130, 131, 141,
162, 165, 168, 173, 174, 175, 180, 187, 202, 203,
212, 219, 220, 221, 240, 241, 242
Dugdales (dealer) - 66, 207
Dunlop Joey - 214, 224
Dunnell Tony - 130, 142, 202, 216, 217, 226
Dunphy Joe - 31, 65, 70, 81, 110, 164
Dunstall - 42, 43, 44, 45, 46, 73, 75, 108, 109, 112,
120, 130, 133, 134, 158, 159, 166, 167, 176, 177,
178, 179, 180, 185, 187, 188, 197, 198, 200, 203,
206, 220, 234

E

Elites MCs (dealer) - 197, 203, 224
Evans Hugh - 48, 101, 102, 103, 119, 122, 135,
144, 153, 182, 194, 195, 218, 219, 235

F

Falcke Graham - 226, 227, 228
Fannon Bill - 153
FIM - 3, 9, 36, 37, 98, 115, 142

G

Gleed John - 80, 81, 88
Goosen Chris - 148, 149
Goss Neville - 9, 81, 82, 209
Gould Rod - 7, 40, 42, 80, 81, 88, 89, 117, 118,
126, 132, 157, 166, 169, 188, 213, 215, 216, 231,
232, 233, 234, 236
Gibson Grant - 200, 202
Grant Mick - 151, 197, 229
Green Gary - 104, 105, 151, 228, 229
Greeves - 34, 40, 41, 42, 73, 126, 207
Gus Kuhn - 173, 191, 197, 198, 199, 204, 205, 232,
234, 235, 236, 237, 238, 239, 242

H

Hailwood Mike - 10, 11, 16, 36, 50, 84, 86, 87, 88,
89, 90, 91, 93, 115, 116, 117, 125, 132, 144, 145,
158, 171, 176, 188, 212, 214, 234
Hanks Norman - 85, 91, 144, 207
Hardy Reg - 35, 48,
Harley-Davidson - 53, 115, 240
Harrington Bob - 130, 131, 168, 169, 170, 186,
187
Harris Lester - 50

The story continues. The King of Brands meeting, Brands Hatch Friday 9th of April 1971. Percy Tait (53) Peter Butler (12) Andrew Goldsmith (105) Barry Ditchburn (34) Ron Smith (82) Alan Clark (100) and Bill Reid (92) line up, production racers mixed in with the thoroughbreds